THE
MYSTERIOUS
LANDS

BY THE SAME AUTHOR

BEYOND THE ASPEN GROVE (1970)

LAND ABOVE THE TREES
  (co-author with Beatrice E. Willard, 1972)

RUN, RIVER, RUN (1975)

WIND IN THE ROCK (1978)

A CONSCIOUS STILLNESS
  (co-author with Edwin Way Teale, 1982)

A DESERT COUNTRY NEAR THE SEA (1983)

JOHN XANTUS: THE FORT TEJON LETTERS 1857–1859 (1986)

DOWNCANYON (1995)

THE MYSTERIOUS LANDS

A Naturalist Explores the
Four Great Deserts of the Southwest

ANN HAYMOND ZWINGER

Illustrated by the author

The University of Arizona Press   Tucson

The University of Arizona Press
⊗ This book is printed on acid-free, archival-quality paper.
Manufactured in the United States of America
01 00 99 98 97 96   6 5 4 3 2 1

Library of Congress Cataloging-in-Publication Data

Zwinger, Ann.
    The mysterious lands : a naturalist explores the four great
deserts of the Southwest / Ann Haymond Zwinger ; illustrated by the
author.
        p.   cm.
    Originally published: New York : Dutton, c1989.
    Includes bibliographical references (p.   ) and index.
    ISBN 0-8165-1650-2
    1. Desert biology—Southwestern States.   2. Natural history—
Southwestern States.   I. Title.
    [QH104.5.S6Z84   1996]   96-7077
    508.79—dc20   CIP

British Cataloguing-in-Publication Data
A catalogue record for this book is available from the British Library.

Grateful acknowledgment is made for permission to quote from four lines
from "The Call of the Wild," by Robert Service, in *Collected Poems of Robert
Service*, reprinted by permission of The Putnam Publishing Group.

To Nana

CONTENTS

ix

CONTENTS

THE MOJAVE DESERT

THE GREAT BASIN DESERT

The deserts should never be reclaimed. They are the breathing-spaces of the west and should be preserved forever.

—JOHN VAN DYKE, *The Desert,* 1901

THE CHIHUAHUAN DESERT

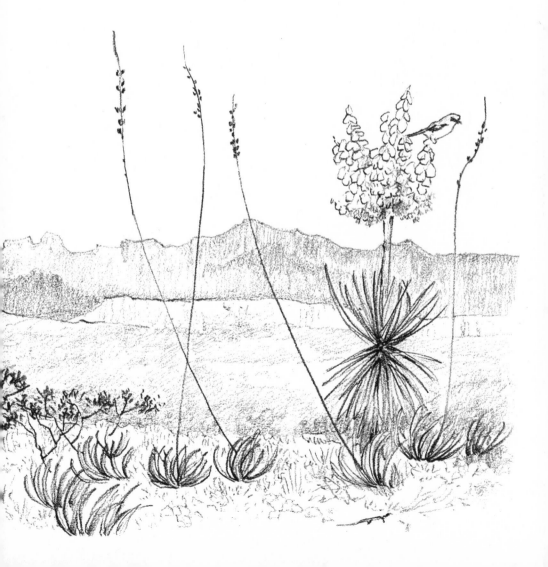

OF BEGINNINGS
AND LECHUGUILLA

The great horned owl calls up the dawn, over and over, a soft *hoo-HOO hoo hoo-o-o,* ribbons of sound weaving through the fretwork of mesquite branches. It is no longer night but not yet dawn, the hinging time between still dark and before light, when the starlight that fell fresh and bright is gone, leaving only three stars in a huge triangle strung across the sky. Finally only Venus walks the twilight of the eastern sky that hoods the Chihuahuan Desert.

Narrow clouds stripe the horizon pink, violet, and cream, a pousse-café of a sky. Over a cusp of rock, one spot of color glows royal rose, deepening and broadening, turning the pink stripe ruddy, the cream to gold. The silhouettes of the Chihuahuan Desert take on interior shapes and color but the mesquite holds jet black, its thorny zigzag branches drawn in India ink by a tense hand incapable of either a gentle curve or continuous straight line.

3

I, for one, am glad to see the dawn. I am miserably cold, having been foolish enough to think that night in early March, in Big Bend at the northern end of the Chihuahuan Desert, would be reasonably warm. It isn't. Forty-five degrees isn't cold until it's all you've got. When the sun fell behind the horizon last night, the air, with no humidity to temper the drop, lost its heat quickly. During the day, such low relative atmospheric humidity allows a high percentage of sunlight to reach the ground, unfiltered by atmosphere and un-blocked by clouds; the pellucid air allows almost 90 to 95 percent of available solar radiation to reach the desert floor (in temperate zones, humidity lowers that figure to between 40 and 60 percent). Con-versely, night air cools quickly, accounting for large diurnal swings of temperature. In the desert, more often than not, it's roast at noon and freeze at midnight.

Adding to last night's chill, a gusty desert wind barreled down the hillside. Ideally I would orient myself so that the wind comes up from my feet, not down my neck. But that downslope night wind meant lying with my head downhill. I chose the lesser of the two evils and contended with the wind gusting down my neck.

As if to make up for the discomfort, moonset was so spectacu-lar that I forgot I was a candidate for hypothermia. The moon delicately lowered itself to the mountain rim and poised there, its brilliant crescent balanced on the profile of the arete. Then it slid behind the rim until only the tip of its horn remained, as bright as a star. The remainder of the globe lingered, lit by earthshine, a darkly bright, still-glowing, cratered moon, light from desert to moon and back to desert again. With the moon gone, the stars cascaded a light as blazingly bright as full moonlight, and I attended to them, scintillating twins and dogs and hunters, red giants and white dwarfs, roaring circles across the sky.

Now I think stars and transition to morning sounds. A wood-pecker drills. A pyrrhuloxia on a close-by branch sings "sweet cheer, sweet cheer." Its vermilion-smudged breast reflects a fiery sun, dawn on the wing. I register the sound of pencil on paper, coffee perking on the hibachi, along with the repartee of two cactus wrens.

4

I pull my yellow mug out of Susan's kitchen basket at my knee and the clatter superimposes human sounds on the morning of the desert. Susan is my eldest daughter. As we warm our hands around our mugs of coffee, we plan our day in the desert. She is giving me this camping trip to the Chihuahuan Desert for my birthday, wrapped up in a desert dawn, tied up with silken strings of pyrrhuloxia song.

Like this day, deserts are beginnings, perhaps because there are so many questions in a desert. Questions are beginnings, answers are endings, and in the desert all the answers come in the form of more questions. Desert beginnings are made up of early-morning sun slanting through the mesquite boughs, fresh wind flickering the creosote branch, an opening cactus flower, a slow-ticking darkling beetle and an intent robber fly, a rattlesnake ending its night hunting and a kangaroo mouse popping into its burrow before sunup, a horned toad emerging to warm in the early sun, a world full of anticipations and apprehensions, possibilities and potentials, quick shadows and careful eyes.

That afternoon, searching for a campsite near Nugent Mountain, one of the peaks in the Chisos Mountains, Susan and I miss the turn and end high up on a cobble-rolling spring-bouncing mountain road. Looking for a place to turn around, we find a pull-off and stop.

We scan a splendid panorama to the south: a broad valley slipping down to the Rio Grande and, across the river, the high rim of the Sierra del Carmen, a magnificent corner of the Chihuahuan Desert's 280,000 square miles. The cliffs are Roman-striped, softened by distance to a rosy cream and lavender gray, lighter walls separated by darker talus slopes. Above them rides a phalanx of cumulus clouds, like the ghosts of Spanish galleons sailing nowhere. A few drag virga, unkept promises of rain left hanging in the air. Behind me the ridgelines are stalked with lechuguilla and sotol and the buggy-whip branches of ocotillo, stalks akimbo.

High up on the hillside is a single century plant, a silhouette that symbolizes the upland Chihuahuan Desert to me. Compared to

5

CHIHUAHUAN DESERT WITH CENTURY PLANT
(*Agave* sp.)

the frequent sotol and ubiquitous lechuguilla, two other agaves, century plants are few and far between and thus possess a solitary dignity, kings of the last century, personages whose ranks grow thinner year by year. These big agaves may be disappearing because the bats that pollinate them are drastically diminished in number, mostly from loss of habitat. The agave's salvation may lie in vegetative reproduction and much less efficient pollination by hummingbirds and some bees. The empty stalk still stands like a giant candelabrum, candles snuffed out, the party over.

We decide to take advantage of our unplanned visit, Susan to hike up the canyon, I to ramble down a sandy arroyo that stairsteps down the west flank of Nugent Mountain. Quintessential Chihuahuan Desert surrounds me. These thorned and spined, crooked and daggered plants were already here some eleven thousand years ago, part of a more moisture-loving vegetation that dominated the area, in place and ready to expand when the climate changed with a drop in winter precipitation and a shift to a summer rainy season. In

6

effect for only about eight thousand years, this climatic transition established the Chihuahuan Desert by engendering a vegetational change from grasslands to desert scrub communities, the most recent major vegetation change in North America since the Pleistocene.

Desert and grassland vegetation was displaced southward when glaciers formed during the Pleistocene epoch, which began two million years ago. No massive glaciers formed in the Southwest, but the greater rainfall and consequent stream erosion filled the intermountain valleys with thousands of feet of sediment and created hundreds of lakes, some of them huge. The Great Salt Lake in Utah is a remainder of ancient Lake Bonneville. As the postPleistocene climate warmed and dried, glaciers retreated from the northern mountains. Plants and animals that survived the Pleistocene in desert areas to the south began their vigorous invasion northward to pattern deserts as we see them today.

Much of this vegetation is difficult or impossible to walk through, armed with spines and thorns of invidious intent, developed in many plant families to conserve water and discourage being eaten by animals. I avoid at all costs the close-packed, calf-high, slightly curving leaves of the Chihuahuan Desert's endemic agave, lechuguilla. *Lechuguilla* is the diminutive of the Spanish *lechuga,* "lettuce," a rather unlikely name for a plant whose leaves can inflict such nasty injury: the sap contains a strong muscle contractor that makes a wound unusually painful. Not only are the leaves edged with gray spines, an eighth to a quarter of an inch long, but at the tip the edges fold together, joining into a finger-length needle that indurates, as lethal as a stiletto, and explains the common name of "shin dagger."

In this upland desert, hundreds of its flower stalks punctuate the skyline. The stalks raise clusters of coffee bean–size seed pods, yucca pods in miniature, a scarce inch long. Seeds tumble out on my sketchpad, shiny black, wrinkled, eighth-inch half-moons. It takes twenty-five to thirty-five years for a lechuguilla to store up enough energy to flower, after which it dies. Lechuguilla also reproduces vegetatively by rhizomes, the close-packed plants forming

7

impenetrable thickets. Although ranchers consider it a nuisance for obvious reasons, it was a useful plant for prehistoric peoples, who discovered in its leaves a major source of fiber; in Mexico today there is an important industry making commercial brushes from them.

Like huge asparagus stalks, the dried stems of sotol, another agave, march up the hillside. The graceful thin leaves fan out from the center in a waist-high rosette, brighter green than the rest of the scrub. Light picots the tiny spines on the leaf margins so that the whole leaf mass glistens in the sunshine. From a distance the top of the flowering stalk resembles a giant bottle brush, dried flower heads now a platinum gray. Up close, the dried flowers are a jeweler's fancy of beaded wire and Florentine finish, the still-attached stigmas delicately feathering the stalk. Sotol husbands its resources, not for a hundred years as folklore would have it, but perhaps twelve to fifteen, making maximum growth for the year during the winter and spring months. Even when well watered, sotol is genetically programmed to grow slowly, although, when ready to flower, the scape shoots up a foot or more a day. Meanwhile, the outer leaves dry and brown, and by the time seed is set the parent rosette is dead.

Sotol was important in prehistoric economy as a food source, and people still chop away the thatch and roast and eat the cabbage-size hearts (the taste is similar to raw cabbage) and brew a powerful alcoholic drink from the sugar-rich sap. Just before sending up its flowering stalk, the sotol's artichokelike heart swells with nutrients. The stored carbohydrates are broken down into sugars, which translocate to the heart. When roasted underground with hot stones, it is good to eat, the heat changing the chemical composition of the heart from an indigestible to a highly edible food.

My plan had been to avoid picking my way through these difficult plants and take an indolent stroll down what looks to be the open, flat, sandy bottom of a dry wash. Within fifty feet my plan comes apart as the arroyo narrows and forces me to swivel between whitethorn branches, whose thorns gleam evilly on mahogany-red branches, and catclaw or mesquite, all of which stalk the banks and lean out into the draw, sometimes blocking it completely. Branches

CHIHUAHUAN DESERT WITH SOTOL
(*Dasylirion leiophyllum*)

with thorns like lancets strike through my clothes, and lacerate my hands and arms until I am as red-flecked with blood as a south-western santo.

The bank runs uneven and rugged, roughened by multicolored rocks—brown, slate gray, rosy red splotched with white, rust, Confederate gray, and Union blue. The plentiful grasses of the Chihuahuan Desert hide small starts of whitethorn and mesquite and catclaw as nasty as their parents. Although I know that it is too early in both day and season for rattlesnakes to be out marauding, rustling leaves and whispery grasses keep me wary, and more than once I stop short, tensed, scanning the stubble for the furtive coil, the telltale tail.

Whenever possible I retreat to the arroyo bed. As it steepens, a twenty-foot-high wall rises on my right. In its layers are all the cobbles and pebbles of eons of river deposits, rough and angular, scarcely worked. Water has ripped and torn and gutted out here; it has not rounded and polished and gentled.

A loggerhead shrike alights on the top of a Torrey yucca flower spike, its white breast, dark back, and bullet-shaped head unmistakable. Shrikes are wont to spike their prey on the stiff terminating spines of yucca leaves. Having been cursed with a raptor's beak but a perching bird's untaloned feet, they cannot grasp their prey and must anchor it by other means. Oddly, prey is never found impaled lower than about twenty inches from the ground, which may reflect either the shrike's preference, or the possibility that opportunistic scavengers pick off the lower ones. Yucca plants with kills usually flaunt more than one horned lizard per plant, each impaled on a different leaf—one researcher found a yucca decorated with twenty-three.

The Torrey yucca sports a big rosette of leaves almost as tall as I, the leaf margins frayed with white fibers curling off in graceful curves and loops and Spencerian flourishes. From the center of the leaves rises an opulent stalk of close-packed creamy flowers whose thick waxy petals feel like oilcloth; unlike agaves, yuccas do not die after flowering. Soft red stains the sepals, stocked with red anthocyanins (the pigments that make beets red), which absorb heat and hasten blooming at this cool end of the season. Minute flies speckle the one fully open flower. As I watch them, out of the corner of my eye, two threadlike legs disappear around the corner of the stalk as a large brown-and-yellow-striped *Polistes* wasp probes for pollen.

Farther on down the slope, blooms of tiny straw-yellow cones cluster the spiky branches of Mormon tea, and the limber dark red stems of leatherplant bend and snap back at my passage. Both are traditional medicinal plants. Leatherplant, so named because of its supple, tough branches, is also called *sangre de drago*—dragon's blood—for the reddish juice it exudes, a sap painted on ailing gums and used to treat sore eyes.

The medicinal use of plants by prehistoric peoples fascinates me: how many fatal poisonous plants were ingested before the knowledge of their toxicity was secure? How did people without knowledge of the complex chemistry involved, through trial and error and visions that we have lost, find plants with healing properties? How many generations did it take for the connections to be made? How was the most effective use found: decoction, poultice, tea, or simply eating? What were the incantations necessary to ensure their efficacy?

The same questions intrigue present-day botanists who work with native healers, the *curanderos* who have an encyclopedic knowledge of native plant cures and are themselves as endangered as many plants. Today's researchers have documented that many of the plants of primitive remedies contain chemicals that help in diabetes and heart disease and dozens of other human ills, and new research indicates that some of these plant products also have anticancer properties. Some compounds are so difficult to synthesize that their only source may be the plants themselves. And no one knows how many plants have healing properties yet to be discovered.

How important the passage of information in prehistoric times must have been, the transfer of precious knowledge from generation to generation: this leaf or stalk helps with childbirth, this one helps with sore gums, be careful not to rub your eyes when you pick this one, and here, this one right by my foot, this pretty white flower, will give you a vision of heaven. One way or another.

Another draw comes in from the left, three feet wide, with a flat, even, gravelly bottom that crunches pleasantly underfoot. The bed is relatively clean and fine-grained and must get a good sloshing out now and then judging by the fact that there is so little vegetation in it—occasionally a grass plug, a single buckwheat with flat-to-the-sand gray spatulate leaves, but mostly just empty floor in which the crisp, precise, teardrop imprints of collared peccaries register sharply. Peccaries are common in the Chisos Mountain area of Big Bend and most likely to be expected in this catclaw–sotol–prickly pear habitat along a twisting dry streambed. As much as I would like to see one, I am chary—I would not like to surprise a boar or matriarch at naptime. Although they are not likely to attack, I don't fancy being trapped in the way of those saber-sharp tusks in a confined area.

These small relatives of Old World swine travel in limited herds, usually half a dozen or so, needing areas with both free water and prickly pears to provide moisture in their diet. Unlike most animals, which find such food unpalatable to poisonous, peccaries relish both oak leaves and acorns and tolerate the amount of oxalic acid in prickly-pear cacti through modifications of their kidneys.

Different herds may have overlapping territories and mark their boundaries with secretions from a gland on their back, which must be removed to make them edible. Although many early Americans used them for food, James Ohio Pattie, a mountain man in the early 1800s, wrote that they were as offensive as polecats and that they "killed a great many, but could never bring ourselves to eat them."

The easy walking is but a momentary respite. Watching ahead and congratulating myself on the easier passage, I walk right into a catclaw, one of the several "wait-a-minute" bushes, because that's what it takes to disengage yourself from their clutches. The draw

COLLARED PECCARY
(*Dicotyles tajacu*)

cuts deeper, the banks grow higher. Turning again walks me into the sun. All the empty grass seed heads, all the sotol spines, burn with backlight.

A patriarchal prickly pear grows on the bank and down into the draw, one pad stuck out like a flagman's arm in warning, blocking passage. Its center has become corticated and browned, supporting a wreath of green pads. Not only inch-long spines but fine bristly hairs called glochids tuft the pads. From sad experience I'll take the spines any day: they hurt but can be extracted. Fine as angel's hair, glochids slip into the skin and then fester for days. Even worse is blind prickly pear, which has no spines, only glochids. A strong wind loosens them and blows them into the eyes of cattle, eventually causing blindness.

When wood rats nibble cactus pads, or peccaries jog down the wash, they frequently break off pieces of opuntia cactus joints because the joints detach so easily. Since even the bits and pieces root, fragmentation contributes to rapid spreading—overgrazed range is beset by prickly pear and cholla for this reason. If mature, a cactus pad can withstand desiccation until roots develop from its areoles, the points of spine growth. Roots also sprout easily where branches languish on the ground, and both cholla and prickly-pear thickets form lethal hedges in this way.

I sit down in the gravelly bed to catch up on notes, and the prickly pear defines my view of the world. Its rounded silhouette interrupts the Sierra del Carmen in the distance, displaces the profile of Nugent Mountain close by. Shooting from off its neat scalloped outline are the yucca and sotol stalks on the rimline, mesquite boughs and creosote bush branches on the bank, and a shaving brush of Mormon tea growing in the sand behind.

Sun lights the bold, simple shapes of the pads. Quarter-inch cinnamon-brown dots centered with gray speckle every one. A large hole perforates one pad like a Henry Moore sculpture, and two others have their margins so nibbled that now one is a mitten, the other a heart, probably the work of peccaries, which prefer the new pads for their succulence and softer thorns. Succulence has developed in at least two dozen different plant families as an efficient means of storing water. With such a vital store, protection from thirsty animals becomes a necessity, and along with succulence most desert plants also developed spines and unpalatability. In the case of prickly pear, a layer of insoluble calcium oxalate crystals lies under the epidermis, which both slows evaporation and is toxic to most animals.

While grasses beside me gossip and quiver in the breeze, the opuntia pads are stolid, unmoving, immutable. This old prickly pear has the same enduring character and dignity as a venerable oak tree. In this cactus there are years of sun and very little rain. It has survived insects and flash floods, cold Decembers and sweltering Augusts. Survived them all. It rooted here by chance, made the best of what it had and grew, a pad at a time, a survivor in a desert that takes no prisoners.

Salud.

Opulent cushions of blackfoot, a white daisy with a yellow center, grow where the wash widens and the banks reflect heat onto the sand. Newly opened flowers are striped deep pink on the back. The close-packed disk flowers confirm the joys of a hand lens: the flowers are tiny yellow tubes spreading open at the top into five-petaled stars, each tip fringed.

Big boulders totter on steps of light gray limestone, sometimes stained snowy white. A tiny rock lizard scampers in front of me, the first I've seen this spring. As the arroyo approaches the valley, it flattens, widens, and the channels braid in sinuous curves. Drifts of lupine, a spectacular blue purple, grow in the sand and saturate flanking hillside—the earth has put on its old gray bonnet and decorated it with ribbons of blue lupines. They perfume the air like narcissus.

Mineral deposits stain the flanking hillsides gray green and dark mauve and mustard yellow. Some fine-grained deposits are full of nodules, sparkling with fine crystals on the broken surface. Quarter-inch veins of halite cut one wall, flashing silver in the sunlight. Mudstone crumbles into neat little cubes. A tiny butterfly lands on a patch of dark brown soil precisely its same color.

Suddenly the view opens out to dry, layered hills, colors that

BLACKFOOT DAISY
(*Melampodium leucanthemum*)

change from buff to charcoal, from sienna to umber, names that go
back to when all pigments came from the earth. In the distance a
row of dust devils lifts off. Studding the terrain are the same
rounded and ragged plants familiar at the top of the arroyo, now
spread out and separated. And sometimes there is nothing at all in
the desert's ultimate economy of means—obstacles removed, trees
dispensed with, objects discarded along the way, just to get down
to this precise, bare-bones landscape.

I turn back to rendezvous with Susan and stop dead in my tracks. All the sandy channels look alike, and for the life of me I can't tell which one that disappears around which hillock is the one that will deliver me back to our meeting place. Not for the first time the implications of being alone in the desert and the potentials for disaster strike me: stumbling onto a rattlesnake, spraining an ankle, confronting an irritable peccary, or getting embarrassingly lost.

And my next thought is, Good. *Good.* The desert grants me expanded time, time to perceive, to enjoy, to ask questions, to learn. I may get to be here for a while by default, the sensible, responsible housewife freed into a maze of dry channels that feed only into each other. As Ed Abbey says, "the desert, any desert, suggests always the promise of something unforeseeable, unknown but desirable, waiting around the next turn in the canyon wall, over the next ridge or mesa, somewhere within the wrinkled hills."

Perhaps someday someone will pass this empty spot and watch a swirl of dust and wonder who evanesced here, spun upward in a fine spinning flurry of contemplation.

Instead, I concentrate for a moment, choose my channel, and walk up to meet Susan.

2

OF DESERT RIVERS
AND PIPISTRELLES

A dozen of us embark on a week's river trip down the lower canyons of the Rio Grande, an eighty-five-mile reach from La Linda to Dryden Crossing, Texas, under the auspices of the Chihuahuan Desert Research Institute. We are to check out the reptile fauna on both sides of the river, and to corroborate or extend current known ranges in an area that has been little studied before and, in some places, not at all—only four lizard species are currently recorded for this area. Both physiology and limited mobility bind desert reptiles to their region, and their distribution closely reflects the influence of both ecology and history.

A group of herpetologists setting off on a lizard hunt looks like a scene out of the "The Hunting of the Snark," a motley file dressed in varying degrees of desert shabby, accoutered with collecting bags tucked in their belts, and an assortment of "zappers," zappers being

17

two half-inch-wide rubber bands looped together, operated sling-shot fashion. I suspect herpetologists enjoyed misspent youths, rubber-banding tin cans off the back fence. The trick is to snap the lizard hard enough to stun it but gently enough not to damage it, a fine and delicate art.

Lizards are plentiful in deserts because, with their nearly impervious skins, their ability to excrete almost solid uric acid rather than liquid urine, and their propensity to get most of their moisture requirements from the food they eat, they were physiologically "preadapted" to dry seasons twenty-five to forty million years ago, and slipped with relative ease into living under desert conditions year round. With further adaptations in behavior, such as aligning their bodies to or away from the sun to warm or avoid heat, they moved quickly into the rapidly expanding habitat of the Chihuahuan Desert.

Along the Rio Grande, the ground is riven with runoff channels, cacti are legion, the sun unremitting, and I find it hard to look ahead for a lizard and not become impaled on a pencil cholla or tasajilla, the spines of which are covered by a sheath that remains painfully in the skin long after the spine is removed. Only one lizard, a marbled whiptail, streaks across the hot sand and escapes, uncaptured.

We return empty-handed, a state that becomes more common than not this spring, for it is very dry in trans-Pecos Texas, and there is a dearth of insects. Walking in the grass alongside the river I would expect to see thousands of grasshoppers flying up at every step and yet there are so few as to be notable. No rain has fallen in this part of western Texas since last October, and it is now nearing the end of May. The dark green leaves of the incessant creosote bush have tarnished to yellow. Vegetation provides not only food for the lizards' insect and spider prey but increased cover and protection as well. Both prey and vegetation populations fluctuate with rainfall. In years lacking sufficient prey, lizards curtail their aboveground activity and do not reproduce. The atmosphere is crusty. My throat feels as if I have swallowed a dirty dust mop. Nearly every plant, even the vindictive cactus, is a desiccated wisp.

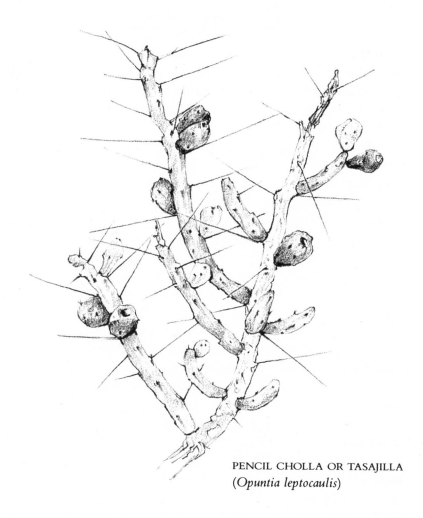

PENCIL CHOLLA OR TASAJILLA
(*Opuntia leptocaulis*)

Herpetologist Jim Scudday estimates that we are seeing only about a third of the lizards he expected to see. Even the tiny pipistrelle bats fly in full sunshine, foraging long after their usual hours. Seeing them out during the heavy heat hours (it's over 90 degrees in the shade every day) underlines the stress that the lack of rain brings to desert inhabitants.

The next morning, while we wait for the rafts to be packed, Scudday sketches a map in the sand and says in his soft West Texas accent, "If you want a line on the ground for the eastern margin of the

Chihuahuan Desert, I'd draw it down the Pecos River on the basis of plant communities. Lechuguilla and creosote bush both run out just east of the Pecos."

On his sand map Scudday limns a couple of scallops to the north where desert intergrades with grassland, a dynamic transition band where in some years the grassland gains and in others, desert. A squiggly line defines the amorphous western boundary, a broad doming of land straddling the New Mexico–Arizona line, where many species of the Chihuahuan Desert reach their western extension. Having delineated the 200,000 square miles of Chihuahuan Desert, with a flourish he marks the heart of the Chihuahuan Desert in north-central Mexico with an X. Only the northern rim, some 10 percent of its total land area, lies in the United States, the remainder being in Mexico. The Chihuahuan Desert is the most upland of the North American deserts, with half of it above four thousand feet in altitude, the lowest part where we are, along the Rio Grande.

The raking light casts sharp shadows in the sand grooves, and even early in the day the sun sears my shoulders. I look up to see a blatantly blue sky and know that by lunchtime the temperature will be three figures, a "typical" desert day: no clouds, full sun, hot wind in the afternoon, no shade.

Spinning bubbles on the river's surface gleam in the morning light, coalescing and separating, shiny as Christmas-tree balls on the pewter sheen of the water. Damselflies perch on every branch leaning over the water, their gossamer wings glittering on narrow bodies of lavender, gray, green, black, rusty red, and light blue with black markings.

We push downstream; the current is so lethargic that the raft has to be rowed. Spring is the low, slow time of the year for the Rio Grande. So much water is taken out upstream for irrigation that essentially the Rio Grande dries up after El Paso, and the river we travel is fed by the Rio Conchos, up from Mexico. We move so slowly down the river that there is ample time to plant watch.

Our slow wending downriver emphasizes the richness of life along riverbanks in the midst of desert dryness. Like all desert

20

rivers, the Rio Grande nourishes a belt of rich riparian vegetation, behind which unmitigated desert takes over. Within that narrow green ecosystem, seep willow and giant reed grow too thickly to push through. Most of the flowered cane stalks are upright but many tilt out toward the river, lances in a Renaissance battlepiece by Uccello.

The lushness, the leaf patterns, are those of a Rousseau primitive painting, the verdancy sparked with exotic flashes of color—in this case, hooded and Scott's orioles that ring orange, competing for sheer brilliance with cardinals and summer tanagers. Say's and black phoebes flit along the bank. Canyon wrens carol the whole day long, cascades of melodies. The varied songs of the yellow-breasted chats hanging in the canes float out over the water. Whenever we leave a lunch site, Chihuahuan ravens check it out. Smallish ravens, they show their diagnostic white breast-feather tips only up close.

RIO GRANDE

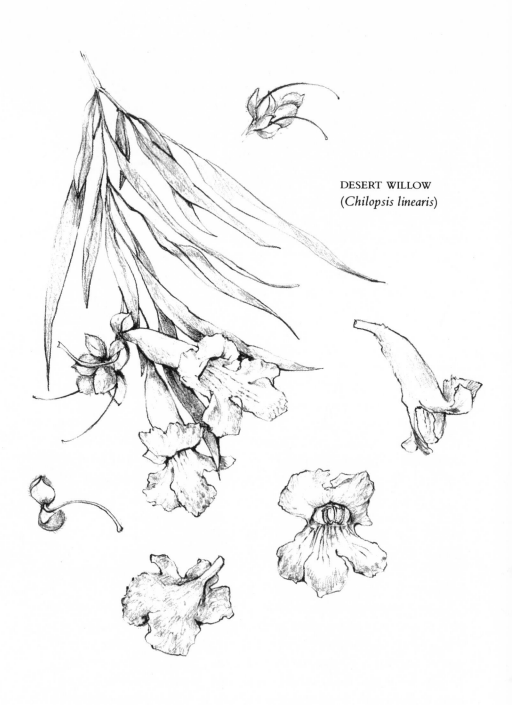

DESERT WILLOW
(*Chilopsis linearis*)

Once six wild turkeys pick across a river terrace, making short-hop flights but mostly just waddling.

Birdsongs, interknotted like beautiful lace patterns, grace the river. The continual diapason reminds me of one of those onomato-poetic children's books in which the cow says "*moo,*" the mourning dove says "*coo,*" the catbird says "*mew,*" and the white-winged dove says, "*Who cooks for who?*" Or, south of the border, "*Cucu-rucu-coo.*"

Away from the riverbank the Chihuahuan Desert radiates heat like a wood stove. Numerous holes perforate a mound of sand built up under a desert willow; Sammy Marshall identifies them as belong-ing to pocket mice. Sammy (from his middle name, Sammons) is doing graduate work in mammology, and pocket mice are his specialty. Each mouse has one or two entry holes, which often get drifted over during the day, causing the resident considerable cleanup work but at least keeping it safe from marauding rattlesnakes.

The entry holes are smaller around than a broom handle. Pocket mice weigh but a few ounces and are tiny enough to sit in the palm of one's hand with room to spare, a smallness that presents them with tremendous problems of thermoregulation because of the large surface in relation to volume. Even more than the legendary kangaroo rat, pocket mice are independent of water. They excavate deep burrows, sometimes up to five feet deep, which provide them with a more favorable environment of lower temperature and humidity that may be triple or more that above ground. Beneath ground they undergo daily cycles of torpor any time their food supply slips below normal. Torpor cuts down on food consumption and undoubtedly contributes to the longevity of this genus com-pared to most rodents, which have an almost annual population turnover.

One morning Sammy finds a cactus mouse in his live trap, a wee gray mouse right out of a fairy-tale illustration, with huge eyes and an unfurred tail much longer than its body. It quickly swivels out of Sammy's gloved hands and darts for the bush so swiftly I hardly see it go. Restricted to low, arid desert, cactus mice cope with high daytime temperatures and a drop in food or water supply

23

WESTERN DIAMONDBACK RATTLESNAKE
(*Crotalus atrox*)

as pocket mice do, by becoming torpid. Their metabolic rate, already low to begin with, lowers further and their body temperature drops several degrees below normal. Such daily estivation extends from a few hours in cooler weather to eight weeks in summer. This rapidly adapting genus of rodents has been around only a million years or so, and has quickly acclimated to desert conditions.

Scattered around the burrow openings, shells of *Rhabdotus* land snails litter the sand, empty and bleached white, a coiled nothingness in my hand. Beyond exposure to high temperatures and lack of water, the desert habitat poses other survival problems for snails, such as the absence of suitable food except during the short rainy season. Snails emerge to feed only at night after rains, and during the day keep to damper, cooler microhabitats: the shade under shrubs or buried an inch or so below the surface, or cloistered in the more humid interstices of ground litter.

During dry times the live snail pulls itself into the smaller upper whorls, seals the opening with an airtight papery cover, leaving the largest bottom whorl filled with insulating air. The thin, crisp shell rocking in my palm reflects well over 80 to 90 percent of the total solar radiation hitting it. The cushion of insulating air combined with high shell reflectivity allows a snail to remain within tolerable temperature limits despite desert heat. In such a state they may exist for months without water, losing only 0.5 milligram a

24

day (since it contains around 1,400 milligrams of water it can still survive for years). When enough moisture is available, an activated snail can ingest about forty-five times as much water in one day as it loses hibernating the same length of time.

Still, from the number of shells littering the ground and crunching underfoot, longevity is not a snail's lot.

The first time Scudday points out candelilla they look like nothing so much as thick, clumsy clumps of grass growing out of the gravelly limestone slope. Farther downstream we stop to look at one of the many abandoned candelilla "factories" along the river. Endemic to the Chihuahuan Desert, candelilla is practically leafless, its pencil-thin stalks a dull waxy green. When I pull a stem to draw, it breaks off at the ground, dripping its milky sap (like all Euphorbias) onto my sneakers.

Except for grasses, which are very plentiful in the Chihuahuan Desert, candelilla used to be the most utilized plant in the Big Bend area. A century ago, when the price of wax was higher, it was a most important part of the local economy. The gray wax coating that forms on the stems is undoubtedly a protective device that helps prevent the evaporation of moisture; plants growing in areas of least rainfall produce the most wax per unit weight (many desert medicinal plants also produce more chemicals per unit weight in the desert than when grown under ideal conditions).

In the old days, laborers pulled up whole plants, bound them into bundles, and then packed them by burro to the rendering vats. The most primitive vats were built and set near the river. The plants were dumped into a solution of water and sulfuric acid and boiled, loosening the wax that then floated to the surface as scum. Skimmed off, it hardened as it cooled; when refined it was water resistant, hard but malleable. Before synthetic waxes, it was used for waterproofing and phonograph records, in automobile and floor waxes and shoe polishes, and is even listed on the label of the multivitamins I take. Its scientific name, *Euphorbia antisyphilitica,* indicates a belief in its medical prowess by some native peoples.

Now limestone walls bound the Rio Grande, gutted and punc-

WHITETHORN
(*Acacia neovernicosa*)

tured by crevices and niches. I feel as if we are figures in a Piranesi
stage set, full of rococo grottos and blind arcades, holding the
bizarre shapes of pencil cholla and candelilla, the curious ocotillo and
singular lechuguilla, any one of which could be a plant more of the
imagination than of the real. Adding a further theatrical note, the
prickly-pear pads reflect the light like metallic disks precipitously
balanced, one on the other.

Kneeing the air out of my mattress, I count dozens of curly pods of
whitethorn littering the sandy ground. The outer sides of the pods is
reddish brown; the inner, light tan pink, always empty, seeds sprinkling the soil like rough-ground pepper. Seeds remain only in pods
still swinging on the bush.

   A click beetle scuttles onto my ground cloth, recognizable by
its slender shape and the way in which the pronotum is prolonged

backward into spines on either side. When it goes too quickly across a pleat in the plastic it tips over, folds its legs over its abdomen, and flips upright.

On the underside of its thorax is a plate with a tab on the forward end, a small projection that fits into a socket toward the back. When supine, it arches its back so that it pulls the tab almost out of the socket, and then quickly snaps it back in by straightening its body. The forceful movement pops it into the air and, most of the time, it lands right side up. I cannot resist flipping it over on its back time after time to watch its acrobatics. When it finally lands off the plastic onto the ground, it flees to the protection of the nearest acacia with, I fancy, a sigh of "Enough already."

Next a thistledown velvet ant careers across the sand. Half-an-inch long, it staggers as erratically as a vagrant cottonwood seed. Velvet ants are not ants but wasps, the females wingless, the males winged and somewhat larger, both densely covered with pubescence—white hairs coat this black wasp so heavily that it appears hoary. Velvet ant young are external parasites of the larvae and pupae of various wasps, bees, beetles, and flies. The adults, despite the fact that they look cute enough to pick up, have one of the most painful and dangerous stings of any insect in the desert.

Lacy insect tracks pattern the beach, laid by the endless searchers after the Holy Grail of food. The insect fauna of Big Bend and the lower Rio Grande canyons is relatively unstudied. Someone suggests that this is because this is not an agricultural area so there are no "pests" to damage crops and justify large expenditures for research and control. Insects certainly abound here. There isn't a bush that doesn't have either perforated or rolled leaves, or branches clotted with tubes of white spittle. One plant of bicolor mustard growing on the sandy beach is so beset by ants, moths, bees, and bee flies it practically vibrates.

When we stop for lunch, Steve Levey always disappears immediately, on the prowl for lizards. This time he returns with a regretful look and a limp side-blotched lizard. He stepped on a piece of wood under which the lizard lay and unintentionally dispatched it.

27

BICOLOR MUSTARD
(*Nerisyrenia camporum*)

Spencer F. Baird, building up an unparalleled natural-history collection as Assistant Secretary of the Smithsonian Institution, named
this small, ubiquitous species *Uta Stansburiana* for Captain Howard
Stansbury, who first surveyed the Great Salt Lake.

Scarcely as long as my palm, the lizard's skin gleams like an
enameled Cellini fancy, silver tan clouded with bluish gray down
the spine. I run my finger up and down the clean smoothness
of its back; in reverse, the scales, laid with fine keels, snag my
finger. On the top of its head I can barely make out its parietal eye,
which registers light intensity, synchronizing its rhythmic daily
activities with different intensities of light, inhibiting activity when
light is too strong or too dim. The fine spiny feet with their hairlike
black nails look much too delicate to carry this little clockwork
creature scurrying across the hot desert floor.

The "blotch" on either side of the body, just behind the front
legs, is charcoal gray; placed low on the sides, it can be difficult to
see when the lizard is on the move. Unable to cope with extreme
midday heat like most lizards, side-blotched lizards are active in the
cool hours at either end of the day, taking refuge in the shade during
the heat of the day—with fatal consequences for this one.

As it is early in the year, this may be a very young lizard,
generally less well coordinated and skilled in avoidance behavior
than adults. In this treacherous desert environment, survival to
maturity must be the exception. Mortality rates peak a few days
after hatch and a scant 10 percent live longer than a year. The
average life span of this little creature is but four to five months,
making it an "annual" species particularly able to respond to the
vagaries of the desert environment.

The imbricated covering of scales looks protective, but considerable moisture escapes from the hinge areas between scales. The
greatest danger to this side-blotched lizard (or any small desert
animal, for that matter) is desiccation. To remain in water balance, it
must account for losses that occur through the skin, or through
elimination and evaporation. Many desert animals get by without
free water by eating moisture-containing food such as insects, or by
actually creating free water through metabolism. When foodstuffs

are metabolized, fats and carbohydrates are created, which in turn break down to carbon dioxide and water.

The problem for this tiny carnivore is that the end products of eating protein are carbon dioxide, water, and nitrogen, the last a toxic metabolite that must be gotten rid of. Mammals excrete urea, a nitrogen product that requires a great deal of water to dilute its toxicity, more than a desert creature can afford to lose. To avoid this, lizards do not excrete urea but uric acid, which is nontoxic, almost insoluble, and requires little water for elimination. Molecule for molecule, twice as much nitrogen can be excreted in uric acid as in urea. Mammals have a very limited capacity to concentrate urine; lizards and birds go through additional steps utilizing enzymes that mammals do not have, and produce this semisolid uric-acid excrement.

I wonder, at this heavy-heat noontime that leaves me awash in perspiration, why this little lizard wasn't underground and safe. As do most desert rodents, side-blotched lizards utilize underground burrows during very hot hours to take advantage of the higher relative humidity. Side-blotched lizards frequently use wood-rat nests for shade and shelter and, ultimately, population size may depend on the availability of these nests. In some areas, which otherwise provide good habitat, these lizards may not be present if there is no wood-rat population. In the absence of wood-rat nests, side-blotched lizards have to burrow directly into the ground beneath bushes.

Another noon, looking for any shade at all in which to have lunch, we climb up the riverbank to a shelf backed by a high rock. Steve scoops up a bark-colored tree lizard resting upside down on a pale boulder. Judging by its lethargy, Scudday thinks that it may be out of its usual habitat because of stress. Like all lizards, in wet years females develop good fat reserves and produce large litters; in drought years, as this one is, when insects are scarce to absent, tree-lizard populations are reduced.

Occasionally we pull ashore to investigate the Indian middens that remain all along the river. One ancient midden, blown over with sand, is patched with dog cholla, whose joints break off easily, depress when stepped on, and then spring up and grab you on the back of the ankle with spines made of spring steel. Usually these middens are nothing more than heaps of dirt containing burned rock, or shattered metates and broken manos with which corn was ground. It always gives me pause that such undistinguished mounds radiate such a feeling of the presence of those who lived here in the desert in a way that modern man cannot.

Farther downriver the lunette opening of a large cave, three hundred feet up on a cliff face, looms darkly. To reach it we must scramble across a treacherous, loose slope where every dry paper-flower rustles like a rattlesnake, and where there is nothing to hold on to unless I want to have a handful of every kind of spine there is. The cave is shaped like a big clam shell, eight feet high at the opening, sloping back ten feet, the ceiling blackened. Unlike most utilized caves, it does not open to the south or southeast but to the northwest, its size and the relative lack of living sites in this area making it attractive despite its unfavorable exposure. Probably a winter home, it still offered some protection against the cold storms that can drop temperatures to below freezing here.

At the cave's lip are holes that must have started out as metates and then became worn down so deeply that a pestle rather than a mano was needed for grinding. The cave was undoubtedly occupied by Big Bend Basketmakers, who shared many attributes with Basketmakers to the northwest, weaving baskets and sandals, living in caves and, later, in pit houses, growing some corn and beans and possibly squash.

The study of coprolites, or petrified feces, documents that primitive man may have lived better than modern man has given him credit for. Coprolites preserve microscopic evidence as fine as pollen breathed or parasite eggs carried and, by extrapolation, permit an accurate and detailed reconstruction of individual prehistoric life and its environment. They witness that gathering was more important than hunting, and that the Basketmakers exploited their environment efficiently, maintaining a varied diet of both animal and vegetable foods: prickly pear, agave, seeds, identifiable bones of young rodents (primarily wood rats), rabbits and raccoons, lizards and snakes, birds and fish. Many of the animals they caught and ate then are no longer present here.

Modern myth has it that these early dwellers were undernourished and parasite-ridden scavengers who lived at the edge of starvation. But the coprolite evidence indicates a good state of health. Despite a rough diet dominated by fiber, seeds, and the epidermis of prickly pear, there are no indications of intestinal laceration, or of parasites. Prehistoric man enjoyed a sturdy digestive system, likely a great deal hardier than modern man's.

San Francisco Canyon crawls with more infinitesimal ants than I ever knew existed. Inexorably they stream into, over, around, and through everything I own. The ants scurry up the small bushes of evening stars just getting ready to bloom and explore the big leaflets of cassia, closed when we arrive but opening as the sun goes down, leaves so thickly haired that they appear silver-frosted. Other ants busy themselves about a mimosa that looks like a miniature acacia, its leaflets less than an eighth-of-an-inch long and minute spines rimming scant inch-long pods. Ants that don't have anything else to do swarm over toothbrush and toothpaste and everything else I've set out for the night.

With the temperature close to 100 degrees and an annoyance of ants, I do the only sensible thing: I head for the river to cool off. I am concentrating on seeing how deep I can sit in the river and not float downstream when I see a darting shadow out of the corner of my eye. I turn just in time to see a whiptail lizard slither into the rocks. I wait. It returns, head sweeping from side to side, long tongue flicking out as it prowls, searching for food. It scarfs up many kinds of insects as well as insect eggs and larvae, its wedge-shaped head especially useful in flipping over the twigs and rocks that shelter termites, its favored food (today I hope it's after ants). At any movement on my part the lizard skitters into hiding though I am at least twenty-five feet away, testifying to its excellent vision.

When I go back up the hill I alert Scudday. A master zapper, within a few minutes he holds a Texas spotted whiptail, a handful of lizard around nine inches long from snout to tail tip. In color it is

32

somber, almost dark gray with black stripes and dashes down its back and on its flanks, a blue wash on its legs and a rusty wash on its rump. The tail is easily twice its body length and drapes well down Scudday's arm; the scales on it are keeled. Its underside shines brightly, a reflective white.

No markings bar the tail or large back legs, while its back patterning continues down onto its front legs. Its large muscular hind legs indicate a fast-moving bipedal species, in which the shortened forelegs contribute little to its rapid movement, and make it look like a miniature brontosaurus. By contrast, legs of equal length, such as those of a tree lizard, are characteristic of slow-moving or arboreal lizards where both pairs of legs are more or less equally involved in movement, the forelegs pulling and the hind legs pushing.

It revives, black eyes blinking, and Scudday pops it into a damp collecting bag. Out of the same collecting bag Scudday hands me a greater earless lizard before he frees it, a slender animal with its back speckled tan and gray, and pairs of dark square spots down the middle. Bright inky-blue stains, like large Cs, are a startling contrast against its white patent-leather belly.

At dusk the nighthawks come, swooping low for their allotted time, then leave. Then come the bats. One minute there are none, the next minute they plait the sky with their high-speed barrel rolls and outside loops.

The tiniest bats are the western pipistrelles, which forage for but a short period at night and again before sunup, marked by their erratic flight as well as their minute size. Their small size gives them a greater body surface area in proportion to their mass, making them vulnerable to temperature extremes. They remain inactive or dormant at low air temperatures when they lose body heat too quickly. High temperatures put a severe strain on their thermoregulation; sweating is too expensive a way to cool—an animal this small loses almost a third of its body weight in moisture per hour. Long-term hibernation and short-term daily dormancy, both periods of reduced metabolic rate, help in survival, as well as time spent in a hibernal (where bats hang out) of relatively constant air temperature and high humidity.

Pipistrelles additionally conserve energy by reducing their metabolism while in flight, thus lowering the temperature gradient between body and air. The metabolic rate of desert bats relates to their diet; those that depend upon an almost pure, high-cholesterol insect diet have a much lower metabolic rate than those that feed on fruit, nectar, and pollen.

The pipistrelles soon disappear, and half a dozen Mexican free-tail bats take the sky, larger in silhouette, flapping like ornithopters. When most flying insects disappear at night, so do the insectivorous bats, leaving that single mosquito, which invariably nails me.

The next morning, while I sit on the beach sketching, Sammy brings over a pipistrelle he found on the ground with a broken wing bone. He thinks it probably ticked the tip of a branch diving for an insect and snapped the threadlike bone.

It lies comatose, barely breathing, in my hand, its body no larger than a pecan, its blond fur as fine as velvet. Its ears are dark brown, against which the tragus, a small projection that aids in echolocation, is prominent. The tiny feet are less than a quarter-inch long.

Its delicate, wizened wings lie closely pleated to its sides. Sammy gently stretches them out to reveal the pouch at the tail end with which it scoops up insects. Hairlike bones thread the gossamer membrane of the wings, now translucent when stretched, threaded with parallel veins; vasodilatation of these wing veins provides one pathway for heat loss.

As I hold this exquisite creature, I grieve at the accident that brought it to this pass at the same time feeling selfishly grateful to have this chance to examine it close up. It beggars my imagination to understand how something so small can be so complex. I think of all the things it can do that I cannot, of what I know that it does not, and of what we share, a common chromosome perhaps, or a retinal cell. Because it cannot fly I know that it will not, cannot, live, that the wing cannot be splinted and healed. Such a small miscalculation to be so fatal.

On this fresh sunshiny morning a chill draft unfurls from the river, reminding me of my own mortality.

34

3

OF HORSE LUBBERS
AND CREOSOTE BUSHES

Out in the Chihuahuan Desert with me this fall day are my husband, Herman, and my cousin Earl Milner, who, unaccountably, has never been exposed to the desert. Because he is from the neatly trimmed town of Colonial Williamsburg, it pleases me to show off the high horizons and rock-bound canyons that the Colonists never dreamed of.

Unlike the other deserts, which have spring blooms of annuals, many Chihuahuan Desert flowers appear after summer rains, making a splendid show in September and October. Late fall mornings in the Chihuahuan Desert are halcyon—flowers still in profusion, comfortingly warm but not breathlessly hot, sky spotless, air sparkling.

Black vultures hunch on fence posts, shrugging their shoulders at the coolness of the morning. One facing the sun clasps a fence post and holds its wings, elbows crooked, out from its sides. When it straightens them, the feathers fringe gracefully. Then it slowly pivots, displaying its primaries to the sun like a Las Vegas chorus girl in full costume.

When I sit down to draw one plant, I find it impossible to concentrate because the dozens of other flowers at my elbow distract me. Gaura, a small evening primrose, blooms profusely. Pink windmills spread big patches of intensely lavender flowers with sticky stems: creeping and climbing plants are frequent in the Chihuahuan Desert. A mat of ground cherry tangles across the ground, little Japanese lantern seed pods just forming.

Trailing stems of angel-trumpet vine catch in my boot laces, embellished with flowers that look like small, delicate, very long-tubed morning glories, adapted for a hawkmoth's long proboscis. Like many other moth-pollinated flowers, they open at sundown and close after sunrise. The Chihuahuan Desert is one of the greatest areas of diversity for the morning glory family, in which many species have self-pollinated flowers that never open but are pollinated in the bud stage. In early summer, when there are few insects, this plant is strongly self-pollinating, but when adult moths leave the cocoon, the plant shifts to producing flowers appropriate for moth pollination. Self-pollination may be an adaptation to seasonal drought and in moth-pollinated plants, like this one, is insurance against the uncertainty of hawkmoth pollinators, who may not fly on cool evenings or may be scarce in drought years.

When I stand up and sight across the top of the vegetation, the illusion is of solid growth. When I look down at the ground at the actual number of plants, there is by far more parched, mud-cracked soil than there are plants. Black swallowtails and white cabbage butterflies skywrite above horizons of yellow and lavender.

There must be thousands of bushes of Texas silverleaf, loaded with big lavender flowers. Where many flowers cluster on top of the bush the name becomes understandable as they haze the desert with a silvery lavender. Local lore has it that this is Zane Grey's "purple sage." The only trouble is, silverleaf is neither purple nor true sage, which belongs to the mint family, or sagebrush, which has tiny

TEXAS SILVERLEAF OR PURPLE SAGE
(*Leucophyllum frutescens*)

yellow flowers and belongs to the daisy family, but a figwort, cousin to snapdragons and penstemons and Indian paintbrush. If so, Zane Grey has forever and indelibly fixed this figwort in literature by the wrong name and the wrong color—so much for the power of the printed word.

Earl, his first time out, wishes to see all those threatening denizens of the desert, particularly a tarantula, with which viewers of every desert film have been entertained. When I espy a large dark object on the sand in the distance, I head toward it eagerly, expecting to find a large furry spider but find instead a monstrous shiny black grasshopper plodding along like a spent windup toy with un-grasshopperlike lethargy.

When I pick it up, its two-inch body is surprisingly heavy, and it startles me by hissing—a sound made by the air and fluid being expelled through the spiracles through which it breathes, a fluid that contains an antipredator foam. A dapper devil indeed—a yellow-orange line down its center back and bright yellow markings on its face and legs, a yellow netting on its cover wings and bright rosy-red underwings, vividly mark its body. It bears the sodden name of horse lubber and is endemic to the southern part of the Chihuahuan Desert in the United States.

After Herman photographs it, I set it at the base of an agave rosette, thinking it will take shelter in the shade beneath. Instead it pulls itself slowly upward like a six-legged mountain climber, its feet sensitively tapping and reaching. Unable to get a foothold on the leaf's waxy surface, it locks its feet and clings hooked to the margin. There it remains, sides bellowing slowly in and out.

The waxy coating of the agave leaf comes off like a powder on my fingers. The coating, formed by a deposit of hydrocarbons, protects the large leaf surface by reflecting up to 75 percent of both ultraviolet and near-infrared heat radiation, and lowers the chance of damage when the leaves are dehydrated. It also slows down evaporation, conserving both the water and minerals within.

This impervious coating, while it saves water, also prevents the absorption of the carbon dioxide required in photosynthesis. In photosynthesis water and carbon dioxide are united to form sugars and starches and oxygen in the presence of sunlight. To do so, most nonsucculent plants open their stomata, the ducts through which gaseous exchange goes on, during the day, in the most widespread method of photosynthesis, called the Calvin cycle after its discoverer or, simply, C_3 photosynthesis.

Two other methods of photosynthesis have evolved: one occurs in plants of tropical origin, a two-cycle system called C_4 photosynthesis. The other, first discovered in succulent plants, is called

Crassulacean acid metabolism, or CAM for short, which allows up to a 70 percent saving in water use. Succulent plants are those whose leaves contain unusually large water-storage cells. Succulents like agave open their stomata and take in carbon dioxide only at night. During the day they utilize it for photosynthesis inside the leaf while the stomata are closed, and thus avoid water loss when water stress is high. Although growth and productivity are low because the rate of carbon gain is low, persistence and endurance, not fast growth, are the name of the game.

Open stomata during the day allow evaporative cooling and these thick-leaved agave plants run the danger of overheating on hot days. Nor are rigid, thick leaves capable of movement to avoid sunlight as are, say, the folding leaves of mesquite. But the latter, under water stress, must either wilt or close their stomata and cease photosynthesis. The stolid succulent leaf endures.

But even this seemingly impervious coating is vulnerable: on another leaf is a huge leaf-footed bug, a handsome insect with a flattened chocolate-brown body an impressive inch long, with orange feet and orange-tipped antennae. A Hemiptera, it has sucking mouthparts for feeding on plant tissues, and not even the thick waxy coating of the agave deters it.

I remove the obviously stymied horse lubber and put it back in the grass, where it lumbers away. I have always thought of grasshoppers as quick to scatter, fast to flee, high to hop. This one has a good case of the slows.

Drops of rain pick my rainjacket like a banjo. The clouds are so low I grab a handful of soft damp air and watch it puddle in my palm. A gray quilted October sky holds the horizons of the Chihuahuan Desert together, cuestas and ragged ridges, one behind the other, notched into curious smoky shapes frayed ragged by the rain. Cliff faces glisten and rain jigs off the desert pavement. A usually dry arroyo spins water the color of café au lait, ruffling over rough rocks, spinning in foaming ovals and circles.

The air breathes rain. The small fine drops hiss as they fly through the air, overlaying the sounds of leaves catching rain, the sounds of roots reaching for it, responding to plant knowledge of the drought to come. The leaves and branches shift gently as rain-drops hit in sequence, the nodding and bowing of a vernal string quartet. Most of the Chihuahuan Desert's precipitation, between 60 and 80 percent, falls during the heat of the summer months, often brought by tropical disturbances sweeping up and in from the Gulf of California hundreds of miles to the southwest. This third of an inch of rain turns out to be the last of the summer season.

The Chihuahuan is a rain-shadow desert. The Sierra Madre Occidental and Sierra Madre Oriental in Mexico arose during the long period of mountain building that marked the end of the Meso-zoic and the beginning of the Cenozoic Era sixty-five million years ago, a period during which the Rocky Mountains were also raised. The new mountain barriers blocked the moisture-laden winds that had swept in from the Gulf of California and the Pacific Ocean, cooled them as they rose, and caught their precipitation on their western flanks. On the eastern side, the same winds compressed and heated as they descended, approximately 4 degrees Fahrenheit (F.) for every thousand feet, and arrived hot and dry. The rain-shadow effect is the most fundamental factor in creating the Chihuahuan Desert, causing a dry season that extends from late October into early June.

Summer rainfall exceeds winter rainfall in both amount and predictable occurrence, making up most of the annual average index of less than ten inches. Although plants and animals in the Chi-huahuan Desert must endure nearly eight bone-dry months, they also enjoy a longer and more certain growing season than any other of the U.S. deserts because rain comes during summer's warmth, in contrast to the Great Basin and Mojave deserts, which get most of their moisture in the fall and winter.

Traveling westward, North American deserts form a virtual east-west continuum, from western Texas and the Chihuahuan Desert to the Sonoran Desert in southern California. In the western reaches, the Mojave and Great Basin deserts, winter rainfall pre-dominates, while the central Sonoran Desert is blessed with biseasonal rainfall, shifting to a summer regime in the Chihuahuan Desert.

Rain-pruned petals confetti the ground and cling to my boots. The petals of a small rushpea are rain-shot, and the open flower cups of a lavender rose mallow fill with water and begin to droop, the petals water-soaked and transparent. I brush by a creosote bush and a common sulphur, a butterfly with black-rimmed yellow wings, flushes out in fluttery flight, hovers here, hovers there, and takes thirty seconds before it finds a spot to re-alight. The rain that touches me so lightly must thud like drops of lead onto those delicate, scaled wings.

I lean down to watch a ladybug pick its way down a grass stem and water drizzles down my neck. In my concentration I gradually become aware of silence. The plucking of the rain is gone and it is so still that I hold my breath, afraid that the sound of aspiration will violate the quiet. In the whispery stillness I listen for the resins to gather on the surface of the creosote leaf and leap off into the air. A breeze stirs the branches and the aroma swirls out of every leaf. I inhale that marvelous scent that graces the air, not cloying, not sweet, but resinous and clean. It's what the world ought to smell like when it rains.

I have become quite fond of this unprepossessing feathery, aromatic shrub that covers thirty-five million acres, 6 percent of the land of the coterminous United States. So attuned to the desert environment is it that its range coincides with that of the Chihuahuan, Sonoran, and Mojave—the warm deserts. Its Mexican name, *gobernador*—"governor"—pays tribute to its dominance.

Creosote bush's ancestors and closest relatives grow over five thousand miles away in South America. A few other genera have this same immense gap in their ranges, all plants of arid regions, among them iodine bush, mesquite, and paloverde. I pull off one of the round white furry seed clusters and separate the five dark seeds. Although seeds could have reached southern Mexico and dispersed from there, there is also the possibility that they made the leap in one jump. The South American diploid is apparently self-compatible, so all that was necessary was one pioneer seed to sprout, mature, and self-fertilize. And once it was in place, already preadapted to desert conditions, it quickly became dominant when these conditions

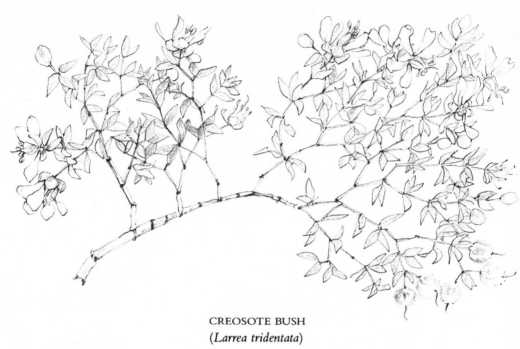

CREOSOTE BUSH
(*Larrea tridentata*)

42

arrived. How it arrived on the North American continent may never be settled and is a fascinating subject for speculation.

When I contemplate the untold number of creosote bushes, the horizon-to-horizon creosote bushes, the is-there-anything-else-but creosote bushes, it is difficult to realize that their arrival in North America is so recent, within the last ten to eleven thousand years. No fossils, no remnants in ancient middens of wood rats that foraged, as they do today, within several hundred yards of their nests and left a record of local vegetation, exist to indicate the creosote bushes arrived till after the Pleistocene.

In the United States all creosote bushes are of a single species, *Larrea tridentata,* but each desert has a different chromosome race. In nature, this increase in chromosome sets, or polyploidy (often artificially induced in hothouse plants for bigger blooms, greater hardiness, and so forth), is most likely to take place during times of climatic instability such as existed during the rapidly warming and drying post-Pleistocene environment into which the creosote bush rapidly expanded. In a polyploid series of this sort, the new polyploids usually have different ecological requirements from the original diploid, fitting each to survive in a different new habitat. Part of creosote bush's success in populating three different deserts is undoubtedly owing to the development of polyploidy. The oldest are the diploids of the Chihuahuan Desert, with two sets of chromosomes; compared to creosote bushes in other deserts, they germinate more rapidly and make faster early growth, can tolerate lower temperatures, and form denser populations of shorter bushes bearing sparser foliage and incurved leaflets. Those of the Sonoran Desert are triploid and less angular in appearance. Those of the Mojave are bushier and may have thicker leaves with more surface resins, presumably in response to greater stress.

The leaves are fresh and dark green, sticky to touch, leathery and dense, with a protective coating that prevents water loss and discourages grazing animals. Spines and thorns (spines are modified leaves; thorns are modified branches) have developed in many desert plants to conserve water and discourage browsing and grazing animals, but creosote bushes are protected by the resins in their leaves, which neither wild game nor domestic cattle can stomach, so unpalatable that "even mules will not touch [it], when so hungry as to eat with avidity the dry twigs of all other shrubs and trees," according to Lieutenant William H. Emory who crossed the Chihuahuan Desert in 1846. When these resins are chemically removed, cattle relish the leaves, which have a nutritive value nearly equal to that of alfalfa.

When grasslands are disturbed, creosote bush arrives promptly and, because it is not browsed, quickly outcompetes native vegetation and, as might be expected, is anathema to ranchers, especially because it is ingeniously resistant to herbicides. One botanical wag suggests that the only way to get rid of creosote bush is to try to cultivate it as a crop.

The major leaf resin, about 15 percent of its weight, is nordihydroguaiaretic acid (NDGA), one of the most powerful antioxidants known. NDGA reduces digestibility in much the same way that tannin does; it is effective against molds and may be effective against dental caries. Creosote bush was, until 1967, when it was synthesized, the best source for NDGA. The most important use of NDGA has been to protect refrigerated and frozen foods, particularly meats, and to retard rancidity in lard and vegetable oil. NDGA is but one of hundreds of natural compounds that make up half the weight of its leaves and stems.

A breeze wafts creosote bush's slightly medicinal aroma and reminds me that the Mexican name *hediondilla* means "little stinker." Long used as remedy for various of man's ailments, creosote bush produces an unusually varied and plentiful supply of natural products. Edward Greene, a botanist slogging across the Sonoran Desert in 1880, reported that the "Indians and Mexicans journeying across these parched wastes, chew them, and even tie bunches of them to the bits in the mouths of their ponies with good results in cases of extreme suffering from fatigue or thirst."

Indian *curanderos* used it as a treatment for arthritis by making a strong decoction of the leaves and upper stems, and immersing the patient in a tubful. Others rubbed the dried leaves on rheumatic limbs, or used it as an antiseptic and a styptic to soothe cuts and bruises. The Pima, Tohono O'odh'n (as the Papago Indians now prefer to be called) and Paiute used it as an emetic and in poultices for sores.

Creosote bush extracts are of interest to modern scientists. In experiments, the lives of female mosquitoes have been almost doubled by receiving extracts of creosote bush. It is thought that NDGA may trap the free radicals, those chemically active atoms or molecules with an unpaired outermost electron, which cause the kind of mischief in the body that hastens aging.

4

OF BARCHANS
AND COTTONWOOD

One October night, Susan and I camped in the dunes of White Sands National Monument. Susan, who slept in her tent, is dry and warm and busying about breakfast. I chose to sleep out and made the mistake of putting my corduroy jeans over my feet for a little extra warmth in the bitterly chill night. This morning my sleeping bag is drenched by a heavy dew. So are the corduroys. I sit swathed in my sleeping bag while they dry. My bones feel made of ice, my fingers as frangible and ready to shatter as icicles. I am as cold and damp as if I had been sailing in an open boat on the North Sea, as immobilized with the cold as an early-flying bee. No wonder one Spanish settler of New Mexico wrote in 1812 that "frequently the milk freezes almost as soon as it leaves the udder of the cow, and we can carry it in a napkin."

Last evening I sat here on this gelid dune and pondered who had first seen these spectacular snowy sands stretching into the night. Perhaps it was Álvar Núñez Cabeza de Vaca, who had been ship-wrecked in 1531 on the Texas Gulf Coast and taken captive by Indians, and in 1536 trekked more than a thousand miles to free-dom. Or perhaps it was one of Francisco Vásquez de Coronado's men, on whose map the entire area between the San Andres and Sacramento mountains that bracket the valley is labeled simply, "Las Salinas." Or was it the Mescalero Apaches, who later raided the impoverished Spanish colonists, beleaguered people who soon found life unendurable in New Mexico and gave up—too cold, too little water, and too many Apaches.

Drizzling through my fingers, the cold sands separate like grains of sugar, faintly gritty, fine and superfine. The hard-packed sand measured 34 degrees a few inches below the surface when I got up, and now at seven-thirty it is still a frigid 40 degrees two-and-a-half inches down. Such sudden cooling presents a problem for animals that must cope with the wide range of temperature within a twenty-four-hour period here, and this may account for the fact that of the White Sands fauna 90 percent are insects and highly mobile birds.

Gypsum sands are soft, most grains angular to subrounded, predominantly medium-size. Gypsum is easily scratched and the myriad furrows on the grain scatter the light, endowing these sands with their eye-glazing whiteness. The gypsum washed out of for-mations deposited some 300 million years ago by an arm of an ancient Permian sea whose waters contained large amounts of cal-cium sulfate, commonly known as gypsum. Some 70 million years ago the same geologic pressures that created the Rocky Mountains also buckled this area gently upward into a high, rounded plateau, followed by another shifting of pressures that shot a pair of fault lines north and south for a hundred miles. Between these lines of weakness the plateau dropped intact as a graben, leaving the paired mountain cliffs of the Sacramento Mountains on the east and the San Andres Mountains on the west facing each other across the basin.

Last night, even while the mountain profiles to the east and west faded to fawn gray, the sands retained their pearly whiteness. The sky remained bright along the rim of the San Andres Mountains, a pale yellow-green sky like Chartreuse in the glass, rolling up to a deepening blue. Then, beyond a waning moon tracking to another station, one star pricked a hole in the blue tent, then a second, then thousands. All around me were peace, serenity, a perfect meshing of sand grain with star track, and the soft warbling of sandhill cranes heading south.

This morning, just before I think I'm finally going to congeal, the sun finally begins to heat my left shoulder, and the air warms enough for me to take off my gloves. The first fly cruises by with an annoyingly loud buzz. I look westward through an arch formed by two cottonwood branches to the San Andres Mountains, whose sooty gray-blue façade emphasizes the whiteness of the dunes.

Several cottonwood trunks, each about eight feet high, spring out of a sand pedestal on the windward side of the dune on which I sit. Their roots, running just under the surface, web the sand twenty feet out. *Populus wislizenii* is the only tree in the Monument. It was named after Frederick Adolphus Wislizenus, one of several European naturalists who traveled this area in the mid-nineteenth century and made notable collections of flora and fauna. Wislizenus arrived from Germany in 1835, traveled south along the Rio Grande to Mexico in 1836, just in time to get caught in Mexican-American hostilities.

Three feet away from me, a leafy stalk from an underground root appears as if out of nowhere. Leaves on the main stalks are average to small for a cottonwood, but the leaves on the branches from outlying roots are ample. Only a few leaves are fresh and whole. Most bear the ravages of insects: some stuck together by leaf rollers, many nibbled on the edge or partly perforated, and some so gutted that only a lattice of veins remains. With such sparse greenery available, insects here must give praise for cottonwoods in their prayers.

On its downwind side, the dune breaks away from the cottonwood roots, revealing a multitude of thin sand layers laid wind by

48

wind, embroidered with hundreds of threadlike roots. The main trunks and larger branches react to sand burial by producing adventitious roots, essentially a floodplain adaptation that also works well in the moving-sand situation of dunes. Most of the cottonwoods in a particular flat or dune are connected by a common shallow secondary root system. With enough moisture for germination present only in the flat interdune area, they start life there, but must soon cope with the encroachment of the sand. Interestingly enough, cottonwoods do not grow in the desert outside the dunes, pointing up the amount of moisture held for long periods in the dune sands.

The cottonwood leaves quiver without making a sound. I sense rather than feel the intangible wisp of a breeze, the one that just after dawn wanders through on its way somewhere else, heralding a subtle notice of change, a transition, a never-again-now, a good morning.

Dunes form when wind blows and transports sands in one predominant direction. They usually develop on the downwind side of pluvial lakes, or playas, the common term for dried-up Pleistocene lakes, because the lakes contain a huge supply of fine dried deposits. The dunes of White Sands are no exception. The basin was once inundated with a vast lake geologists named Lake Otero. Torrents of water attacked the mountain flanks, flushing highly soluble gypsum from the strata into the lake, creating a briny pool saturated with calcium sulfate. With the post-Pleistocene change from a cold-wet to a warm-dry climate, the lake began to evaporate, leaving a mineral-laden remnant, today's Lake Lucero.

Prevailing south-southwesterly winds winnow the gypsum grains out of the ancient lake's deposits and sweep them into dunes. Irregularities in dune shape result from shifts in wind direction during winter storms, shifts that are short-lived but of great strength. These cold northern storms, coming as they do in February and March, are strong enough to rearrange sand crests and shift dune orientation. White Sands is a textbook case in the progression of dune types, distributed in broad bands that extend roughly at right angles to the prevailing winds. Beginning at the edge of Lake

Lucero, huge dome-shaped dunes dominate, melting into transverse dunes that break up and become reshaped into barchans. Finally, at the outer eastern edge of the dune field, the barchans reverse into massive parabolic dunes.

Barchans form out of transverse dunes because sections of the latter move at different rates. Eventually one section lags behind or becomes vulnerable to wind breakthrough. When wind breaches a transverse dune at two points, it pushes curving horns of sand forward: *barchan* is the Arabic word for "ram's horn," a perfect description of their shape.

At the farthest edge of the dune field, parabolic dunes replace the barchans. Vegetation from the surrounding desert encroaches on their flanks and stabilizes the shallower arms so that it is the center of the dune, not the horns, that advances. Bearded and tufted with plants that halt them in their tracks, they are the last outliers. One could, I suppose, hike across these dunes in a couple of days, but then all the fascinating things that go on here would literally be lost in the shuffle—the constant sense of implied movement, the continual argument between sand grain and plant root, the blending, melding shapes and active flowing of the dunes themselves, the continual tango between plant and blowing sand.

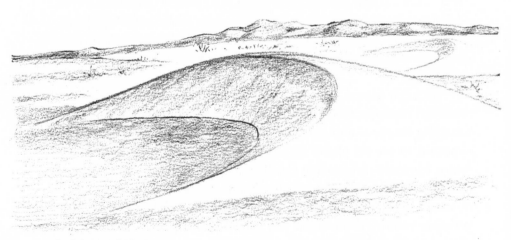

BARCHAN DUNE

□

I reach the boundary between the edge of the dune and an interven-
ing flat before another dune. Small fringes of fresh pale sand dust out
onto the darker, damper floor of the flat. While the dune sands are
nearly pure gypsum, the flats are darkened with other sediments,
creating more livable soils for the few grasses and small plants that
grow here. The darker pustulated relief of the interdune surface
contrasts sharply with the flowing white smoothness of the dunes
rising above it. These prominent swales between dunes cover more
area than the dunes themselves but they are ephemeral, disappearing
and appearing as the dunes creep over them and pass on. Aerial
photographs show big hooks and swirls on today's flats that are the
fingerprints of earlier dunes—remnants of shapes that indicate the
direction of bygone winds, even the amount of the deposits that
were formed in a single storm.

Mormon tea webs linear shadows over small evening stars and
rabbit brush. Little bluestem grass brushes my knees. With its
contradictory rosy stems, it intermixes with ricegrass, which has
long since set seed. Rodents avidly seek its protein-rich kernels and,
in husking the seeds, remove the hardened outer shells that protect
the seeds from sprouting. Seed production is important in these
flats. Except for species tolerant of burial such as soap-tree yucca,
cottonwood, and squawbush, vegetation generally does not survive
being inundated by blowing sand, and most herbs occur chiefly in
the interdune flats. They survive largely by seed propagation since
they lack any specific adaptations to cope with being buried by
sand.

Between plants the sand is puckered and peaked with new
seedlings, each protruding above a vamplatelike cone of sand surrounding its stem, and some of these minutiae are in bloom. I had
expected to see no plants in bloom in October. Instead there are
many. Most are annuals that escaped the heat and drought through a
compressed life cycle, able to sprout, flower, and set seed in a matter
of weeks in the moister habitat of interdune flats. Bright pink sand
verbena, yellow rabbit brush and greenthread, creamy yellow evening stars, and a scraggly evening primrose with eight glorious

flowers color the flat. There are fewer than seventy plant species here, compared with nearly eight hundred in an area of the Lake Michigan dunes of comparable size.

Insufficient water is not the problem—here the water table varies between two and three feet below the surface. Waterlogging is a far greater hazard than the lack of water. The extra moisture that engenders this bloom brings its own limits, for these sands are not only deficient in potassium, nitrogen, and phosphorus, but gypsum has such high solubility that all water absorbed by plant roots is a near saturated solution of calcium sulfate.

Some of these plants are "gypsophiles." There are more endemic gypsophiles in the Chihuahuan Desert than in the other three deserts. Although gypsum limits plant growth, the limitation is not as restrictive as that of saline soils, and often a distinctive flora develops. Many nongypsophilous species can tolerate gypsum, but few can tolerate an equally concentrated saline environment. Interestingly enough, it is not known whether gypsophiles require extra sulfates and if other soil factors play a part, or if they just avoid competition by growing where other plants cannot.

Marks from a recent rain dimple the sand. The sand is not solid and cohesive, as I expect, but crumbly and friable on top. When I dig down, a faint green striping appears an inch below the surface. Subterranean growths of algae, mostly blue-green algae, are found throughout White Sands and after rains may tint the dune surface green from their rapid proliferation. Their importance in these sterile soils is immense because they provide almost the only organic matter available in the center of the dunes. Their interwoven filaments create a stable surface crust that improves moisture filtration. Blue-green algae fix nitrogen, important in these nitrogen-deficient soils. Were it not for the nutritional role played by the little-understood algae and bacteria found throughout the sands, few plants could grow here.

Algae are prominent dwellers in desert soils because they can withstand both extreme heat and desiccation. Their dry encysted cells can survive up to eighty years in desert sands. Growth occurs in soil layers according to the amount of light received, with numbers dropping off sharply according to depth. Filamentous blue-green algae are more likely to be near the surface, the green algae deeper, hence the Roman stripes.

A small mite ticks across the sand and takes shelter in the tunnel of my boot's lug sole. Generally, not a lot is known about the role of algae, and less is known about the microarthropod fauna—the myriad mites, sand fleas, springtails, and other small crawlers and poppers that generally go unnoticed—but extensive studies in the Chihuahuan Desert by a distinguished group of scholars make these soil minutiae better known here than anywhere else. Algae fuel the beginning of the food chain; these decomposers reprocess whatever organic remains there are at the other end of the chain, providing basic food for the producers.

That a minute mite is the largest soil animal indicates the impoverishment of the substrate. But, despite the smallness of scale, microfaunal activities are complex and intricate: some inoculate the soil with fungal spores and then graze on the fungi; others feed on nematodes and bacteria in the meager litter. This predation partly decouples the process of decomposition from its requirements of moisture and heat, and contributes to the stability of this Lilliputian community. Windswept and relatively clean these dune surfaces may be, but beneath is a nibbling, creeping, multilegged life of endlessly busy particulars.

I would have thought that the flat, firm floor between dunes would be a preferred surface for walking, but I notice that we laboriously keep to the loose sand of the dunes and I wonder why. Is it the dampness of the flat that registers our lug-soled footprints too clearly for those of us who are loath to leave a trace of passage in this pristine place? Or just the eternal enchantment of dunes, and we but kids in the ultimate sandbox?

Although it is still cool, I scan the dunes for the small lizard called the White Sands swift. This lizard is a uniquely whitened form, marked on its belly with a broad light-blue stripe. A prominent blue throat patch extends to and covers the back of its head, but other-wise its back is pure gypsum-sand white.

The reflectivity of desert lizards exceeds that of other species, an adaptation for life on the hot side, but may have more value for protection from predators than for heat economy. A lizard can adjust its heat load easily by simply moving between sun and shade. Background color matching develops through predator pressure; the darker lizard, more obvious on white sands, seldom survives to pass on its dark genes.

White Sands supports other whitened forms: an earless lizard, a whiptail lizard, and the omnipresent side-blotched lizard. The pallid forms have all been derived from "normal"-colored (and darker) animal populations in the Alamogordo Valley close by White Sands. Even White Sands mammals—coyotes, rabbits, pocket mice—bear lighter fur compared with their relatives in surrounding deserts. Paleness may even be of use on moonlit nights when lighter-colored rodents are not as easily seen on the sand.

The tendency toward background color matching is not so common in insects and other invertebrates, although on the dunes at White Sands there are snout beetles and tiger beetles lighter than elsewhere, plus one nearly transparent variety of cricket—at White Sands, survival and paleness are synonymous.

Except for darkling beetles. I follow Susan's footprints and find her tracking a broad-necked darkling beetle that toddles across the sand, quite oblivious of her scrutiny. The darkling beetle is by far the most common of the nearly 370 insect species found here, as it seems to be in every North American desert.

Just the opposite of the white animal forms at White Sands, this beetle is completely black. Possibly the greater heat absorbed allows for an increased metabolism rate and therefore a faster growth rate. An insulating air pocket beneath its elytra, the hard wing covers of the beetle family, protects the body from excessive heat. Black coloration may also enhance heat retention during cold desert nights, and provide some peripheral advantages in prevention of water loss, and possibly act as a shield against excessive ultraviolet radiation. Melanin, the pigment that causes the dark coloration, strengthens the outer shell, of help in this abrasive habitat.

Toward the edge of the dune field, a dark hole gapes near the bottom of a barchan. I am curious about the occupant but find no clues, although from the size of the opening it must be a kit-fox burrow. On the surface, sand constantly blows and shifts, but inside, close to the base of this dune, lies a lens of damp sand firm enough to dig a burrow in. When rain falls on the porous dunes, it penetrates rapidly. Because of capillary tension, water sinks to a certain depth and no lower, and there it abides as a moist, unsaturated zone for months, sometimes for years, while sand above and below remains dry. Fine-grained sands, like these gypsum sands, hold considerable water, making it possible not only for plants with deep-probing roots like cottonwoods and yuccas to survive here, but for burrowing animals as well.

Heat and dryness are not the only limits to animal populations in the dunes. Nonleafy solitary plants, such as cacti or grasses, Mormon tea or yucca, cast meager shadows and provide little in the way of food. Although there is underground water for plant growth, it is unavailable to mammals, which must garner moisture from the plants (and animals) upon which they feed.

The mammals that do succeed here do so through some changes in physiology and morphology, but mainly changes in behavior. Of the more than a dozen rodents, as well as the kit fox and badger, that inhabit White Sands, most dig deep and often complex burrows and are active only at night.

Larger vegetation appears, usually a single yucca or a squawbush or a small cottonwood, often raised high on its individual pedestal. A huge squawbush towers above me, leaves mahogany red on gray branches. It crowns a mound of sand four feet high, the bush itself another eight. Like cottonwood, it is not common in the surrounding countryside. It duplicates the yucca's system of extending its stem above inundating sands and proliferating adventitious roots. A trio of horned larks, feeding inside on its red-orange berries, explode out of it. Probably the only fruits available here now, they are all the more relished by dune animals.

Plants that survive in the dunes proper and are well adapted to do so are few in species and number. Some plants endure temporary burial of the crown, or withstand exposure of their root systems, or can develop rhizomes from which new plants sprout. Others simply grow fast enough to keep ahead of the accumulating drifts. Although burial usually results in defoliation and death in most plant species, in others it stimulates stem elongation, which keeps young, leafy portions of the crown enough above the sand for survival. Some have stems that sprout random roots at any level touched by moist sand. Such adventitious roots develop very rapidly, often within twenty-four hours of rain, and sometimes sooner. These plants' adventitious and secondary root systems, proliferating below ground, and their closely grouped stems above ground contribute to dune stability. After the burying dune passes them by, they retain an indurated pillar of sand that, in its subtly striped layers, reveals all the sheets of sand laid down through millennia of wind.

Although vegetation is sparse, there is still a surprising amount of it—isolated pedestals of yucca and islands of shrubs peg the dunes in every direction. Without organic matter to serve as nutrient material, one of the possible solutions to the shortage of nitrogen may have been solved by yucca and several other plants, whose roots have well-developed mycorrhizae, fungal threads that can fix nitrogen, which then becomes available to the plant.

The high winds of spring that bury plants also carry sand that abrades them. Sandblasted stems and roots, exposed on the windward side, are as shiny as if polished. Most of the sand blows within three feet of the ground and injury is severest there. Desiccation compounds the mechanical injury. Exposed leaves and branches catch the wind and act like sails or vanes, causing the plant to twist. The resultant strain causes (wonderful word) thigmomorphogenesis, strengthening the stem by making it thicker and sturdier, and probably reducing stem height.

I pick the largest dune in sight to enjoy one last vista of White Sands. Climbing it turns out to be both formidable and ridiculous. The angle of repose of the slipface, that angle at which a pile of loose material remains without slumping, is very steep. Sand constantly sifts down in slithering streams that tuck and pleat and shirr the smooth rimline. There is no possible way to get up the dune on this side without risking self-burial. The windward slope rises more

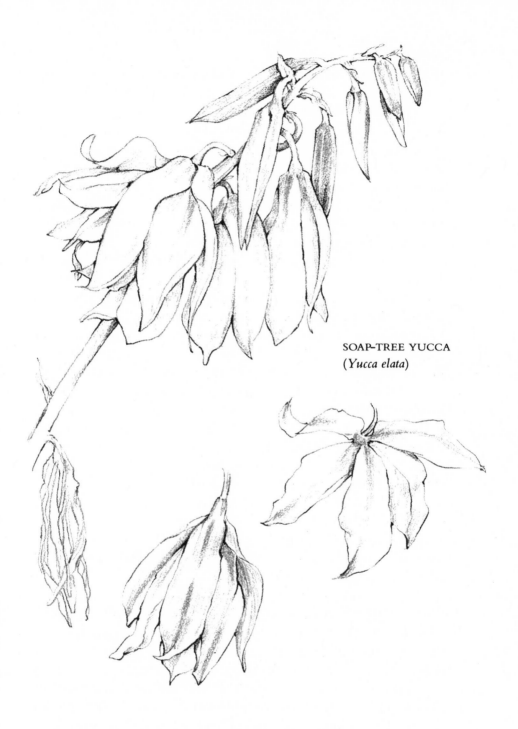

SOAP-TREE YUCCA
(*Yucca elata*)

gently. Sand moves up it by saltation, making it a much easier slope to climb, but only relatively so. It's still one step up and two back, and a pound of sand per boot.

On the crest, I reflect that there must be no more harmonious shape in nature than a barchan dune. It calls forth sibilant *s* words, such as sinuous, sublime, silent, soothing, serene, sigmoidal, satisfying. My view spans clusters and rows of them in the middle of White Sands, their serpentine curves extended in sphinxlike arms that reach out in front, interlocking crescents, flowing shapes so mysterious that the eye follows without being aware, a calmness of horizons. A plume of sand in the distance, poked up by a heating air current, reminds that the dunes are not immutable but whimsies of the wind.

Across my feet, blowing, moving sand blurs the whole crest. On this seething surface a chrome-yellow, very furry, heavy-bodied spider speeds across, spinning an anchor line as it goes. Several stilt bugs, which look more like crane flies in configuration and flight pattern than true bugs, cartwheel over the dune, sand grains stuck to their hairlike legs and half-inch bodies. Plant feeders, they must have been blown up here by the quixotic morning wind and now, at the wind's mercy, tumble like scraps of straw, then pop upright whenever the wind calms.

On quieter spots of the crest, half-inch holes with quarter-inch collars of dry white sand dot the sand surface. A two-inch band of tiny beetle shells ring one, obviously the leavings of a recent meal, suggesting a wolf spider might be the seigneur in residence. Opportunists, feeding on both dead and live animal material, they dig three feet or so straight down into the sand, stabilizing the walls with silk. During warm weather the female brings her eggs to the surface to sun them, surely a quality that should endear her to even the most hardened arachnophobe.

So much life goes on here, hidden from the world above. I no longer think of sand dunes as empty, barren mounds of dry sand, but as honeycombed with life, burrowed and tunneled and excavated, drilled and dug and tamped, full of scratchers and hoppers and tickly walkers.

5

OF DEAD MEN
AND MESQUITE

A scraggly creosote bush is the only wreath garlanding a pitifully derelict gravestone at San Marcial, New Mexico. Dated 1883, it and another grave are surrounded by a small picket fence of satin-weathered wood. The broken adobe walls of what is left of San Marcial, a village repeatedly wiped out by rampaging floods of the Rio Grande, stand like larger headstones.

On this chill March morning, mists rise off the river and frost sheathes the low grasses. A rising sun glows like a full moon behind a cloud bank that shows no interest in dissipating. A rooster crows wildly again and again; a chorus of yipping, yodeling coyotes echoes in the distance; strings of warbling geese float over in ribbons like the flagellae of some monstrous organism, beating across the sky. Sights and sounds must be much the same as those heard by the apprehensive nineteenth-century traveler, waiting to set out on

the Jornada del Muerto—strictly, the Day's Journey of the Dead
Man, truncated to the Journey of Death, the trail between Santa Fe,
New Mexico, and Chihuahua, Mexico. The Jornada acquired its
bitter name in the sixteenth century from some beleaguered colonist
following Juan de Oñate, the first governor of New Mexico, on his
way to lose his fortune trying to colonize this hostile land.

Added to the desert hardships were the fierce Mescalero
Apaches, so called because of the young agave stalks (*mescal* in
Spanish) they cooked and traded. They migrated into the Jornada
around A.D. 1400, driving out the hunter-gatherers who had been

JORNADA DEL MUERTO AND WHITE SANDS

there for at least five thousand years. When they acquired horses from the Spanish in the 1600s, they began murderous raids on traders and ranchers in southern New Mexico.

From Santa Fe south to San Marcial, the road followed the west bank of the Rio Grande. At San Marcial the river begins its broad sweep west, pushed there by the Fra Cristobal Mountains, which block further passage along the river edge. The Jornada cut a straighter line inland, away from water, and took a day off the trip between San Marcial and Chihuahua, Mexico. To travel its ninety miles required a day bracketed by two nights without water, a journey of such hardship that passage was usually made only at night. The terrain is so short-hilled and steep it had to be wearisome for man and horse and almost impossible for sutler's wagon and ox, and the unnumbered creosote bushes provided no forage for stock.

San Marcial was one of the last places to get water for humans and stock before facing the Jornada. Partway down the slope to the river that so ill-treated it, San Marcial is a place of leavings with no one there to whom to say good-bye. Anyone traveling the Jornada dreaded it, its reputation built from truth and rumor, fact and fiction, each worse than the other. The loss of life and property and stock to marauding Indians, plus tempers quickened by apprehension, all intensified the horrors of the journey. Today no amount of sunshine can stanch a foreboding that even I, here in this desert over a century later, feel as I take into account the isolation, when letter deliveries were measured in months, when major events weren't called up on the evening news, when small mishaps could be fatal, when you couldn't get in touch with anyone on the instant, when there was plenty of time for rumor and hearsay. I have to think what it was like *not* to know, and even today this desert teaches you that.

My view must be much the same as that of Colonel Philip Kearny in 1846, on his way to take possession of California from the Mexicans (it was assumed that United States naval forces would be in possession of all ports by the time he arrived, a grave miscalculation). Until Kearny's trip, only the north-south strip along the Rio Grande was known with any accuracy, and the desert country between Santa Fe and California was completely unmapped.

The young surveyor who accompanied Kearny, Lieutenant William H. Emory of the U.S. Topographical Engineers, provided the first accurate record of distances and geography. Rather than relying on transit and triangulation, Emory attached a viameter to the wheel of a howitzer and measured the up and down and all-around distance that travelers would actually have to tread across this fearsome desert.

Kearny took nearly three days to travel the Jornada. His dragoons went miserably hungry, animals gave way by the score, and wolves tracked the column to down the weakened mules. After that he stubbornly marched two hundred more miles with wagons before he read the brutal truth of traversing the desert, abandoned his wagons, and continued westward with only mules for transport. In a letter to his wife he penned a dour assessment of the landscape:

> It surprised me to see so much land that can never be of any use to man or beast. We traveled many days without seeing a spear of grass, and no vegetation excepting a species of the Fremontia [creosote bush], and the mesquite tree, something like our thorn, and which our mules eat, thorn and branches to keep them alive.

The Jornada has not changed. As I walk Kearny's somber path toward the river, I work my way from creosote bush to creosote bush, each one beckoning with its branches like some Lorelei, promising water and green shade and peace, and delivering only dust, more thirst, and disappointment. They have replaced the old grasslands. Now aridity, combined with the gypsum that lies just under the surface, makes vegetation sparse.

Few birds take flight out of the bushes and shrubs. The bird assemblage of the Chihuahuan Desert historically is little known. To date no endemic bird species have been logged. Explorers of the mid-nineteenth century, both Europeans and North Americans, were more interested in collecting exotic tropical or semitropical birds, or went west the easier way by sea or railroad or followed the few main roads, none of which crossed the Chihuahuan Desert, where distances were as vast as the transportation was meager.

Chihuahuan bird life, because of the paucity of vegetation, is not as rich as that of the Sonoran Desert, particularly in breeding species. The total density of breeding pairs is low in comparison with other deserts largely because of the lack of diversity of small shrubs and trees for protection and nesting, and especially the lack of variation in plant height. Creosote bush provides little in the way of food or cover, and creosote-bush communities everywhere generally have depauperate bird fauna. One night I slept in a hollow where creosote bushes grew on a low rise. Silhouetted against the sky their open and delicate branching was completely revealed, little suited to cradling or supporting even the smallest nest.

Running of cattle and sheep in this area diminished the grasslands and encouraged the invasion of creosote bush as well as the opuntia cacti, both equally unwelcoming to breeding birds. By the mid-nineteenth century, overgrazing, along with clearing for agriculture, doubtless eliminated many birds and animals, especially in the northern reaches of the desert, where grassland and desert scrub interweave in a shifting border.

But many birds winter here. There is nearly always a harrier, skimming the creosote bush, hunting, white rump spot flashing. Some years very large flocks of Brewer's sparrows, mourning doves, lark buntings, longspurs, and horned larks congregate here, ample food supply for hawks. When higher rainfall than usual produces large blooms of annuals and seeds in excess of those that can be harvested by rodents and ants, large flocks of migrant seed-feeding birds gather in the desert. The intensity of their feeding so exhausts the supply of seeds that they seldom occupy the same areas two years in a row.

A branch quivers in a creosote bush ahead and I catch a glimpse of the black-and-white-streaked head of a black-throated sparrow. This sparrow is the only bird that frequents creosote bush with any regularity. It has the unusual ability to reduce the water content of its droppings when water is limited. In mammals, kangaroo rats have remarkably efficient kidneys that can excrete urea in concen-

63

trations twenty to thirty times that in the blood; birds, excreting uric acid, achieve concentrations some three thousand times greater.

More or less restricted to arid regions, black-throated sparrows feed largely on seeds and are better adapted to desert life than almost any other small seed-eating bird. If green vegetation or insects are available they do not need to drink, even if temperatures soar. When only seeds are available, they still survive without free water. The animated hopping of the sparrows is a welcome flicker of movement in an otherwise preternaturally still day.

On the east side of the river, Susan and I track the Jornada. Thickets of western honey mesquite clot the landscape, not so much trees as a scrubby, mean-looking barricade.

Like crows, cockroaches, creosote bushes, and coyotes, honey mesquite has captured attention through its nuisance value. Ranchers and range managers deplore its tenacity and ability to crowd out good pasture. Since the genus originated in South America some fifty million years ago, it has expanded into some fifty species, three of which—honey, velvet, and western honey— occupy millions of acres of the southwestern United States. When it arrived from South America, mesquite spread rapidly in the arid and semiarid lands of the Southwest because it can grow almost everywhere—on ground that is alkaline or saline, in soil that is gravel or clay or sand or loam, under rainfall from a sparse six inches to a more generous thirty—makes no nevermind to a mesquite. It can reduce its transpiration rate, and therefore its water use, and can even enter a resting mode, a kind of vegetal hibernation. It can withstand winterkill to the base of the plant.

To ranchers, the most annoying thing about mesquite is its ability to withstand being burned out or frozen out, since pre-formed buds sprout the minute that any primary part of the tree is injured. The tangle of mesquite's spreading trunks and interlock-ing, zigzagged thorn-set branches knits an impenetrable thicket. The characteristic zigzag pattern begins after the first year of growth. Lateral buds on the branch produce leaves, stem, spines, and inflorescence at each node. Terminal buds develop at the ends of the twigs, but when mesquite stops growing for the year, the terminal buds abort. When growth resumes in the spring, it begins at a node to the side. The quirky branches interweave like rolls of barbed wire in a no-man's-land.

No wonder Kearny's surgeon, Dr. John Griffin, thought "most annoying, was the chapparal [sic], this has long thorns on it, and we found it pretty thick in the high lands, this annoyed our mules in the team greatly, and if there be much of it ahead it will be impossible to pass through it. The leaf of the plant looks like the honey locust."

The clouds break at sunset and shafts of light slant through them, illuminating the mountain peaks. Low mounds of dry snakeweed green up, punctuated by tall, shaggy stalks of yucca, most with buggy-whip flower stalks. Whitened cottonwood leaves, caught in shrub stems, look like exotic seedpods. The low, raking afternoon light frosts patches of low grass. Dark cone mountains lurk behind a straight-line horizon whose straightness is enhanced by distance. In reality the ground is anything but even, it is broken and clumped, set with hostile plants that are just the right height to rip the shoulder of a horse or the leg of a rider.

There is little change as we drive southward, a countryside that seemingly stretches on and on, hardened by the sun into an overall sameness, here today, here tomorrow, here forever. Once, when we stopped, we were enveloped in our own dust, and as I breathed I knew what it must have been like to be at the end of a line of oxen and wagons, inhaling a choking gray air. Susan and I make the transit of the inimical Jornada in a few hours, and as we approach the Rio Grande I feel an unanticipated relief.

After we make camp, coyotes sing all night long and the sound comes from every quadrant, the harmonies of nomads. The barking begins high and rapid, with an urgency that comes in ten- to twenty-second pulses. The ululation that follows begins low, almost gutturally, then rises in pitch like a siren until the note is lost beyond sound, dust devils of song, spinning upward and dissolving in the night air.

65

6

OF CACTUS WRENS
AND PLAYAS

Following on the route Lieutenant Colonel Philip St. George Cooke took in 1846, I unconsciously slip into the role of contemporary observer, listening to the creak of saddles and the irritable braying of mules. In a long wind plume of dust a mile or so ahead I see the flickering figures of the marching column. I watch for the new plants and animals to collect that will go back to Spencer Baird, Assistant Secretary of the Smithsonian Institution, who was building an unparalleled collection of natural-history specimens out of the discoveries of these western expeditions. I walk with beginner's eyes, seeing the flora and fauna as they saw them, as if I had never seen them before—and indeed, a great deal of them I have not.

In 1846, Cooke marched southwest with Kearny, who, at the loss of the original commander, put Cooke in command of five hundred Mormon volunteers, under orders to establish a wagon road across the desert to California. Cooke went south as far as the present town of Rincon, New Mexico, then turned west into what was still Mexican territory. His discovery of a route over which wagons could go south of the then boundary between the United States and Mexico was a powerful incentive for the Gadsden Purchase of 1853.

Cooke's road passes through low, undulating sand dunes stabilized with broom dalea that the observant Emory described as "a much branc[h]ed shrub, three feet high, with beautiful purple flowers," a plant first collected on the Jornada del Muerto. The crusted sand in which the broom dalea grows still retains its coolness from the night, pitted with the intaglio of raindrops from a recent shower. A handsome young coyote trots ahead of us, crosses into a wash, and sits down in the grass on the other side. In excellent pelage, with rufous ears and white covering its throat and chops, it sits in the grass and watches us through slitted eyes. So its ancestors must have watched Cooke's company.

Honey mesquites rise out of ample hummocks, their bare zig-zag twigs silhouetted against the morning sky. A cactus wren hops up inside one stunted mesquite tree, branch to branch to branch, teetering on the topmost twig. Band-winged grasshoppers furnish

CACTUS WREN
(*Campylorhynchus brunneicapillus*)

67

BLACK-TAILED JACKRABBIT
(*Lepus californicus*)

primary food for cactus wrens and their young, and the grasshopper in turn feeds on annual plants, which fluctuate with rainfall of the previous autumn. Female wrens somehow register the paucity or plethora of grasshoppers available just before laying and adjust the size of their clutches accordingly. Most laying is instigated by a rise in air temperature that endures for three or four days. If temperatures are too low, the wren must devote more time to brooding, which subtracts from feeding time. It is to the wren's advantage to time her laying so that she has to spend the least time on the nest and has the most time to gather food.

A jackrabbit bounds out from beneath a creosote bush, sun shining through its ears, and the alacrity of his lope says something about the freshness of the day—in summer heat it would go only a few feet before turning back to shade. Scraps of a jackrabbit carcass lie beneath another shrub, an important food source for the decomposers within the desert ecosystem, as well as for the predators and parasites.

A definite sequence attends the decomposition and tissue breakdown of a carcass in the desert. The fresh carcass is visited first by ants, which attack the eyes and associated membranes. Coyotes and foxes, as well as vultures, dismember it, while several species of beetles, some of which require putrefying flesh to complete their life cycle, move inside the corpse itself. As the carcass ripens, many more insects make the body hum with insect sounds. Fur loosens from the skin. Odor becomes stench, then disappears after six or seven days. Various insects, in sequence, continue to work on the carcass as it dries into a state of advanced decay. Remaining tissue shrivels and separates from the bones and the bones fall apart. Teeth drop from the skull, leaving only the clean, disciplined curve of cranium and eye socket.

White legs showing, tail switching, a roadrunner perches on a stump, the first time I've seen one anyplace but on the ground. It fluffs its feathers, pivoting to get as much sun as possible on the black patches on its back; its dark skin absorbs more calories than that of a light-skinned bird and gives it a greater saving in metabolic heat production when temperatures are cool. At our approach it drops down, struts a circuitous path through clumps of low creosote bush, alternating three seconds of walking with three seconds of looking. Each time it stops, its tail snaps up, its head swivels around for a sharp look, and seeing nothing of interest, off it bustles again, looking as if it has distant errands of great importance.

As this splendid day warms, an almost minty fragrance perfumes the air, and it becomes a contest to see who can identify the source. Between us, we sniff the flowers and rub the leaves of every herb we walk past. There is no odor from the threadlike stems that lace bushes of buckwheat. Nor is there odor in a delicate sand penstemon growing in the shade of larger shrubs. Four-wing saltbush quivers with papery seedpods. No odor there. Spectacle pod has a delicate alyssum-like fragrance, as does peppergrass. Perhaps it is the leaves of paperflower that leave a fragrance on my fingers when I rub them. Some of these still bloom—fresh flowers with yellow centers intermixed with dried ones, which remain whole on the plant, the pale, papery tan petals netted with dusky veins.

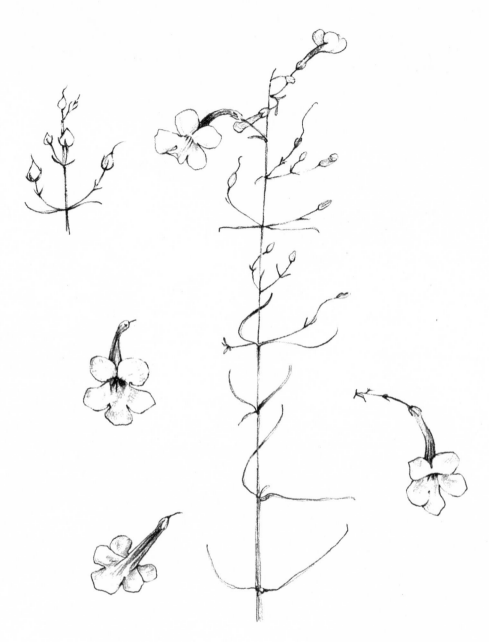

SAND PENSTEMON
(*Penstemon ambiguus*)

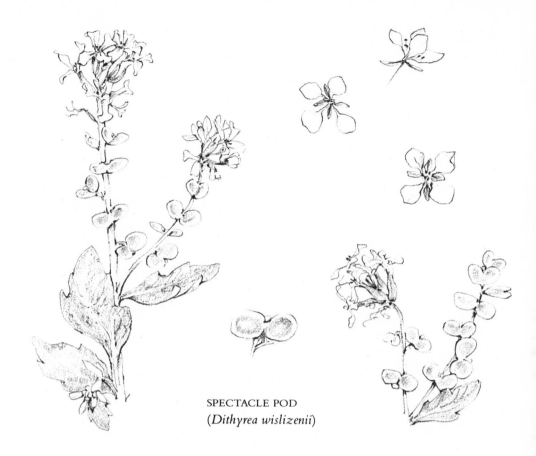

SPECTACLE POD
(*Dithyrea wislizenii*)

Buffalo gourd stems loop across the ground and trip me up more than once. Capable of prodigious vegetative growth, buffalo gourd yields both a massive enlarged taproot with a considerable subterranean water-storage capacity and multiple annual shoots that seem to whipsnake across the soil, sending up huge triangular leaves, all of which it delivers in a short five-month growing season. Growing through one tangled plant, the antithesis of its gross stems and leaves, is a delicate pale-blue longleaf phlox.

There are so many fall flowers that the Chihuahuan Desert seems oddly out of sync. Here it is autumn and it might as well be spring. And I will always be teased by an eternal mystery: what was that lovely scent, blossomed upward by the warmth of the sun, that haunted the air and perfumes my memory?

□

Cooke's road continues west and my boots scuff up the same desert dryness as those doughty Mormons. I wonder if raptors were as legion in Cooke's day as they are this morning. For every one I spot, Susan adds two. They commandeer fence posts and mesquite, blockade the road, picking at a dead jackrabbit, rocket through the sky ready to stoop on the first unwary rodent—in this country the early bird doesn't get the worm, it gets a ground squirrel. An American kestrel shoots into a six-inch-diameter hole in a sandy bank. A loggerhead shrike teeters on a creosote bush, checking out the lizard population's propensity to sleep in on cool mornings. A golden eagle anchors the top of a telephone pole like a flag finial. These man-made additions to the desert provide unparalleled

PEPPERGRASS
(*Lepidium fremontii*)

PAPERFLOWER
(Psilostrophe tagetina)

73

LONGLEAF PHLOX
(*Phlox longifolia*)

perches for raptors, which formerly had only low mesquite for surveillance posts. Attending to the eagle on the pole, we almost miss seeing the immature eagle that flushes out of the high grass below. As it takes flight, it flashes white on its tail.

The fresh morning steams itself into a hot midday. The bare, glaring ground between the sparse shrubs radiates the sun's heat. Lavender and pink mountains notch the western horizon, looking like a candy-colored Maxfield Parrish illustration. They are dry-rock desert mountains left out to dry in a New Mexico sun, blessed with names like Animas and Peloncillo, lost souls and sugar loaves.

Cooke crossed the Continental Divide in one of the two places in the United States where it is not a mountain ridge from whose crest waters are drained to opposite sides of the continent, but a low, broad basin. Waterways to the Atlantic begin from high ground along the west side of the Rio Grande, and rivulets to the Pacific begin from the crest of the Peloncillo Mountains. In between lies a vast 125-mile-wide basin with interior drainage across which flowed the ancestral Rio Grande.

During cooler, wetter pluvial periods, the connected desert fauna from the west (Sonoran) and the east (Chihuahuan) were periodically split while more cold-adjusted faunas migrated southward and became established. Drier interpluvials, as now, allowed the eastern and western warmth-loving species to connect or reconnect. For some species it allowed range expansion; for others, the development of sibling pairs, such as the two subspecies of tiger whiptail lizards or the two black-tailed jackrabbits. Across this southwestern corner of New Mexico and southeastern corner of Arizona, some 20 percent of the Chihuahuan Desert fauna reaches the western edge of its range.

Lunchtime. Colonel Cooke would have said "nooning." Susan fixes lunch while I stalk a lesser earless lizard, glad to find something moving at this stupefying lead-heavy-heat time of day. A creature of wide latitudinal distribution, it ranges from as far north as South Dakota, south to Mexico. It is difficult to see because its back, flecked with tiny darker chevrons, perfectly matches the soil. But once spotted it is easy to identify because of its lack of ear openings. Depending on vision to detect its prey, it is absent from heavily vegetated areas. Often it climbs into bushes both to escape pursuit and to get a clearer view of what's going on. The earless lizard is one species that can withstand an extended period of submergence during heavy rains; it can even shift into anaerobic respiration for the duration. I follow as it dashes from bush to bush, swift and quiet as a shadow, while I, Brobdingnagian-footed, crunch dried twigs and desert millipede shells with every step.

Impossibly tiny leggings attach to each segment of the whitened desert millipede rings, each about one-quarter inch in diameter. Millipedes are one of many arthropod species whose physiology and behavior—possessing a chitinous waterproof exterior and keeping hidden during the day—render them "preadapted" to desert living. The living relatives are doubtless in the debris under the mesquite scrub waiting out the dry season, as their main feeding coincides with summer rains. Although they scrape bark from shrub stems, this does not supply enough moisture, and they also regularly consume moist soil. They spend most of their life underground, where they maintain their water balance during both dormant and feeding seasons. They also molt underground, after which they are very vulnerable to desiccation. If they begin to dry out they can quickly rehydrate during periods of rain, when they take up water anally, a rapid way of accumulating and storing moisture. Possessing a "repugnatorial gland" that emits an offensive vapor, they are not often bothered by vertebrates; their main enemy in the Chihuahuan Desert seems to be an immature stage of a glowworm beetle, which dotes on them.

I return to a beautifully arranged plate of tabbouleh, lemon wedges, tomato slices gleaming with balsamic vinegar, and artichoke hearts. Our tablecloth impinges on the territory of a robber fly, stiletto-bodied and goggle-eyed; a deep indentation on the top of the head forces the large eyes far out to the sides, giving it a sweeping field of vision.

From its bare patch of ground it jumps straight up in the air like a helicopter, flies a foot or so, a bare inch off the ground, and alights. The robber fly repeats its seemingly fruitless forays, over and over, just keeping its wing in so to speak, until a yellow butterfly wafts into view. The fly plows the air straight for it, and that movement galvanizes the butterfly, whose desultory flight instantly becomes swift and highly erratic. The fly's efficient aerial darts thrust it beyond the short zigzag flutters of the butterfly like an F-16 trying to make contact with a Piper Cub. The fly makes corrections in the air and sharp reversals of direction but never even comes close. It gives up, sets down. The butterfly larks off with a shrug of wings.

A strange, rather large, black-and-red-striped insect teeters through the stubble near my foot. Its ludicrously tiny wing covers leave much of its bulbous abdomen uncovered. Under my hand lens, the creature is a deep blue black; its wing covers are thick and punctate, and the head is beetlelike. When Susan asks what it is, I opt for Coleoptera. It does my maternal prestige a lot of good when it turns out to be a beetle that Howard Ensign Evans, an entomologist, describes as "one that even an entomologist finds it hard to love." It is, of course, a blister beetle, which lacks hind wings, and is of such distasteful odor and taste that it enjoys almost total immunity from predators.

The substance that renders it repugnant to bird or insect is cantharidin, better known as "Spanish fly," long reputed to be an aphrodisiac, which, according to Evans, was mixed into the love potion mistakenly slipped to Tristan and Isolde. Although its utilizations are probably more fable than fact, a poultice of the crushed insect is irritating enough to blister human skin. Pairs of quarter-inch beetle elytra, bleached white, joined like two little clam shells, are scattered across the ground, indicating that blister beetles are not totally invulnerable.

A blister beetle larva, unlike the usual lethargic wormlike creature, is long-legged and active. After hatching it immediately crawls to the top of the nearest flowering plant to lie in wait for a pollinating bee. When a larva senses the plant quivering, it moves to the edge of a petal, where it positions itself with its legs free, ready to latch on to a pollinating bee. Without sight or hearing, it depends on subtleties of smell or touch, and will as eagerly attach to a piece of Velcro as to a bee. Carried home to the bee's nest, the larva parasitizes its host's eggs and begins a series of transformations—a "hypermetamorphosis"—during which it becomes more wormlike. Some species of blister beetles are doubly damaging to creosote bushes when the larvae both infest the flowers and attack the bee larvae, the adults of whom are the creosote bush's most important pollinators.

Odd mounds of fresh dirt are piled all about, many punctured with three-inch holes, some battered closed by recent rains. While rain greens up vegetation for the herbivores, it also flattens and floods small exposed burrows, especially those that were in the open and went more or less straight down. Fresh repair work shows around many entryways. At one, three Paul Bunyan ants, thwarted by the lumpy fresh dirt, haul away a one-inch light-green creosote-bush grasshopper, dispossesed both of its life and its usual perch in the shady branches of a creosote bush. Ants, seed consumers as well as predators and scavengers, are the most numerous insects in the Chihuahuan Desert with the possible exception of termites. All around me the hills of harvester ants dot the flat. Each one is a mound a couple of feet across, encircled by bare ground.

When abundant annual plants are available in the desert, most ant groups eat seeds. When only a few annuals are present, they shift to being omnivores. Harvester ants take different seeds as various kinds come in and out of season, and the amount they consume is considerable. Despite their small size, ants by their sheer numbers strongly impact the ecosystem. They effectively compete with and influence desert seed-eating rodent populations (who may them-selves carry off 75 percent of seed production), as well as limit plant populations by leaving so few seeds to germinate. Some plants, like a species of datura, get around this by producing seeds that attract ants by providing tiny carrying handles, but prevent the ants from utilizing them by arming the seeds with a thick coat that they cannot penetrate. The datura takes advantage of the harvester ants' predilection for seed carrying to get its seeds scattered far away from the parent plant before rodents have a chance to remove and cache them. My burdened ants negotiate the hills and valleys of the dirt heap and finally reach solid ground, setting off with their bounty in triumphant procession.

Thin adobe tunnels and tubes cover a complex of twigs on the ground utilized by the other most frequent insects in the desert, the termites who nest in wood and in the ground. In some areas they may, out of sheer numbers, be the most important consumers in the desert ecosystem. Desert termites (which are more closely related to cockroaches than to ants) do not build huge castles but modest meandering tunnels: this one spreads about a foot across the ground.

By covering small objects with mud and sand, termites construct a protected haven in which they can consume the weathered surface of the objects covered.

In the desert termites work mostly on dead material (they avoid mesquite or creosote bush when it's fresh) or mine cacti and other plants, and can consume over 90 percent of available wood litter in a year. Through symbiotic protozoa, bacteria, and probably fungi in their hind gut, they are able to digest cellulose and recycle the debris of the desert. Their workings in the soil enhance water infiltration by increasing soil porosity, influencing the amount of grass and shrub cover. By number and activity, they deserve the ecological designation as a "keystone species," indispensable in maintaining the structure and integrity of the desert ecosystem.

Poised at the edge of a vast playa that Cooke crossed, I am as full of anticipation and as happy as if I had good sense. I am enamored of playas. I have been known to go miles out of my way to walk one, so it is a matter of great interest to me that a cluster of them stud the valleys between the mountain ranges in the southwestern corner of New Mexico.

The Spaniards who first crossed this country called these vast flats *playas,* their word for "beach." The geological meaning is slightly different, referring to a dry lake bed or ephemeral lake in an arid environment, of which there are hundreds in North America, particularly in the areas of California, Oregon, Nevada, Arizona, Utah, and New Mexico known as the Basin and Range Province; they are numerous everywhere but in the Sonoran Desert.

In a generic sense, playas are much alike: one of the flattest land forms in existence, they were created from thousands of cubic feet of silts and clays washed down from the surrounding mountains into a basin lacking external drainage. But they never are the same, and they never fail to have some individual and distinctive quality— a new plant, a new silt pattern, a new wind, a new way of spelling playa, a new way of defining desert.

Nearly all the now-dry basins cradled lakes during the Pleistocene epoch. Although beyond the reach of continental glaciers, the cooler and wetter climate fostered greater runoff that dropped heavier rocks and debris, often impregnated with salts, on the hillsides in sloping bajadas, and carried the finer silts to the center of the basins, where often they were covered with a permanent skim of water. With the warming and drying post-Pleistocene climate, most of these areas evaporated, exposing the bottom silts, which hardened into cementlike flats that John Russell Bartlett, following Cooke's wagon road while running the Mexican Boundary Survey in 1852, described as a surface of "indurated clay, so hard that the wheels of our wagons scarcely made an impression."

Ribbonlike pools from a recent rain edge the playa and double the distant mountains. At my feet, silt-filled strips of water reflect lavender sky; farther away, reflections replicate a hedge of luxurious saltbush. Between puddles is a viscous, gluey silt, which coats my boots with the tenacity of peanut butter.

Dry patches are shot with cracks forming irregular polygons, nature's tangrams. In some places the top layer of silt dries and curls up, paper-thin. Where slight indentations have held a modicum of water a little longer, the silt is thicker and the curls have rolled into cylinders. Peeling begins at a crack where drying air penetrates and separates the layers. The topmost layer dries more quickly and curves upward like a thermocouple, pulling an underlayer with it, revealing the deeper-colored grainy underside.

I wonder, given the basics of silt and water, how many styles of curls can be manufactured. Most cylinders are small enough to be a tight fit on a skewer, but some are larger, thick as orange rinds, but still fragile. One patch holds sturdy tubes with the diameter of a rake handle. The outside is like fine sandpaper, the inside as smooth as glazed porcelain. Thick, loose plates in a long puddle resemble prehistoric pottery shards in their curve and thickness. A perfectly circular puddle splits into pie-shaped pieces, each peeling back from the middle like a croissant.

In some places the dry surface is so shiny that the sun glares off it as off glass, created by a combination of wind polishing and shallow sheet runoff. In other places the fine-as-talc silt imitates polished marble, swirled with the same discreet mottlings. Made visible only by its moving shadow is a half-inch silt-colored weevil. It travels between coin-size moon craters of silt, each circle rimmed with a thin line of silt left when a tiny bubble collapsed.

Striding toward the center of the playa is great walking—no cacti to run into, no vines to trip over, no rattlesnakes to watch out for. I leave the pools and puddles behind, cross through the rimming saltbushes, and stride out onto its hard-packed surface. Even though there may be a couple of feet difference between the edges and the middle, the slope is generally about 1 percent, so gradual it wouldn't roll a marble, kept level by periodic flooding. In two hundred yards I stand, like the pivot point of a compass, in the center of the universe—a place to dance, to hoot and holler, to rearrange mountains, to count the rollicking stars at night. To redesign the world.

For 360 degrees I mark not a tree, not a shrub over three feet high, not a glint of water, only a light-absorbing heat-inhaling landscape that translates heat into wavering light and light into shimmering heat so that one inhales, smells, touches only heat, listens only to heat drying skin and cracking silt. No wonder Bartlett questioned why the United States wanted this country anyway:

> As we toiled across these sterile plains, where no tree offered its friendly shade, the sun glowing fiercely, and the wind hot from the parched earth, cracking the lips and burning the eyes, the thought would keep suggesting itself, Is this the land which we have purchased, and are to survey and keep at such a cost? As far as the eye can reach stretches one unbroken waste, barren, wild, and worthless.

THE
SONORAN
DESERT

OF SAGUARO
AND ROADRUNNERS

One December morning, botanist Karen Reichhardt and I explore the interfingering of the Chihuahuan and Sonoran deserts in the southeastern corner of Arizona. She is a delightful companion and, because she lives in Arizona, a very knowledgeable one. For both of us, crossing a transition area between two deserts is slow going—there is so much to see: what was, what is becoming, what is, and what yet may be. We keep to the east bank of the San Pedro River, traversing the alternate uphill and down-dale crests and gullies that drain to the river, looking for the signal sign of the Sonoran Desert, a saguaro cactus.

Saguaro symbolize a living desert that covers approximately 120,000 square miles of North America. The Sonoran Desert lies mostly below 3,000 feet at its eastern edge, sloping to sea level near the Colorado River, crossing it into southern California, extending southward into both mainland Mexico and Baja California. It is the only North American desert with sizable "subtrees" and treelike cacti, along with numerous deciduous and evergreen shrubs, and a marvelous variety of succulents. This particular assemblage of desert plants has been in place only about four thousand years. An Egyptian ecologist, seeing the Sonoran Desert for the first time, exclaimed that this was not a desert at all but a veritable flower garden.

Part of the richness of the Sonoran Desert flora is made possible by a bimodal precipitation pattern. In the western Sonoran (and northward into the Mojave and Great Basin deserts), Pacific frontal storms break over the coastal mountains, bringing winter-to-spring rainfall; in the eastern Sonoran and into the Chihuahuan, tropical

CREOSOTE BUSH AND SAGUARO
(*Carnegiea gigantea*)

summer convection storms predominate. A great part of the central Sonoran catches both rainy seasons. Summer rains tend to be brief, torrential, and highly localized. Winter rains, from December to the end of March or mid-April, are gentle, prolonged, and usually occurring over wide areas.

Karen sights the first saguaro, a meager stalk halfway up the facing gravelly slope. Further evidence that we are entering the Sonoran Desert follows quickly: the first mesquite big enough to be called a tree, the first green-trunked paloverde. Two more saguaro appear, low on a south-facing hillside where temperatures are warm, then two more. Prickly pear grows lower on these slopes, creosote bush higher. Mesquite grows in the lowest areas near the river.

The first saguaro rises but five or so feet high, probably twenty-five to thirty years old. If not damaged by frost, within another foot or so of growth it will shift into a "wine bottle" shape as the plant puts out its first blooms. When saguaros begin to flower, at about this height, they divert almost half of their potential stem growth into the energy needed for reproduction.

The massive semaphore arms and the imposing stature of mature saguaro are more instantly recognizable than any other aspect of the Sonoran Desert. Saguaro are such a fixture here that it is difficult to understand that they may be disappearing from the northern reaches of the desert in Arizona. Nearly every cactus looks as if a string had been tied around its stalk and pulled tight. This sharp indentation results from freeze damage that collapses internal tissue and destroys the plant's ability to take up water. These saguaro grow north of the freeze line and may spend a great part of their lives simply recovering from the last cold shock. Although they do not freeze at 32 degrees F. but supercool (that is, temperatures within the plant cells go lower than 32 degrees but do not crystallize into ice), they can briefly withstand temperatures in the 20s. More severe temperatures that cause permanent damage occur frequently enough in Arizona to threaten this whole population, although even after a severe freeze the giant plant may continue to grow and produce seeds for another decade before it dies.

Mature saguaros that survive unscathed are long-lived, some as old as 150 to 175 years. Despite immense seed production, saguaro populations have been decreasing for some decades because the number of younger plants is inadequate to replace those that die. Within another century, unless there is a change in establishment of seedlings, saguaro may no longer be the trademark of the Arizona Sonoran Desert.

Karen finds a saguaro seedling beneath a matronly paloverde. Saguaros commonly associate with large trees, especially paloverde, needing a nurse tree under which to become established, often with fatal consequences for the latter. Every large saguaro in view rises close to or within the crown of a dead or dying paloverde, which is faster-growing and shorter-lived.

The nurse-tree status of paloverdes may depend upon birds that frequent cactus groves during the day to feed on saguaro seeds and return to roost at night in its limbs. They void the indigestible seeds, which fall at the foot of the tree where they germinate in a gentler environment than that of the open desert. Paloverdes considerably soften the winter climate for the cold-sensitive saguaro seedling by retaining daytime heat within their canopies at night, and shade them from severe summer sun.

So needful of shelter are saguaros that at least half of those standing alone are dead. If a seedling can establish roots out to a fifty-foot radius and acquire its waxy waterproof outer coating, it likely survives, but until then it is at risk. A single voracious larva of the granulate cutworm can consume all the fleshy parts of a saguaro seedling in a matter of hours, and ravenous rodents and rabbits often take out a whole year's crop.

The paloverde's distinctive trunks and branches are a startling, unnatural, light olive green because most of the tree's photosynthesis goes on there. In times of drought, like many desert plants, paloverdes drop their twigs, analogous to leaf fall in deciduous trees, to do away with water-losing surfaces. Leaf growth comes only after rains, and the leaves seldom survive longer than six to ten weeks. The leaves are so tiny that even when the tree is fully leafed their total surface area is still smaller than that of the green stems and twigs.

□

A roadrunner flares out of a big silvery brittlebush, scaring the daylights out of me—I must have nearly stepped on it. I may have disturbed its nest building, although Karen reminds me it is a little early. Generally roadrunners nest shortly after the winter rains, with often a second start after summer rains. With other North American desert birds, a second attempt at summer breeding is made only if the spring attempt fails. The roadrunner commonly produces two clutches of eggs, the second one larger, possibly an adaptation to the abundance, after summer rains, of whiptail lizards and arthropods, upon which it feeds.

It easily outdistances me because it dashes through and under the scrub, while this awkward human picks her way carefully between. Having dispensed with me, it continues its regular rounds, darting about in search of a succulent lizard. Before swallowing it headfirst the roadrunner often dispatches it by whacking it against a rock or the ground. If the lizard is too big to swallow, the pragmatic bird will go about its business with the lizard's tail dangling out of its mouth until the front end is digested, then gulp down the rest. Roadrunners also eat a great many other desert inhabitants, from mice to grasshoppers, which they stir up from the grass and then make mad leaps and dashes to catch. They have been, according to fossils, around for some 33,000 years, a forest-evolved species preadapted for life in a more arid environment into which they quickly moved when the climate warmed and dried after the Pleistocene.

Another roadrunner sprints out from beneath an ocotillo, leaving a haphazard nest of sticks a few feet off the ground tucked in the shadows of a cholla. It may be protected by thorns there, but little protected from the strong sun. Unfeathered nestlings have strikingly black skin, which acts like a black-bulb thermometer in response to heat; they cannot survive in an unshaded nest before they are three or four days old, during which time the parents must tend them continuously. As soon as the young are able to adjust their body temperatures, the parents can spend more time hunting.

The eggs hatch asynchronously so that young of various ages may be in the nest at the same time. Older hatchlings are more persistent in begging for food than their younger siblings, of telling importance if food is in short supply. The undernourished, smaller nestlings do not survive and are eventually eaten by their parents or by siblings, a "Cainism" that also occurs in other bird species. If food is ample, all survive to strut the desert floor.

Karen and I strike out across a bare arroyo that wriggles its way out of sight. Just as we clear it three collared peccaries break out of the scrub in front of us and rustle off, sounding like a pack of four-legged rattlesnakes. They trot quickly and lightly down the wash on impossibly little hooves, overplump dowagers mincing across the sandy drawing-room floor of the desert. There used to be so many in the area that the other name for the San Pedro River was "Hog River."

A forest of chollas lines the ridgetop. The white spines of new growth, thickest on the ends of the branches and the nubbins of new joints, halo them with light. Little hedgehog joints, the size of small potatoes, litter the ground beneath the parent plants, some loose on the ground, others already rooting. One cholla blooms with brilliant magenta flowers, whose masses of light yellow stamens quiver with pushy beetles, and whose mossy olive-green stigmas spread like the tentacles of a tidepool anemone. Beetles pack into the joining of stamens and petals, flying between flowers, looking like tiny flies because they appear to be two-winged. When they alight, they crawl to the dark bottom of the flower or insinuate themselves between the dark petals. Beetles are not effective pollinators because they muck about in any flower with enough pollen to attract them, and do not visit flowers of the same species as bees do, nor do their often smooth, hard bodies catch and transport pollen grains as a bee's furry one does. One on my finger does not fly but wanders over my hand while I try to sketch it in my notes.

A gray shadow streaks into a huge nest constructed in the base of a creosote bush and shingled with detached joints of cholla. The mound measures four and a half feet across, about two high, a noble architectural effort with its own modest air conditioning of cooler temperature and higher humidity. It has four eight-inch openings, plus three others. A forest of chollas surround it and scatter new joints loose on the ground.

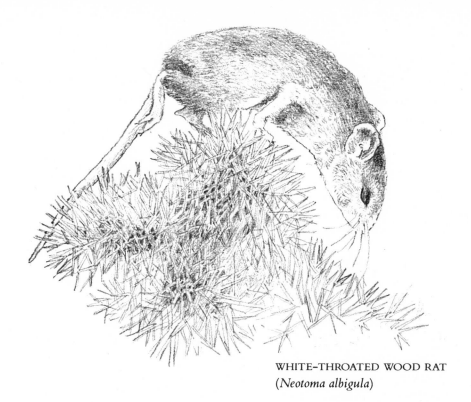

WHITE-THROATED WOOD RAT
(*Neotoma albigula*)

The occupant is a white-throated wood rat, not a true rat but more closely related to mice. Its other name, "pack rat," describes its propensity for operating a trading, collecting, and trash business, out of the proceeds of which it fashions a monstrous well-insulated nest. The wood rats' habit of busying together a nest cemented with urine and feces, "middens" containing readily identifiable organic remains that can be carbon-dated and that endure for hundreds of years, has provided geologists with a method of fine-tuning climatic variations since the Pleistocene. Because wood rats forage within three to four hundred yards of their dwellings, they obligingly compile an index of local plants and changing environment, and have documented the shift from more mesic plants in a damper environment to today's desert flora.

How does a wood rat transport those thickly spined cholla joints studding its nest, a joint of which I personally have had leap untold inches through the air just to attach its spines to my innocent hand or leg? How does a wood rat climb its stems, clamber over the joints with impunity, and even manage to bite into the flesh without coming up with an extra set of whiskers, and thrive on its poisonous oxalic acid, finessing the succulent's otherwise effective defenses? I have no answer other than wood rats and chollas just go together. Arizona wood-rat numbers correlate well with cholla density, because cholla provides water and food as well as protection. Although wood rats do not need free drinking water, they need more moisture than kangaroo rats and pocket mice. This they achieve with a diet nearly 50 percent cactus, augmented with leaves, mesquite pods, and fresh grass.

Karen and I repair to a cool green bosque along the San Pedro River, grateful to be out of the noonday sun. Black mesquite intertwine like Gothic tracery, the black trunks like ruins of ancient cathedral columns against brilliant emerald grass. These soothing respites from the harsh desert outside are disappearing. Bosques used to be frequent along Sonoran Desert streams but a lowering water table from arroyo cutting has robbed them of their water, leaving grave-yards of mesquite along the watercourses.

Fifteen feet below us, at the foot of a straight-cut, raw dirt bank, the San Pedro trickles northward to the Gila River. Instead of the meandering perennial stream where Cooke's Mormon Battalion caught salmon trout in 1846, now only a thread of water runs intermittently through high, nearly impassable banks. Early Span-ish journals as well as mid- to late-nineteenth-century accounts describe streams and rivers flowing through large oases full of riparian forests and marshes. Water sparkled over many miles of stream bottom where now it appears only after major rainstorms. *Ciénagas,* natural spongelike marshes that absorbed runoff peaks and released stored water slowly, dried up.

Irreversible arroyo cutting began in earnest between 1875 and 1895, triggered by several factors in varying combinations: in-creased heat and aridity, overgrazing, fire that denuded fields and allowed heavy runoff, and water-diversion projects that eliminated riparian woodlands. Floods began to gnaw at the soft soil of the banks, undercutting them so that huge chunks fell, rapidly widen-ing the gullies. Dry arroyos are so much a part of the desert scene that it is impossible today to imagine the verdure of desert stream-sides only a century ago and the vastness of the change.

Although there is close association between the onset of arroyo cutting and the increase in cattle running in the 1880s, some arroyo cutting has occurred where cattle have never run. Records kept since 1898 reveal a change in rainfall and temperature patterns: winter rainfall has diminished, summer has remained the same, and there has been a sharp rise in both winter and summer temperatures. These changes alone are sufficient to cause changes in vegetation, and have altered desert watersheds as much in a hundred years as geologic effects that lasted half a million times longer.

From those who knew these streams and meadows when they were verdant and productive just over a century ago, we have only their evocative words and images to superimpose upon a dry dusty landscape.

8

OF DESERT PAVEMENTS
AND KANGAROO RATS

If not sequestered in a national park or monument, the sparse plant growth of unprotected desert is frequently miserably overgrazed. One March night I camp in southern Arizona with Karen Reichhardt and her husband, ethnobotanist Gary Nabhan, and botanist Judy von Ahlefeldt, a friend of many years from Colorado. Tired and running out of daylight, we grab the first possible spot beside a dingy little wash. I've thrown down a sleeping bag in some scruffy places in my life, but this cow pie–studded terrain is one of the dreariest. A landscape I know as so satisfyingly beautiful, so in balance, is here so tattered and beleaguered.

The area is heavily grazed and all the annuals—minute grasses, white forget-me-nots, phlox, and blue waterleaf—grow in protected areas beneath creosote bushes or mesquite trees where hooves cannot reach. Creosote provides islands of fertility, where litter and more soil moisture accumulate because water infiltrates better near them than into the surrounding hardpan, and temperatures are moderated. The larger bushes spring from mounds gaping with kangaroo-rat or ground-squirrel holes, whose digging may be responsible for creating these yard-wide mounds where their inhabitants are also protected from being crushed by cattle hooves.

I kick away cow pies to pitch my tent but opt to sleep outside, watching a half-moon flow across the sky while the clouds stand still. I awake again to see no stars at all; all are hidden behind thickening clouds. Barefooted in unlaced boots, I gather up my sleeping bag and move inside to await the raindrops that come just before dawn, scampering on the tent roof like pocket mice, lulling me to sleep. I awaken to bright sunlight and birds all over the place: singing birds, flying birds, chirping birds, squawking birds. The sky is as clear as if it had been scrub-brushed. The ground is as dry as it was before the shower. A small fluttery caddisfly catches in a damp spot on the tent. The whole world seems to be on the wing.

As we stand eating breakfast, I try to ignore how chill it seems to me, until I see ice on a cup of water left out overnight. I chide Gary, who, in response to my question of what kind of a sleeping bag to bring, had assured me that it would be "just like early summer!" I am chagrined that this far south, this low in altitude, this late in the spring, it should be so cold.

A phainopepla beats against the wind, barely holding its own. Now, in late March, these birds are undoubtedly entering their breeding season; they winter primarily in the Sonoran Desert, where they breed in March and April. They have a unique cycle in that they breed twice annually, once in their winter range and once in their summer. Ornithologist Elliott Coues, on duty as an Army doctor in Arizona in the 1870s, found the phainopepla "a beautiful jet black creature" that "sang such a requiem as touched every heart."

Baskets of mistletoe hang from every mesquite tree in the wash, glowing with translucent salmon-red berries upon which the phainopeplas feed. A leafless, slender-stemmed parasite, mistletoe not only drains the vitality of its host but occasionally overplays its cards and kills it. Botanist Edward Lee Greene, crossing the

Sonoran Desert in the 1870s, reported that the flowers had a scent "with precisely the fragrance of pond lilies," which graced the air for miles.

At the witching hour of five o'clock that afternoon we wait outside the fence of Cabeza Prieta National Wildlife Refuge. Established in 1939, it is an 860,000-acre wedge of land in extreme southwestern Arizona lying along the United States–Mexican border and, paradoxically, also an aerial gunnery range. Yesterday we turned in our permits at headquarters, along with a waiver that if we are blown to kingdom come by running over a piece of live ammunition we will not sue the government.

The landscape changes markedly the minute we enter the cloistered area. Although unmistakable desert in its openness, stalked with great regiments of saguaro and ocotillo, there are so many more plants, so much more variety in size and shape, such a wealth of colors, compared to the overgrazed area outside the fence. On the bajadas, the characteristic slopes that apron the ridges and are the transition between vertical mountain and horizontal desert, creosote bush and bur sage are regularly arrayed like chessboard figures, pawns in rank, with saguaros the kings, ocotillos the queens.

Once inside the refuge, we travel as Father Eusebio Kino did, El Camino del Diablo, the route from Altar and Caborca, Mexico, via Sonoyta, to the Pacific, the road that also carried the shell trade of prehistoric Indians. Father Kino traversed this shortcut from inland Sonora to Alta California (on the way he discovered that Baja California was a peninsula, not an island) with his friend Juan Mateo Manje, planning cities and dreaming dreams about baptized Indians and shipments of grain, and redrawing maps. Juan Bautista de Anza followed Kino's trail to California in 1773–1774, and would later extend it to San Francisco Bay. Forty-niners, the eager and the ill-prepared, blundering their way west to make a fortune, died by the dozen on this dread waterless byway, not knowing that the only water was hidden in canyons and draws, in natural-formation water pockets and water holes called *tinajas* or tanks (from the Spanish *tanque,* a tank or reservoir). These water-eroded depressions, primarily in granite or basalt, hold water for days, weeks, or months after rains, and occasionally all year round.

This narrow sandy rut of a road looks no less formidable to me today than it did to them, and indeed will prove to be so for us.

All night long a great horned owl floats his warnings on the night air. Its call is an interrupted, almost syncopated *hoohoo—ah hoo hoo*, soft as a dove.

The sharp clarity of the icy desert night air chisels the stars, lifts sounds for miles, and cuts through my sleeping bag like a knife. I have on every piece of clothing I can get on and still move. The unclouded sky sucks up soil heat and drops the temperature unceremoniously. In the frigid dawn, the raking sunlight blazes the spines on a particularly hirsute cholla and haloes the edges of its unopened blossoms. I separate the petals of one of its waxy flowers and a bee blunders out—a perfect place to spend the night, wallowing in pollen, cosseted from the cold.

This morning only a dove coos, compared to the many birds we heard before dawn yesterday. Without trees for nesting, few bird species are permanent residents. Except for black-throated sparrows, almost no birds nest in the creosote; the saguaro are home just to Gila woodpeckers and small owls, and only cactus wrens and thrashers can abide the cholla. Since it is too early in the year for those nesters, all is quiet.

A thin, sandy wash threads through the desert pavement, with saguaro and cholla, small paloverdes, big ocotillos, and bur sage rooted in it. By contrast, the desert pavement contains only scattered tiny plants. Lilliputian annuals beard the ground around my sleeping bag, one-inch buckwheat with thread-fine stems bearing pinhead flowers, and two-inch-high woolly plantains. Most grow wide-spaced, feet apart, but sometimes crowd three dozen to the square inch. As soon as the leaves develop, desert plantains are able to accumulate carbohydrate reserves and set seed more rapidly than annuals growing in wetter regions, an admirable adaptation to the minimal desert growing season.

This early in the year, the pale-green spines on golf ball–size

97

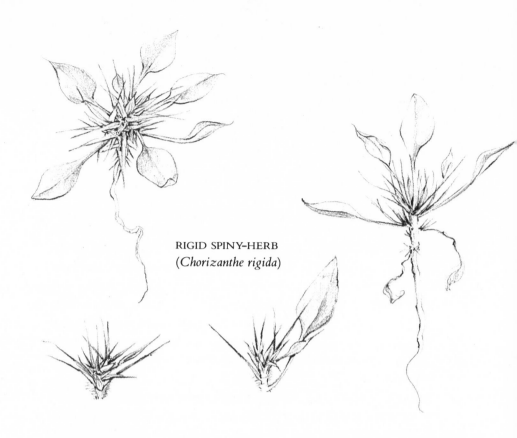

RIGID SPINY-HERB
(*Chorizanthe rigida*)

spiny-herbs are still soft. As the plants dry, they turn dark reddish brown, strewn across the desert like a handful of clinkers, and the spines become sharp as needles. There are very few plants that can withstand the heat load of these reflective desert pavements, where only a fraction of rain reaches the soil beneath, and remains on or near the surface, subject to quick evaporation. Pavements are generally devoid of perennial plants and usually support only a few small annuals, such as these woolly plantains and spiny-herbs.

Stone pavements are so common in deserts the world over that they have acquired local names: in Australia, gibber plains; in North Africa, hammada; in central Asia, sai. Desert soils the world over have the top horizon filled with tubelike air holes formed by the rapid expansion of soil gasses that occurs when summer rains wet the hot ground. I scratch away the pavement and find a puffy, porous soil, full of holes, beneath. Rain dissolves minerals already in the soil and heat causes gasses to form and expand, giving the top layer of soil its particular sponginess. Such desert soils swell and heave when wet, shrink when dry, an alternating contraction and expansion that works stones upward to the surface in a process very similar to frost heaving.

Pavement stones come down in the sands and silts of the alluvium washed off nearby mountain slopes, stones from quarter-inch pebbles to six- or seven-inch cobbles. Once on the surface the stones settle further with each influx of silt after a rain until they are quite firmly fixed. The age of a pavement is reflected in the color of the stones; if reddened beneath, they have been there long enough to become chemically altered, and if with a dark patina on top, long enough for desert varnish to coat the surface. The gleaming pebbles fit so neatly together that they appear to have been laid by some Byzantine artisan's hand, tesserae then polished to a high gloss by dark desert varnish that leaves them shining in the sun, a gleaming desert flooring.

A fractured cobble exposes, in cross section, its thin black coating of desert varnish, a veneer of iron and manganese oxides. Iron gives a red-brown color, while manganese stains dark brown to black. Certain bacteria and lichens as well as blue-green algae may also play a role in the deposition of iron and manganese. Dampness soaking into the rocks works to the surface, where it evaporates, leaving a residue of minerals. Lichens, fungi, and blue-green algae, living just beneath the surface crust, oxidize the minerals deposited on the surface. Rocks darken as they become more varnished and absorb more heat, which encourages the growth of more micro-organisms. Some rocks do not varnish well—for instance, quartz pebbles have neither good blackbody radiation nor the roughness to trap the necessary nutrient dust.

The warm stones from the pavement clink pleasantly in my hand. I pocket a few pebbles, the nondescript along with the descript, the ordinary dime-a-dozen along with those perfectly shaped and satin smooth. Many are varnished dark bronze, sounding as well as looking metallic as they clink against each other in my

MOJAVE DESERT STAR
(*Monoptilon belloides*)

fist. Other pebbles are ruddy, some tawny, one apricot-colored. Some drear, short-houred winter day I shall pave them out on my worktable, place my hand on top and close my eyes, and be back here, feeling the sun's heat in the stone and the firmness of the pavement under my feet, smelling the desert breeze and remembering the expanded sense of well-being.

On its way westward, El Camino Diablo skirts the northern edge of the Pinacate Lava Flow, the northernmost part of a volcanic field centered in northern Mexico, pronounced by Ed Abbey to be 750 square miles of "an iron-hard, iron-hued wilderness of craters, cones, congealed laval flows" and "the bleakest, flattest, hottest, grittiest, grimmest, dreariest, ugliest, most useless, most senseless desert of them all." I can hardly wait.

It lives up to its reputation, black rock too hot to stand on, rough enough to shred Vibram-soled hiking boots, yet full of tiny early daisies taking their warmth where they find it. Humans took warmth here also. Gary points out a low, rough wall, a "sleeping circle" that protected a Sand Papago from the drafts of a winter's night.

On the way back, we recross the Pinta Sands, an area of buried sand dunes blown up from the Gulf of California, and prime habitat for Sonoran pronghorn antelope. One of the trucks slows down and mires in over the hub caps. Permanently. Irrevocably. We get out and survey disaster. The sand goes all the way to China. Digging out is out of the question. The only solution is to build a firm base upon which the wheels can get purchase. No Roman slaves ever scanned the surveyor's stakes on the Appian Way with more dismay.

We need rocks, wood, anything solid, and there is nothing. Judy, Karen, and I search farther and farther afield, while Gary sets the jack on the lug bolt of each rear wheel in turn, raising the wheel above the surface of the sand, ready to slip underneath what meager stones we find. Sand engulfs the stones and wood with each engine-screaming, rubber-burning attempt to power out. We dig them out to use again. A scorpion stalks across the sand after I move a rock, tail curved and at the ready, and then two more scramble out. I wonder uneasily how many more cousins by the dozen are hidden there.

On rock-gathering treks, I note the well-trodden paths of Merriam's kangaroo rats webbing the ground, conspicuous sandy lanes in the scrub, always ending in a cholla-topped mound full of fist-size holes. These kangaroo rats were named for C. H. Merriam, who developed the ecological concept of life zones, and are the darlings of desert researchers, exhibiting distinctive morphological alterations as well as physiological and behavioral adaptations to desert life, making them the quintessential desert rodents.

Kangaroo rats' remarkably efficient kidneys excrete urea in concentrations twenty to thirty times that contained in their blood, about five times what the human body achieves. They live without any free water, creating metabolic water from atmospheric oxygen and the carbohydrates in their largely seed diet. Green plants furnish the extra water required during mating, and may also contain substances that stimulate estrus in the female; during lactation the female produces a concentrated milk that also conserves water.

MERRIAM'S KANGAROO RAT
(*Dipodomys merriami*)

They have no sweat glands through which to lose water, since they might lose up to 15 percent of their body weight in moisture in an hour, too high a price to pay for cooling.

Around my feet small paired imprints tell of bipedal locomotion, which has developed in several desert rodents, such as kangaroo mice and kangaroo rats. It is an adaptation that gives them greater speed and mobility with which to avoid predators. The large hind legs power great springs in any direction and spurt the animal out of harm's way quickly. Its long tail dampens the torque that comes with swift bipedal locomotion. Several species sport a tuft at the end of the tail, which may further act as a rudder to enhance midair turns. The tuft, sometimes contrastingly colored, is often what a predator grabs for, and like the lizard's tail, it is often regrown. Some of the tracks in the sand here are punctuated at a sharp turning with a big *C* swept in the sand, where the wide-swinging tail dragged ground in a high-speed reversal of direction.

I inventory the number of holes in a large mound and try to envision the complex burrows underground, connected with runways and stocked with flask-shaped hollows, often requiring several years to construct, to hold caches of seed, which gain more moisture for being stored in the relatively humid air of the burrow. Although the air in the burrow is not saturated with moisture, it is considerably damper than the air outside, alleviating the water loss through nasal passages the animal would suffer breathing the drier, hotter air outside. Long nasal passages, with a configuration that permits heat and moisture exchange, allow a kangaroo rat to maintain an almost perfect moisture balance while underground. There they also undergo patterns of daily torpor, which conserves energy and moisture.

Toward evening, on another endless rock-collecting sojourn, I nearly step on a tiny Merriam's kangaroo rat lying in the middle of a path, so newly dead that it has not yet begun to stiffen. A small puncture in its left haunch suggests it was felled by a rattlesnake, probably a sidewinder, not too long ago; the snake, disturbed, abandoned it where it lay. A sidewinder, lying coiled in its pallet just under the sand surface, is most likely to have been waiting quietly for just such an unwary victim.

The kangaroo rat is so light when I weigh it in my hand that I judge it to be very young, a scant two-inch body plus a two-inch tail. Its fine coat is brindled, soft tan-gray with intermixed black and white hairs, the belly white, the tail thinly furred. Transparent claws the size of needles, set in four long pinkish toes, identify it as a Merriam's. Fur does not fully cover its long back legs with their long tibias and feet.

Its delicate ears press flat back against its large head, fully one-third of its body, with a large ear opening. The head enlargement allows room for an inflated auditory bulla, a middle-ear echo chamber that magnifies hearing, especially in the low-frequency sound range of owls and rattlesnakes. Kangaroo rats have large eyes and keen night vision, and their hearing is so acute that they can avoid capture even in total darkness.

Middle-ear enlargement leads to other modifications. It pushes the mouth low on the head, which keeps its seed-holding paws low and out of its line of vision when it eats. Its front legs are shortened, not much use in running, but the paws are nimble and dexterous in seed gathering and pouch loading. They are capable of "high-speed pouching," rapidly stuffing seeds into their fur-lined cheek pouches

(pouches have been found stuffed with up to nine hundred seeds) while at the same time skillfully distinguishing between food and nonfood objects. Such efficiency allows a kangaroo rat to load its pouches quickly and retreat to its burrow, to eat in safety or to cache its seeds for later use. Kangaroo rats prefer annual seeds when available, but may also snag beetles and moths.

This very young kangaroo rat may have had the physiological adaptations but not the behavioral ones to survive. It was neither wary nor swift enough to avoid the quick, accurate fangs of the footless hunter who also tracks the same runways. When I pitch my tent, I zip up the fly very securely.

By noon the next day, some twenty hours after getting bogged down, we are on our way out, having learned more than any of us ever wanted to know about traveling El Camino de Diablo.

9

OF WHITE-WINGED
DOVES AND
DESERT BIGHORNS

Cabeza Prieta means "dark head" in Spanish, and the peak that inspired that name blocks the horizon in front of us, a pyramid of pearly-tan schist draped with a hangman's hood of black lava. It identifies the Cabeza Prieta Mountains, a forbidding fault black mountain range rising from an endless, boundless desert beset with a dryness and heat that devour colors and horizons and fade outlines until all that is left is shimmer.

This third week in June I enter the Cabeza Prieta National Wildlife Refuge with Chuck Bowden and Bill Broyles, both of whom have a desert fixation. When someone asks them why they go to the desert, they figure it's like J. P. Morgan's being asked how much his yacht cost. Bill, who in his sensible life is an English teacher, drives this road with an insane joy in the required high-clearance, four-wheel-drive vehicle. We enter the Cabeza from the north, and it seems to me we have come thousands of miles from refuge headquarters, where we have been briefed on bighorn sheep counting, driving first on highways, then narrow roads, then dirt roads, and now this ridiculous track.

"Road" is a euphemism. When wet, it imbibes rear axles. When dry, it buries you in sand for hours at a time. It has tracks with ruts that snap a wheel, high centered enough to batter a crankcase to oblivion. Washboard is too complimentary a word. We're talking lurching, jolting, tilting, loose-rock or deep-sand, kidney-busting roads that just don't care whether you travel them or not. Ocotillos, rude toll takers, thrust their thorny hands into the open window with intent to rob. On this questionable road, not only does one eat dust, and smell an overloaded and overheated engine, but also has to endure the squeals of vegetation dragging its fingernails along the sides of the truck, thorny plants as ill-tempered as the road itself.

We have volunteered to take part in a formal yearly desert bighorn-sheep count that has been done here since 1961. In 1939 ninety bighorns were estimated to be on the refuge; today the number is approximately three hundred.

Desert bighorns roam the mountain range of the Cabeza in male and female bands (young rams are included in both) throughout most of the year, getting enough water and vegetation. They combine and come in to water holes only during the driest months of the year, May and June. The commingling announces the onset of the herd's breeding season, correlated to producing lambs at the most propitious time, a timing that varies in each desert bighorn herd according to the particular mountain-range climate in which it lives.

We bounce into the small east-west valley that holds the tank where I will be stationed. The valley is narrow, rising to a notch between two high granite ridges to the west. Without gentling bajadas, the mountains bolt out of the floor, rubbled and pitted, short and steep, boldly tilted, roughed out with a chisel but never worked down or refined.

Bill offloads three jerry cans of water, enough for my six days here, a folding chair, and a cot. He and Chuck will go on to their own stations twenty miles away. I heave my duffel down, eager for them to be gone, anxious to set up desert housekeeping, ready to begin these days of immaculate isolation. The truck disappears in a cloud of dust, and for a moment I just stand quietly, blissfully alone. Then I unfold my chair, set up the tripod, and mount and focus the spotting telescope on the far slope, where I hope the sheep will be, wire the thermometer at eye level, and survey my kingdom.

The blind is half-hidden beneath an ancient mesquite tree. Open in the rear and with a window facing the natural water pocket of the tank, it is made of four steel posts faced with saguaro ribs. The plywood roof has wallboard nailed underneath, and, in the space between, a heaping of mesquite twigs and pods hints at a wood-rat nest, a suspicion soon confirmed when the occupant itself sashays off to forage.

The tinaja itself is invisible from the blind. It is tucked to the right against a vertical wall, two hundred yards up the draw. Huge boulders flank it on the left; one, fifteen feet high, provides a provident perch for the several dozen birds that frequent it. Tomorrow I shall walk up to record its water level.

Promptly at 7:00 P.M. bats begin cruising the campsite, looping lower than I'm used to seeing bats fly, whishing right past my ear, winnowing the air for insects with great efficiency. After they leave, I get bitten. The light fades so gently that my eyes are adjusted to starlight by 9:30 P.M. when I go to bed. The air is a comfortable 86 degrees F. The quiet is soporific. An infinitesimal breeze feathers my ankles and face all night long, the gentlest whisper of air in a great friendliness of night. Gazing up through the lacy canopy of mesquite leaves, I try only to doze, unwilling to miss anything. I do not succeed.

In the midst of a sound sleep, a sudden gust of wind looses an avalanche of mesquite twigs and pods and I shoot awake. The moon fingerpaints the sky with clouds. The Milky Way forms a great handle to the basket of the earth in which I lie. It is deliciously cool, enough so to pull up my sleeping bag. When I awake again, a big old saguaro hoists the near-full moon on its shoulder. By 4:30 A.M., when sheep watchers are expected to be sentient and at their task, pearly-gray light seeps into the valley.

Mesquite pods litter my sleeping bag and shoes. My cup holds three like swizzle sticks. These mesquites have longer, slimmer fruits, smaller leaves and leaflets, and a larger number of leaflets than those in damper climes. Unlike other pea family pods, these do not split open but retain the seeds embedded in a hard covering, and an animal that eats one must eat pod and all. So important were they to the prehistoric Seri Indians who inhabited Sonora, Mexico, that they had names for eight different stages of fruit development. The Seris even sifted through wood-rat nests several months after harvest to recover the mesquite seeds; their high protein and carbohydrate content made them a significant addition to their diet. Other desert Indians, the Amargosa and Pinacateño, developed a special gyratory crusher for grinding them. All I can say from experience is that the fruits are as hard as rocks, dry as bones, fall like lead weights, and truly do taste sweet.

I settle into my watcher's chair, in which I will spend so much time I will come to feel as if it is annealed to my behind. Immediately in front of the blind wends a dry, sandy streambed about eight feet wide, in the middle of which grows a twenty-five-foot saguaro with one massive arm raised in greeting. Some fruit remains on the cactus, looking like red blossoms—indeed, an early botanist mistook them for blossoms—but most have fallen to the sand and seethe with ants. George Thurber, botanist for the Mexican Boundary Survey in the early 1850s, who first collected saguaro seeds, followed the Indian practice of rolling the coarse fruit pulp into balls for storage; the seeds he thus preserved later germinated in distant botanical gardens. A mature cactus can produce more than two hundred fruits, each with some thousand seeds. Of these, perhaps half a dozen will be left after birds and rodents and ants have devoured them. Not only are they nutritious but they fulfill the water requirements of most animals.

Behind the blind a low divide centers the valley between two narrow, wiggly sandy draws. The soil of the small divide, without

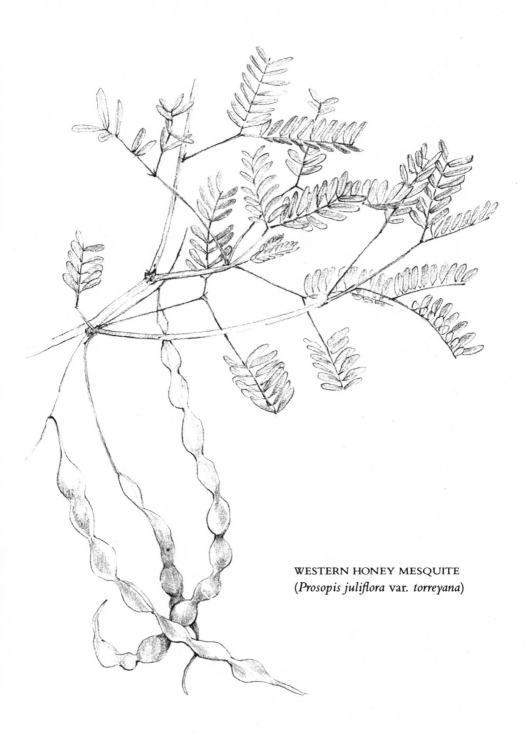

WESTERN HONEY MESQUITE
(*Prosopis juliflora* var. *torreyana*)

benefit of shading mesquite or protective creosote bush, is cement hard, paved with rough granite chips from the flanking and flaking mountains. Anthills stud it, a cholla or two, a few bristly borages, and many spiny-herbs, but mostly it is bare.

On the crest of the divide is a small hill of harvester ants, whose twelve-inch-wide stream of foragers was busy long before I found them this morning. With the temperature well above their threshold of 50 degrees F., they likely were out at first light. They swarm on a small gilia with cottony heads, harvest white forget-me-not seeds, explore peppergrass, and cart back not only seeds but leaf scraps and bracts, anything detachable. Thus laden they totter back to the nest's dime-size opening, rimmed with a foot-wide circle of salt-and-pepper debris. There they disappear underground to feed the larvae that serve as the colony's collective stomach. Although the adults gather the food, chew it and prepare it, it is the larvae that digest it and regurgitate part of it to the adults, and the colony cannot survive without their services.

By nine o'clock, when it is 90 degrees, not an ant is to be seen.

The white-winged dove contingent begins calling as the day warms, a repetitive call, not the familiar measured "who cooks for who" but an erratic, petulant "don't tell me, don't *tell* me!" Their calls intermingle with those of the mourning doves in antiphonal sound.

The air between the blind and the water tank begins to waver and shimmer. More doves arrive on the big rock overlooking the water. Throughout the day they gather, sometimes twenty or so in plenary session, sometimes playing musical chairs as they drop down to drink and return. But always in full sun.

Judging from their numbers, white-winged doves are exceedingly successful desert dwellers. The whitewing's clutch size is always two, and population increase depends upon how many clutches are laid and reared. They are capable of producing throughout the year, apparently oblivious of the usual environmental spurs, such as day length and rain, that govern many birds. Very resistant to dehydration, they can lose up to 20 percent of their body weight,

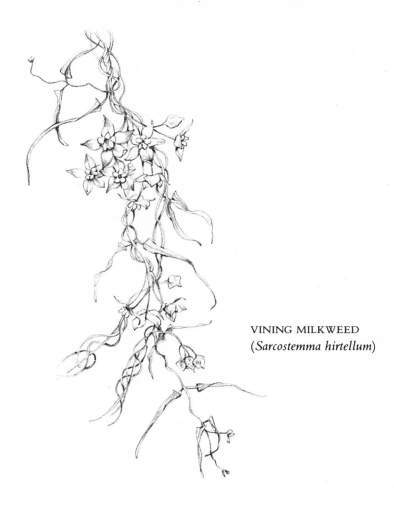

VINING MILKWEED
(*Sarcostemma hirtellum*)

and go four to five days without water. With access to water, they can tank up within five minutes. The doves' mobility makes it possible for them to water long distances away from where they nest.

Whitewings throw together a haphazard nest that provides little in the way of insulation or protection from sun when there are eggs in the nest. A "brood patch," a small area of bare skin on the bird's breast, serves as a heat sink for the eggs that prevents them from overheating. Most desert birds maintain elevated body temperatures; white-winged doves have a lower body temperature and are able to maintain it during incubation. Males have an even lower body temperature during the day than females and do most of the egg tending during the highest heat periods. In the Sonoran Desert in Arizona, even in direct sun, brooding birds never leave the nest unattended.

When they take off as a flock, their white wing patches shine while their dun-colored bodies fade into the background, and from a distance they look like a flock of small white birds. But I did not come to watch birds. I came to watch desert bighorns. And not one has shown itself.

In the noon stillness, the heat presses down, lies as heavy as a mohair wool blanket on my head, on my shoulders. It's only 108 degrees; knowing it can get up to 130 degrees in these close canyons, I am thankful for small favors. The air around the rocks near the rock tank wavers with banners of heat. I feel stooped and bent with heat

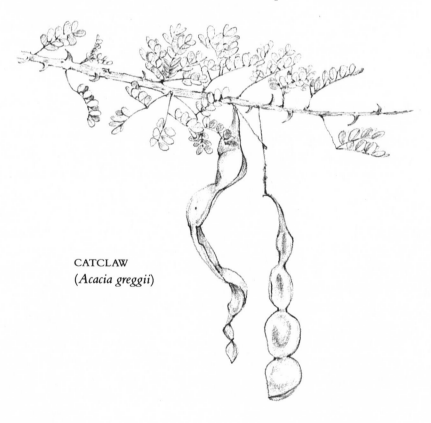

CATCLAW
(*Acacia greggii*)

as I leave the shade of the blind to walk up to the tinaja. I need to record the tank's water level so I can see how much water evaporates during the week (it goes down $3^1/_4$ inches). Bur-sage leaves disintegrate as I brush by them. Where there is shallow groundwater, mesquite and big clumps of saltbush outline the wash, many of them festooned with vining milkweed, twined and twisted in great heaps like a giant-size helping of vermicelli. Seed pods load catclaw, how ripe the seeds are depending on where the bush is set. By the blind the seeds are still green and held tightly in the pod; lower, they are drying to a salmon color, and in the hollow at the foot of the draw, they are dark brown and shiny, rattling in the twisted pods.

Up the slope, a four-foot-high elephant tree has found a purchase in the rocky slope along the trail, leaves just perceptible, ready to unfold the moment it rains. The papery-barked trunks, fat for water storage, give off a familiar turpentine odor. Hollyleaf bur sage, endemic to the lower Sonoran, marches up the slope to the ridge crest. This bur sage retains its scalloped leaves for years, the oldest faded nearly pure white. Now nettlelike seed heads remain, blooming over for the year.

The granite surrounding the water tank is pale gray, crystalline, flecked with sparkling black mica and roughened with large quartz crystals. Like most tinajas here, it lies in the crease of a small stream channel. A silt-holding wall has been built above the pool, and some cementing at the lower end provides an apron where animals can safely approach the water. Higher water levels limn the rocky sides with gray lines, and an inch of vivid green algae circles the present pool. It swarms with bees, ravenous for water to replace the large amount they lose in flight. I hesitate a long minute, then make my measurement as quickly as possible because in recent years I've become allergic to bee stings.

Anaphylactic shock, due to bee or insect stings, is not common, but on a percentage basis, it kills more people than venomous snakebite does. While it would take over a hundred stings to affect a nonsensitized person, just one sting can cause anaphylactic shock within minutes in one who is sensitized. Mellitin, a basic protein composed of thirteen different amino acids, is the chief toxin. It

GILA MONSTER
(*Heloderma suspectum*)

affects the permeability of skin capillaries, instigates a drop in blood pressure followed by a swift rise, can cause severe asthma, damage nerves and muscle tissue. In fatalities, the allergic reaction to the sting causes a drop in blood pressure so massive that no oxygen gets to the heart or brain. With immediate medical help a necessity, and none within a hundred miles, I am exceedingly conservative.

On the way back to the blind, still thinking about venomous bites, I round a boulder and gasp: five feet in front of me, on a large flat rock, is a Gila monster, a fearsome-looking lizard because it's so big. The size of my forearm, its tail is massive and thick, a repository for fat and water. Vivid warning colors of black and light yellowish orange pattern its beaded skin. With only two venomous lizards in the whole wide world, I nearly have to fall over one of them.

After a Gila monster locks onto its victim with its jaws, it chews. While doing so, it injects venom from glands set just under the skin of the lower jaw. Each tooth has sharp flanges flanking the grooves through which the venom flows, making its virulent bite very painful. In small animals death comes from respiratory paralysis. Although the bite brings severe pain and swelling, quickly followed by nausea and weakness, it is not usually fatal to human beings.

Gila monsters generally hunt at night during hot weather and are out during the day only in cooler seasons. Their metabolism is so low that they need to eat infrequently, and then prefer the eggs of reptiles and birds and the young of small rodents. I cannot imagine why it is out at this time of day. I back off with more speed than grace and leave it to its meditation.

An innocent little four-inch zebra-tailed lizard, perhaps more tan-and-white than zebra-striped, scampers across the sand, its ringed tail curled up over its back like a pug dog. One of the fastest lizards around, it has a chevron pattern on its back and legs that blends in with the flickering shadows and becomes invisible when it skitters under an acacia. I watch it dully. By comparison, my legs feel made of lead.

I spend well over an hour out of the blind, most of it by necessity in the sun. The temperature is 100 degrees F. when I get back at noon, despite a high overcast. Not only does air heat envelop me but heat billows up from the ground and radiates from everything around me: the ceiling of the blind, the sand in the wash, the desert pavement.

I gulp down a half bottle of fruit juice, made highly conscious of the necessity to drink lots of liquids by a packet of articles thoughtfully presented to me by Bill Broyles, harrowing accounts of death by thirst in gory detail, including "tumid tongue and livid lips," "unclean blow-flies" that will gather on the eyes and ears of my "already festering carcass," pierced again and again by the cruel spines of cholla.

My pulse rate is up to ninety. My face is flushed. Small blood vessels at the skin's surface dilate in order to radiate heat back to the environment because skin temperature stays cooler (around 92 degrees F.) than the surrounding hot air. The dilation of skin vessels also ensures an ample supply of blood to activate the two million sweat glands on the body because, when air temperature reaches between 86 and 92 degrees F., the only way the body can lose heat is by sweating. No amount of training, no amount of acclimation, alters the amount of water that is needed to replace water lost in perspiration. Because the body can neither store water nor reduce its need, water supply is critical.

Sweating makes it possible for human beings to exist in the desert and is controlled by centers in the hypothalamus that have set points keyed to temperature. Overheating can be prevented by the loss of one cup of sweat per hour, but it's easy to lose more without sensing it because in the desert sweat evaporates the minute it reaches the skin surface. But there is a limit to how much cooling can be provided by sweating because sweat removes not only water but salts in the blood, upsetting the electrolyte balance. The loss of these components of the blood—sodium and potassium chlorides and lactic acid—can bring on the muscle cramping, headache, and fatigue that come with severe electrolyte imbalance.

Acclimatization helps by increasing the perspiration rate and volume, lowering body temperature and heart rate, beginning sweating at a slightly lower temperature, and up to a tripled capacity to transfer metabolic heat from the interior of the body to the skin. Circulating blood increases in volume, urinary sodium and chloride are better retained, and salt concentrations in perspiration decrease. But, no matter how much one is acclimated, water remains critical to well-being.

Paradoxically, even with ample water available, it is difficult to drink and recover the amount lost immediately, because thirst becomes satiated before one's intake equals water loss. A person, voluntarily, drinks only a third to half of what is needed for replacement. This feeling of satiation may serve as a natural governor that prevents serious upsetting of the concentration of salts in the blood. Complete restoration usually comes when water is taken with food, and food replaces the lost salts. While it is almost impossible for someone to replace in one draft the full amount of water lost, animals do so by drinking greater quantities in shorter periods of time. A mourning dove can drink ten times (per body volume) what a man can drink in the same amount of time, and bighorn sheep can gulp down enough water at one time to recover their original weight.

If water loss from sweating is not replaced, sweat glands extract water from blood plasma, and body temperature rises. The loss of plasma water increases the viscosity of the blood, placing an additional stress on the heart, requiring more work to pump thickened blood through arteries and veins, also raising the pulse rate. Even though the heart beats faster, the amount of blood pumped out per minute remains nearly the same. In turn, retarded blood flow fosters a continuing rise in temperature in the inner core of the body where the temperature needs to be stable (the temperature of the peripheral tissue can vary without causing problems). Pulse rate and rectal temperature increase, breathing quickens. (The same reduced blood volume does not affect the heart rate in dehydrated bighorn sheep.)

At 2 percent loss of body weight due to loss of body water, thirst for some may already be fierce, accompanied by anorexia, flushed skin, and increased pulse rate. Small increments of debit have large symptoms: at 4 percent the mouth and throat go dry; by 8 percent the tongue feels swollen, salivary functions cease, and speech becomes difficult. After 10 percent the ability to cooperate, or even to operate, disappears. At 12 percent loss, circulation becomes so impaired that an explosive heat rise deep in the body is imminent and deep body temperature rises dangerously fast. Death follows, although lethal limits may be as high as 18 to 20 percent loss of body weight. When liquid is available, recovery can be nearly complete an hour after drinking.

At 104 degrees F., one must evaporate an equivalent of 1.5 percent of one's body weight per hour to maintain a constant body temperature. I do a quick calculation: at 110 pounds 1.5 percent of my body weight is 1.65 pounds. Because a pint's a pound the world around, to replace what I lost means at least a quart of liquid because, in addition, the body produces about eighty calories of heat per hour through metabolic activity. Dissipating this through sweat requires another five ounces of water per hour. In other words, an hour's wandering has started me toward a 2 percent deficit.

I look with new respect at the bighorn sheep that can lose 20 percent of its body weight (or a 30 percent loss of total body water), or the white-winged dove that can lose 25 percent, with no ill effects and even drink salt water, or the quail that survives 50 percent loss of body weight without succumbing.

I had anticipated some anorexia. Normal enough. I had also anticipated some of the psychological by-products of dehydration, such as lethargy or depression. Lethargy just may be the better part of valor in this heat, and as for depression, I have done nothing but walk around with a grin on my face the entire time. Like one of Carl Lumholtz's creosote bushes (Lumholtz traveled the Cabeza three-quarters of a century ago), I feel "radiant with health and good cheer."

Nevertheless I take another slug of juice. It ensureth my well-being.

The sheep do not come in until the second day, as if they were waiting to be sure their intruder was from a friendly planet. As I periodically scan the mountain slope with binoculars, it is some moments before I realize that the "rocks" are moving. I nearly tip over the spotting scope in my delight and eagerness to get it focused. The bighorns come downslope with a deliberate, mea-sured tread, pausing occasionally to stand and look about or pull off an acacia twig. Either eight or nine gather at the tinaja, and they change places just often enough to make them exasperatingly diffi-cult to count.

My first impression is of smallness and grace. Less than four feet high at the shoulder, they move easily over what I know to be a ruggedly steep and treacherous slope. With their smooth coats and long legs they bear little resemblance to domestic sheep, to which they are *not* related. The genus *Ovis* originated in Eurasia more than two and a half million years ago, migrated, as man did, across the

Bering Land Bridge, and became isolated into different groups during glacial periods. Today desert bighorns inhabit the arid mountain ranges of the southwest deserts.

Although I observe no pushing or shoving, clearly there exists a hierarchy at the water tank. A large, mature ewe waters first, taking two-minute and then four-minute drafts, and then stands aside. She has shed most of her winter coat but a continuous remnant cloaks her shoulders like a shawl, making her easy to identify when she appears again. Bighorn shedding begins at the rump and moves forward. All the other sheep have less old pelage clinging, suggesting that this ewe may be an older animal. She is accompanied by two lambs with their mothers that never do go down to drink. The ability of desert bighorns to go without water exceeds even that of the camel. Their extensive rumen complex—the first stomach of ruminant animals—holds and supplies enough water to support their needs. They produce a concentrated urine and to some extent resorb moisture from their feces. They can drink rapidly enough to get back into water balance within five minutes.

The next morning the large ewe again waters first, taking two long drinks before she leaves. Other sheep move in, young ewes and/or yearling rams—their size and horn shape are so close that I cannot differentiate at this distance. Mature rams are easy to identify, as the horns are much more developed and the four-year mark is usually a very prominent and readily visible groove on the horn, especially visible from the back. From that line one counts rings back toward the head for a fairly accurate age estimate, as each ring marks the cessation of growth for one year. The sheep remain at the tank, either drinking or standing around, for half an hour, and then slowly amble up the hill.

After they leave, a single large ram comes to drink. His horns have almost a full curl with the ends broomed off, leaving the tips worn and blunt (brooming results from rubbing the horns against rocks and dirt). The ram takes almost ten minutes to come down the hillside. After reading about their prowess in leaping rocks and sheer cliffs, covering ground with astonishing leaps and bounds, I am struck by his extreme deliberateness, which I take also to be a measure of his serenity. I dutifully record that he drinks for two minutes, then six, then two more minutes before mincing his way back up the hill.

Meanwhile the earlier crew reach the crest of the ridge to the east and disappear over the rim. The ram stops twenty feet or so below the top, where a ewe and her lamb lie hidden in a shadowy niche. He nuzzles the lamb, which tags along after him over the hill. The ewe remains, entering a deep overhang I have not noticed before, disappearing from view in the shadow.

I am inordinately pleased. I feel as if the sheep have honored me with their presence and I find myself smiling as I write up my observations.

IO

OF RED-TAILED HAWKS
AND BLACK-TAILED
GNATCATCHERS

Three concerns haunted me before I came on this bighorn sheep count: that I would be uneasy alone, that time would hang heavy, that I could not endure the heat. Instead I have felt at home, there have not been enough hours in the day, and the heat has become a bearable if not always welcome companion. The words of Joseph Wood Krutch, also writing about the Sonoran Desert, come to mind: "Not to have known—as most men have not—either the mountain or the desert is not to have known one's self. Not to have known one's self is to have known no one."

At noontime I am concentrating so hard on taking notes that when a cicada lets off a five-second burst like a bandsaw going through metal I jump. When there has been no activity at the tank for over an hour I opt for a can of tuna sprinkled with the juice of half a lemon.

No sooner do I open the can and get my fork out than all the birds explode from the rocks on which they've congregated. A red-tailed hawk bullets straight toward me, talons extended, tail spread. No sound, no screaming. It breaks off, rises with no rodent in its talons, wheels, spirals upward, and stoops again. Again no luck. It makes no third try. Its disappearance is followed by a great shocked silence. Half an hour passes before the doves venture, one by one, back to their sentinel rock.

I see only this one hawk stoop. The only time redtails are quiet is on the attack. Otherwise I hear their eerie *KEEEeeeer KEEeeer* that ricochets off the sky itself long before they come in to water. One afternoon a redtail sits on the steep cliff to the right; a couple of feet below it perch some house finches; a black-throated sparrow searches the bush beside it; a pair of ash-throated flycatchers rest above it; and across the tank, a batch of doves roost peacefully on their rock. All birds must be vulnerable to attack at the water hole and many avoid too much exposure by being able to drink very quickly, or coming in early and late when raptors are not hunting. Yet there are also these moments when the lion and the lamb lie down together.

I put aside my field glasses and lift my fork. This time a turkey vulture alights on the big rock. The rock is nearly vertical on the side overlooking the tank and this is where it chooses to descend to water. It gets about a quarter of the way down, contorted in an awkward position, big feet splayed out on the rock, tail pushed up behind at a painful angle, as it looks intently down at the water, a hilarious study in reluctance. Gingerly it inches down (vultures have no claw-grasping capability as birds of prey like eagles and hawks do) until it can hold no longer and crash-lands so ridiculously onto the apron to drink that I laugh out loud. The closeness of the rocks around the pool impedes the bird's maneuvering space because of its broad wingspan, and so it edges as close as it can to ensure dropping upon the only place where it can stand and drink.

Four species of this misanthropic-looking bird existed in the Pleistocene, and this creature looks like one of the originals. On the ground, vultures are hunched and awkward bundles of feathers, but

HARRIS' (YUMA) ANTELOPE SQUIRREL
(*Ammospermophilus harrisii*)

in the air. where I watch them during much of the day, they are magnificent, graceful soarers. They ascend with the updrafts coming off the hot desert floor, floating and lifting to cooler air, where visibility is superb; at five hundred feet the visible horizon is twenty-seven miles away, and at two thousand feet, fifty-five miles. Such big raptors generally get as much water as they need from the carrion they consume.

One more try on the tuna fish. A Harris' antelope squirrel scuttles down the wash to nibble on saguaro seeds. Tail held high over its back for shade, a single white stripe on each flank, it has quick, jerky movements typical of the ever-watchful. It stands slightly hunkered up on its hind legs to eat, but its rear end never touches the hot sand. It spends little time feeding and soon tucks back into the brush near the blind, where it undoubtedly has a burrow. There it spread-eagles on the cool soil and unloads its body heat, before taking on the desert again. Still, it withstands unusually high heat loads because of a lower basal metabolism.

The next day, emboldened, it hops up on the iceless ice chest in the blind and puts its head in my empty plastic cup, which tips over with a clatter, sending the squirrel flying.

I eat lunch at a fashionable three o'clock. By four o'clock, shadows cover the tank and the blind is in sun. A cloud cover that has kept the temperature relatively low all day has disappeared and the sun has an unobstructed shot at my back. Until the sun drops behind the ridge, it is the most miserable time of the day.

The resident robber fly alights in front of me, makes a slapdash attempt at a wandering fly, misses, and returns to watching. Flies are widely dispersed in the desert, more prevalent than any other insect order, and of these, bee flies and robber flies are the most numerous. The huge eyes of robber flies give them peripheral vision; with streamlined stilettolike bodies that allow swift flight, and needlelike beaks, they are efficient predators on the desert wafters and drifters. I've watched this one impale a smaller fly in flight, almost too quickly for the eye to follow, then alight to suck out the juices. Today it seems scarcely to care.

In the evening a caterwauling of Gambel's quail issues from the mesquite trees, where they perch in the branches. Their fussing is interspersed with a short soapsudsy cluck, embellished by a silvery *tink* at the end. The first night I was here they scolded and fumed about the stranger in their midst. The second night they gossiped and fussed, and the third night I awoke to find them within a few feet of the cot.

They visit the big mesquites only in the evening, always after sunset, and they are always noisy. I would think a predator could hear them a mile off. Their drinking patterns have evolved to avoid predators: they commonly come in to water twice a day, one period beginning at dawn, the other ending at dusk. Birds of prey tend to arrive around noon, so the quail's watering time does not overlap.

Quail have been termed "annual" birds because of their variable yearly populations. In the Sonoran Desert, the number of young quail per adult found in the fall correlates to rainfall during the previous December to April; in the Mojave, the same high correlation exists between young and October-to-March precipitation (a relationship that exists in other desert animals, among them bighorn sheep). Their reproductive activity begins before green vegetation becomes a part of their diet, the amount of which would give them clues to the amount of nourishment available, and hence the clutch size that could survive. Although quail do not breed at all in exceptionally dry years, they are one of the most prolific of birds.

They remind me of charming windup toys, painted wooden birds bustling about with staccato movements, officiously giving each other directions as they bustle among the creosote bushes. As I watch them, I remember the Kawaiisu Indian story about the tear marks on Quail's face because her young died, one after the other, when she made her cradles out of sandbar willow—a wood that the Indians therefore do not use for cradles.

The day dims and I stretch out to count the stars framed in a triangle of mesquite branches. Content, I realize I have reached, as Sigurd Olsen wrote, "the point where days are governed by daylight and dark, rather than by schedules, where one eats if hungry and sleeps when tired, and becomes completely immersed in the ancient rhythms, then one begins to live."

Yes.

Early in the morning, and again in the evening, bees create an unholy cantillation around the blind, some working the few mesquite and creosote flowers that remain, but most of them just circling in holding patterns of their own devising.

The number of creosote bushes in the western deserts make it a prime source for pollen and nectar. Several bee species are closely associated pollinators of the creosote bush although it does not depend on any single species for successful pollination. The most numerous pollinator in the summertime is *Perdita larrea,* a tiny bee just an eighth of an inch long. Because of its small size *Perdita* can harvest pollen larger bees cannot, but smallness may also curtail its value as a pollinator. Smallness prevents it from making reliable contact with a stigma, and its foraging range is modest and limited.

While the bees are outside the blind I remain quietly inside, hoping that the shade will discourage them from visiting and, most of all, from stinging at some imagined insult. With great relief each day I watch the bees move toward the water tank as the day heats. A thin black cloud of them is visible through the spotting scope. More than once I see a bighorn sheep make a hurried withdrawal from the tank, shaking its head vigorously from what I assume to be a bee's umbrage.

This morning bighorns remain at the tank, either drinking or standing around, for more than an hour before they leave. I follow them with the field glasses as long as I can. When I begin recording my stopwatch notations on the work sheet, I hear a strong bleating at erratic intervals. Search as I may, I can neither see around the saguaro to identify the activity nor locate the source by sound.

By default, I see a great deal of the old saguaro for the next quarter hour. The cactus is badly riddled about eight feet off the ground, so that daylight shows through the ribs, undoubtedly the work of the resident white-throated wood rat. Wood rats are the only animals that consistently eat cactus; other species may feed on it occasionally but cannot make it a steady diet because of the high content of malic and oxalic acids, created by the cactus's CAM photosynthesis. Oxalic acid is in the form of insoluble calcium oxalate crystals that, in humans, cause severe renal problems. For six months cactus is the wood rat's major source of food, reaching a peak in late May when it may comprise more than 90 percent of its diet.

The saguaro is closely pleated, waiting to expand when the rains come. The bellowslike action, which permits expansion of the stem without tearing the inelastic skin, allows precise adjustment to water storage, an action that starts with even very light rainfall. Water loss during the dry season reduces the volume of storage tissue, shrinking the stem; as the diameter becomes smaller, the ribs draw closer together, hence the pleated look. After a rain the process reverses rapidly, with more intensity on the south side of the stem, probably because water-conducting tissue is more prevalent there; the north side does not begin to swell until a few days later. About three feet off the ground on the north side facing me, an extra rib has been added to the basic number of twelve ribs. This onset of radial growth, or bifurcation, doesn't occur until the trunk grows to at least twelve inches in diameter.

A cactus of this immense size can absorb 95 percent of its total weight in water, sometimes up to a ton, expanding for up to three weeks after rains. Confined to the upper three inches of soil, tough ropelike roots may extend outward fifteen or twenty feet, placed to suck up as much water as possible before it evaporates. Lacking a stabilizing taproot, a saguaro topples if these lateral roots are severed.

The south and north sides of the cactus are measurably different. Ribs on the south side are deeper. Receiving the greater amount of direct sunlight, the deeper furrows provide a modicum of shade, reducing the time that direct sunlight heats the surface. Spine lengths on the south side are longer, and may provide an insulating layer of air. Fruits ripen first on the south side. Branch ends are usually colder than the main stalk during the night, and since single flowers form at the tips only, more rapid development occurs on the warmer side. Dryness promotes the formation of flower buds; plants growing with a favorable water supply make handsome vegetative growth but tend not to bloom.

Flowering is, after all, not an aesthetic contribution, but a survival mechanism.

The variety of birds in the Cabeza Prieta has been a surprise, especially at this hot, dry time of year. A pair of ash-throated flycatchers, tails a bright reddish brown, forage in the mesquite. Only gullies and washes with larger shrubs and trees support enough insects to attract the flycatchers. Three verdins squabble in a saltbush, their yellow caps bright but their bodies blending and disappearing in the fretted background. Feeding on insects (as most migratory birds do) they can exist without free water as long as insects are available. Subject to more water loss because of a less advantageous ratio of surface area to volume than that enjoyed by larger birds, they spend the day closeted in shade and shadow. Females weave ball-like nests in the thorniest of bushes, catclaw and sometimes cholla, and line them with down and feathers for the young, while the male builds a simpler nest for protection against the chill of desert nights. A wreath of spiny twigs around each entrance protects the relatively low-placed and vulnerable nests.

Wings whir close by as a Costa's hummingbird checks out my hanging red nylon stuff sack, then perches on a mesquite twig. This three-gram female loses nearly half of her body weight on hot days, making dependence on surface water and succulent food greater than that of large birds, which lose much less. When nectar from ocotillo and Indian paintbrush, as well as agaves, is available, hummingbirds obtain moisture in their food, but at this dry time of the year, when no flowers bloom, they must have access to free water instead.

At dusk a desert cottontail rollicks down the wash, which is now in partial shade. This cottontail is lighter than the mountain cottontails with which I am familiar, illustrating the tendency of desert mammals to be paler in pelage, somewhat smaller, and with longer ears and legs than their cooler-climate counterparts. It does not hop; its front and back feet move together in a rocking motion like a hobbyhorse canter. It nibbles some fallen saguaro fruit, then beds down on the other side of the sandy strip in a thicket of saltbush. Another one appears. The first returns. They face each other three feet apart, feinting. The first one dashes for the other, who levitates straight up while the first dashes beneath, and then both bucket off. To me it looks like great good fun and I enjoy their silly antics.

My band of bighorn sheep prefer morning watering. They come with some precision to the tank. This morning there is a considerable amount of amatory exercise going on between the young rams and the ewes. Breeding season is not far off and mating behavior patterns briefly interrupt the more unstructured ambles to the tank.

A ram follows a young ewe downslope, nose so close to her tail that he trips for not watching where his feet are going; the scent of a ewe's urine communicates whether or not she is in estrus. The ewe appears to ignore him, stopping to browse along the way or simply look about. I watch three different pairs, and each female, at different times, stops and urinates, a behavior that occurs only when a ram closely follows.

A group of six sheep come in early today, with some I've not seen before. They remain two hours, most of it standing around and mountain watching, before they move back up the hill. Busy recording, I hear the cracking of branches close by, and suddenly there are five right in front of the blind, noisily cracking mesquite pods. Although they prefer grass, there is precious little of that here and so they have become more opportunistic in their feeding. The group includes both a young ram and the big mature ram, two lambs, and a female. They are obviously aware I am here, look at me with less than the curiosity I feel I deserve, but otherwise pay no more attention to me than to the saguaro. I hear them crunching mesquite pods as they move downslope.

Sweeping the slope with binoculars, I spot more sheep on the hillside. As I switch to the spotting scope to watch them more closely, I hear a jet coming in low. A sonic boom rips the air and reverberates so close the whole blind vibrates, and even though I know it's coming, I still jump when the sound hits.

The bighorns on the hillside never turn a hair. The ten white-winged doves on the sentinel rock never move. The mourning doves never stop calling. I later find this to be generally true, that the frequency of a sonic boom resembles that of a thunderstorm, and that wildlife here generally is not disturbed by either. This observer is.

At midday, when tank activity has closed down and the temperature reads 106 degrees F., the metal of the spotting scope burns my fingers. The water I take from the jerry can to drink is hot enough to brew tea with. I can't complain. Early travelers had it much worse; John Durivage, crossing the same desert in 1849, found

> the water was detestable and at any other time would have proved a powerful emetic, but now it was *agua dulce*. A tincture of bluelick, iodides of sulfur, Epsom salts, and a strong decoction of decomposed mule flesh were the component parts of this delectable compound.

A western whiptail lizard patters out from behind a water can and prowls the edge of the blind, snuffling the dirt floor as it goes. I puzzle over the dark color, an allover deep smoky brown with a checkered back pattern, a good-size lizard with a long tail, the last three inches of which are almost black—until I realize that the soil

129

under the mesquite tree where it forages is brown from the humus of leaves and pods and twigs built up over the years. Western whiptails are very variable in color, tending to match the ground upon which they travel. When the lizard reaches my bare right foot, to my delight, it tickles right over my toes.

I pour four inches of water into the bucket, put my shirt in, wet it thoroughly, and put it back on wet. Even though the water is hot it chills immediately and sits on my skin like salvation. It refreshes and energizes me enough to take a walk. When I return, hundreds of bees have found the water I unadvisedly left in the bucket. My blue sleeping bag is the dearest object of their desire. They cling to my blue shirt with ecstasy or joyously explore every object in the blind.

I sulk outside in the flimsy shade of a creosote bush for forty-five minutes while they enjoy my grudging hospitality.

Behind me, the next morning, are the subtle sounds in the brush that indicate small-animal movement, but peer as I may, I see nothing. Finally I pick out a dull-brown robin-size bird, which scratches the dirt, pauses, disappears, pops up on a branch and down again, difficult to see and to follow. I finally get a good glimpse of a fierce yellow eye and an almost raptorlike gaze: a curve-billed thrasher. With something in its beak it flies to a nearby cholla and solves a mystery: at last I know who built the large messy nest in the cholla in which I found three fully-feathered, grayish-brown young, eyes tightly closed, beaks like hand-drawn brackets too big for their heads, so nondescript as to be unidentifiable. A high percentage of desert birds nest in inaccessible cavities, spiny trees and shrubs and cacti, symptomatic of the strong predatory pressures on nesting birds here, but only cactus wrens and curve-billed thrashers regularly brave the cholla.

By noon the temperature is 102 degrees F. and climbing. I was going to walk, for there are things I want to check out. I was going to draw, but even with a paper towel beneath my arm I still perspire enough to buckle the paper, and the drawings are out of proportion and awkward. I was going to do a lot of things, but the heat, combined with my usual after-lunch low metabolism, saps my ambition. A white-winged dove calls, repetitive, insistent, annoying. A thankless breeze comes through the blind. The little ground squirrel arrives, unnecessarily spry and lively and perky. I feel listless to the point of stupor.

Actually I may have reached the point where I can live with this heat, this everywhere, this without-respite hot. My skin feels cool so evaporative cooling is working. It would be heaven to pour a pail of cool water over my overheated head, but all the water is hot. Not warm. Hot. And I yearn for every ice cube I ever heedlessly rinsed down a drain.

The silence of noon is palpable, more an onerous, enveloping physical presence than a lack of sound. A female Gila woodpecker lands on a mesquite branch, mouth agape. When a mourning dove coos, it has a lunatic overtone. A fly's drone sounds like a freight train.

The white-winged doves sit on the sentinel boulder above the tank, in full sun. The heat radiating off the rocks must make the cul-de-sac in which the tank sits unbearable, yet the doves appear unperturbed. The thrasher, beak agape, sits on her nest, lit by full sun. In this high-heat time of day she must be there to shield the young, enjoying none of the comforts of a shaded nest but also not vulnerable to attack, a brutal trade-off.

Rather than evaporating water to lower body temperature, most desert birds allow a passive rise in body temperature. Birds ordinarily have a higher body temperature than mammals, well above 100 degrees F., and this higher temperature allows them to dissipate heat by radiation. Birds, with the exception of burrowing owls, cannot utilize burrows for cooling, nor can they sweat. They can sit in the shade and extend their wings to expose bare patches of skin; they can compress their plumage to reduce its insulating value; or they can gape, which is a means of evaporative cooling.

When ambient temperature rises above body temperature, there is one more option: gular flutter—fluttering the thin floor of the mouth and the soft skin under the throat. Gular flutter increases evaporation and is highly developed in several desert bird species, among them doves, quails, nighthawks, and roadrunners.

But sometimes even that doesn't suffice. On the last afternoon I check the thermometer at three o'clock, already 108 degrees on its way up to 112 degrees F. Heat rolls down off the surrounding ridges like a *nuée ardente,* consuming everything in its path.

Hopping up on a bough of the mesquite against which the blind is built is a tiny black-tailed gnatcatcher, not much bigger than a hummingbird. Illustrations in bird-identification books show such plump, neatly feathered creatures. This little soul is waiflike and thin, feathers disheveled and tufting out, the Edith Piaf of the bird world.

She walks up the branch in front of me, less than an arm's length away. She stands with her body high off the branch, tail quivering. As I watch her, her head nods forward in that familiar "I can't hold my head up another minute" droop. As soon as her head drops she jerks it up and opens her eyes in a gesture so reminiscent of a child fighting sleep I have to smile. She moves to stand beside my duffel bag, which is wedged up against the tree trunk and, as I watch, slowly lists until she leans completely against it as if exhausted by the heat. Her head drops forward and she starts awake several times more. Finally her head remains down. She sleeps.

In time my head falls forward and I too jerk awake, and finally, very quietly, scoot down in the chair so that my neck can rest on the back, and then I doze as well. I awake with a stiff neck just as the little gnatcatcher stirs. She pulls herself upright, shakes her feathers flat, looks about perkily for a moment, and in leisurely fashion, hops into the brush.

My last evening here. I walk up to the divide that separates my valley from the desert flats to the west, winding to the top, flushing a lizard, climbing over granite boulders, avoiding the barbed and the spurred. When I reach the top I climb up on a boulder that is set out of the wind that hollows through the defile. Below, saguaros stalk down a dry wash and then disappear as the land levels out into a wild, open emptiness.

Looking out over the pure sweep of seamless desert, I am surprised to realize that the easy landscapes stifle me—closed walls of forests, ceilings of boughs, neat-trimmed lawns, and ruffled curtains of trees hide the soft horizons. I prefer the absences and the big empties, where the wind ricochets from sand grain to mountain. I prefer the crystalline dryness and an unadulterated sky strewn from horizon to horizon with stars. I prefer the raw edges and the unfinished hems of the desert landscape.

Desert is where I want to be when there are no more questions to ask.

II

OF SAND FOOD
AND PALM TREES

The Cabeza Prieta stretches westward almost to Yuma, astride one of the few crossings of the main desert river, the Colorado. Although in 1538 the Spanish navigator, Francisco de Ulloa, laid claim for Spain to all the area drained by the Colorado River, not until 1774 was this desert crossed on foot when Juan Bautista de Anza, commandant at Tubac, scouted a route west, forded the Colorado River, and trekked across the Salton Basin as far as San Gorgonio Pass. The next year he took this route all the way to San Francisco Bay and established a path used for years. Seven years later Don Pedro Fages made the exceedingly difficult southern crossing to San Diego Bay, a route little used until Kearny and Cooke brought Army contingents through in 1846–47. Present-day California highways across the desert largely follow their routes.

Lieutenant Emory crossed here in November 1846, and

134

AJO OR DESERT LILY
(*Hemerocallis undulata*)

SAND VERBENA
(*Abronia villosa*)

"encountered an immense sand drift, and from that point until we halted, the great highway between Sonora and California lies along the foot of this drift, which is continually but slowly encroaching down the valley." That great drift is called the Algodones Dunes, a massive dunefield of two hundred square miles that runs roughly north and south athwart the travel path, paralleling the western edge of the river.

I walk the Algodones Dunes late one companionable spring afternoon with Anita Williams, a gracious woman who knows and writes about the Cocopa Indians of northern Mexico. Late light softens the flowing flanks of the dunes and low light pushes our Giacometti shadows ahead of us. The fluted white trumpets of desert lilies luminesce in the low-shafting sunlight. The plants are large, the flowers opulent, much larger than the usual calf-high lilies I just saw in the Cabeza Prieta, as are some of the creosote bushes

BIRDCAGE EVENING PRIMROSE
(*Oenothera deltoides*)

and evening stars, a gigantism that frequently occurs on dunes because of the lenses of deeply-held moisture these plants can tap.

In the hollows of the dunes, yellow evening primroses trace volutes, sand verbena lays deep pink serpentines, and hundreds of birdcage evening primroses unfurl. In 1846, when he brought Mormon troops across the desert, Philip St. George Cooke noted the last as a plant "which grows into a pear-shaped basket frame, the stems or branches all uniting as if tied above. . . . The bushes furnish a small fire for making tea and frying meat."

Cooke was referring to the skeletons of the evening primrose, which endure from season to season, some of which lie fragmented in the sand beside us. As the plant grows, it does so by adding stalks around the periphery of the original rosette. As they dry they curve upward to meet toward the top, forming an open basket of seed pods, giving rise to its common name of birdcage primrose. When the tubular capsules pop open at the top, some seeds spill out while others remain attached. The drifting sand eventually buries the skeletons with their cache of half-filled capsules. With rains, the capsule-enclosed seeds germinate in place, often in a circle following the outline of the buried skeleton.

The white evening primroses, like the pearly desert lily, luminesce, their luster intensified by the tawny color of the dunes themselves. Red iron-bearing minerals are common in sand, and some dune sands acquire a coating of ferric oxide concentrated in pits on the grain surface, becoming darker with age. The Algodones Dunes have acquired, over the centuries, a lovely resonance of color.

One dune crest looms behind another, a heavenly disorder of line and flow. To see order I have to remember how they looked when Herman and I flew over them: nearly parallel ridges defining the western edge, long, almost straight ridges bending slightly eastward, extending for eight or nine miles, five hundred to six hundred feet apart. Or to recall the even greater simplicity of a Landsat photograph, where the western edge is merely wrinkled, and the main body of the dunes themselves mere ripples, facing neatly southeast. To the south the ridges curve into immense barchans, some of which may have horns up to a mile apart. The blended shapes flow in elegant sinuous patterns with a purity of line absent in the surrounding piled-up and turreted mountains.

The prevailing winds blow from the west-southwest, but the orientation of the dunes—both in their slipfaces and general trend—indicates that the preponderance of dune-forming winds comes from the north-northwest. Such strong northwesterlies probably blew during the Pleistocene, and drove large amounts of sand inshore from the beaches of Lake Cahuilla, the much larger Pleistocene predecessor of the Salton Sea, and built the Algodones Dunes to their present configuration. Now there is little movement. Plotted on aerial maps, the present-day dunes travel some three inches a year.

I had no reading of magnitude when I first saw them from the air, no sense of scale. They might as well have been ripples on a beach. But on the ground, this floating evening, the dunes are impressive and massive, unforgettable. Wherever I trace a horizon, I follow an elegant line that protects and defines, brings order and serenity into a chaotic world.

Anita and I are meeting Gary Nabhan to look for sand food. The name of this well-camouflaged parasitic plant comes from its intensive use for food by local Sonoran Desert Papago, the Hiach-eD O'odham: the Sand People. The easiest way to find sand food is to find the plants upon which it is parasitic, especially pleated tiquilia. This tiquilia, noted by William Emory in 1846 as "a low bush with small oval plaited leaves, unknown," is itself not all that easy to find. The sand-drifted rosettes, splayed flat on the ground, with its spare quarter-inch leaves, tend to disappear in the vastness of the dunes.

We scuffle a lot of dune, looking for sand food. Gary's eye is better attuned to subtle changes in sand texture and infinitesimal shadows, and soon he cups sand away from a flattened golf ball–size head, exposing the stem. Beset with small bracts, the stem is the diameter of a man's thumb and exactly the color of the sand. The flavor of the stem is described as melonlike, and early travelers, as well as Indians, relished its freshness of flavor and texture. Potential hosts are close by: six feet separate it from a pleated tiquilia, ten feet

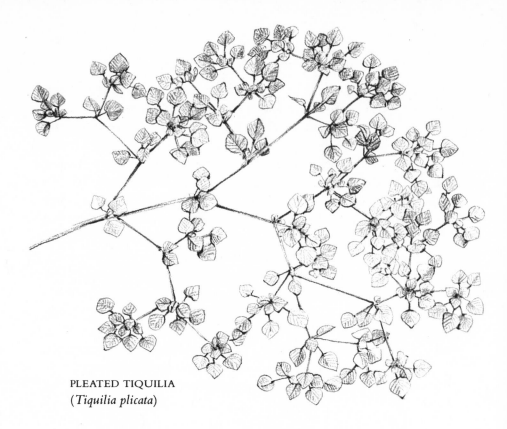

PLEATED TIQUILIA
(*Tiquilia plicata*)

from another, five feet from a dune peabush. A sand-food root need barely touch the host plant with only a few root hairs to tap into its moisture and sugar.

How sand-food roots locate a host, without which they cannot survive, no one knows for sure. Possibly desert kangaroo rats, the only species present here in any numbers, bury the seed heads near a host plant, where contact can be made on germination. Or sand food's dry seed heads break off and tumble, peppering the sand with thousands of seeds, and with odds that some of this number will catch around the base of a potential host and work into the sand. Or vice versa, seeds from other plants snag in sand food's dried head and germinate there, bringing the mountain to Mohammed. Or perhaps they are simply part of the vast reservoir of seeds in the top few inches of desert soil, galvanized to germinate by exudations given out by germinating seeds of potential host plants.

Given the good health of its hosts, sand food's classification as a parasite may need to be revised. Sand food imbibes and stores moisture from infrequent rainfall in its succulent stem, moisture then possibly available to its host plant, providing it with a better supply than it could have achieved on its own. Excepting parts of the Mojave Desert and Death Valley, the 250 square miles of the Algodones Dunes are the driest part of the United States. Rain falls occasionally in the winter and in spasmodic torrential summer rains, but the mean annual precipitation here is less than three inches.

The plump disk of the two-inch flowering head is lost in the vastness of sand around it. Just beginning to bloom, sand food's few tubular flowers are scarcely a sixteenth of an inch across, nestled in the dense plumose pubescence of the calyx. Since ultraviolet photography picks up the flowers' lilac hue, they must be clearly visible to pollinating bees, and some additional pollination undoubtedly occurs at night when the majority of dune insects are active.

Like sand food, all the sensitive plants of the Algodones Dunes have evolved unusually long stems, forced by the continually blowing and drifting sand. Elongated stems develop shortly after germination in Wiggins' croton, dune sunflower, Pierson's locoweed, and dune buckwheat, as well as in sand food. After buckwheat seeds germinate on moist dunes, only a leaf tuft shows on the surface, while the rapidly growing stem may anchor ten feet or more into sand.

Pierson's locoweed displays another adaptation to dune living. Although it is a perennial that matures into a small shrub, it can flower and fruit just two months after germination, assuring seed survival even if the plant never reaches shrub status. It produces seeds larger and heavier than those of any other southwestern locoweed. Housed in inflated seed pods, they tumble and bounce across the sandy hillocks, gathering in hollows or piling up against other plants, confined by their weight to the place they grow best.

All these plants are threatened. Sand food has almost totally disappeared from Arizona because of a combination of agriculture (desert soils can be very fertile when irrigated) and off-the-road-vehicles (ORVs); dune buggies also destroy the habitat and seedlings of croton, sunflowers, and locoweed.

Gary fills in the hole and sprinkles some sand across the top and, if I didn't know better, I'd swear he murmured some Hiach-eD O'odham incantation for its longevity.

The Coachella Dunes pile up on the east side of a narrow valley extending some sixty miles from the Salton Sea on the southeast to the summit of San Gorgonio Pass to the northwest. The booming winds that pour out of San Gorgonio Pass and funnel down the Coachella Valley are legendary (attested to by the numerous wind-generator "farms" at the throat of the pass). Desert areas of lower barometric pressure draw relatively cool air in off the Pacific, creating an inversion at around three thousand feet over the pass. The narrow configuration of the pass creates a Venturi effect: air pressure drops and wind accelerates, unleashing high-velocity and extremely desiccating winds into the basin below, and whisking sand into low, rolling dunes against the Coachella Mountains.

The day has built to full blaze when I reach the dunes at noontime. I loathe hats but clamp one on my sweating forehead anyway, and check to see that my water bottle is full, knowing the water will soon be as unappetizing as warm dishwater. I roll down my sleeves and turn up my shirt collar to keep off the sun—loose clothing that does not hinder perspiring can halve the radiant heat load and cut water loss by two-thirds. I pick up my notebook, take a deep, reluctant breath, and push my way into a desert blanched with heat.

The dunes are so light in color that they reflect and focus the heat on any object above ground. Small dunes, the largest but twenty-five feet or so above the interdunal flats, face mostly south and east. I tromp through a rich growth of dune plants stabilizing small hummocks on the dunes' apron, laced with rabbit and fox tracks. Ladybugs clamber on desert yellow primrose and over desert four-o'clocks.

I bend over to admire a clump of yellow evening primroses and find myself contemplating instead a desert iguana tucked away neatly in the shadows. A stocky medium-size lizard with a five-inch body plus a five-inch tail, its buff-colored body is patterned with brown spots that form varied patterns across its back and coalesce to form lines around the tail, pied patterns that render it part and parcel of the broken shadows. A diagnostic row of beaded scales runs all the way down its back and onto its tail. It has a narrower range than that of creosote bush, which makes up almost all of its diet. It often climbs into the bushes to feed on the blossoms although it avoids the unpalatable leaves.

Desert iguanas are beautifully adapted to life on the desert. They may drink water if available, but can exist with only the water contained in their food. As they are primarily vegetarians, desert iguanas must have some extrarenal mechanism to get rid of the sodium and potassium salts they pick up in their diet. This they do in much the same way sea birds do, through a pair of glands opening into the nasal cavity that act as accessory kidneys and remove salt ions with a minimum loss of water.

In this afternoon heat the iguana operates very close to its tolerable limit. It regulates its body temperature within rather narrow limits by behavior, as it is doing now. It began its day in its burrow, waiting as long as two hours after sunup before emerging to forage, remaining nearby its burrow until its body temperature reached its optimum, a high 111 degrees F. Unlike most lizards,

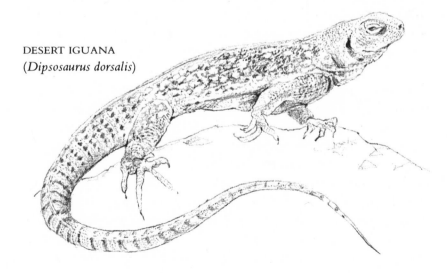

DESERT IGUANA
(*Dipsosaurus dorsalis*)

which tend to take over old rodent burrows, desert iguanas usually dig their own.

I lean closer to see it better and it bolts off across sand so hot I feel the heat through my soles. It runs with such a peculiar shuffling, swimming gait that I think it has a bad leg, before I realize it is brushing the hotter surface sand aside to bring its body into contact with cooler sand beneath. As the day cools—and I fervently wish it would—it will spend more time in the sun, orienting its body to receive the rays at a more perpendicular angle, until it finally tucks into its burrow for the night.

When I reach the dunes proper, I find them well used by ORVs, tire tracks superimposed on the chained imprints of lizards. Although it is windy now, it is nothing like what it can be, for which I am thankful. Fast-moving hot air quickly adds to heat stress. Because the winds from San Gorgonio Pass are so powerful, accumulations of larger grains and pebbles in the troughs emphasize the spectacular ripple patterns. Smaller-scale patterns crosshatch larger ripples going in another direction, as if the wind constantly wearied and shifted, quixotically rearranging the patterns to its liking every hour or so.

Small cylinders of damp sand dot the top of one dune, an inch or so high, as if tubes of sand had been piped up. Smaller ones are sealed. Several dozen stud the area, always several feet apart, probably belonging to large female wolf spiders, who find happy hunting on the dunes.

The distinctive and extraordinarily even track of a sidewinder loops across a sand flat. The impressions in the sand sit at an oblique angle to the rattlesnake's direction of travel, arcs with little walled ridges of heaped-up sand on the outer arc of the curve. Each impression has a hook made by the head and neck and a T by the tail, which is to say that this snake was heeding Horace Greeley's advice.

Sidewinders are specialized for living in dunes by this peculiar type of locomotion, not by any anatomical or physiological alterations. The principle of sidewinding is that of a sidewise rolling screw, touching ground with only two sections of its length at a time, efficient for fast travel in a loose substrate like sand because the force exerted is vertical, better than a horizontal force, which is inefficient in loose sand. I follow the tracks until they peter out, only to emerge a few feet farther, going in the other direction, looping around a bush, setting out straight again, and finally disappearing. They have no rhyme or reason and there are interruptions where I think this crazy snake must have been airborne. Where tamarisks have formed copses in the dunes, the hummocks are riddled with holes, oases for the sidewinder's favorite prey of small mammals and lizards.

What I have come here for, am enduring this fiery furnace for, is a glimpse of a fringe-toed lizard, one of the most highly specialized vertebrates of North America sand-dune habitats, a lizard endowed with distinctive anatomical adaptations to living in this flowing, unstable medium. Its sloping snout is wedge-shaped, with a countersunk lower jaw to slip easily into the sand. Its eyelids are thick and overlap and interlock to keep out sand. Scales form protective flaps over the ears, pressing back as the animal burrows. Elongated scales fringe its toes, which increase the surface area of the feet and therefore the traction, allowing greater purchase in loose sand by doubling back when its leg bends forward and flaring outward as its leg extends. Fringe-toed lizards are the only reptiles limited to and totally dependent upon dunes.

Fringe-toed lizards' ability to bury themselves on the instant is legendary. They wiggle their heads sideways and push strongly with muscular hind legs, holding their front legs close to their sides to reduce resistance as a scuba diver, arms held back, powers through the ocean with his legs. A U-shaped nasal passage prevents sand grains from penetrating its head. A cavity of air under its body keeps sand from falling in about it and constricting its next inhalation.

I follow endless tracks chaining the dune rims and skidding down over the edge into loose sand, where there are dark burrow holes on the slope face. But not a lizard is in sight. Possessing exceptionally keen eyesight, they may have spotted me long before I could see them. Or, being so closely matched to the sand that sometimes sophisticated optical equipment cannot differentiate

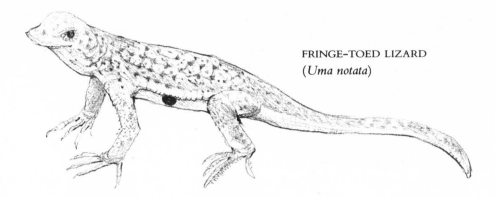

FRINGE-TOED LIZARD
(*Uma notata*)

between lizard and background, perhaps I couldn't see them even if they were out. I scan the dune crest for movement. Nothing.

Even though I know they bask only in early morning and late evening, the eternal optimist in me bids me wait. I sit down on the dune. Perspiration streams down my nose and drips on my notebook. I drain my water bottle. The sun notches another degree to the west, cleaning out the shadows, encouraging the wind, blowtorching my shoulders. If I don't get up I may be glued to the sand. After an hour, it takes great effort to heave myself to my feet and admit defeat. No lizard in its right mind would be out.

Disappointed, I shuffle my way out of the dunes, pondering the impossibility of fringe-toed lizards. I can see where one went to market, where they held the Olympic games, where one had another to tea, where the chorus line formed, but they themselves have sensibly retired beneath the surface, waiting for a respite from the heat. I envision dozens of them studding the lee side of the dunes, all neatly tucked beneath the sand, front legs folded close to their sides, hind limbs flexed for action, pineal gland shuttered, eyelids locked closed, all perversely, unreasonably, and inconsiderately keeping out of sight.

The 13,000-acre Coachella Valley Preserve protects not only fringe-toed lizards, but also a palm oasis, the anomaly of the Sonoran Desert. The flickering shade of the palm oasis is the complete antithesis of the unmitigated heat of the dunes. The shade is as much aural as visual. The fronds converse quietly, rustling like taffeta, from an air flow that moves through treetops thirty feet above but scarcely reaches me below. I can almost hear the whir of cameras as Rudolph Valentino gesticulated through *Son of the Sheik* or Cecil B. De Mille filmed *King of Kings* in this very palm oasis.

The only way in which early travelers survived crossing the desert was to know where there were tinajas, springs, or oases. On the first major crossing, when de Anza trekked the desert in the 1770s, he took with him an Indian as guide to direct him to water, and survived the trip. These oases are still marked on the map but now they are towns, among them Twentynine Palms, Thousand Palms, Palm Springs.

Native desert palms have been present in western North America for 100 million years, and at this time may be actively expanding their range. The genus developed in the Pliocene, probably in Baja California, and spread northward, retreating southward during the cooler, rainier times of the Pleistocene. When climate warmed after the Pleistocene, they again migrated northward, increasing their range, able to establish where there were springs and seeps. Every canyon with enough water to support a desert palm grove is on a fracture or fault that allows, or forces, water to rise to the surface.

The kind of soil in which the palms root is not as important as permanent water. If runoff and seepage increase, so do the number of desert palms; likewise, successive drought years decrease grove size. These groves look as if they are all the same height and the same age, but after reaching thirty feet the palms slow in growth, limited by the ability of the vascular system to pump water any higher; between seventy and eighty feet seems to be the limit. While close in height, they may actually be varied in age.

Since the seeds are so heavy, long-range dispersal depends on coyotes, which eat the whole fruit, passing the seeds through their digestive tracts unharmed—those seeds germinate better than uneaten ones. In the fall, coyote scat is filled with desert palm seeds, most of which are ready to sprout. Robins have been seen with seeds in their beaks, and possibly other birds may help in distributing palm seeds. Over eighty species of migratory birds frequent palm oases.

147

Fire is the most important factor, other than water, in maintaining desert palm oases. Palm oases are very flammable from the large skirts of dry fronds that thatch the trunks. Without burning, palms eventually decline in number, crowded out by plants with more extensive root systems. Fire eliminates the above-ground portion of competing plants so that palms can outgrow even the grasping tamarisk with its incredibly dense and shallow water-usurping root system. Although tamarisks will return by sprouting from rhizomes and roots, at least three years pass before they reach their former growth. Meanwhile, the industrious desert palms, growing one to two feet a year, will have produced multitudes of new seeds, which will have enjoyed ideal germinating conditions.

The cambium layer, which produces new growth, in deciduous trees is near the surface and thus vulnerable to fire; in palms, such transport tissue is scattered throughout the trunk. Even though the green leaves are killed when the dead hanging skirts catch fire, the palm generally survives and puts out new fronds in two to three weeks.

With no plants except desert palms transpiring, the soil actually becomes more moist, creating a perfect situation for palm seeds to germinate. In response, desert palms produce twice as much fruit after a fire. The survival rate of new palms is enhanced by arming the petioles of tender new fronds with spines, which discourage browsing. The large grove at Palm Springs burned in 1980; now, half a dozen years later, it has regained its lushness. Only blackened bark recalls the blaze. Nevertheless, each fire removes a little more wood, destroys a few more vascular bundles, eventually weakening the tree and making it vulnerable to boring beetles.

Nearly every tree has thumb-size exit holes, made by the two-inch larvae of the giant palm borer beetle on their way out. Once a desert palm is well-started, few insects attack it, but this beetle can literally reduce the core of a tree to sawdust. The fat, pale-yellow larvae spend up to six years eating their way through the trunk. Seventy to 90 percent of the palms are done in by these beetles, either directly or indirectly. The only control is fire, which decimates beetles close to the surface. The palm borer occurs in every palm oasis except the two remote ones in Arizona to which the beetles have not yet spread.

My cultural belief that fires are one of the evils of nature has required some massive rethinking on my part to discard, in order to accept that fire has always been a natural part of certain of the North American biomes, even a necessary part. The burning of the prairies fertilized and kept the tall grasses vigorous. The Indians who lived near the palm oases—and each oasis had its own group—often fired them to promote new growth. Plant and animal populations are adjusted to fire. Man is not, and has contrived to remove fire as much as possible from the ecosystem, frequently to its detriment.

But before there were careless campers there were, and still are, careless storms with careless lightning. Nature has its own cadence, in which there is little tolerance for houses built in floodplains or flammable chaparral, little consideration for cities built on fault zones, or irrigation works that turn the desert green. Nature acts without calling in a consultant or submitting an environmental impact statement.

12

OF OLD SEAS
AND NEW SEAS

From one of the tufa-coated boulders that makes up Travertine Point on the western edge of the Sonoran Desert, I gaze out over a panoramic view of the Salton Sea and the Chocolate Mountains beyond. This place invites looking back and looking forward, for there is so much visible evidence of past seas, past plants, past animals.

There was a time when the land around me was not desert. At my feet are the familiar Sonoran Desert plants—tiquilia and pincushion plant, four-o'clocks and brown-eyed primrose, California chicory and burrobush, whose bracts cast a satiny sheen. These plants did not grow here fifteen million years ago for it was much too wet. What did grow here was a rich woodland with numerous live oaks and walnut, mountain mahogany and sumac, all of which require frost-free winters and twenty to twenty-five inches of

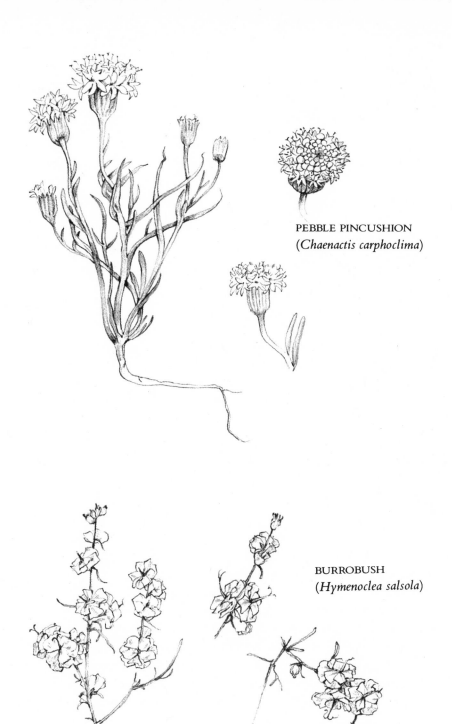

PEBBLE PINCUSHION
(*Chaenactis carphoclima*)

BURROBUSH
(*Hymenoclea salsola*)

151

BROWN-EYED PRIMROSE
(*Oenothera claviformis*)

annual rainfall (today's flora gets along with barely three inches). In fact, woodlands covered the whole vast area of the Southwest until recently when the area now called Mojave Desert was uplifted as a block, breaking the continuity.

Nearly three hundred feet above the northwest corner of the Salton Sea, Travertine Point was once connected to the Santa Rosa Mountains by a tombolo, a sandy spit on the shoreline of the Salton Sea's ancient predecessor, Lake Cahuilla. Actually, Travertine Point is misnamed, since travertine forms from calcium carbonates precipitated around hot springs and is different in appearance and formation from tufa, which coats the rocks here. When the waves of Lake Cahuilla lapped these rocks, they were covered with algae. In summertime algae take in great amounts of carbon dioxide in photosynthesis. Tufa forms when turbulence and wave agitation rob the algae mat of carbon dioxide, leaving calcium carbonate that spontaneously precipitates out and coats, in this instance, the beige quartzites that mark the high-water level of Lake Cahuilla.

This Pleistocene sea exceeded the Salton Sea in area and depth, being some three hundred feet deeper. An ancient beachline beneath me is drawn but a few feet above present sea level and likely represents the former northern limit of the Gulf of California, before the delta of the Colorado River diked the basin. This lake did not fluctuate with climate, as other pluvial lakes did during the Pleistocene; rather its water level depended on the Colorado River—how its channels ran and whether or not there was an outlet through to the gulf. The lake existed long enough to produce beach deposits of considerable extent, particularly those along the northeast shore that supplied the sand for the Algodones Dunes.

Today tufa wraps the rocks with softly pillowed shapes, as abrasive as coarse sandpaper, hot to the touch, full of centuries of sunshine. Encrustations coat the rocks to a depth of 20 inches in a 120-foot vertical band. Where the tufa erodes away, frond patterns ice the granite surface or form imbricated patterns on the sides of the rock, leaving lacy dendritic tapestries. On others the tufa looks like

SALTON SEA, COACHELLA VALLEY, ALGODONES DUNES

spongy dough, risen full of huge air holes. Sometimes the coating resembles dried shaving cream, the foam dried into little holes and thousands of little empty wiggly tunnels. Lichens, black as iron filings, darken the interstices of the tuberculated surface. Big rinds of tufa lie on the ground, some nearly a foot thick. I work out a tiny snail shell trapped within the tufa, an algae grazer that plied its trade thousands of years ago, and think of its modern cousins who have adapted to survive in a place without water.

The rocks lie like old lizards piled on top of one another. Bulldog faces guard crouched frogs. All kinds of eyes look out from the rocks, baleful, slanted, downcast, deepset, smiling, and in one profile a Janus face, looking back and looking forward.

In reading a landscape no longer here, it is as if I have access to an understanding of change beyond the span human eyes can reach to scan the future. When Lake Cahuilla dried up around 500 years ago, it left a desert valley some 110 miles long and 34 wide, a structural trough bounded by two mountain ranges and deeply filled with erosional debris from their granites, gneisses and schists—sediments so deep that borings 1,700 feet through interbedded sands and clays do not reach bed rock. So much salt accumulated here that it was an item of trade for the Cahuilla Indians, and the conspicuous salt beds were worthy of note in the Pacific Railroad Survey reports. The desert stretched from the Colorado River west to the coastal mountains, north from northern Baja California to the end of the Coachella Valley.

To cross it was a nightmare. In 1849, the *New Orleans Picayune* sent a reporter, John Durivage, to write about the rigors of this desert crossing. When Durivage's group reached the desert, they waited until the morning to set off

through the dreariest road imaginable. The heat was intense, and reminded one in many essential particulars of a portion of Goldsmith's "Deserted Village.". . . By ten o'clock in the morning the rays of the sun poured down upon our devoted heads with the utmost intensity. The animals faltered and staggered in their tracks; one half of our little party were on foot; and the signs of the times around us were such to alarm the most intrepid. The scorching, seething sun provoked the most intolerable thirst, and none had that with which to allay it; those who had supplied themselves most liberally with water having exhausted their precious store. The dejected countenances, the unnatural brilliancy of the eye, and the inflamed veins in the face gave token of the sufferings of the men.

Afterward he acknowledged that "until one has crossed a barren desert without food or water, under a burning tropical sun at the rate of three miles an hour, he can form no conception of what misery is."

William Blake, geologist on this segment of the Pacific Railroad Survey in 1853, recognized that there had once been a very large amount of water here and named the ancient Pleistocene lake Lake Cahuilla because it lay in the Cahuilla Valley, in turn named after the local Indian tribe of itinerant farmers and fishermen who lived there when the lake still filled the basin. Blake named the desert the Colorado Desert for its proximity to the river, a confusing name that must be qualified with "of the Sonoran Desert" since there is now a state of Colorado.

Blake returned in 1905 to find a desert he had named now inundated, found his "old-traveled trail across the desert lay 15 fathoms deep under water, where before not a drop could be found." He saw what I now see below me: a placid body of water sparkling in the sunshine, a shimmer of liquid blue over a desert pavement.

And how the Salton Sea came to be is a product of "making the desert bloom," one of those patriotic slogans like "God, mother, and apple pie," tied up with hopes and dreams, avarice and ignorance.

In the 1880s and 1890s the empty Colorado Desert provided impoverished grazing. It was a dry, empty basin where a meager living could be made if you liked sun and wind and heat and living by yourself. The first Southern Pacific Railroad train crossed the Colorado Desert to Indio in 1876. Within a few years, more than twelve thousand people had moved into the desert, determined to have agriculture by building an irrigation canal from the Colorado River to the valley. Capital was so difficult to come by that the canal was not finished until 1902, but it was, from the start, a powerful impetus to settlement, and was built despite a 1902 United States Department of Agriculture circular in which a soil expert reported that the land was too full of alkali to grow anything.

By 1909 the canal had silted up. After two years of heavy rains and inadequate canal maintenance, the Colorado River breached the canal's headworks, rampaged into the lowest part of the desert, the Salton Sink, and defied desperate efforts to stanch the flow. Tons of rock and heroic effort finally contained the river, but not before millions of gallons of water had poured into the Salton Sink, creating the Salton Sea. Today the Salton Sea has a net evaporation loss of five feet per year, and a salinity quadruple that of the Pacific Ocean.

A section of the Colorado Desert south of the Salton Sea was reclaimed for agriculture and named Imperial Valley, a name that would become synonymous with an almost continuous growing season that produces fine fruits and vegetables. In 1928, Congress passed the Boulder Canyon Project Act creating Hoover Dam, Imperial Dam, and the All-American Canal System, and put the Colorado River behind cement. By 1940 the All-American Canal conveyed water 125 miles from the Colorado River, irrigating 450,000 acres of desert. When the Coachella Branch was finished in 1948, more than 80,000 desert acres were added, much of the valley lying below sea level.

"Making the desert bloom" is not a happy-ever-after story. It blooms, but at a price. Successful reclamation is possible in inland salt deserts but tremendous "soil amendment" is necessary. Once a crop is planted, it must be irrigated. An efficient drainage system is essential to avoid the buildup of subterranean salts, which gradually work up to the surface, making the land unfit for crops. The natural flora of the Salton Sink is differentiated from the general flora of the Colorado Desert by the preponderance of saltbushes and other halophytes, diagnostic of highly saline soils.

Yesterday I involuntarily watched crop spraying, trying not to inhale the acrid fumes. Little planes like smart yellow dragonflies flew to the end of a field, pulled into a tight left turn, tilted their wings, then buzzed back down the next row, leaving a mist of chemicals hanging pungent in the air. Along with its fruits and vegetables, California also grows rapidly adapting, voracious, quick-breeding insects, encouraged by the seldom-rotated single-crop plantings of large agribusiness. Although some farmers are abandoning synthetic fertilizers and pesticides, information on crop yields and the costs of conversion are not yet widely available.

Even with good irrigation practices, many of the fields in the Imperial Valley that I see both from the ground and from the air have empty moth-eaten spots shaved out of the green. Salt is not only present in the soil but is carried in solution by the Colorado River, and desalinization is becoming a major concern in the valley. The gloomiest estimates are for only twenty years more life before the valley is no longer fit for crops and the desert takes back its own. Once there was desert here, and here there may be desert again.

At the turn of the century, John Van Dyke, an eastern art historian who came to the desert for his health, was captivated by the dry heat and clear air, and became concerned for its preservation. In *The Desert* he wrote prophetic words: "The deserts should never be reclaimed. They are the breathing-spaces of the west and should be preserved forever."

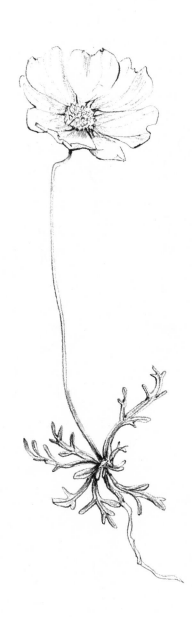

THE
MOJAVE
DESERT

13

OF NIGHT LIZARDS
AND SINGING DUNES

Less than twenty miles north from the Salton Sea, as the raven flies, the Mojave Desert begins. The transition is abrupt, brought on by a sharp change in altitude. Originally the Great Basin, Sonoran, and Mojave were a more or less homogenous stretch of arid land. About two million years ago, the Mojave Desert uplifted as a block, rotated, and became a transitional desert, intermediate in climate and elevation. The change in altitude separated the Mojave from the Sonoran Desert to the south by excluding warm-climate species (mostly succulents) and accepting the more northerly species from the Great Basin Desert. Present-day vegetation patterns are less than ten thousand years old.

Basin-and-Range topography, essentially the geography of all four deserts, is more marked in the Mojave and Great Basin deserts. Flying from Yuma to Barstow, California, I look down on an aesthetically satisfying landscape, the right contrast between crimped and smooth, vertical and horizontal, united by graceful alluvial fans and bajadas in just the right proportion, a visual balance that nevertheless portends landforms in transition, mountains rising up and mountains wearing down. The landscape that flows beneath the wing is a landscape of form rather than color—restrained, subtle, played on by light, a few shades alternately warmed and cooled.

Exquisite landforms, yes. But intimidating. Frightening. The encapsulating airplane, the white noise of the engines, all at once seem very safe and very secure. The landforms below offer succor for the eye and the soul but nothing for the body. The body needs all kinds of life-support systems to survive out here, and this landscape provides none.

Strange how a landscape so unwelcoming and intolerant of life can be so inexplicably and compellingly beautiful. This place is beautiful in the same sense that a rattlesnake is, patterned with a perfection of design lifting it above its potential for death. Or perhaps confirming it.

"You got lost," says Dr. Kenneth Norris, zoology professor at the University of California, Santa Cruz. His big grin somehow makes it seem like the wisest thing we ever did. What can Herman and I say? We have managed to see a great deal more of the Mojave Desert—defined as that desert east of the San Andreas Fault, south of the Garlock Fault, and west of the Colorado River—around the Granite Mountains, than we had planned. Since I frequently get misplaced in a one-way canyon, getting lost has become such an intrinsic part of my life that I've been forced to make a virtue out of it, realizing that it enables me to run across a great many things I would otherwise miss.

I immediately ask Norris if there are any *Xantusia* about, the tiny desert night lizard named after John Xantus, a Hungarian naturalist who collected for Spencer Baird at the Smithsonian in the late 1850s. "Oh, plenty," he reassures me, and we start out to look for one, expecting to be back in five minutes.

Norris bangs one yucca stump after another to rout out an elusive night lizard, and gives me a running résumé of the genus: its smallness, its lack of eyelids, how it sheds its skin as a snake does, that it is so incredibly sedentary that one may stay under the same bush or Joshua tree for much of its entire life and, being strongly thigmotactic—needing to keep in contact with the world about it— will always try to keep its back against a solid protective roof. Night lizards bear live young, usually two, and are placentate; when the mother breaks the membrane, the offspring appear live. They covet termites but also relish other insects and spiders.

I stumble along behind, trying to take notes, keep up with Norris, and not trip over the Joshua-tree logs that litter the ground. When I see a small movement under a piece of bark, I whomp my hand down in a reflex based on eagerness, not on care. And there, under my hand, is the little night lizard, and there, outside my hand, swiftly wiggling off across the ground all by itself, goes its tail.

I am appalled by my clumsiness and not a little relieved when Norris chuckles. He shows me where the sphincters shut off blood supply at the base of the tail and the tail breaks through the center of the vertebra, a handy protective device, since that's where most predator attacks focus.

I hold the tiny charcoal-gray creature as gently as possible. It is scarcely longer than my third finger. Its large head scales gleam softly. The lacy pattern of scales on its body have much less contrast than most lizard patterns, appropriate since it spends most of its time in dim light and probably does not need the camouflage of those subject to constant predation pressure from hawks and mammals. Still, it does undergo daily cycles, darkening during the day, paling in the evening. Being thin-skinned, it must avoid desert desiccation and does so by remaining in the shade and hunting only at night.

I set my tailless charge back on the gravelly ground. For a second it does not move, then swings its head once—and where it was it isn't.

□

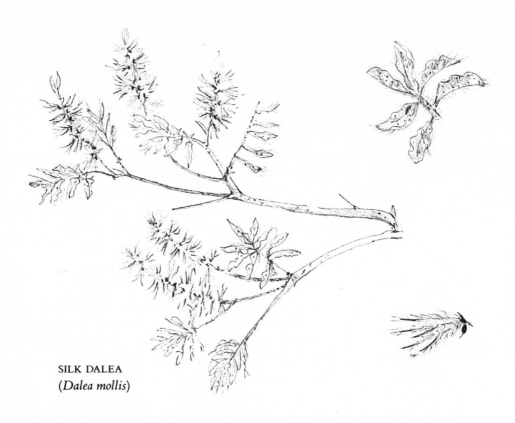

SILK DALEA
(*Dalea mollis*)

Herman and I camp in one of the many niches that scallop the edge
of the Granite Mountains, where cold bubbling water springs out of
the rock. At five o'clock in the morning a half-moon still hangs in
the sky, a canyon wren sings, the sky glows rosy, and the wind has
been up for hours. It frets the junipers, worries the Joshua-tree
flowers, quivers the stiff bushes, so gusty that I expect to see the
granite rocks shift.

The wind blusters the shrubs studding the wash, most of
which are in bloom, breaking up the color patterns into pointillist
dots. Dark red tints the buds on Mojave yucca, tinted by anthocyanins, which warm the tissue inside; spines border its spiky
yellow-green leaves. The tiny flowers of silk dalea nestle in a furry
calyx among hirsute leaves, the hairs so long they almost obscure
the flowers. Lavender flowers hang on turpentine broom, its stems

and fruits heavily dotted with pungent oil glands. Yellow flowers soften the rigid branches of blackbrush, and sparkle the creosote bushes, whose open flexible branches wave giddily in the breeze, adding a kind of silly gaiety to the whole scene. Magenta colors the rhatany bushes, and pale violet flowers enhance the Anderson's desert thorn.

Most of these Mojave plants are drought-enduring, evergreen perennial shrubs, a growth form fairly restricted to deserts. Most flower only in the spring, stimulated by lengthening daylight hours and warmth. Most of them never quite drop all their leaves, but put out new growth after rains; they may lose most of their leaves during drought but retain enough of them to justify being classified as "evergreen." Under severest conditions, these shrubs shed many of their stems and branches as well as leaves, and as much as a quarter of the plant may die back. In wetter climes, these dead parts would decompose within a few years. In the desert, insects and decomposers are not present in the numbers necessary for rapid breakdown. When flowers catch the eye, the dead wood is not so evident, but the rest of the year, when such color is absent, dead trunks and branches tinge the landscape gray.

In last night's twilight I hung my shirt over a wolfberry bush— an Anderson's desert thorn—to my regret this morning. My shirt bears its imprint with three small snags. Thorned branches distinguish Anderson's desert thorn from other members of the nightshade family. This morning's flowers will give way to juicy red berries; its leaves, which contain high concentrations of calcium, strontium, and magnesium, are almost round in cross section. Desert thorn photosynthesizes only in the cooler temperatures of spring and fall, with only a modest ability to withstand high temperatures and drought; when the desert heats up, it drops its leaves. Desert thorn is one of the first plants to become active in the Mojave Desert in the springtime when temperatures are still around freezing at night and daytime temperatures are just reaching 60 degrees F.

The last species to break dormancy in the Mojave Desert is rhatany, which requires minimum air temperatures above 40 degrees F and daytime temperatures in the eighties. A small rhatany

ANDERSON'S DESERT THORN
(*Lycium andersonii*)

RHATANY
(*Krameria parvifolia*)

bush beside which I left my boots last night is in full bloom, dark reddish-purple flowers poised like tiny butterflies on the stems. Unlike desert thorn, it carries on photosynthesis during the heat of summer (even though photosynthesis rates are low), and no matter how severe the drought conditions, it does not go dormant. Rhatany is a much-utilized browse for wild animals, all the more important because there are so few palatable shrubs. Nibbling prunes it, and new growth proliferates from the old root system, resulting in a dense low bush. Its fruits are covered with barbed spines, adapted to be transported in fur.

These tough small shrubs endure where soil moisture is least, where air temperatures near the ground in summer are extreme. Since leaves do not sprout from stems until well up off the ground, they escape heavy heat radiation as well as catch cooling wind. That these small shrubs are the largest deciduous plants able to grow under such conditions indicates the severity of the Mojave climate, and that they cover 20 percent of the desert demonstrates their success in meeting these conditions.

This festive and ebullient morning is worthy of a Shakespearean sonnet or a Dufy painting, confettied with color—in short, another splendid desert morning with that particular clarity of light and color that so pleases the eye. But for one thing: having chased my ground cloth four times this morning, I could do without the wind.

On the northern piedmont of the Granite Mountains lie the Kelso Dunes. On a March day-before-spring afternoon, somber clouds back the mountains as I walk northward toward the dunes. Two-inch-high white linanthus spatter-paint the sand between shoulder-high creosote bushes and uncountable bur-sage bushes.

I slog a cattle trail in which the soil is deeply pulverized. Even though it is hard walking, my conscience prefers it to stepping on and destroying the turrets of dark soil lichens that bind the sand beside the trail. As I trudge along, I make an informal count: for every one creosote, three bur sage. Just ahead of me a rounded ridge of sand runs parallel to the main dune massif, seven or so feet across

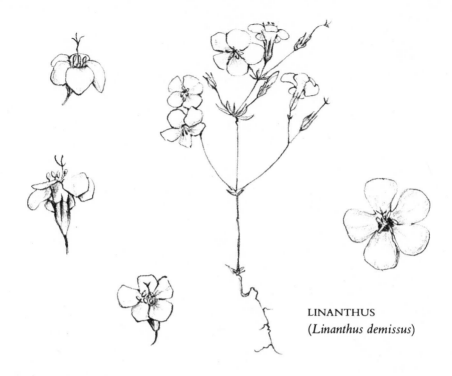

LINANTHUS
(*Linanthus demissus*)

and as high, set with huge creosote bushes, each with a multitude of trunks springing out of the crest, the result of vigorous branching by one bush nourished by underground pockets of moisture.

Ricegrass flickers in the breeze but all the linanthus has disappeared—in fact, no more annuals grow past this elongated hummock. Judging from the rippled surface, wind action is much stronger here. The prevailing westerly winds fashion ripples with a marked asymmetry. Some are small, a few inches separating the crests, while others stretch up to ten feet apart, almost a foot high. The sand, though it has dried, is fine enough to retain the recent rain's fingerprints, and the wind has not yet scrubbed them away.

Spring is just getting underway in the dunes. California croton reveals new gray sprigs, and Borrego locoweed, endemic to Mojave and California dunes, begins its yearly growth. The stems and roots of both loop and arch over the sand, polished shiny from windblast but still water-bearing. New sprouts of dock show green, and last year's papery rosy fruits cluster in small drifts.

DOCK
(*Rumex hymenosepalus*)

Big galleta grass, a coarse grass, greens up. Its runners web the sand, reaching out many feet before sending up new shoots. Only perennials can cope with the onslaughts of the sand by elongating their stems or producing rhizomes. Sending up new shoots and reproducing by vegetative means is an effective means of survival in unstable dunes areas, avoiding the tenuousness of seed reproduction and the concomitant hazards of germination.

White collars fur the galleta-grass leaf sheaths, and the new leaf tips are not soft and pliable at all but stab my finger like spines. Big galleta is a C_4 plant, able to photosynthesize best under high temperatures, increasing the amount of carbon dioxide fixed as temperature rises. Because fixing carbon dioxide in photosynthesis is coupled with water loss, desert plants have evolved different methods of photosynthesis to make more efficient use of sparse water.

The Calvin cycle, or C_3 photosynthesis, is the most common mode of photosynthesis outside the desert; more prevalent within the desert are Crassulacean acid metabolism (CAM) and C_4 photosynthesis. CAM is more water efficient, and C_4 is more energy efficient per unit of biomass produced. The C_4 cycle is a two-cycle system that allows the plant to absorb carbon dioxide effectively, even at low concentrations, and then feed it into the regular C_3 cycle to continue and complete the reaction. The double-cycle photosynthesis of C_4 plants produces more sugars for spurting growth, enabling the plant to grow quickly enough during hot days to escape burial by drifting sand. The difference between C_3 and C_4 photosynthesis is the despair of gardeners: Kentucky bluegrass and creeping bent, cooler-weather C_3 grasses, get overwhelmed with exuberant crabgrass, an annual C_4 grass, with its grasping growth fueled by summertime heat.

Like CAM, C_4 photosynthesis evolved independently in several plant families, primarily in summer-active desert plants. The catch-22 is that the leaf adaptations that improve water conservation reduce the rate of photosynthesis when water is plentiful. It is as if C_4 plants are locked into growing at the most severe time of the year, unable to photosynthesize as efficiently under more kindly conditions.

Beyond the sand ridge I climb up and slide down huge hummocks with blown-out hollows between. With their stubble of
wind-trimmed plant stems, the mounds have a scarecrow look.
Huge bird tracks, as large as my hand, trail across the sand. Incredibly, they must be the imprint of a great blue heron, a bird I associate
only with water.

In sheer enjoyment of this luxuriously solitary day, I whistle
along with the wind, and somewhere out of the never-never land in
the back of my head comes a snatch of Robert Service:

> Have you wandered in the wilderness, the sagebrush
>   desolation,
>   The bunch-grass levels where the cattle graze?
> Have you whistled bits of rag-time at the end of all cre-
>   ation
>   And learned to know the desert's little ways?

I traverse an area of firmer gray sand overlaid with paler dry
sand in lacy ripples. The closer I get to the main mass of the dunes
themselves, the more the mounds increase in size and the sparser
the vegetation becomes, although a stubble is visible almost to the
top of the dunes, a long way up from where I stand—nearly six
hundred feet.

At least one hundred thousand years were required to accumulate this volume of sand (these dunes cover forty-five square miles)
and one geologist estimates them to be a million years old. Winds
sufficient to blow this much sand into dunes, from the playa of
Pleistocene Lake Mojave some thirty-five miles away, may have
blown only between glacial periods. Ancient wind regimes seem to
have been characterized by opposing winds like those of today,
which may have been necessary for building dunes to the unusual
height of the Kelso Dunes.

The Kelso Dunes are one of a handful of "singing dunes" in
North America. Singing dunes entertained and mystified travelers
in the Middle East at least fifteen hundred years ago, but have been
explained only in recent years. To sing, sands must be dry, well-

sorted, of medium size, spherical, and highly polished. Such grains are produced by winds that work them over long periods of time.

Sand of this ilk, if put in motion by wind or a lot of people stomping on it, produces sound. High dunes with steep slipfaces that can be easily set moving reverberate best. The sound begins with a single frequency, but after a few seconds vibrations within the sand elaborate it into a low-frequency drone, unpoetically described as sounding like a low-flying bomber. R. A. Bagnold, a physicist and student of dunes, described the booming of African dunes on a still night:

> a vibrant booming so loud that I had to shout to be heard by my companion. Soon other sources, set going by the disturbance, joined their music to the first, with so close a note that a slow beat was clearly recognized. This weird chorus went on for more than five minutes continuously before silence returned and the ground ceased to tremble.

What looked from the distance to be shrubs studding the lower slopes turns out to be mesquite trees. The first mesquite is a twenty-foot tree, six big trunks splaying out from a buried base, with new leaves but three-quarters of an inch in length, a fragile and ethereal green. Old pods dangle, in various stages of desiccation. They range from the original shape, with only the color changed, to twisted and curled and splitting, most speckled with insect drillings and tunnelings. I settle in for a pleasant hour of amateur entomology when thunder gutters and for the first time I look up and notice the ominous, burgeoning clouds over the Granite Mountains. Behind my back as I walked to the mesquites, they now fill the whole southern quadrant, grasping greedily toward the dunes. Heart in my throat, I am on my feet on the instant. Dunes are too exposed, not the place to be in a thunderstorm.

A little side-blotched lizard scoots in front of me, leaving raindrop tracks. A darkling beetle lies dead, feet pointing to the sky, rocking on its black back. Lightning snaps the mountaintops. I quicken my pace. I have at least a mile to shelter. Thunder avalanches down the mountains. As I hurry along I look for hollows in which to hunker. A single bolt of lightning, worthy of Zeus in a fury, bangs in front of me. The air ripples and crackles. I clap my hands to my ears, and the thunder erupts out of the sand. The first drops of rain hit like gravel.

I reach the band of creosote bushes, soaked. Cymbals of lightning flare, sound made light, light made sound. Drops saucer the sand about me, sending up minute sprays of sand when they strike, each interrupting the last perfect depression until the sand is a series of tiny puckered peaks. Despite the sound of the thunder, the rain is almost silent, absorbed by the sand, falling through the open creosote-bush branches, absorbed by the granular dryness.

On the instant the rain stops; it does not lighten and diminish, it simply stops as if someone had turned off the faucet. Rain still fingers the dunes, turning them dark, and then they disappear in a glowering cloud that obliterates their contour and inters the desert.

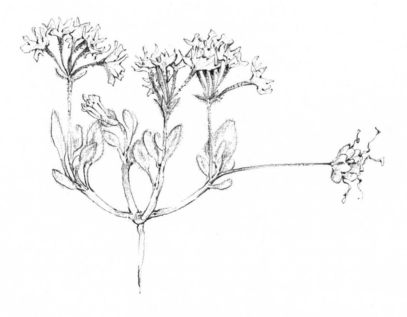

14

OF JOSHUA TREES AND
RED-SPOTTED TOADS

Zzyzx sits on the edge of Soda Lake, southwest of Baker, California. The name "Zzyzx" was coined in the early 1940s by Curtis Springer; one of the possible reasons for such a bizarre name being that Springer wanted to be the last name in the telephone book so that those wishing to patronize his health spa could find it easily. The pools he built held healthful waters that were supposed to cure everything from backache to fallen arches, hangnails, and asthma—but judging from the clientele, the most important cure was for loneliness. Palms flank the entry road and a listing signpost reads THE STREET OF DREAMS. Now, in its later years, Zzyzx is the Soda Springs Desert Studies Center, twelve hundred acres administered jointly by the Bureau of Land Management (BLM) and the California State University System.

Herman and I meet Alan Romspert, a zoologist and botanist, who today wears his hat as coordinator of the center. He clangs the BLM gate shut, climbs back into the truck, and we bucket off across

Soda Lake, now mercifully dry but all the more corrugated for being so. The questionable route that we follow, innocent of tracks, is the old Mojave Indian trail that connected the Mojave Indian villages between the Colorado River and the California coast, a well-used trade route across the desert that the Indians showed to Juan Bautista de Anza's group on their way to colonize California in 1775. Jedediah Smith and Kit Carson trod it in the early 1800s. In 1857, Lieutenant Beale brought camels across this trail which was by then heavily used by the military and the postal service as well as wagon trains going to the coast. As it must have looked to those travelers, so it looks to us, a desolate strand brightened with desert poppies and lavender asters.

We are on the way to see another kind of desert, the Cima volcanic field. Ahead of us an array of black cinder cones punctuate the sky, and dark lava flows mark the volcano field, one of several late Cenozoic basaltic fields in southwestern North America. The afternoon heat radiates off the black rock, and it would take an Indian fakir to walk barefoot across it. The surface temperature of these rocks can reach 170 degrees F. or more, and I feel as if I were standing on top of a sizzling griddle. The younger flows are abrasive and rough and surely must have been belched up from one of the lower levels of hell. Because individual flows can be dated with some certainty, the rate of erosion has been calculated to average less than an inch per millennium.

Basalt stones form the desert pavement, a dark veneer on the light sandy soil. In the older pavement, most of the basalt pieces are reddened underneath; stones in newer pavements lie loose on the surface. Despite the heat ballooning off the dark lava, a whole garden of annuals blooms against the ebony background, each in its own pocket of soil—white rock daisies, small pink monkey flowers, desert five-spot, and spotted langloisia are only a few of many species. By the time the lava heats up to lethal, they will be in seed.

The Cima volcanic field is but part of the East Mojave Desert Scenic Area, a million and a quarter acres so designated in 1980, the nation's first. Ranging from mountains to enormous bajada slopes to basin, the variety in elevation provides habitat for bighorn sheep

ROCK DAISY
(*Perityle emoryi*)

BIGELOW MONKEY FLOWER
(*Mimulus bigelovii*)

DESERT FIVE-SPOT
(*Malvastrum rotundifolium*)

and mule deer as well as all the smaller desert mammals. Elements
of both the Sonoran (at least a quarter of the flora and also its reptile
fauna) and Great Basin deserts are here, intermixing with those of
the Mojave, emphasizing the Mojave's aspect of a "transition
desert." Yet the Mojave also has characteristic endemic species, and
the most prominent of all are the Joshua trees.

Early travelers called them "dagger trees," the Mormons called
them "Joshua trees," and William Manly, traveling west to seek his
fortune in 1849, called them "a brave little tree to live in such a
barren country." In the Kawaiisu Indian legend, Coyote and his
brother were pursued by enemies who were eventually turned into
Joshua trees; Coyote and his brother escaped and found their way
eastward to the end of the world, where they turned into two
stones. When the two stones move, they cause an earthquake.

My first encounter with a Joshua tree was the same as that
experienced by many other people—it was hiking over a far ridge
with a pack on its back and waved at me in greeting. I waved back.

And wondered why it didn't respond. A typical Joshua tree, so configured that, from a distance, it assumed the stature and gesture of a human. As I met more of them I realized that they are characterized by a lack of balance, perhaps a branch stuck out too hastily, a certain awkwardness of stance, yuccas with aspirations to be trees.

If many are missing grace, it is because of the way in which they grow. Dicotyledons, like roses and ivy, have repeated branching and leafing patterns that provide coherence, a stability of design. Not so monocotyledons. A Joshua tree pokes out an arm here or an arm there when vertical growth has reached a certain height. Usually the first side branch breaks out about ten feet from the ground, others following more or less at random. Many years elapse before flowering branches appear, although new leaf growth is relatively rapid. After blossoming, growth terminates at the end of that particular stalk. On this April morning many of the trees bear masses of creamy-white flowers, the individual flowers of which

JOSHUA TREE
(*Yucca brevifolia*)

open only for a single night. Thinking they must be exotically fragrant I sniff one, only to find that it smells cool and dank, somewhat like a mushroom.

Fissures channel the thick corky bark that sheathes a bole of solid wood without growth rings. Its roots, like those of the saguaro, spread across a wide, shallow area, and adjacent small trees may have sprouted from the roots of this one.

Joshua trees stalk the desert from horizon to horizon. No wonder they, despite their rather limited range, dominate visually, a dominance more perceived than true, for several shrubs and herbs exceed them in number and cover. Because they require more moisture, they grow along the cooler, higher, and wetter periphery of the Mojave Desert, sometimes along with species of the desert scrub from the Great Basin Desert, or in patches in northwestern Arizona where, with Mojave Desert scrub, they form two islands that extend eastward from the Hualapai Mountains. Here they often intermix with saguaro, so similar are their habitat requirements.

On a smaller Joshua tree, some of last year's capsules hang within reach. Each has at least one hole in it and rattles with thin black seeds. Yucca moths fertilize all yuccas, including Joshua trees. A female gathers and packs pollen into a ball under her head. At the next flower she inserts her ovipositor into the flower's ovary and lays her eggs, then continues to the top of the pistil and brushes the stigma with her head, thereby transferring some of the pollen she carries. The larvae develop in the seed pod and eat part of the seeds. Then they bore through the pod and drop to the ground, where they form a cocoon, to emerge the following year. The female moth receives no benefit from this procedure because she feeds neither on nectar nor on pollen; she does assure however, by her action, food for the larvae. The relationship between moth and yucca has evolved over time to such a nicety that each species of yucca has its own species of moth.

As the three of us go down the long bajada slope into the valley, the soil becomes drier, the heat of the day increases, and the Joshua trees thin out, shorten, regress to single branchless stalks. Creosote bushes multiply. Woolly marigolds and desert dandelions strew the desert with an abandon of gold coins.

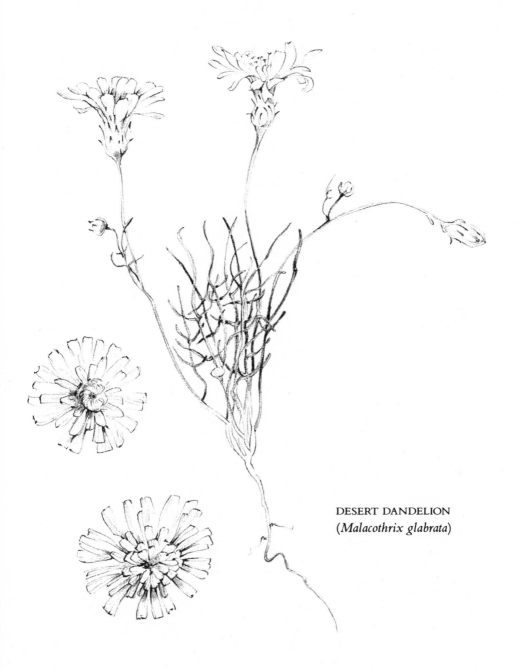

DESERT DANDELION
(*Malacothrix glabrata*)

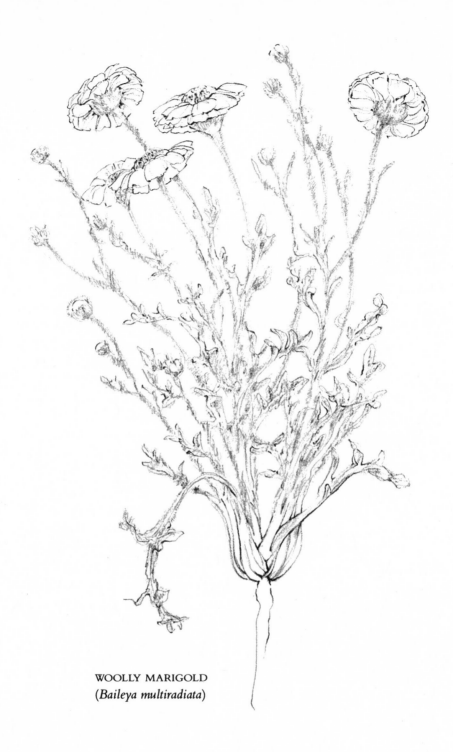

WOOLLY MARIGOLD
(*Baileya multiradiata*)

We traverse acre after acre of classic Mojave Desert creosote bush–bur sage flats that stretch to infinity, a remarkably uncluttered landscape. The single- or few-stemmed creosote bush catches no debris and a street-cleaner wind sweeps the pavement. Bur sage is in full bloom, unnoticed, until I pick a sprig, because of the insignificance of the blossom. A crushed leaf releases a faint pineapple odor.

Such extensive stands of creosote tend to be single-age, the result of some single massive germination. Germination requires an abundant moisture period of at least twenty-four hours, a condition not often realized in desert topsoils. Rainfall may soak the mericarp but still be insufficient to instigate germination. In the laboratory, remarkably moist conditions are required for germination, suggesting that it may be rare under today's dry desert conditions.

At noontime a whiptail lizard hightails it for the shade of a gold-poppy. Dust billows around the lurching truck like heat made animate.

Al takes us to a small wash that contains a great horned owl's nest. The nest, a disheveled mass of sticks, is stuffed in a low rock-wall crevice alongside the sandy wash, but disappointingly empty. Soft feathers drift and waft along the sand. A big new nest is stuffed into a nearby ledge, large and unkempt, perhaps that of another raptor.

Pinks and yellows and whites, the flowers of annuals, fill the wash. White stemless evening primrose, goldenweed, pink storksbill, Pringle's woolly daisy, desert chicory, wing-nut forget-me-not, and lavender lupine contrast with a profusion of yellow desert marigolds. Tiny lavender gilia with yellow throats bloom next to orange mallow and Stansbury phlox; tiny gold-poppies drop their petals at a touch.

Dodder drapes many plants like some peculiar yellow-orange cotton candy spun over the crown. It parasitizes more than a dozen different vascular plants and has the ill-mannered habit of sometimes killing its host. Vermilion buds hang pendant before opening into cadmium-yellow desert evening primroses. Tiny white linanthus spatter the ground, and among them is a single one-inch-high plant, another genus of phlox, with a huge pale-lavender flower out of all proportion to its size.

DESERT GOLD-POPPY
(*Eschscholtzia glyptosperma*)

186

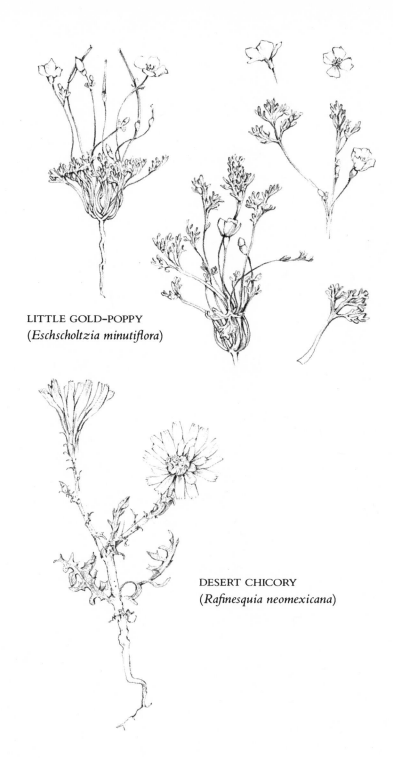

LITTLE GOLD-POPPY
(*Eschscholtzia minutiflora*)

DESERT CHICORY
(*Rafinesquia neomexicana*)

187

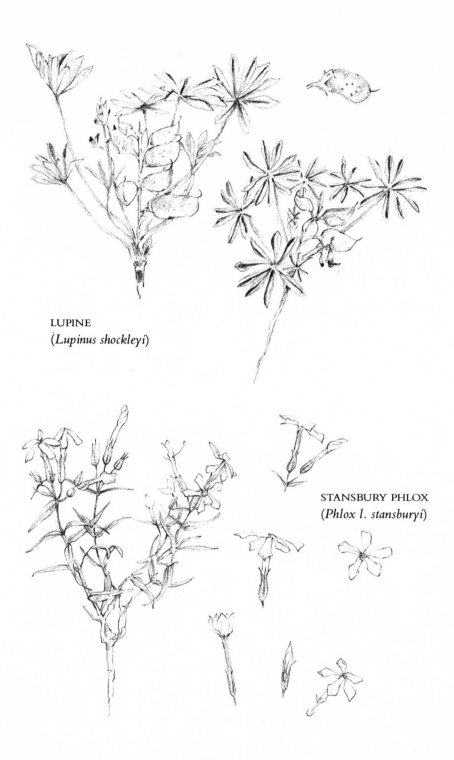

LUPINE
(*Lupinus shockleyi*)

STANSBURY PHLOX
(*Phlox l. stansburyi*)

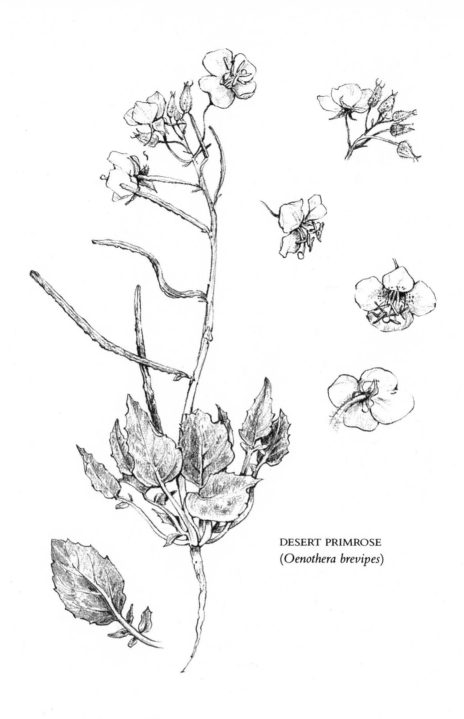

DESERT PRIMROSE
(*Oenothera brevipes*)

To me, this looks like a marvelous show of annuals; Al shrugs his shoulders—he's seen better, he says. Every year does not produce a superb show; generally every sixth or seventh year is one of spectacular bloom.

The Mojave Desert luxuriates in annuals, with over half of them endemic. Generally the number of annuals, as opposed to perennials in the flora, increases with both aridity and the uncertainty and variability of rainfall. Since desert plants can grow only when there is water available, perennials have many morphological and physiological adaptations to tolerate drought, for example, modified leaves, root systems, vegetative reproduction.

Annuals, although they too have some modifications for desert stress, particularly in seeds and germination controls, strongly resemble plants of moister climates and show remarkably few morphological changes to withstand drought during the green-and-growing-plant phase. They largely avoid drought by growing only during the available water season. Yet none of them grows outside the desert's perimeter. Evolution for desert life has worked, not on the leaves and flowers, but in germination control on the seeds. Protection of the seed is paramount. With annuals it provides the only method of reproduction. But when they finally do sprout, they appear in massive numbers and create vivid shows of color.

Rainfall causes the yearly variations in annual bloom, both its amount and when it falls. The winter rains that nourish these annuals come from Pacific storms and a winter change in air circulation, known locally as the "Nevada high" and the "Mojave low." During the winter the usual high over the Pacific slides eastward, allowing moist Pacific air to flow inland, often bringing gentle soaking rains. Occasionally, true winter storms sweep across the desert, laden with heavy winds as well as water. These rains are absolutely essential to desert survival, not only for plants but also for animals, directly affecting lamb survival of Mojave Desert bighorn sheep. The most common annuals are those that germinate only following autumn rains, then bloom the following spring, the "winter annuals."

The numbers of seeds locked away in these sandy soils is truly prodigious; in good years, anywhere from 100 to 2,400 seeds may pepper every square foot of desert. I sift a handful of soil and find an anonymous round brown seed. I roll its incredible knowledge in my hand. During a dry year, this seed likely remains dormant, steadfastly refusing to germinate even after a rain unless it is of at least half an inch. Nor will it respond to water soaking up from below, as from a rising water table, because only water leaching down from above removes the seed inhibitors in the seed coat and washes them down away from the seed. Many seeds need a series of rain to break dormancy. Some seeds decline to germinate if the soil holds a perceptible amount of salt; when heavy rains leach out the salts, they sprout. Seed germination is often restricted by hard coatings that need scarification, alternating heat and cold, or leaching.

The seeds of some winter annual grasses hold off germination for a few days after rain, for if the soil remains moist that indicates that rain was ample enough to support continuing growth. Still other seeds require a period of prolonged moisture for bacterial action to remove inhibitors. Most of the time a seed germinates only when it registers that there has been enough rain to complete its life cycle without depending upon unreliable "follow-up" rains. This one seed in my hand, smaller by far than a peppercorn, carries all these codes and responds precisely when the time is right.

Countless plants of storksbill, a tiny pink-flowered geranium, grow along the edge of the wash. Storksbill, also called crane's bill and filaree, is a typical winter annual: it germinates abundantly after late-summer or fall rains, remains in the rosette stage until February, when new stem leaves and flowering stalks appear. The wonder is that there are so many plants, for kangaroo rats often clean out 90 to 95 percent of its yearly seed crop.

Storksbill's ferny leaves snug close to the ground in a markedly warmer microenvironment, the typically dissected leaves of many winter annuals. This irregularity and complexity of leaf surface may provide a greater surface area for the exchange of air and the absorption of carbon dioxide for photosynthesis.

Most winter annuals share a characteristic growth pattern and phenology: sprouting in the fall, developing slowly during low

STORKSBILL OR FILAREE
(*Erodium cicutarium*)

winter temperatures, simply maintaining themselves until sufficient warmth and daylight hours arrive, when they are already in
position to make a jump start. Intricate "crane's bill" seed pods
already form among the numerous pink flowers. I separate a seed
with its attached filament that snaps into a spiral the second it is free.
The amount of humidity affects the tightness of the coil, which
literally screws the seed into the ground, protecting it from wind
and hungry rodent alike.

The quick shift of growth from flat rosette to raised stems and
flowering may be a valuable adaptation to an arid environment, for
it too is timed to the amount and spacing of rain. If rains are light,
just enough to allow germination, the plant flowers almost immediately and remains dwarfed. For plants to grow large and luxu-

192

riant, there must be a sturdy initial rain followed by more rains. Then the plant makes longer vegetative growth, puts forth many more leaves, and only changes over to the reproductive mode after it is well foliaged. Even under the poorest growing conditions, each sturdy little plant usually manages to produce at least one flower.

I choose one of a thousand storksbills to draw. It pulls out of the sand easily, scarcely anchored by its rudimentary roots, which drip with sand grains. Ordinarily, such a paucity of root development would limit plant growth. Not so in the desert, where fungal hyphae permeate the top few inches of soil, enveloping the sand grains. The combination of the fungi and the roots of the plant form mycorrhizae, which reach farther out into the soil than the plant's roots can, increasing the plant's absorbing surface tenfold. The fungus gets food from the plant and in return delivers some nutrients to its host, such as the essential phosphorus, zinc, and copper in such short supply in desert soils.

The timing of desert annuals brightens the desert hour. No plants are more finely tuned to their world than these to the vagaries and whimsies of the desert's demands.

During Al's elegant alfresco dinner the other evening, peculiar bleatings issued from inside one of the ice chests, where a small cloth bag tried to elbow its way elsewhere. The bag contained three red-spotted toads, each of which carried an implanted two-gram transmitter, on their way to rejoining their brethren in a filament of a stream up a canyon in the Avawatz Mountains, south of Death Valley.

Red-spotted toads were probably once present in the canyon a few thousand years ago when there was more water but have disappeared in recent dry times. The canyon makes an ideal study area because it is limited and self-confining. In 1979, Dr. Lon McClanahan, then head of the Soda Springs Desert Studies Center, stocked the toadless creek with eighteen toads, of which two were female. The toads have burgeoned into a population of a few hundred. Today McClanahan and his zoology class will track the transmittered toads with an antenna to find how far they go from the

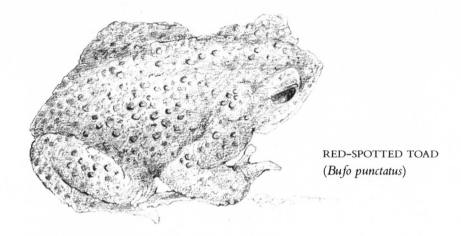

RED–SPOTTED TOAD
(*Bufo punctatus*)

stream during the day (all three turn up within seventy yards of their release point).

Last evening, before Al freed his charges, we walked up the canyon, catching toads. During the day they stay hidden in the moist shadows under rocks or bushes, coming in to water in the evening. They hop slowly enough to be easily hand caught although many maddeningly managed to hie themselves to safety inches beyond my grasp before I could bag them, disappearing into the black shadows outside the flashlight beam. In the darkness I splashed into unexpected hollows of water and stumbled into willow thickets. One elusive hopper persisted in hiding deep in the bottom of a cluster of willows. In the darkness, I thrust my hand again and again trying to grab it and ended up empty-handed and frustrated.

This morning I watch Al record the thirty-four captured toads. He unloads a triple-beam balance out of its packing case, balances it with a plastic cup on one side, opens his notebook, and begins work. He cannulates each toad before he weighs it, using a small pipette called a cannula to remove the urine, which is nearly pure water. These toads use their urinary bladder for water storage, sometimes storing up to a third of their body weight. They also withdraw bladder water for use when under water stress, tolerating a water loss equal to about 60 percent of their body weight.

Scrabbling and beeping emanate from under the plastic cups as he puts one unhappy toad on the scale after the other. The plastic cup doesn't always work: one bolts, cup and all, right off the pan. The males' piteous bleat, a short, high-pitched query, sounds like an electronic cash register. If a male mounts another frog and it bleats, he knows it's a male, breaks off his amorous advances, and goes on to the next, possibly taciturn and female, object of his affection.

I pick up a little nothingness of a toad. It nestles into my palm, cool and pulsing with life, skin a rough gray green embossed with orange to vermilion spots of varying intensity, a miniature blinking Buddha with horizontal pupils. When I turn it over, the translucent pelvic patch, a delicate thin section of skin, pink to almost lavender, stretches between the back legs and extends one-third of the way up the abdomen. So thin is the skin that the underlying musculature shows through the patch. Although the pelvic patch makes up only 10 percent of the body surface, it is responsible for 70 percent of the water intake. These toads' capacity to rehydrate is phenomenal. When a red-spotted toad gets to water, all it needs to do is hunker down and take in moisture through its patch.

Red-spotted toads have adapted to desert living by maintaining an adjustable breeding season dependent on temporary water, not on time of year. Rainfall, not temperature or length of daylight, triggers calling and breeding behavior. Al says that this canyon was filled with trilling toads a few weeks ago. Eggs hatch within a few hours after laying and tadpoles develop very rapidly, metamorphosing into adults in forty to sixty days, one of the shortest periods of all amphibians, an alacrity demanded by their highly temporary habitat.

McClanahan, a casual, energetic man dressed in sandals and shorts, arrives with his class. He assembles the antenna, shows his students how to tune the receiver, and they walk up the canyon trying to pick up the transmittered toads. One student, poking into the willow thicket where I had been reaching for an elusive toad last night, lets out a shout and jumps back. Coiled in the willows is a pair of speckled rattlesnakes. McClanahan picks one up on a stick to show it to the class. The sharply narrowed tail segment before the rattles says this is the female, and a gravid one at that. McClanahan stands there, barelegged and virtually barefooted, with a writhing, irritable rattlesnake a foot away from his hand.

I gulp. It never occurred to me that rattlesnakes might be cosseted in a cold, wet willow thicket in the middle of a chilly stream. *Cave Crotalum.*

We camp halfway up the canyon. I position my sleeping bag in order to have an unparalleled vista in the morning. I awake before the sun is over the horizon and face a voluptuous view of the Panamint Mountains, sleeping lavender on the horizon, fronted by a high ridge line of smoky mauve just now taking shape on its surface. Colors shift as I watch, contours form, dissolve, re-form as the light plays on them. I would stop the light metamorphosis, play it back, watch the day emerge again from its chrysalis of dawn. I would stop time to gather up this desert morning, fold it neatly, slip it in my pocket, and carry it away with me. (I did, in words.)

A heavy buzzing thrums the air, bee flies searching the brittlebush that surrounds me. More brittlebush, the commonest shrub in the area, colors the canyon below in blurs of yellow. Myriad flower stalks extend high above the leaf-defined mound. The bees hover, checking a flower head here, one there, seldom alighting, evidently finding little to feed on, opportunists too early for nectar production. The brittlebush grows from a single stem, branching above ground, with clusters of crisp leaves at the ends of its branches. Like many desert shrubs, its summer leaves are thicker than its winter ones.

Behind me, sunlight creeps down into the coolness of the canyon. I relish the moment, knowing it is only a matter of minutes before the day heats up. The flies sound noisier, bustlier. Birds twitter up the canyon. A light, sweet aroma perfumes the air—the brittlebush? Whatever it is, when I smell it again, I recall this gleaming desert morning in April.

Since no one else is awake, I put my head down again to find that, right under my ear, a mine is being excavated by heavy earth-

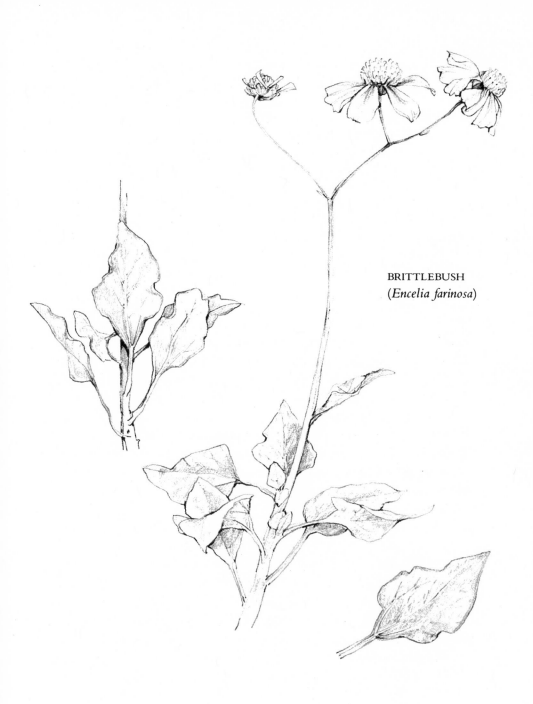

BRITTLEBUSH
(*Encelia farinosa*)

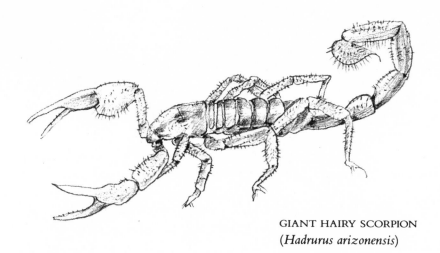

GIANT HAIRY SCORPION
(*Hadrurus arizonensis*)

moving equipment. Or else a giant with boots on is crunching down the canyon, the sound growling through the ground. I sit up. Everyone still sleeps. I put my head down again. This time it sounds as if the San Andreas Fault were giving way. I pat the ground, rearrange my pillow. Search as I may, I find no answer.

Until I take up my ground cloth. A small prehistoric-looking creature totters hesitantly out from underneath. Before it reaches shelter in a pile of rocks, Al scoops it up into a vial and identifies it as a young giant hairy scorpion. Ancient Egyptians believed that scorpions came out of decaying crocodile corpses; I know better—they come out from under ground cloths.

I examine it, safely inside the vial, and marvel that such a small creature could have made such a horrendous noise. Even in the vial its tail, curled over its back, stabs the air. A scorpion holds its prey in its pincers and paralyzes it by bringing the tip of its tail over the prey and, with a quick downward thrust, injecting venom. The curved barb is backed by two venom glands encased in smooth muscle fibers at the base; a violent contraction of the muscles ejects venom from the gland into the duct of the barb. Generally the venom is like a very bad bee sting but, being neurotoxic, it can cause convulsions, paralysis of respiratory muscles, and heart failure.

Scorpions are omnivorous, practical in the sparse-prey desert,

198

pouncing on whatever tidbit passes their way; they will eat anything they can hold on to long enough to sting it into submission. (Much of scorpion behavior is easily observed at night because they fluoresce in black light.) Like rattlesnakes, scorpions husband their venom, stinging only when necessary. Despite its sting, it is in turn gobbled down by desert mice and elf owls.

A scorpion hunts not by sight or sound but by feel. Sensory structures on its legs not only detect prey but determine direction and distance as well, homologous to the structure in web-spinning spiders that detects prey on the web through vibrations. Sensory organs, embedded in hairs on the bottom of the feet and skin folds on the tarsus, may sense distance by differentiating between the times that different waves reach each of the two organs. At about four inches or less, a scorpion seldom misses.

I consign this fascinating creature to Al's care, knowing that he already has an adult giant hairy scorpion in an aquarium and thinking mine might provide company. I find later that his scorpion ate *my* scorpion. The certain logic in the situation escapes me.

15

OF ALLUVIAL FANS AND DESERT TORTOISES

Death Valley, from ten thousand feet on a warm September afternoon, elongates flat and arid, stained with thin patches of vegetation, bound by mountains, smudged with cloud shadows that
mottle it like Carrara marble. Judging from the erosion patterns,
nature abhors a straight line. All the lines at the very least waver.
Most kink like frayed rope, retaining the curve of the twist. Creosote bush and scrub stipple the high ground, scribed with clean
drainage lines wriggling their way downhill.

Green would seem out of place here. Green symbolizes flickering leaves, gentle sounds, quiet dusks. But this rocky landscape is
silent, immutable, changing not in the span of our eyesight,
although in my imagination I hear groanings and cracklings, see it
as it might have looked a hundred million or so years ago—eight
thousand feet above sea level, draining out its southern end into the

Mojave River at Soda Lake; see it as it is now, the valley sunk below sea level, those same mountain peaks half buried in their own sediments.

Fault lines, tears in the earth's surface clear from this altitude, run the length of the valley, shear lines that began to give way some two million years ago. Between these lines the valley dropped intact, as a graben, and so it lies now, a low hammock flanked by the Panamint Mountains on the west and the Black and Funeral mountains on the east. Since the valley subsided faster than it filled, the floor is now below sea level. On the west, the Panamint Range tilted eastward. On the east, the Funeral Range and Black Mountains tilted likewise. The alluvial fans at the base of the mountains verify this—kicked askew by the eastward slant, fans along the east side are short and steep, fans along the west, longer and gentler. With no exit, no outlet, the valley gathers into itself and focuses the heat toward its center as a lens gathers and focuses light.

The floor looks like an old washtub, once half filled with water, forgotten and left in the sun to dry up. Lines of white salt annotate the edges, the lake bed dry as a bone except for some furtive glints of unnatural blue in the salt flats. Once a Pleistocene body of water, Lake Manly was only one of several Pleistocene lakes that successively lapped the valley. At its maximum it was 90 miles long, with a surface some 310 feet above sea level, and 600 feet deep. When the Sierra Nevada rose to the west, bringing a rain shadow, the lake dried, leaving behind the most difficult kind of desert.

Just to rest in the shade here in July requires nine quarts of water a day to remain alive.

Don't send love, send water.

Missing in this objectively cool, hawk's-eye view is the desert's assault on the other four senses. I understand Death Valley in a way I will never understand it on the ground, but lacking are the breath-sucking, abiding heat, the sand crunching under and in my boots, the taste of dryness in the mouth, the pungent odors, a shimmering of horizons that is almost audible, the tendrils of silence woven into the searing wind.

From the air, Badwater is a chalky smear; on the ground the white surface glaze is so blinding that I must pivot to cast a shadow before I can look at the salt. Only then can I see the cursive lines of salt scribbling the surface in one-inch-high relief and the minute red spider that threads through them. Crystalline threads cling to the surface tracery, furry filaments three-quarters of an inch to an inch long. Most point to the northwest but in some spots they frizzle every which way. I feel as if I'm walking on an angora sweater.

Salt flats are characteristic of western deserts, but usually the salt is mixed in with clay and sand. Here the flat *is* salt. Puddles glisten everywhere. In one, salt precipitates out in plates one crystal thick. In another, soldier-fly larvae wiggle across the bottom, and small, fat bronze water beetles search for algae, occasionally popping their antennae through the surface for air. In still another, perfect sixteenth-inch cubes flash in the sun. The high water table keeps much of the salt in solution. Ground water rises through capillary action, and when it reaches the surface it evaporates, leaving the salts on top. Flooding, although infrequent, spreads the salt evenly over the surface. With flooding these sodium chloride crystals dissolve and recrystallize, always maintaining the perfect signature of their shape.

I stoop down to watch hundreds of brine-fly larvae squiggle and snap and curl. Some have aggregated into shirt button–size clusters; some spin around the pool like iron filings chasing a magnet. Brine flies are ubiquitous in salt and alkaline pools and lakes throughout the West. After the larvae hatch from eggs deposited on the water, they drop to the bottom and use the curved hooks studding the ends of their false legs to anchor themselves. The larvae develop a long, usually branched anal tube that reaches to the surface and serves as a gill. They pupate under water and the emergent adults escape to the surface in a bubble of air.

The change in life structure—from the ability of the larvae to survive in these pools so loaded with salt that they are brinier than the ocean, to nectar-and-pollen-feeding adults—is incredible. I watch the tiny insects scoot across the water surface like stilted water striders, not believing it possible to imbue such a small package with such sophistication.

□

The following March I fly out to join Mary Savina and a Carleton College biannual winter seminar in Death Valley. Mary, the geologist in charge, greets me and tells me that tomorrow we go out to the alluvial fans in Chicago Valley, a north-south valley a few miles east of Death Valley itself, literally "the pits" day when students who have been doing studies on the soil profiles in alluvial fans go out and fill in the pits they have dug.

Alluvial fans possess an aesthetic completeness. They unify vertical and horizontal, mountain and flat, the repository of untold debris given up by the mountains, and are magnificently developed in the Mojave Desert. Beautiful simple forms they may be from a distance, but up close they are intricate and complex.

I walk up the slope of the alluvial fan on the west side of Chicago Valley with Jan Schlamp and Nancy Braker, following a narrow wash that dissects the face of the fan. Nancy, with a degree in biology specializing in entomology, is the cook for the session; Jan is a geology major. The ashen color of the soil, the gray desert holly, the loose rocks coated with dirty white caliche, bur sage with stems and dried leaves the same color, create a lunar landscape. I do not realize how far we've walked uphill until I look back and see how far the crease of the valley is below us, so gradual is the slope.

Neatly constructed pupation chambers dangle from a creosote bush, little tubes three-quarters of an inch long, fashioned of leaf fragments arranged spirally starting from the tip, the whole case attached to the branch with silk. When Nancy fingers the tough silk apart, the inside is feltlike. The larvae of the creosote bagworm, moth larvae, construct these neat little cases. In one, the minute pupal case of a bracconid wasp remains, the unwelcome intruder who parasitized the original inhabitant. In another the chitinous pupal case of the moth protrudes from the bottom. While males possess wings, the female spends her entire life within the case, hatching, pupating, mating, laying eggs, and dying there. As my eye becomes accustomed to the pattern, I spot many more pendant within the creosote bush's open foliage. After hatching, larvae construct their own cases and lug them about. When they reach full growth, they attach the cases to twigs and pupate inside. How

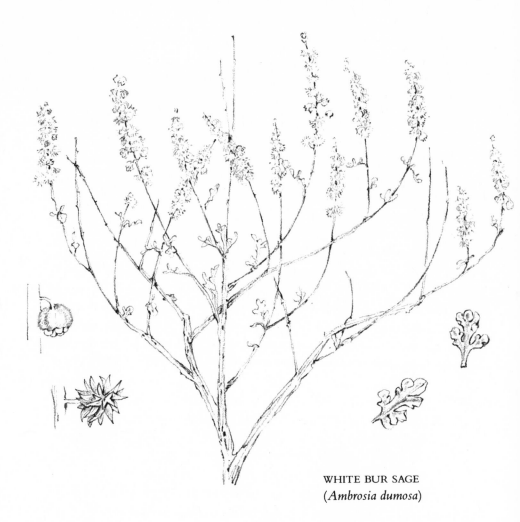

WHITE BUR SAGE
(*Ambrosia dumosa*)

bagworms colonize different bushes is a puzzle. It seems unlikely
that they are able to crawl far across the dry hot desert floor between
far-spaced bushes, toting cumbersome cases. Wind dispersal seems
even more improbable—just one more of the hundreds of questions
the desert poses.

Nancy picks a scale insect off a creosote bush branch, its flat,
dark body encrusted with a furry white covering. The migratory
young emerge as minute "crawlers." When they settle down they
change form, become sessile, and excrete a waxy or scalelike covering over themselves. They deposit a reddish-brown resin on the

branches that local Indians used to mend pottery, waterproof baskets, and glue arrowheads.

As with the creosote bagworm, only the males are winged. The female remains inside her covering and mates there. Each coccid is adapted to the chemistry of its particular host plant, and recognizes unerringly the proper plant upon which to lay its eggs, possibly by odor. The young, if not in place on the correct food plant at the time of hatch, unable to fend for themselves, will perish.

Like an ostracon, a piece of limestone annotated with an embedded chert nodule catches my eye because of its color, cinnabar against pearl gray. The hard chert stands in high relief since the limestone dissolves more quickly; because of this it also holds no varnish. The chert, being smooth and stable, does. A small chunk of quartz rests among the other angular rocks, stained green on the underside from a skim of algae. Algal growth on the underside of translucent stones—milky quartz, chalcedony, gypsum, agate—is characteristic of the desert. It also grows on calcareous objects like bones, fossils, and snail shells. Nearly every piece of quartz I tip over rewards me with a green astonishment that such water-dependent plants should be so prevalent in such a dry desert.

These algae occupy a specialized niche in the desert, growing where no other plants grow. When desiccated, they withstand high temperature and drought without damage (which higher plants cannot), and take in water quickly when it is available. They can also absorb water vapor from the air, turning that bright fresh green that looks so startling against the pallid desert palette. They are able to photosynthesize at the very low light levels that exist under the stones on which they grow. The price of survival is minuteness.

Farther up the slope of the fan, the wall of a wash rises ten feet above my head, layered like a torte with the cobbles and gravels and sands of centuries of runoff. At eye level, caliche cements a layer of sands and gravels laid down by flowing water, the larger cobbles completely coated by dirty white calcium carbonate.

Caliche, a type of cement deposited on rocks, is common in arid regions. Over 80 percent calcium carbonate, it can form quite quickly. Caliche develops in sequence, first forming coatings on

pebbles and then entire soil horizons, where all the rocks are completely coated and the interstices solid with "calcrete," basically a
mixture of lime, sand, and water. If any of these various layers are
exposed, weathering breaks the calcrete into chunks, which are
sometimes recemented into a new layer; formation and re-formation
of caliche is so erratic that no dating of the deposit is possible.

The wash wall shows little tendency to give way; calcrete holds
it stable and aridity keeps it solid. Its stability is further proved by
pepperings of brown lichens on many of the shaded rocks, slow-
growing plants that could not survive were they continually disturbed; like algae, they can endure long periods of desiccation in a
dormant state and resume growth within minutes when moisture
becomes available. Their rhizomes infiltrate any cracks and gnaw
away at the calcrete. Where calcrete exists, it markedly affects the
topography. This wall would long since have broken down had it
not been for the cementing calcrete.

All this calcium carbonate, thousands of tons of it, enough to
have settled on the ground and to account for all the calcium carbonate in the soil, came largely from the numerous playas in the region
whose fine lake-bed silts were loaded with carbonates easily picked
up by the wind. A documentable increase in the amount of calcareous dust in the atmosphere during the early Holocene coincides
with the time period in which the Pleistocene lakes were drying.
Soil layers clearly indicate that most of this eolian material came in
pulses, correlating with known climate shifts. Once the silt dusted
the land's surface, rain washed it down between pebbles and into
voids between rocks. There it collected, alternately wetting and
drying, causing the soil to swell and shrink.

I plod up the wash until I reach the oldest surface on the fan. To
my surprise, it is soft and spongy underfoot, because of increased air
spaces in the soil. Caliche fragments lie scattered over the surface.
White beards of it coat black rocks. Many chunks look like thick
white orange rinds, negative casts, smooth on the inside, coated
with mini-stalactites on their outer surface, broken free of the rocks
upon which they formed. Rocks lie loose on the soil surface, not
firmly embedded in a pavement as they are below but free, ready to

FLUFFGRASS
(*Erioneuron pulchellum*)

tumble. Here weathering is active—fracturing, splitting, heaving. This upper slope receives the heaviest runoff, has the smallest plants and the barest ground.

At my feet, a miniature garden of fluffgrass sprouts. In the warmer deserts it flowers in the summertime. In the Mojave it becomes a spring annual. All plants grow dwarfed here: a bur sage bears infinitesimal leaves; a few wide-spaced creosote bushes do not even reach to my knee. Their branches flare like fans, two-dimensional, turned toward the sun, leaves glistening from their resins. They remind me of the dwarf willows of the alpine tundra, espaliered against the ground, their size belying their great age. I speculate how old these dwarfed bushes may be, and how they happen to be this high on the slope.

Growth rings, reliable indices of age in trees, are no help in these slow-growing plants since rings in creosote bush probably indicate growth only in favorable years. Some of the oldest creosote bushes in California, thought to be older than the previous holder of "oldest" title, White Mountain bristlecone pines, are estimated to be several hundred to several thousand years old. Some recently radio-carbon-dated creosote bushes are 11,500 to 12,000 years old. These clones resulted from vegetative reproduction: as the lower branches spread and touched the ground, they rooted, spreading outward in very slow increments, perhaps requiring 120 years to grow an inch.

Numerous three-foot-wide dry washes feed down the alluvial fan into the valley, flattening out and broadening as they reach the flatness of the valley floor. Odd sticks poking out of the sand of many of them turn out to be the dusty chocolate-brown stalks of broomrape, a brown-purple flowered parasitic plant, now rare. Pulling the sand away, I uncover a pale yellowish stem, without chlorophyll, two fingers thick; the roots were once employed as a cure for skin ulcers. The stem snakes underground to join two more to form a root the size of a small parsnip, then trails toward the nearest bush, which is bur sage (broomrape is also parasitic on burrobush).

Mary Savina, with whom I'm walking, stops suddenly and points. About three yards in front of us in the sandy arroyo is a dark-brown hardhat suspended above the surface on four posts: a desert tortoise. At our approach it draws in its legs and the shell drops to the sand. Not fully withdrawn, its flippers with their formidable black claws remain visible.

Close-up, its shell is tannish gray, bluish around the edges of the scutes, flushed with brown. The repeated rings in the scutes come from fits and starts of growth, but cannot be correlated with age like tree rings; new shell growth extends beyond the former growth by a fraction of an inch, forming a fine line.

DESERT TORTOISE
(*Gopherus agassizii*)

Like most day-active lizards, turtles regulate their temperatures by sun basking. They hibernate in permanent deep horizontal dens during winter, and this one is likely just out, a month earlier than the usual April emergence date. They favor sandy, gravelly banks in arroyos for both winter dens and temporary summer burrows (which are usually shared with numerous local snakes and usually tick-infested). Summer burrows are more casual affairs, and there are about four times as many, providing a network of easily available escapes.

Falling temperature triggers the tortoise's retreat underground for the winter. The deeper the tortoise goes into the burrow, the more slowly outside temperatures register on it, and those that are deeply buried are generally the last to emerge. During the heat of the day it takes shelter in either shade or the numerous burrows available in a shallow wash like this.

The tortoise does not move despite the fact that full sun blasts it. Mary and I instinctively move to cast our shadows on it. It survives without free water, getting all the moisture it needs from either its food or the production of metabolic water. Its food contains large amounts of carbohydrates, which are stored as fat and,

209

when it is metabolized, releases water. A total vegetarian (which does not preclude a few insects picked up accidentally), it browses on a wide range of desert plants, mostly the shrubs that have succulent buds in the springtime low enough to be within turtle reach, such as brittlebush and bur sage. They especially dote on grasses, and when annuals are available, feast on those. In addition, the heavy, armored shell prevents evaporation and conserves whatever moisture it does have. Like all reptiles it excretes uric acid rather than urea. Its greatest water loss occurs through breathing, a loss that is ameliorated through occupation of a humid burrow—which is where we hope it will go after our brief rude interruption.

As long as we can see it, it remains there, baking in its own oven in the middle of the wash. Doubtless, in its own plodding but purposeful way, it will find a close-by burrow. Its protruded neck and heavy-lidded eyes convey an air of weary patience and resignation with having evolved an interminable forty million years ago, and having been bottom turtle of the turtle stack ever since.

At the edge of the Death Valley dunefield early in the morning, when a fly buzzes or a raven calls, each sound rings distinct and crisp. If I close my eyes, it is so quiet that I can almost hear leaves unfolding and larvae spinning webs.

The dunes undulate to the west, low transverse dunes, none over eighty feet high. Local wind eddies and cross winds coming off the Tucki Mountains decrease in speed here and drop their sand loads from the west-northwest at the same place over long periods of time. Now seasonally opposing winds continually work the dunes, their northeast spring-summer advance canceled by strong winds from the north, the seasonal conflict maintaining the dunes in one place.

A cluster of western honey mesquite trunks rise, half alive, half dead, out of one hummock twenty feet across and at least ten feet high. Like others on the many hummocks along the periphery of the dunes, this half-buried tree leafs only on its lower branches. The leaflets are narrower than on most mesquite, and this characteristic makes them a subspecies, *Prosopis juliflora* var. *torreyana*, after John

Torrey, the famous botanist of the mid-nineteenth century and one of the first to study mesquite.

Most leaves are infested by larvae, probably those of small moths; they spin gossamer webbings that bind the leaves together, and then mine the leaves, eating the leaf out between the veins. Each branch bears one or two colonies. One small black-and-white beetle picks its way up a twig. Webbing drapes every leaf node, and insect depredations twist and crinkle the leaves. A few flowers hang open, crawling with aphids. An Edwards' blue butterfly, a small female with white-rimmed wings and small dark dots edging the hind wing, flutters down onto a branch, one of the butterflies whose larvae are known to feed on mesquite. The mesquite girdler, a beetle with marvelously long antennae, also attacks these trees. Because mesquite is considered of little economic importance, their insect fauna is little studied.

Mesquite taps underground lenses of fresh water, maintained by rainwater from winter rains that holds throughout the year in pockets in the sand. A seedling must project a root down thirty feet through sand before it reaches water, requiring a seed with a great deal of nourishment, and honey mesquite seeds sprout only when there is enough water to guide roots downward to damp soil. Judging from the lack of seedlings or young plants here, these conditions have not been met in the last century or more. Most Death Valley mesquites are venerable in age, probably hundreds of years old.

These mesquites must tolerate the highest air temperature recorded in the Western Hemisphere, 134 degrees F., and grow here at the limits of adaptability for terrestrial plants. Soil surface temperatures can reach 180 degrees F. or more, or drop below freezing in the winter. Some years there is no precipitation whatsoever and, in all years, evaporative water loss exceeds rainfall a hundredfold. Surface water is almost nonexistent, and what there is, is salty. This ancient tree leafs out as if it were still in the springtime of its life, all but inundated by the dunes, its fresh green growing tips outracing the blowing sand.

□

Picked out by the raking sunlight, quixotic little ridges tangle across the dune surface, passages made last night by the small desert cockroaches that feed on the mycelia of the fungal mycorrhizae associated with the roots of honey mesquite.

Confined to sand dunes, the females are wingless, the males winged. They only slightly resemble ordinary cockroaches, being much smaller and plumper. They develop to adulthood very slowly, a condition that may be linked with their ability to withstand periods of starvation. They withstand greater water loss, and tolerate temperatures from 120 degrees F. to freezing for limited periods, a wider range than even the ubiquitous common cockroach endures. Unlike their city cousins, they sport thin coats of fine hairs, which may prevent sand abrasion; even minor abrasion destroys the impermeable lipid layer of the shell that protects them from desiccation.

Desert cockroaches have the remarkable ability to rehydrate when relative humidity is high, and this ability to absorb water in vapor form is an important adaptation to desert living. They have only to propel themselves deeper into the sand to reach that hospitable degree of humidity. Burrowing in the darkness, they need a way to maintain their gravity orientation underground, accomplished via equilibrium receptors on their cerci, small protruding spines positioned at the posterior.

I scoop away the sand by double handfuls at the end of one trail, rapidly reaching a cooler level. After I have a washbasin-size cavity, I give up. Either these little six-legged raisins can burrow faster than I can dig, or they are buried elsewhere.

Wreathing the edge of the dunes is one of the handsomest of the Mojave Desert endemics, desert holly, a globose saltbush that is one of the most drought-resistant, most xerophytic, plants in Death Valley. A highly variable and flexible species—I swear there are no two leaves alike on any plant—it is unusually able to adjust to different and difficult environmental conditions. It conducts photosynthesis with great efficiency via the C_4 pathway, making most of its growth during the summer months. It possesses two types of leaves according to season: in late winter the leaves swell with stored

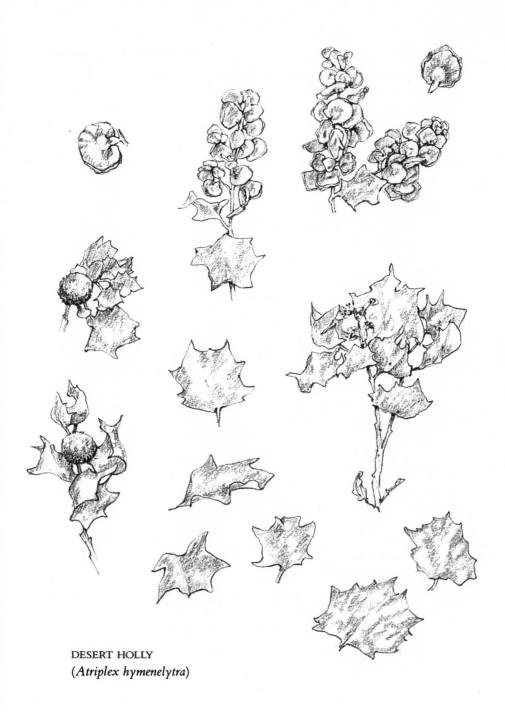

DESERT HOLLY
(*Atriplex hymenelytra*)

water and become greener; in summer the leaves turn thicker, smaller, and more reflective, with cuticles thickened and stomata sunken. At high temperatures salt, held in solution in water-filled winter leaves, crystallizes and becomes trapped within the collapsed cells. The high reflectivity of sodium chloride tints desert-holly leaves their peculiar platinum summertime sheen. Protected beneath the desiccated leaf surface, photosynthetic cells remain hydrated and active. Such leaf dimorphism may be the main reason behind the predominance of "evergreen" shrubs in the Mojave Desert. The neatly formed shrub that I examine holds a desert self-sufficiency that epitomizes Death Valley.

Around it, grasshoppers arc up and sift back to the sand, soundless. No clatter breaks the feverish stillness.

16

OF PUPFISH
AND DESERT RESORTS

Sara, my youngest daughter, and I have directions on how to get to Ash Meadows on the eastern edge of Death Valley, frontward and backward, from Johnnie and Crystal and Pahrump, from Shoshone and Death Valley Junction, a sure prescription, given her mother's sense of direction, for getting lost.

When we find Laxalt Playa beyond Crystal and know we're on the right road to Ash Meadows, I am pleased on several levels. Sara has never seen a desert playa and it is my pleasure to give her one to wander. Our boots practically clank, so smooth and hard is the playa floor. Because the surface is so hard, most rainfall runs off before it can percolate into the soil. A harmonious pattern of fine, nearly perfect, hexagonal cracks spider the surface. Such evenness occurs only when the salt content does not exceed 5 percent, and the silt is of uniform texture. Were there more salt, the surface would be puffy, and were the sizes of soil particles more varied, the cracks would be irregular. Silts and clays still wash off the surrounding mountains but at a more sluggish rate than they did during pluvial times; now less than one millimeter accumulates in a thousand years.

Unworked cobbles pave intermittent low mounds, pieces of mountains, in color bronze red, chocolate brown, burnt umber, ocher; in shape angular. Striped and splotched, each adheres by a single contact, ready to tumble away with the first fence-lifter rain. Ample source for all these rocks circles us, 360 degrees of mountains shouldering up the horizons. Sara picks up a black rock speckled with tan dots that turns out to be a piece of heavy black lava riddled with holes, each filled to the top with buff-colored sand. There are many more, evidence of the sand- and soil-catching ability of porous volcanic material.

Other than a few inkweeds and whitetops, a mustard with thick glaucous leaves, the rest of the plants are shad scale, neatly wind-trimmed into perfect half-basketball-size hemispheres. These globose shrubs have no pliable branches of foliage to bend and curve in the wind like weeping willows, no round leaves to rustle like cottonwood leaves, only tough, short limbs on close-knit, tough, short shrubs, shrubs that quiver as an entity with a gust of wind, and even then scarcely give more than a convulsive twitch.

Tent caterpillars and galls decorate every branch, presenting an odd illusion that the bushes are leafed out. Old leaves hang so dried and curled that they look like seed pods, pendant from the stiff, spiny branches. Nearly every shad scale tops a low mound riddled with rodent holes. Kangaroo-rat scat is plentiful, despite what looks to me like minimal vegetation to feed on.

I look around for Sara and see a small figure far away. Watching her scuffling along on this lonely, lonely flat, head down, pursuing her own puzzles and observations, relishing a natural world that so ballasts my life, gives a poignant pleasure to the day.

Just over the ridge is the natural tank that is the remaining habitat of the Devil's Hole pupfish, PROBABLY THE MOST RESTRICTED ENVI-

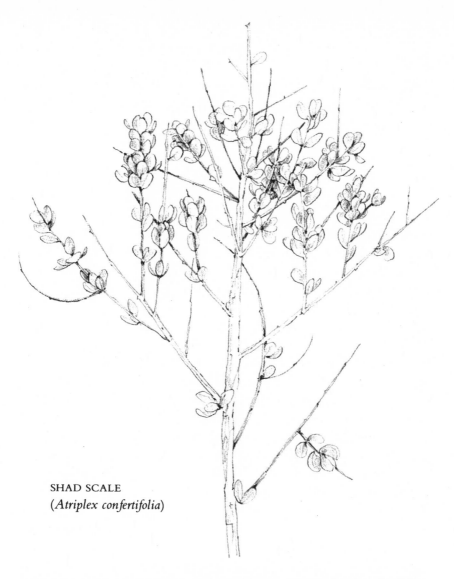

SHAD SCALE
(*Atriplex confertifolia*)

RONMENT OF ANY ANIMAL IN THE WORLD, reads the Death Valley
National Monument sign. We peer through a high chain-link fence,
down forty-five feet to a small, still pool rigged with measuring
devices, a limestone cavern that contains the entire population of
pupfish, a lively (hence the name) tiny transparent fish with blue
eyes, measuring an inch and a half full grown. Thirty-one fish are on
the endangered-species list of the United States Fish and Wildlife
Service, and of these, twenty-three are desert species. The scene
here is somehow shocking: the pool looks like a terminal patient,

ringed with tubes and shot with medications, kept alive after life is gone. In requiem, a big Mojave aster blooms on the warm wall. The water level in the pool is court mandated and maintains the minimum fish population at a constant temperature of 92 F., one hundred fifty to two hundred fish in the winter to three hundred to nine hundred in the summer, linked to the seasonal food production of algae.

The Devil's Hole pupfish are the most famous of a series of small fish, technically cyprinodonts, that once lived in the connected Pleistocene lakes that filled the desert valleys of California. Many desert fish are now confined to isolated pools that have persisted since the pluvial lakes disappeared. Such pools are relatively stable but very fragile habitats. Spring-fed, they are little affected by variations in precipitation, but are vulnerable to drawdown from deep well pumping. What makes the Devil's Hole pupfish of such interest to researchers is their relatively fast adaptation from cool freshwater fish to fish that can survive in water whose salinity may be up to six times that of sea water, an amazingly rapid evolution that has implications for all living creatures. Because they live in such calcium-laden waters, researchers are looking for the physiological shields they must have to protect their renal system; an overload of calcium salts is one of the main causes of kidney stones and kidney failure in humans.

More than half of the desert fish, except for a few ancient relics, are recently developed, just predating the Pleistocene. The exception is the Devil's Hole pupfish, which may have been isolated earlier in pre-Pleistocene times. Cyprinodonts of the Amargosa Valley, Salt Creek, and the Owens River are nearly identical. The same species also live today in distant tributaries of the Colorado River, all habitats interconnected during Pleistocene times. The physical isolation of these ponds and holes and springs prohibits both genetic exchange and recolonization. In response, endemic forms have developed, species known only from a single spring or from related spring complexes, as here, or below in Ash Meadows.

The problem of deteriorating habitat for the Devil's Hole pupfish began in 1960, when a nearby slough was drained and mined for

MOJAVE ASTER
(*Machaeranthera tortifolia*)

peat. This was followed by extensive agricultural development that by 1970 lowered the water to the danger level for the surviving pupfish. The National Park Service took the farming company to court, and in 1976 a Supreme Court ruling mandated a minimum allowable water level for Devil's Hole, but the ruling applied only to Devil's Hole pupfish and only to withdrawal of agricultural water. The property was then sold to a developer who envisioned a resort at Ash Meadows of 20,000 homes, put in roads and augmented pools, altering their outflow, again affecting the pupfish. When other options failed, the Nature Conservancy bought the property and turned it over to the U.S. Fish and Wildlife Service, which administers it as a national wildlife refuge.

On this April morning, Ash Meadows stretches before us, a low, open landscape, confining mountains pushed far away. From the height of the divide on which we stand, a lake lying ahead gleams an odd, chalky turquoise. A ruffling of wind sweeps across a full breadth of sky, flourishing a freshness and coolness that will disappear in another month. With an average of less than three inches of rainfall a year, Ash Meadows well qualifies as a desert. What makes it unique is the discharge from an underground aquifer that, flowing a hundred miles from the northeast, surfaces in open water and adds another dimension to life here.

On our way down we walk through a grove of big cottonwoods and ash—hence the name Ash Meadows. Despite the white alkali stains on the ground, the vegetation is relatively lush and, in April, just leafing out. Outside the bars of tree branches, the wind tantrums. From a puddle somewhere in the grove comes a tentative amphibian question, "*Creeek, creeeek?*" In answer comes a flat "*crk crk crk crk,*" evenly repeated.

When we return a month later, screwbean mesquite sports vivid, piercing green leaves, and the ash trees are leafed out and in bloom. A small pool, half a foot of warm water, flows from a spring upstream. Reed grass, seven feet tall, and sleek, green cattails, grow thickly around the edge. Dragonflies patrol the periphery, and blue forget-me-nots nod over the water that garbles sound as it works

LEATHER-LEAF ASH
(*Fraxinus velutina* var. *coriacea*)

across the pool. Only feet away, salt grass, shad scale and inkweed root, scattered on ashy gray soil encrusted with salts.

When we set out to hike, it is across this desert soil that we traipse and stumble, alternately sinking into soft spots and thumping on hardpan, crossing a salty, silty, beleaguered landscape that seemingly exists only in transition. Manly, crossing the desert

in 1849, quoted a Kansas "Jayhawker" he met who was so un-
enchanted with this area that he declared

> this was the Creator's dumping place, where he had left
> the worthless dregs after making a world, and the devil
> had scraped these together a little. Another said this must
> be the very place where Lot's wife was turned into a pillar
> of salt, and the pillar had been broken up and spread
> around the country. He said if a man were to die he would
> never decay on account of the salt.

Where the ground is higher it is putty-colored, soft, and friable;
where lower, it is deeper tan and hardened, paved with mud curls.
On top of low hillocks dark pavements stud the blanched soil, the
pebbles on end, loosened by frequent ground heave. No pavement
forms on the areas between, subject to swift water flow and runoff.

A western meadowlark sings from a dead snag, and half a
dozen more soar and swoop above us like gold nuggets tossed in the
sky. A white cabbage butterfly probes a white-flowered peppergrass. The new leaves of goldenbush are so resinous that they
stick to my fingers; under my hand lens the glands glisten. A
jumping spider's web festoons a tall prince's-plume. The spider
itself hangs on the stem nearby, its three-eighths-inch black body
vividly patterned with orange and white spots. Mojave thistle rosettes are already over a foot wide, lethal-spined leaves arched
downward, last year's stalks as tall as I.

We search for the Ash Meadows endemic plants that bloom in
the spring, plants that grow nowhere else and endow a special
quality of place. Streaked mariposa lilies emerge out of low rabbit
brush or saltbush, the bare-stemmed flower surrounded by a gray-
green doily of someone else's foliage. The flowers are a delicate
pinkish lavender, cleanly lined with purple, tufts of ascending white
hairs surrounding the gland at the base of each petal. Each mariposa
grows in an "island of fertility," offered by a shrub that affords
greater protection and greater nutrient turnover than in the open
desert; under shrubs water infiltrates up to ten times faster than in
the open clay soils.

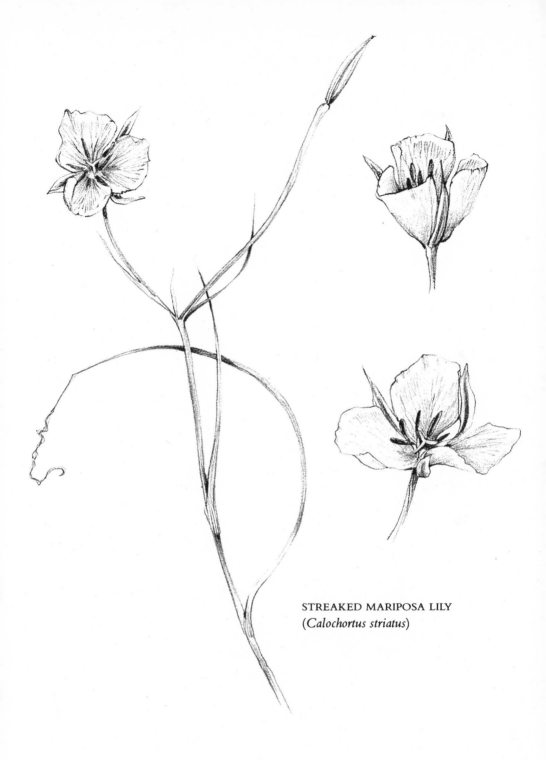

STREAKED MARIPOSA LILY
(*Calochortus striatus*)

BEAR POPPY
(*Arctomecon merriamii*)

On a damp saline flat, the tight overlapping leaf growth of Ash Meadows ivesia looks like little green caterpillars upon the ground; they will not bloom until fall. These ivesia have a very limited habitat indeed, confined to a single specialized soil situation. I also look for Ash Meadows milk vetch, which grows in the same barren saline clay flats. I wander its habitat and query the plants with which it consorts, rhatany and saltbush, but find no milk vetch. But I do find one rare (although not endemic) bear poppy, a large frowzy plant whose petals fall at a touch, and I am somewhat mollified.

We look for a sheltered place to eat lunch. Every bush twig and dried grass blade fidgets in the wind. "I don't like eating wind," says Sara. My problem goes further. I don't like eating salty silt. We finally find a narrow break of tamarisk, which gives precious little protection, near a defunct street sign tilted forlornly to starboard that reads, SPRING MEADOWS DRIVE. Salt-grass stubble frays along the ground like an old falling-apart scrub brush. As usual I wander, eating on the hoof, plant identification book with mayonnaised pages tucked under one arm.

A ten-foot-wide rill with a hearty flow braids through the dry ground, the water deep amber. Near the bank, webbing binds an inch-wide spider-hole opening. Salt deposits fringe the edge of the water where the ground is marshmallow soft, so consistently saline is the soil. Small mounds of sand heap around every saltbush, but not one single creosote bush is to be seen. The only green sprigs belong to inkweed and salt grass. The wind worries the grass and waters my eyes and hassles the universe, mischievous, annoying, petulant. A restless time of year, full of questions, among them why anyone would want to convert this beautiful, empty salty desert into anything other than what it is.

THE
GREAT BASIN
DESERT

17

OF BLACKBRUSH
AND SAGEBRUSH

The wind twitches the short, stiff branches of somber blackbrush and sets them scratching at my shins. Here, on this high ridge, the transition zone between the Mojave and Great Basin deserts, the contrast between the warmer southern desert and the cooler steppe desert could not be more marked. The giddy creosote bushes with their graceful branches are replaced by these angular-branched shrubs with twigs sprouting stiffly at right angles. Their color is darker green, more somber.

Even the sky is overcast. A mizzle falls. A cold wind bites the air. I miss the sunshine of the Mojave, the brilliance of the Sonoran, the glow of the Chihuahuan, as I stand poised on the threshold of a far more severe and stringent landscape with a different beauty.

Creosote bushes and Joshua trees persisted into Nevada. Then creosote bush disappeared, and with it the distinctive color and growth patterns so much a part of the three southern deserts. The landscape looked odd without creosote bush. Joshua trees still arrayed the hillsides, scattered and gesticulating, and then they too thinned out until only single stalks remained, sentinels without regiments. Along with those humanoid arboreal forms went a certain animation and spontaneity. With Joshua trees gone, the visual change was complete.

Although the northern Mojave greatly resembles the Great Basin in its limited life forms and the simple composition of most communities, the rise in altitude of the basin floor plus a latitudinal step northward shuts out the warmth-loving plants of the Mojave. Rainfall, on the increase, and temperature, on the decrease, control this transition zone in which I stand and shiver.

Blackbrush dominates here, a plant community restricted to the upper bajadas, occupying an intermediate position between the creosote bush of the Mojave and the big sagebrush of the Great Basin, replacing a more mesic juniper community some 7,500 years ago.

Boundaries like this one fascinate me. These visual boundaries augur the invisible ones: where stands the last creosote bush and where grows the first sagebrush? Where does the last saguaro become a mere armless post in the ground and finally give up its footing? Where does the kangaroo rat pause, one well-adapted desert foot poised in the air, nose twitching toward a wetter, lusher existence, and not cross over? Where is the line beyond which the desert cockroach does not tunnel? Where is the barrier that keeps the sidewinder and the fringe-toed lizard at home on the hot sands? Where does the desert tortoise blink its slow eyes and turn back to the only home it knows? In trying to define where a desert is not, one learns where it is.

The soaking mist that blurs the air molds a subtle series of silhouettes and softens the hard mountain outlines. Sixty percent of the year's moisture arrives during the long winters, falling on frozen ground, when it brings the least blessing; if spring or summer rain does fall, its amount and length are highly variable and unpredictable. Trapped in the interior of the continent, the Great Basin Desert

230

BLACKBRUSH
(*Coleogyne ramosissima*)

suffers some of the most severe desert conditions in North America. Behind the rain shadow of the Sierra Nevada, barricaded from moisture coming in from the east by the Rocky Mountains, the Great Basin is an inland island desert. Although polar outbreaks bring temperatures below freezing, sometimes for extended periods, summer temperatures easily reach over 100 degrees F.

The clouds overhead shred for a moment and pallid shafts of light focus through the openings, highlighting a piece of mountain flank here, an outcrop there, like a good stage set, leaving the rest up to imagination. Then they close in again, a lowering ceiling. The gloomy, melancholy effect prompted Dr. James Schiel, surveying the Great Basin in 1853, to enter in his journal that "the shadows of small clouds obscuring the morning sun were the only living, moving thing in the landscape, and they seemed to heighten the feeling of utter gloom. If the eye of a man of ancient Greece had seen this sight, he would have located the entrance to the underworld here."

Flying over in September, from twelve thousand feet the Great Basin Desert has a past-finished aspect, as if all that could be done to it has been done, and now it is old and tired and worn-out, grizzled and gutted, faded and weatherbeaten. Sometimes the land has a worn velvet look, tucked with arroyos, pleated with mountains, a landscape seemingly without seasons or eternally half past autumn, a landscape left out to dry, forgotten, tattered with rain, wrinkled with sun, and yet, in a peculiar sense I cannot explain, always vital and never forlorn.

Because big sagebrush is the same color winter or summer, the landscape has a changelessness that grants it an aura of stability. It won't slide into the ocean. It may slip with a fault here and there, ooze with molten rock that darkens a slope with basalt, but it itself is the in-between, the middle, the hammock that holds the shores together, creases and adjusts with time to tensions and stresses, heaves up another mountain range, drops another graben, and just gets on with it.

The Great Basin Desert is by far the largest within the continental United States, almost 200,000 square miles, most of it above 4,000 feet, which qualifies the Great Basin Desert as cold steppe desert. It includes most of Nevada and western Utah, reaches into the southern part of Idaho and the southeastern section of Oregon; to the west, a north-south band of eastern California is classified as Great Basin Desert. John Charles Frémont named it when searching for the mythical river that drained from the Rocky Mountains to the Pacific Ocean. When he found none, he realized that he had entered a vast area of interior drainage and, on October 13, 1843, wrote in his journal of "the Great Basin—a term which I apply to the intermediate region between the Rocky mountains and the next range, containing many lakes, with their own system of rivers and creeks, . . . and which have no connexion with the ocean, or the great rivers which flow into it."

Garbed in a March morning, Sara and I hike a nameless sagebrush flat in far southwestern Utah. The incessant sagebrush looks like a collage of torn gray-green paper, one piece laid on top of the other, smallest in back, largest in front, compressed into two dimensions like a telephoto photograph. Winter lingers white under the big bushes. Simple plant communities characterize the Great Basin Desert, uniformly covering thousands of square miles—big sage-brush, saltbush, greasewood, rabbit brush, sometimes stretching as far as the eye can see. Sagebrush itself occupies over half the acreage of each of eleven western states, and has the largest range of any ecosystem in the western United States, spreading over nearly 300 million acres.

Like the other North American deserts, the Great Basin Desert evolved recently, between twelve thousand and five thousand years ago, as climate warmed and dried, and into this expanding aridity, its two major desert shrubs, sagebrush and saltbush, spread as well, laying a gray haze over the landscape. Hairiness provides intermit-tent protection from arid winds and drought for plants that tap a deep water supply, as sagebrush and saltbush do. Waxy or varnished leaves, such as those of creosote bush, or tiny leaves may be more effective at stopping water loss where water supply is more meager. Sagebrush covers all eventualities for water, with both a fibrous surface root system and a deep taproot.

From a distance, the terrain looks deceptively flat, but when we walk it, it is as hummocky and rough as a newly harrowed field. We speculate about how difficult it must have been for emigrants to jockey their wagons through, sagebrush close enough together to thwart easy wagon passage, wagon wheels raised and lowered in a cadence of jerks and bruising lurches. In July 1849, Bennett Clark, traveling from Missouri to California, had enough of it and wrote, "If we once get safely out of this great Basin we will not be cought

233

[*sic*] here again in a hurry. The eye tires & mind wearies of this tasteless monotony of scenery." Still, the sight of big sagebrush was welcome; it indicated land that, if cleared, was suitable for agriculture, with a mean annual rainfall of at least eight inches and non-saline soil.

The hoary, fragrant shrubs not only look old, they often are, enduring up to 150 years. High as my shoulder, a feathering of branches fans out of shaggy-barked, twisted trunks caused by eccentric growth rings. The growth pattern of big sagebrush is typical of Great Basin shrubs: multibranched, soft-wooded, leafed all year round, and spineless. And in the easy swiftness of my pace, I realize a great truth: there are no thorns to scratch and tear, no spines to lodge and pain, that sagebrush desert can be *friendly* desert.

Sagebrush has a tremendous competitive advantage in the Great Basin because it maintains its gray-haired light-reflective leaves all year round. Although the leaves cease growth during the winter they remain on the plant ready to begin growth quickly in the spring, and photosynthesis goes on even when temperatures near freezing (a C_3 plant, it is more productive at lower temperatures). The leaves grow every which way off the stems and bear stomata on both sides, not just the undersides of the leaves as do most plants, making them more efficient in photosynthesis, and the rates of photosynthesis adjust rapidly to match the availability of moisture.

Like creosote bush and mesquite, big sagebrush invades over-grazed range with a vengeance because native bunch grasses and herbs are unable to withstand grazing pressures. Sagebrush populations contain a high percentage of polyploids, suggesting an evolutionary opportunism, with plants equipped to thrive in varying environments. In Frémont's time, grasslands covered three-quarters of the Great Basin. Now sagebrush dominates and, once established, it tends to remain in place because the leaves are unpalatable, containing oils that hamper animal digestion, although cows and sheep will eat it when under duress. Too, it is a prodigious seeder— one plant may produce a million minute seeds. Only fire unequivocally destroys big sagebrush.

234

When the ground becomes sandier, we cross an area of low, rolling dunes that rise and give us a vantage point from which we can see for miles. Big rabbit-brush plants stabilize the dunes and, in the open alleys between, ripples swag the sand. Pockmarked with rain, the sand is in some places a lovely coppery color, in other places, pink shading to salmon. Hummocks have blown up around the rabbit brush, and many of the shrubs have long, gyrating trunks grown to remain ahead of the drifting sand and now blown bare. Round white galls infest most. I open one to find a nondescript, pale-green larva ensconced in a soft, white, feltlike center, insulated, protected from predators, surrounded by a ready food supply.

In the shade of the rabbit brush, lichens coat small pillars and bosses of sand. Wind blows the sand out between the tenacious lichens, leaving them in high relief. Mosses, almost black in color, taking advantage of the considerable residual moisture in these sands, also grow in the shaded protection of the rabbit brush, a microhabitat measured in inches.

As soon as the sand disappears, sagebrush reappears. A furtive glimpse of purple heralds an early larkspur. I find small clumps of plains daisies and a meek yellow parsley bloom, but it is useless to search for more. The colorful annual flora common in the southern deserts is missing here. The brightest colors come from the orange and dirty yellow lichens encrusting the sagebrush bark.

Between shaggy trunks, fresh-peaked harvester anthills rise like miniature volcanoes out of soil spidered with mud cracks. It is so chilly that all the openings are plugged. Two red ants, the only ones out and about, laboriously drag a tiny beetle. A few small cholla mix in with the sagebrush, and drifts of cheatgrass shiver last year's straw-colored heads. White-tailed antelope squirrels flee across the flat; others sit on their haunches, poised to scramble at our approach but not quite sure the occasion yet warrants the effort. A western meadowlark sings in defiance of the season.

Many tiny mosses pad the soil, which is also speckled with gray-green and black lichen, the hyphal rhizoids of which net and bind the soil particles. The coating of these minute plant crusts protects the ground against wind and water erosion. The algal

235

partner of the fungus is often a blue-green alga, which is capable of fixing nitrogen, a plant mineral second only to water as a limiting factor in the growth of desert plants.

All the while we have been walking, we have been conscious of the hawks—perching, circling, always hunting. This must be marvelous hunting country. Ground-squirrel young have just emerged and are everywhere, unwise in the way of silent wings and latching talons. Still here on its winter range, a rough-legged hawk with black wings, black tail barred with white, soars with deep wingbeats. Another roughleg takes off, harried by three ravens, leaving a glimpse of white-pantalooned legs and a streaked breast. We watch it in the air, wheeling and then patrolling in a neat back-and-forth pattern. Suddenly its legs drop, its wings tuck back, and it plummets to the ground—another ground squirrel tallied.

Spring in the Great Basin is emphatically *not* Edna St. Vincent Millay's April babbling down the hill. On an even danker April morning, air laced with dampness, Sara and I search for the dunes north of Tonopah, Nevada. The clouds lie so low that from a distance we cannot see the damp-darkened dunes against the mountainside that backs them.

When we arrive, moisture glosses boulders at the base of the dune. Three horned larks bicker, taking off in short flights and landing back on the ground, hopping back up on the rocks, with a great deal of pushing and shoving. Lengthening daylight brings on mating time, and these respond with a chittering, name-calling, *ménage à trois*.

The top inch of dune sand is soaked, but my boot breaks through to dry sand beneath. A huge ubiquitous darkling beetle plods slowly up the dune surface, but does not catch my attention like the little black pill beetles: round and fat night wanderers out so late. The dampness and the darkness have extended their night, and just now they begin to tunnel back into the sand. When Sara finds one excavating near some grass stubble, I look more sharply. A patch of slightly heaped sand next to a small stick covers one that has insinuated itself just under the surface. Several dozen beetles still wander about but many more lie secreted beneath these quarter-size mounds, one every six feet or so, usually solitary.

Despite the clammy New England chill, they are a lagniappe we would not have had without this dour weather.

18

OF LAKES
AND RATTLESNAKES

It has taken me miles and miles of traveling from northwestern Arizona, at the southern limits of the Great Basin, to its northern limits in Oregon and Idaho, to grasp fully the numbers of omnipresent sagebrush in the Great Basin. Miles stretch into days and still sagebrush. Up a rise, across a valley, and still sagebrush. Sagebrush goes on forever, fraying every horizon.

The Great Basin Desert stretches farther north than the general belt of deserts around the world because of the rain-shadow effect imposed by the Cascade Mountains, bringing true desert conditions to at least one-third of Oregon. Along with the extension go hundreds of square miles of sagebrush, hazing the fields to the horizon or the foot of a mountain with a color that becomes so embedded in the mind that when I see that particular soft frosted verdigris elsewhere, even in a completely different context, I smell big sage.

□

By May the chill has disappeared, and in the late afternoon a softness lies over Oregon's Alvord Desert. There are straw-colored patches of last year's dried cheatgrass, tawny heaps of dried tumbleweeds, and instead of slow-sloping valleys to the mountains, there are mesas and short, rolling hills that, when they disappear, leave broad valleys, sagebrush-stretched and meadowlark-sung.

There are mountains, yes, the constant mountain-after-mountain one comes to expect in the Great Basin, but gentled, as if here the impetus that drove all the ranges of the Basin and Range area upward were damped, the ranges less corrugated, the horizons pushed farther away, less intrusive. On their rolling flanks black volcanic rubble drizzles down the mountainsides in streams and patches. When there is a craggy profile it is singular and notable, not like the more southern mountains, which rise in rugged phalanxes alongside every valley. Blued by the afternoon light, the rim lines appear even more giving—undulating, unbroken, flowing. Bands of sunlight ray through the clouds and fan out, filling the valley with light.

Magnificent clouds overlie the sky, blossoming cumulus, wispy stratus, bird spirits with wings spread, flowing across the sky, edges backlit, an apotheosis of clouds. This deceptively lush landscape is one part hills, three parts sagebrush flats, and fifteen parts sky. The clear light of the desert here is softened from moisture in the air that blossoms the clouds and attenuates the outlines.

The Alvord Desert, part of the high desert that fills the southeastern quarter of Oregon, is one of the least-known parts of the Great Basin, still almost as empty as it was when the first emigrants entered. Emigrants coming west considered this open land to be unrestricted, theirs for the grazing. By the 1880s, the central Oregon range was overstocked and much of it overgrazed. By 1900, watersheds were damaged, erosion was rife, unprotected soils picked up and blew away.

Sagebrush and rabbit brush replaced native grasses unable to withstand such heavy usage and weedy species came in—cheatgrass, tumbleweed, halogeton. Halogeton clusters at the road edge, gaining from the modicum of moisture that collects there from runoff. A tiny needlelike seta tips each fat, crowded leaf. Related to Russian thistle, halogeton is deleterious to livestock because of the high salt concentrations it contains: it requires concentrations of almost six parts per thousand and higher. Dead plants return their sodium to the soil, further degrading it because the salts crust the soil and thwart the sprouting of other plants.

Along with grazing came fences. Out here fence corners are not a simple single post supporting wires strung out at right angles, but four posts making a meter-square enclosure, chock-a-block with boulders, four feet high. Gateposts are the same. I wondered why. Until I faced into an Alvord wind.

In the desert the normal windbreaks are missing, and low desert vegetation does not inhibit and slow the wind. Such sparsity of cover also allows barren soil to be intensely heated during the day, setting up conditions for strong air movement. Winds blow hardest during the day and tend to be strongest in spring and early summer, and many early accounts speak to their psychological effect. Although they average around ten miles per hour (and seldom exceed fifty) they are strong enough and constant enough to cause considerable erosion and to round off the sand grains in the sand dunes they create, and drive researchers and plant collectors to distraction. Wind speeds up evaporation, something with which four-footed animals as well as humans must cope, although small animals have the advantage in that the layer of air closest to the ground in which they operate is often the calmest.

The wind is a constant, shoving, making it impossible to write, blowing my hair in my face, gusting me off balance. Wind is such an ever present part of the desert environment the world over that every country has its name for desert winds: the *sirocco* in Algeria, the *shahali* in the Sahara, and the North African *khamsin* from the Arabic word for "fifty," because that's how many days it supposedly blows at a stretch in the spring months. In Nevada Mark Twain called it the "Washoe Zephyr,"

> a peculiarly Scriptural wind, in that no man knoweth "whence it cometh." That is to say, where it *originates*. It

240

comes right over the mountains from the West, but when one crosses the ridge he does not find any of it on the other side! It probably is manufactured on the mountain-top for the occasion, and starts from there. . . . Its office hours are from two in the afternoon till two the next morning; and anyone venturing abroad during those twelve hours needs to allow for the wind or he will bring up a mile or two to leeward of the point he is aiming at.

The Alvord Basin at one time held a major pluvial lake, Lake Chewaucan, which covered nearly five hundred square miles, with water once three hundred feet deep. Other Pleistocene lake remnants remain in playas and lakes in southern Oregon: Summer and Abert lakes, Warner Lakes, Alvord Lake. Between seven thousand and five thousand years ago, a decrease in effective rainfall shrank the lakes and marshes and most dried up. The flora changed from one that contained a large proportion of herbaceous plants, such as grasses, to one dominated by shrubs. Major pluvial lakes mark the Great Basin Desert—Chewaucan, Lahontan, and Bonneville—and the numerous salt-laden playas they left like pale smudges between every pair of mountain ranges constantly remind the onlooker of times both cooler and wetter, and of the inevitability of change.

When I walk down to Alvord Lake this September day, nearly every rabbit brush has its pair of black-green long-horned beetles, all mating like crazy, or is beset with cinnamon-brown long-horned beetles, most of these mating too. These are only two of many insects, all buzzing, landing, mucking about, taking off, circling in a constant grand right and left. Magnificent big bee flies pop between flowers, holding their wings out stiff and horizontal. Tiny beetles tumble from one flower to another and minute flies dart in frenetic motion from blossom to blossom. Small wasps, landing gear dangling, sample every available blossom.

The slope goes down to the playa in steps, riven with drainage lines full of gravels that are tan, rust, beige, white, ocher, burnt sienna, rose, chocolate, pulverized memories of massive mountains. A black-tailed jackrabbit bounds out from under a sagebrush bush, an animal whose ancestry goes back twenty million years. Its scal-

loping pogo-stick gait is a characteristic sight in every desert in the
United States.

In this cooler climate they breed from early spring to midsum-
mer; in the warmer Sonoran they breed nearly all year long with
larger litter sizes. Their populations tend to fluctuate more markedly here than they do in the more southerly deserts, on a ten- to
twelve-year cycle, directly affecting the coyote population in a
classic predator-prey relationship.

Black-tailed jackrabbits are by far the most important herbivore in the sagebrush desert, utilizing it both for cover and for
food. Although they prefer grasses and fresh greenery when available, they are not put off by the oils in sagebrush and go after new
growth and young woody stems and have even been known to eat
creosote bush. Jackrabbits spend most of their daytime hours sheltered, feeding in the cooler hours of the day, following well-
tramped paths through the sagebrush. Nocturnal feeding helps in
keeping water loss down. They can also withstand considerable
hyperthermia; perhaps in a somewhat similar manner to birds, an
elevated body temperature allows them to lose heat to the environment rather than gain it.

My jackrabbit remains visible across the slope. One bountiful
leap every so often lifts it higher, giving it a better view of its
surroundings. Standing straight up, its huge, lightly-haired ears
catch the sunlight. On hot days its ears, which are one-fifth of its
body length, can radiate around a third of its body heat through
vasodilation. It finally disappears down the slope, only the first of
several I will inadvertently disturb, all of them leaping off with a Le
Mans start.

When I reach the edge of plant growth, ready to stride out into
the playa, I look up and ahead and to my astonishment the whole
surface is in flux. Concentrating on the scene at my feet, I had not
noticed the great sheet of water until I was close—from the distance
it looked as empty as any other playa. Because so much fine silt
hangs in suspension, the water carpet is a soft, opaque coffee-with-
cream color, a quilt of unbleached muslin appliquéd with pale blue
velvet cloud shadows. I stand here with my hands on my hips and

think that if there is one thing I am tired of hearing it is that the desert is always hot and dry. At the moment I am chilled to the bone by the wind and facing a large expanse of annoyingly wet playa.

I should have known. Along with other dry lakes in the northern Great Basin, Lake Alvord has water in it, and the next time I see it I am prepared. In the springtime, frowzy plants of balsamroot are in bloom, big clumps of yellow flowers lighting up an otherwise monotone flat of sagebrush, rabbit brush, and cheatgrass. Closer to the lake, sagebrush gives way to greasewood. Hard-packed paths wind between the shoulder-high shrubs and big clumps of wild rye. Around one turning a pile of gray and yellow feathers flutter across the ground, the remains of a meadowlark from a falcon kill. Around another, tiny black chips of obsidian abound, shiny as glass, some worked with neat conchoidal edges, some just leftover trash from point chipping. There are signs of prehistoric man throughout the Oregon desert, especially around dry lakes that, when full, provided a richer harvest than the desert alone.

A thick wall of hardstem bulrushes fringes the edge of the lake, and then a wide apron of muck, lightly puddled, leads out to open water. I essay a few steps out on areas of cracked silt that look as if they may be hard enough to walk on, but they too are soft and my feet sink quickly into a gelatinous ooze. The lake has been higher, but this winter and spring in Oregon have been dry, and now a hundred feet separate water from bulrush.

Out here the water is a soft gray blue, deepening in color where the wind fractures the surface, then a Naples-yellow strand line divides mountains and water. I stand knee deep in bulrushes, hearing crickets chirrup, watching thousands of spiders thread through the stems. The green shoots come up between the tan, two feet tall, fresh and straight and intent, in contrast to the broken stalks and frizzled heads of old growth.

This was how the ancient lake dried, inch by inch, bulrush by bulrush. This teeming life at my feet, bulrushes so thick I can't see where my foot steps, the ticking cadence of crickets, will disappear as the lake retreats further. Already greasewood stands ready to invade. On drier ground, small anthills swarm with red-brown ants. They too will move into the drying soil. Every nest is around grass stems, surrounded by dry, pulverized dirt, and as the grass moves downward, so will the ants. All the players are in the wings, waiting.

A prairie falcon arrows down the valley, low and fast, going north. While it is still light I am determined to find a horned lark's nest. They nest on the ground, often near some protection—a grass tussock, a cow pie—but what I want most to see is the arrangement of pebbles or mud pellets the female places at one side of the nest like a miniature desert pavement. No one knows why this behavior has evolved, but the oddness of it is reason enough to wonder, especially as another desert lark species builds a small protective wall of stones around its nest.

All day I have watched the larks dart out of the short grass and saltbush where they forage for seeds, usually six pair or so at a time. There was a time when I dutifully looked up these birds every time I saw them; now I don't bother. In the Great Basin, if it's a flock, it's horned larks. Period.

Two swoop with short wingbeats, white bellies sparkling, one right on the tail of the other. The subspecies of Great Basin horned larks are paler and smaller than populations to the east. The most omnipresent Great Basin birds, they are widespread across the West. Like the Chihuahuan Desert, the Great Basin has no endemic birds; rather it supports an assemblage of birds filtered in from outside its borders in unique combination.

The horned larks have been spiraling and soaring, displaying some rather ill-tempered territoriality. I strike off across an area of open salt flat on my way to a slightly more grassy area, where there is more cover. Suddenly a soft "*Trr-rr-rrr-rrrrrr*" stops me short. I suck in my breath. Hold it. Waiting. No loud noise freezes me as quickly as that soft unmistakable whir.

I look hard and see nothing. I take another step. The unmistakable subtle sibilant sound of empty packets striking against each other repeats. The sound remains soft, gentle, but a warning nevertheless. I stand still. The sound ceases. I scan the shad-scale bushes. They are small, well separated, fairly open in growth, no place for a rattlesnake to hide. Yet that's where it has to be.

There are hundreds of dried sticks on the ground, to my eye now all of rattlesnake proportion, but none moves, none holds a string of half a dozen rattles up to the sounding-board air. I try to echolocate the bush, and even when I think I'm on target, I still cannot see the snake, which continues to rustle like a cicada every time I move. I have a somber thought: the rattlesnakes with which I have had intimate contact while working on this book have been in totally unexpected places, such as in a willow clump in the middle of a cool, dank stream in the Mojave Desert, and here in this bare, open salt flat.

Seeing the rattlesnake becomes an obsession, for where it is sets the limits of my movement. I can easily make a wide circle around. But I have a deeper curiosity than that. We have become connected by chance and need to play out our roles.

After an infinity of intense peering I finally separate out a patch of pattern marking the back of a western rattlesnake, coiled in a depression beneath a very small saltbush. From the curvature I estimate a coil perhaps eight inches across, and a body an inch and a quarter in diameter, a snake perhaps two feet or so long. I cannot see the rattle but the whirring is almost constant, fading and intensifying, in an oddly peaceful way. I feel warned. I do not feel threatened. Although I cannot see it, I know, having just seen one of its ilk out on a road, that its forked tongue darts out of its mouth straight up, then bends down, quivering, before being pulled in again, a motion that I find almost hypnotically fascinating to watch.

I am tempted to go closer, believing that it is so entangled in the bush that it cannot strike. It is not good sense that holds me back but good manners: I am disturbing it enough simply by my presence. My guess is that it was coiled there in the meager shade of the saltbush during the day and was just awakening to think about hunting when it was rudely disturbed by the vibrations of an arrogant and heavy-booted trespasser.

Late afternoon rounds to dusk, dusk points toward nightfall. A full moon brightens the salt flat while daylight clouds wreath the horizon, amorphous gauzy pink. The mountains phase to deep lapis blue, making it too late to go searching for horned-lark nests. Instead I ponder my reaction to the rattlesnake, my overwhelming need to see it, to pay my respects, and go on my way.

In Navajo legend, rattlesnakes are guardians of sacred things. I bow it peaceful greetings and wish it good hunting tonight.

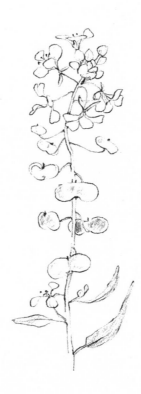

19

OF GRASS FIRES
AND GROUSE LOCUSTS

Herman lowers the flaps over Winnemucca and the aeronautical sectional chart on my lap comes to life. The color and the shadings of map and terrain match. As on the chart, there is no bright green on the ground, only a subtle series of tans and burnt siennas. The resemblance between the two—man's map and nature's map—is uncanny.

But the map records no harvester-ant mounds, no doughnuts of bare soil. Yet hundreds stud the ground below. I feel a quick tinge of superiority: I know something the map doesn't know. Nor does the map acknowledge the scorched and blackened patches of hillsides and fields from last week's lightning fires.

Once we land, the brittle sooty patches are all the more dramatic, ringed as they are by the blond thatch of unburned cheatgrass. In a burned area, charred stems crunch underfoot, the smell as

247

strong as the stale black odor of a doused campfire. Knee-high sagebrush, lower branches like sticks of charcoal, still bear sprigs of growth on the top branches, but in an older burn nearby, everything stands dead. When I scrape the thin black layer with my boot, the soil beneath is sandy and sere. Sand underlies this whole area north of Winnemucca, and before the burn, plants stabilized it. Only a low stubble, flattened and crisp, remains where the fire was heaviest. Slight hillocks mark where roots remain underground even though fire incinerated all that was above ground. Burned sprigs of grass stick out of the ground like inch-high charcoal toothpicks.

A sagebrush lizard darts out from beneath a charred bush, its pale speckled gray scales contrasting sharply with the swarthy background. It dashes to a tumbleweed and stops, its tail switching slowly back and forth. At my approach it skitters out onto a patch of light-gray gravel alongside the road, where it instantly disappears, at one with its background. Surely animals like this one are extremely vulnerable during and after a fire. Not only are they at hazard from the flames and heat, but the background, for which they have evolved to be so carefully matched, has radically changed. And fire reduces, if not totally destroys, their food supply of insects and spiders. But sagebrush lizards have a long history of coping with change and surviving, having endured the dryness of the Pliocene and the ensuing frigidity of the Pleistocene and left their progeny to scamper the desert.

When lightning fires come in profusion out here, there is no way of stopping them. They can only burn out on their own. Although there is something depressing about the unmitigated bleakness, the oxidation of plant materials adds considerable quantities of nutrients to the soil and increases the available nitrogen, at the same time intensifying the water-shedding quality of the soil. Shrubs like Mormon tea and horsebrush, which sprout from roots, appear first after a burn, followed by the more weedy annuals like tumbleweed and peppergrass. Grasses are variously damaged although some, as cheatgrass, thrive and throw copious seed after fire. Rabbit brush and horsebrush, more fire-adapted plants, replace big sagebrush because it cannot resprout immediately after a burn.

HORSEBRUSH
(*Tetradymia glabrata*)

Rabbit brush and horsebrush sprout vigorously, showing a fivefold increase in a decade. The growth of herbaceous cover may double that which existed in the original sagebrush community. The ancestors of the former were neotropical, whereas those of sagebrush were arctic in distribution and less subject to fire—thus the sequence after fire in the Great Basin is often the replacement of the cold-temperature sagebrush with plants of tropical, warm-temperature affinities. Both ancient and modern man have used fire to reduce sagebrush cover and increase habitat diversity.

When native grasses and herbs are removed by grazing or by fire, the remaining shrub community is almost fireproof because of the lack of dried vegetation to burn—until highly flammable cheatgrass invades. Two massive changes have occurred shortly over a century in the Great Basin: the loss of native herbs and grasses and their replacement by sagebrush, and the introduction of an alien plant species, which also expanded to the detriment of native plants.

Cheatgrass turned up in the American West around 1900 when it was introduced from Eurasia. When native grasses cannot withstand grazing, or where they are burned out, cheatgrass elbows in aggressively. As a winter annual, it sprouts in the fall and sets seed early, drying into a fire hazard by mid-June, a vicious circle since it thrives after a fire to the detriment of other plants, outcompeting them for water. In the last decade it has spread drastically, now covering half a million acres south and west of Winnemucca.

Wherever I throw my sleeping bag, it is surrounded by cheatgrass. Wherever I fall asleep, I awake to a fringe of its languid heads at eye level. On some florets the brown stamens and the white frizzled stigmas are still in place, the whole floret glistening with transparent white hairs, but on others the quarter-inch seed has already developed although still firmly attached at the base. Even early in the season the awns are stiff and their backward-pointing barbs assure them a good seat in fur and socks. When I peruse a head under a hand lens I understand why the floret insinuates itself into every piece of clothing I wear. Each floret bears a stiff, finely barbed, rosy awn half an inch long, which will dry into a miniature porcupine quill. Cheatgrass flowers and dries early, and within the month they will be a nuisance, trotting everywhere with the assistance of unwilling hosts.

On the way to the dune field north of Winnemucca, Terry Tempest Williams, a naturalist from the Utah Museum of Natural History whose quick eye is attuned to birds, spots a burrowing owl stationed on a rock by the side of the road, its long legs and short tail making it look as if it stands on tiptoe. Dr. Samuel Woodhouse, on an expedition down the Colorado River in 1852, found them, when approached, to "commence chatting and bowing, presenting quite a ludicrous appearance" before they flew away and took up station "at the entrance of another burrow, where they again commence their chattering."

The whitewash of its droppings daubs its volcanic sentinel rock. Around it are casts full of beetle elytras and some toothpicklike vertebrate bones, testimony to its gourmand tastes as a predator. It times its hunting to the cooler times of the day during summer, returning to midday at the cooler ends of the season.

Its nest is a hole in the low road bank, a dark shadow in the cheatgrass, used year after year, likely the quondam den of a badger or fox. The owl refurbishes it by lining it with manure, possibly in an attempt to disguise its odor in order to disorient its predators. Terry listens at the entrance for the distress call of the young, which sounds like a rattlesnake's burr. Now confined to drier habitats, the burrowing owl is a leftover from the prairie complex of burrowing owl–ferret–rattlesnake–bison. Farther up the road, the somewhat larger female launches herself into the air and circles back to the nest as soon as we pass.

The sand for the Winnemucca dune field probably blew east from an old delta of the Humboldt River, made when it flowed farther northwest than it does now. To reach the dunes we make our way across a burned-out area a year or two old, bountiful with annuals—evening primroses, gilias, white-stem evening stars, desert dandelions, buckwheats, tidytips, the tiny blue phlox flowers set in woolly bracts, and lots of alfalfa. The luxuriance contrasts with both the bleakness of the freshly-burned areas and the

OVAL-LEAF BUCKWHEAT
(*Eriogonum ovalifolium*)

unburned dune sites where the plant cover is simpler in species, supporting mostly cheatgrass with big sagebrush and rabbit brush. What annuals there are in recent burns are stunted compared to the numbers and kinds in older burned-out patches.

Out on the dunes, the finite horizon line blurs with moving sand, urged by better than (on my personal Beaufort scale) a ten-knot wind. Walking across the sand is like being in a popcorn popper with all the grouse locusts—which are actually small grass-

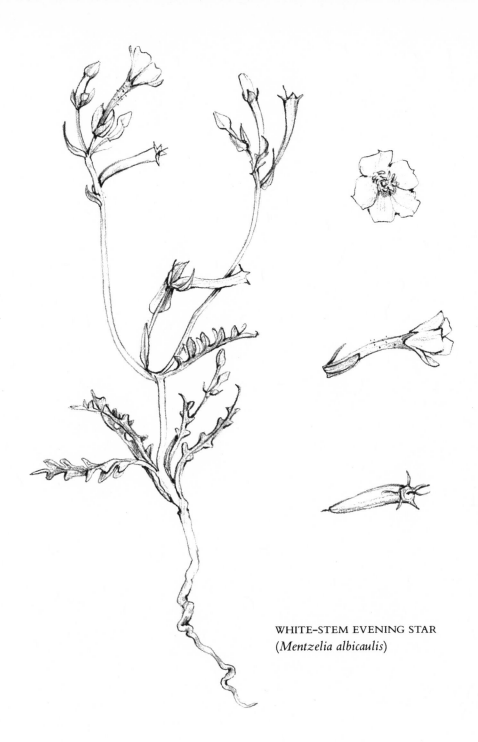

WHITE-STEM EVENING STAR
(*Mentzelia albicaulis*)

TIDYTIPS
(*Layia glandulosa*)

GREAT BASIN GILIA
(*Gilia leptomaria*)

KING'S DALEA
(*Psorothamnus kingii*)

hoppers—spurting up like drops of water on a hot skillet. Unlike
most grasshoppers, a grouse locust's body is flattened horizontally
rather than vertically. Nor does it have the large muscular saltatorial
back legs, which may explain its erratic jumping style. Never
making more than six to eight inches at a leap, they take off and land
helter-skelter, in short, wildly uncontrolled, ridiculous crashes,
landing upside down half the time. The dunes jump and jiggle and
seethe in incessant motion from both grasshoppers and blowing
sand.

A long gnarled root ropes across the sand and disappears, only
to emerge again several feet away, submerge, and surface at last in a
tuft of alfalfa leaves, a plant that has developed a trailing root ability
well adapted to this wind-driven shifting substrate. Small King's
dalea bushes scraggle along and under the ground, purple-flowered,

ropes of reddish roots alternately exposed and buried. Once thought to grow only among sagebrush, and considered a threatened species, it has now been found more widely distributed in dune areas. Just beginning to flower, the plant has not yet developed its full branching. Its characteristic rigidly branched growth pattern shows only on skeletons of last year's plants, not on this year's green and supple sprigs.

Scallops and serpentines, laid in curves of mathematical dignity and physical precision, ornament the dune crest, symbols of moving wind and moving water. I perch close to the knife edge of the slipface and nudge a few grains of sand over the edge. They syrup down the steep face like honey, taking fifteen seconds to reach the base. I push a wider swath and watch it slither down fifteen feet. It's as hypnotizing as watching raindrops chase each other down a windowpane. I push again and watch the gathering stream pull more sand slowly from either side as it moves only part way and then slows. The wind gusts at right angles across the face and feeds more sand into the lethargic stream. It gathers momentum and slumps to the bottom, peeling off a large section of dune in a thin layer, and pulling the support right out from under my feet, cascading me downslope in an avalanche of sand, as ungainly as an oversize grouse locust.

I rejoin Terry. We sit down to get out of the wind, and then, still pestered by sand, lie on our stomachs, and end up spending a delightful hour entranced by a brace of grouse locusts. These little grasshoppers are half hidden in the sand and we stretch out at eye level with them. When I was walking the dunes, the hoppers sprang up at every footstep, but here they have dug in and we puzzle over them—are they grounded too by this irritating sand-laden wind?

Terry drums her finger on the sand. Immediately two small grouse locusts pop out and rapidly dig in again, facing directly into the wind as they burrow, looking like "miniature horned toads," says Terry. Tapping again gets no reaction. A white flange on the thorax makes the body look broad and shieldlike and may be of help in excavating. Three white lines striping the long pronotum (the

257

covering over the thorax of grasshoppers) is diagnostic of the Tetrigidae family.

The sand is predominantly light tan sprinkled with salt-and-pepper grains, and the grouse locusts are the same color. Now that our eyes are sensitized to their particular movement and behavior, we pick out a dozen in the sand.

One particularly large grouse locust (although none is over an inch) braces with its front feet and vigorously kicks out a hole for itself. Its short antennae remain folded down while it digs but at any movement on our part they straighten to attention. For a moment it ceases digging and raises itself up off the sand, its front legs tapping, a more exposed and different body attitude. We speculate: is this a pose for temperature adjustment, to allow some ventilation beneath its body?

Wind snaps the sand and another grouse locust digs itself in like a dog kicking dirt; it shoots out one back leg at a time until it has made a depression, waits a moment, then lowers its body and melds into the background. Grains hopping across the surface quickly bury it but for its antennae and eyes, which remain exposed, two dark grains of sentient sand.

20

OF GREASEWOOD
AND KANGAROO MICE

Nineteenth-century emigrants going from the East or Midwest to the Pacific Coast had two choices: they could go by sea, first by boat from New York to Panama, cross the isthmus, then sail to Los Angeles or San Francisco, or cross the Great Basin Desert. For many of those with household goods and children, shank's mare had to suffice, and by 1852 over a hundred thousand crossed the Great Basin Desert. No other desert lay on a main migration route across the West as the Great Basin Desert did.

The trip was, comparatively speaking, one of reasonable hardship until the Great Basin Desert was reached. Then the Overland Trail feathered out, and cutoffs, legitimate or not, were proffered by every guide, as the way to avoid the dreaded Forty Mile Desert. An ordinarily difficult, miserable, slow-moving, wagon-wrenching crossing was made terrifying by three stretches of desert: the Black

259

GREAT BASIN DESERT SALT FLAT AND SAGEBRUSH

Rock Desert, the Humboldt Sink, and the Carson Sink. All were once covered by the Pleistocene lake system of Lake Lahontan, whose large remnants are Pyramid and Walker lakes.

The Black Rock Desert stretches north from Pyramid Lake in northern Nevada almost to the Oregon border. Across it ran the Applegate Trail, an attempt to avoid crossing the Forty Mile Desert by leaving the Humboldt River higher at its big bend rather than continuing southwestward on to the sink. Established from Oregon eastward by Jesse and Lindsay Applegate (who named the desert in 1846 from the Black Rock Range that split its northern part), the trail was one of several cutoffs that attempted to shorten the trip and, like most of them, brought more hardship to an already onerous journey across the Great Basin Desert.

The sequence of plants, from sagebrush to greasewood to saltbush, signals the increasing saltiness of the soil. Low tufts of winter fat, an ashy-white halophyte, stand out startlingly against darker plants. The more salt in the soil, the shorter, thicker, and hairier its leaves, a more succulent leaf having smaller surface-to-volume ratio to cut down on evaporation. A deep taproot also makes it drought resistant. Winter fat provides valuable winter browse, with a winter protein content almost equal to that of alfalfa, and in addition, most of the plant is edible. The ability to reproduce is the key to being a successful halophyte, and it is likely that its seeds can sprout in this salt-laden soil where the seeds of other plants cannot. The seeds of winter fat are tolerant of a wide range of temperature and soil salinity and, like most halophytes, although they can grow elsewhere, they avoid a great deal of competition by growing in places that most other plants disdain. The only other species in this genus grows in the deserts of Asia.

The last outliers at the playa edge are patches of desert salt grass that web the soil with interconnected roots like steel rods in reinforced concrete. The genus name, *Distichlis,* refers to salt grass's conspicuously two-ranked leaves. Cracks outline polygons twice the width of my handspan, and salt grass, as stiff and as prickly-pointed as a yucca spear, follows their geometry. I tug on a sprig and find it attached to underground rhizomes that heave up soil in several directions at once, one connected plant, going on forever. Saline crusts, the legacy of Lake Lahontan, deter sprouting both because of their imperviousness and their high surface salinity, hence vegetative reproduction is a necessary alternative.

The pallid, dusty arrow of the Black Rock Desert playa points northeastward. The surface results from dry periods, when dust and sand blew across the surface and filled the desiccation cracks, and wet times, when the fine materials on top washed downward and cemented. The last few centuries have been warmer and drier, and deposition continues, cementing the surface with infrequent rains and patterning it with muted colors and marbled designs, whorled like fingerprint patterns. Patches of soil have a raised crust, sometimes formed of thin flakes that crunch like cornflakes underfoot, or sometimes ridged like brain coral. Between the vermiculate ridges are smudges of lichen, charcoal-colored and orange tan, muted in size, muted in color.

Although at the moment the surface is dry and hard, a cloudburst can turn it into a wheel-ingesting, more-slippery-than-grease, tenacious silt, and one surmises that fortunes have been made in nearby Gerlach from prying stuck vehicles out of the muck. No one goes alone into this twenty-mile waste unless prepared for the prospect of a very long and solitary hike.

With a brooding sky, I am content to walk. Clouds adumbrate the playa ahead; shafts of sun strike through low clouds, lighting far hillsides, and rain showers fall behind one screen of mountain range after another. I think of the Reverend Mr. Thornton, who ran out of supplies and claimed that "the young man whom he [Applegate] had sent out with his produce to sell to the emigrants, *scraped* me, by charging me ten prices for that assistance which was necessary to my being extricated from the dangers into which I had been plunged by means of the deceptions practiced upon me."

The desert does not always bring out the best in everyone.

Frémont named the Humboldt River and Mountains after the cartographer Baron Friedrich von Humboldt, who, though he never saw the Great Basin, drew a map published at the beginning of the nineteenth century that literally put the West on the map.

Only in unusually wet years is there enough water to fill the thirty-mile-long Humboldt Sink, known as the "worst place between Missouri and Hell" to the emigrants who had to cross it, or for the Humboldt and Carson sinks to unite. This is one of those years. During Pleistocene times, the Humboldt River flowed all the way to Lake Lahontan, the pluvial lake that flooded most of central and northwestern Nevada until it withdrew some 5,000 years ago. Named after an early French explorer of the West who, like Baron von Humboldt, never saw the landforms named for him, it covered almost 9,000 square miles and its highest watermark scribed a line at 4,378 feet, between 24,000 and 12,000 years ago. Estimates are that Lake Lahontan could return if rainfall increased from the present-day 10 to 18 inches, and the mean annual temperature decreased by 9 degrees F.

Once the Humboldt was a river capable of creating meanders ten times as large as the meander loops in the present-day river. Now it disappears into the sink. It is still, considering that it runs through such arid Great Basin country, a respectable river system and the largest in the region, although Horace Greeley considered it "the meanest river of its length on earth" and Mark Twain thought "one of the pleasantest and most invigorating exercises one can

262

contrive is to run and jump across the Humboldt river till he is overheated, and then drink it dry."

Even though the soil is now close to being saturated, the sink is a saline desert, a waste of alien ground, seemingly bereft of life for miles, with growing conditions that, with the dearth of usable water, match the conditions of an arid desert. I cannot even imagine how it appeared to emigrants who had traversed miserable desert already, jostled and bumped between and over sagebrush bushes, a cacophony of clanking pots and pans with every jolt, the ride so rough it was easier to walk. When they approached this open flat, it must have looked welcoming, a respite from the kidney-springing, backbone-cracking terrain that, as John Bidwell wrote in 1841 on the way to California, could overturn a lightly laden wagon.

Instead it was an even greater ordeal. Walking on this treacherous terrain is like walking on a half-filled water bed, unstable and giving. The viscid soil squishes up over the instep of my boots, a sickly mauve color with an unhealthy funereal cast. A rotting, cloying miasma emanates from the fetid soil. Despite the odor, little organic matter accumulates because of the sparsity of plants and the salinity, which may be anywhere from 10 to as high as 70 percent near the surface.

The soil's saline content limits plant growth to the few plants able to take up water heavily laced with minerals. Although wet, the ground is just as much a desert as an arid dune, with the same problem for plants—that of obtaining sufficient fresh water. To the sink belong the saltbushes and salt grasses, the iodine bushes and halogeton, leaves silvered or succulent, flowers obscure and small.

Most members of the goosefoot family are able to accommodate to the double challenge of physiological as well as climatological drought, and many of these plants have high osmotic pressure, which "pumps" the salt to the leaf surface, where specialized glands exude and get rid of it. Plants sometimes grow separately, sometimes tangle over each other in languid patches. Such are their rank and insidious growth patterns that they seem to strangle anything in their path. Most spread, creep, crawl, even slither. The only "normal"-looking plants are a common weedy mustard called white-

FOUR-WING SALTBUSH
(*Atriplex canescens*)

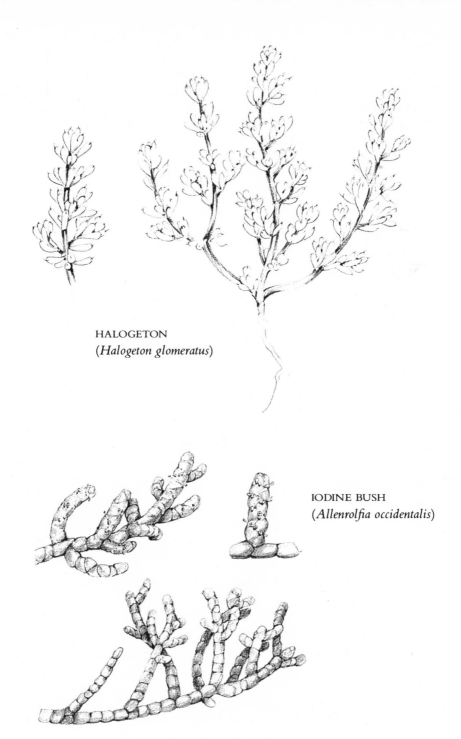

HALOGETON
(*Halogeton glomeratus*)

IODINE BUSH
(*Allenrolfia occidentalis*)

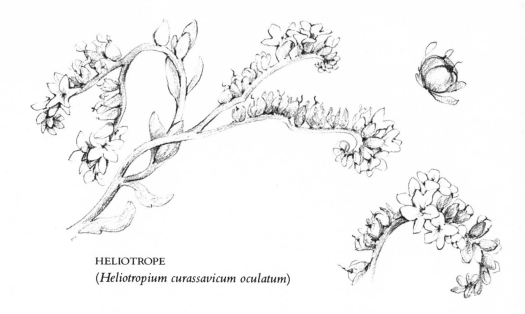

HELIOTROPE
(*Heliotropium curassavicum oculatum*)

top, now in seed, and a heliotrope with small purple-throated blooms.

One bush of honeysweet sprawls eight feet across and grows six feet high. It makes most of its growth during the hottest times of the year because it is a C_4 plant and tolerates the high salt content of the soil, genetic qualities now being explored in agricultural research for their application in arid-land food crops, for the nutritious seeds seldom have the salt content of the rest of the plant.

Where even a slight rise allows the soil to dry, single shrubs of greasewood stabilize patches of fragmentary dunes two to three feet high, outlined by blue-gray salt exudations, while the surrounding wet area glistens like satin. Greasewood seeds will sprout only at cool temperatures, so that seedlings get a good start in the spring rather than during the harder conditions of summer. Greasewood itself may inhibit seed production, for it produces a meager seed crop and the seeds that fall in the leaf litter must endure a microenvironment heavy with sodium. New plants are more likely to start through the production of adventitious roots on the parent plant.

It was across this miserable cloying sink that some 21,000 people and more than double that in heads of stock came in 1849, the

266

year of heaviest travel along the Overland Trail. In that year Bennett
Clark wrote:

> We found the water in holes here that had been dug by
> those before us, and such water we never remember to
> have drank. It was cool but most horrible to the taste—a
> mixture of alkali & Sulpher & no doubt all coming from
> the sink. . . . There is yet a stretch of 45 miles ahead of us
> without grass or water.

Clark refers to the Carson Sink, known then as the Forty Mile
Desert, one of the most dreaded reaches of the emigrant trail to
California; it took its grisly toll of lives and livestock. The Carson
Desert, first described by Frémont in 1844, is a five-thousand-
square-mile swath of Nevada desert laid northwest-southeast.
Immediately in the rain shadow of the Sierra Nevada, it has an
annual precipitation of less than six inches. The dearth of vegetation
makes it extremely susceptible to erosion, so that it is riven by
drainage ways five feet deep and less than that wide. When there is
water in it as after flooding, its extreme saltiness can be toxic to
migrating water- and shorebirds, and in the spring of 1987 thousands of birds died. Mark Twain saw "the road white with the bones
of oxen and horses. It would hardly be an exaggeration to say that
we could have walked the forty miles and set our feet on a bone on
every step!"

Men, animals, and equipment arrived here in weakened shape
to begin a journey that under the best of conditions was desperate.
Wagon wheels that had shrunk with dryness were soaked in water,
every container available was filled with the revolting liquor from
the Sink, and the *jornada* began at night to avoid the heat of day. The
accounts of travelers are wretched case histories of heat exhaustion
and heat collapse, physical duress and mental anguish. Bennett
Clark again:

> Taking the general aspect of this desert into view, and the
> fact that there is an absence of every thing desirable and an

abundance of every thing pernicious here coupled with what we saw, we cannot conceive a hill more full of horrors. It realises all that such a mind as Dante's could imagine.

An ancient volcano spewed black basaltic rock over the bone-white of the Carson Desert, and it is against this black rim that I first see Sand Mountain, a pale, monumental dune set against a dark, ragged background. Sands blown up from the Carson Desert, accumulating between six thousand and two thousand years ago, formed this monolithic mound nearly four hundred feet high. Crosscurrents constantly rearrange the knifelike ridges on the crest according to season. Sand Mountain can be set sounding by a boot stamp on an oversteepened surface, sounds described as so musical as to compare to a fine pipe organ. Today the mountain buzzes with a dozen dune buggies swarming over its flank and crest like angry bees.

To the west of Sand Mountain, a fenced study area protects scattered salt grass and bunches of ricegrass, the clumps a warm, golden tan against the cool background of the sand. The plenitude of ricegrass here may be due to the presence of so many rodents that remove the hard outer shell before they bury the seeds, making it easier for the seeds to germinate. The sturdy stalks of last summer's Palmer's penstemons glimmer light and bright against darker vegetation. Rodent holes perforate every shrub hummock and the impress of busy footprints crochets the bushes together.

These shrubs provide food and cover for an abundant rodent population, with one, the pallid kangaroo mouse, more or less confined to the fine sands of this central Nevada community. For an animal that must emerge, harvest, often husk and eat or transport seeds as rapidly as possible to avoid being caught, the habitat is ideal: open runways, protective shrubs, hummocks to burrow in, and ample food.

Like the kangaroo rat, it has a large head and possesses unusually big and furry hind feet to paddle through the sand. Also like kangaroo rats, the large head allows space for a developed bullar region, which enhances hearing.

Their three-inch size makes temperature regulation difficult. Besides aridity and erratic food supply, the most difficult problem these diminutive rodents face in living in the Great Basin is not the heat, with which rodents in the southerly deserts must cope, but the low nighttime winter temperatures. When food becomes scarce, they respond by going into hibernation in cool weather, or into estivation, a shorter-term sleep, in warm weather. Such a small herbivore must be able to survive at best on limited forage, and sometimes for considerable periods, on nothing at all.

Every kangaroo-mouse pathway ends at a leafless, spiky-branched shrub of smoke bush, which dominates the landscape. This unmistakable shrub was first collected near here by the botanist John Torrey. A fine, dense white felt of downward-turned hairs covers the branches, rendering them a pale, distinctive gray.

Minuscule leaflets decorate only a few, and only a few plants bloom with sweetpealike flowers so tiny they need a hand lens to be appreciated. Although not the normal spring leafing, recent rains have encouraged greenery on these plants. I wonder what insect pollinator is small enough to land on the tiny lateral wings of the flower, and yet weighs enough to push the keel down and expose the stamen and pistil—probably a small bee. Smoke bush, which makes up a third of this plant community, is limited to stabilized dune sands, commonly growing with four-wing saltbush and horsebrush, both likewise intricately branched, nonspiny, small-leafed shrubs. Smoke bush, and the plants associated with it, are more closely allied to plants in the southern deserts of Arizona and southwestern California than to the sagebrush desert assemblage of the Great Basin, and probably moved northward into the Carson Desert with the drying of Lake Lahontan.

Its branches, straight and stiff and sharp, end in points like oversize thorns, and carry on some photosynthesis throughout the year since the infinitesimal leaves appear only after rains. The equally minute flowers produce tiny one- to two-seeded pods, less than a quarter inch long. A chemical in the pod inhibits the seeds from sprouting. When it leaches away or the seed is scarified, germination takes place immediately. A seed sends down a long taproot while above-ground growth goes slowly—a one-inch plant may have a root seven to ten inches long, reaching for moisture.

The whole plant emanates a sharp unmistakable resinous odor from pinpoint golden-yellow glands, a wonderfully penetrating, clarifying fragrance, sharper than sagebrush. Its specific name, *polydenius,* means "many glands." To describe odors, one can only reference familiar smells, and our repertory of aromas is pitifully limited. Smoke bush doesn't smell like anything I recall unless it's another sinus-clearing, pungent, pleasantly unpleasant, smoke bush.

Smoke bush exhales endurance under heat, survival without water, subsistence in sand, and I'm not good to eat. Smoke bush smells like desert.

21

OF SALT DESERT AND
PRONGHORNS

Sevier Lake, in western-central Utah, like a beautiful piece of
Navajo jewelry, blazes turquoise blue in a silvery setting of desert.
The Cricket Mountains back it, their light-absorbent flanks emphasizing the unnatural brilliance of the lake. Pronounced Se-veer' and
usually a dry lake, it has risen in rhythm with the Great Salt Lake in
the mid-1980s. On Baron von Humboldt's famous map of 1804, he
called it Laguna de Miera and, never having surveyed it, drew it
with a wishful outlet that emptied into the Pacific Ocean. Near
here, on October 26, 1853, Captain John Williams Gunnison and
his crew, surveying for the Pacific Railroad Survey, were ambushed
and killed by Pah Vant Indians. Among the dead were Dr. James
Schiel, whose dismal, prophetic words about the Great Basin
Desert were fulfilled. Not until 1872 was the area accurately
mapped as what it always was, a closed basin, the southernmost

271

extension of the largest pluvial lake in the Great Basin, Lake Bonneville.

At its greatest extent Lake Bonneville covered nearly twenty thousand square miles, about the size of Lake Michigan, and inundated one third of Utah with an extreme depth of eleven hundred feet. Direct precipitation and runoff fed it during the Pleistocene, and less evaporation and lower ambient temperatures than today's maintained it. Usually a dry lake with its water usurped by agriculture, it has risen in rhythm with the Great Salt Lake and today sparkles with water.

As I work my way toward the lake, I stroll an indurated salt flat as hard as cement, clean channels threading between mounds of soil paved with dark desert pavement. Of the dozens of harvester ants' nests, most are caved in. Spiny hopsage bushes stud small mounds, greening up with mealy leaves neatly arranged around thin, spiky branches; *Grayia spinosa* was named after Asa Gray, the renowned Harvard botanist, by Joseph Hooker at Kew Gardens in England, an unlikely history for this tough little western goosefoot, which neither man ever saw growing in place.

From under one hopsage a desert horned lizard scurries. I shadow it until it takes cover in another open bush, through which the patterns on its back are visible, light beige overlaid on tan in stylized patterns like Chinese cloud paintings, dotted with salmon. Salmon is a breeding color brought on by hormonal change triggered by lengthening daylight. Small, it's not larger than the palm of my hand, with a short broad tail and body with fringes down its flanks. A row of triangular spines crown its head like a coronet; they may be of use to the male in clasping the female in mating. It seems such a little fellow to have engendered John Russell Bartlett's description that they, "as if conscious of the security afforded by their own hideous ugliness, sullenly remove themselves out of the way of the horses' hoofs, and regard the passer with malicious eye."

At first, horned lizards poke only their heads out to the sun, for head temperature may be more important than body temperature in signaling its time of emergence. They remain with only head exposed until their head blood warms; during that time a shunting

SPINY HOPSAGE
(*Grayia spinosa*)

arrangement of the jugular vein slows the loss of warmed head blood to the body and prevents it from being exchanged for cool. When sufficiently heated, the warm head blood is slowly released to the rest of the body, ensuring that when the lizard emerges it will be ready to move with alacrity.

The presence of this predator of ants likely explains the number of damaged harvester-ant nests about. Ants make up almost the entire diet of horned lizards, although they are more likely to lie in ambush beside ant trails than to take on the whole nest, where ant

273

bites discommode them. I gently pry apart the branches to get a better look. The horned toad rises up on its legs and elevates its crown in display, and then, wisdom being the better part of valor, scuttles to another bush.

Closer to the lake, the increasing salt content of the soil alters the texture of the crust. Instead of being flat and webbed with wrinkles, the soil looks like an endless pan of rising biscuits. On top of the hand-size domes are dime-size black lichens, and small black pebbles outline the wide cracks between in a precise tesselated floor pattern.

A slightly higher ridge, stalked with greasewood, divides the flat from an apron of soft, damp ground that borders the lake. John Charles Frémont first collected greasewood and John Torrey named it *Fremontia vermiculatus* until he found that the genus had already been named *Sarcobatus*. Fresh leaves cluster on stems accented with spiny white twigs. Cottony webs infest every plant, the insect occupants departed, leaving gray-green frass and bent, curled leaves inside its filmy walls.

Its succulent leaves become shorter and thicker with an increase in chloride salts. Greasewood bushes look like a Van Gogh drawing, the short curving strokes of the leaves identical with his splayed pen strokes, curling upward in repeated, restless patterns. A windrow of small snail shells, most of them broken, leaves a wavering white line across the ground, hesitant movers unable to outpace the slow expansion of the lake.

White salts blotch the apron of the lake, and in it dozens of young plants of inkweed flourish. Mormon-tea plants, in full yellow-coned bloom behind me, here stand dead and gray, replaced by the halophytes. A faint fishy odor carries on the wind. My sneakers sink in a salty soft muck embedded with dark pebbles. Countless small insects—small reddish wasps, ladybugs, small metallic beetles and numerous flies—lie caught in the death trap of a band of sticky surface silt. Crimped ridges of salt, an inch high, all point toward the lake. Ahead, the surface shines with a lavender cast, covered with what look like fish bones. When I reach them, the "bones" turn out to be spikes and slivers of salt, some three or four inches long. The mauve coating on which they lie is but a thin crust over a cardboard-thick sandy layer, and beneath that, wet wet, black black, muck with a rank smell to match.

Where I step, my sneaker sinks deep, and a foot away the soil bubbles and hisses. My weight is enough to unequalize this saturated soil and set it burbling and hiccuping. I mince, trying to keep from slipping in this alive terrain. An insinuating clamminess warns me that I am sinking deeper and deeper and I finally retreat, clomping out with Frankenstein boots carrying ten pounds of adhesive gray silt on each foot. When my sneakers dry, they look as if I've had

GREASEWOOD
(*Sarcobatus vermiculatus*)

them bronzed, and the laces so starched with salt that even when they're untied they look tied.

Taking a different route back, I cross terrain padded with plant tussocks. Inkweed headstones mark long raised hummocks that look like graves, bedecked with salt crystals catching the light in a flashing, blinding whiteness. Beyond, domes, from the size of a quarter to a dinner plate, spot the flat. Curious, thinking they have formed over rocks, I pry one open. The top layer lifts like a pillbox lid, lined in a rusty color, and covers a small hollow floored with silky gray-green silt. Curious, I peel up the covering of one of the foot-wide ones. This top comes off like a half-inch-thick blanket, striped with distinct layers of green algae and gray-green silt. The air inside is very warm, sun-heated enough to expand the entrapped air and to elevate this layered dome. The floor is again wet silt with the cool consistency of cold cream.

Across the way a little snowy plover, white-breasted, with a silt-colored back, pokes around for brine flies. A summer resident, it is so tiny and matches its background so perfectly that for a moment I see only its dark bill, probing away in the saline flat. In this shadeless, inhospitable flat, the female scrapes a shallow nest in which to raise her young. On very hot days, the brooding parent often stands above the eggs and shades them, or wets its breast for evaporative cooling. Despite its adherence to this saline habitat, the snowy plover has no kidney adaptations for drinking saline water or salt glands for getting rid of salt.

Black flies and mosquitoes blacken my clothing and bite every exposed bit of flesh, ravenous; on this deserted flat they must be ecstatic to find all that easily perforated skin. They attack my eyes, my ears, my hands, my face, until I look like the last stages of chicken pox, and should a phrenologist do my head, he would declare me either a phenomenal genius or a raving idiot by the number of welts I carry. Hoping to escape their depredations, I camp as far upslope as possible on an outlying ridge of the Confusion Mountains. From the rise, I look down over Tule Valley to the phalanx of the House Mountains, marked by the severe north flank of Notch Peak. Beneath me the land rolls down to the salt flat, an amorphous white blur in the valley. Over it forms an immense cloud, a-stab with lightning, single-streak bolts that jab like javelins into the earth. The mountains behind the storm have turned a deeper blue gray while the House Range to the south remains in the sun, revealing all its rocky colors and shapes.

A rainbow drops out of the cloud, reaching from flat to above the mountains, or perhaps it rises out of the lake bed. I would be hard put to tell. Transparent, it stripes the mountains behind with thin orange, thin green, thin lavender. It evaporates as I watch, clarifying the mountains, reverting the multicolored flat to ash again. Just a barely perceptible ruddy vertical band remains on the mountain and then it too is gone. The sky dries up, the late sun comes out.

I go for a walk down a dirt track that might have been threaded across the desert yesterday or a hundred years ago, so enduring are these scars. The wind is vociferous, plastering my clothes to me, sounding like waves running down the beach hissing and crashing. In this landscape no vegetation is taller than I and the knowledge brings on an odd sense of freedom.

Horned larks trill and twitter; late sun warms the deep orange mallows and picks up a single yellow ragwort. Ricegrass is in full leaf, different from the way I usually see it, as a dried bunchgrass with zigzaggy filaments holding seeds in diaphanous heads. This evening the flower heads are still ensheathed, enclosed in the stem. Lovely small plants of fleabane, narrow white rays and neat yellow centers, lurk under shrubs. My eye is caught by a fresh wet spot in the road with a large amount of black scat near it, the spoor of an animal with which I am not familiar.

Band-winged grasshoppers jet into the air, red wings bright. I follow their arcs but seldom spot them on the ground, for their gaudy wings fold beneath wing covers that are the same indeterminate color as the soil. They crepitate as they fly, making a smart clacking clatter, the only family of grasshoppers that does so. The Indians sold a tasty candy to Frémont's men, which they much enjoyed until they discovered bits of wings and heads and legs in what was, in truth, a gummy grasshopper divinity.

PRONGHORN
(*Antilocapra americana*)

While trying to find where one landed I step back from an orange-and-black velvet ant that prowls the hardpan. Every time it stops, it quivers its abdomen and I back away another few inches. It tracks beneath a huge locoweed, full of red-splotched inflated pods, that spreads across the road. The small lavender flowers are worked by bees and ants and many ladybugs. I get on my knees to watch. Underneath, pulling and chewing on a storksbill leaf, is the most stalwart black darkling beetle I have ever seen, an inch and a quarter long, as are its stiltlike legs.

Engrossed in watching the beetle, I feel a pounding through the ground that snaps my head up. A pronghorn antelope bounds across the road ahead of me on spring-loaded legs. I scramble to my feet to watch it bounding down the slope, surprised at its smallness but not its fleetness—there are reports of pronghorns being able to maintain fifty-five miles per hour for fifteen minutes. At two hundred yards it stops and turns toward me. It looks in my direction for a moment, then leaps away again, stops and wanders across the slope, pulling at the spring herbs as it goes. At least a quarter mile away, its white rump is clearly visible. The erectile white hairs serve as a signal, either to attract and lead a predator away from a young pronghorn, or as a flock danger signal. Pronghorns need these open lands that remain free of snow for running and for grazing.

There is no mistaking a pronghorn, with its short dark horns, roan back, big white patches on the flank, and its white rump patch. A single, strictly North American species, they have hollow horns around which a new sheath grows each year, developing in time for rutting season. Because pronghorns are more likely to travel in groups, I am curious about this single male; was it one that was vanquished by a more powerful male and has not made contact with its group again?

When I reach where it crossed the road, its double-teardrop tracks are clear in the dirt along with more urine-dampened sand and copious scat. By this time, the wind is down, the biters and drillers are up. Pulling my collar up over the nape of my neck and continually swatting, for the first time in recorded history I am sorry to see the wind go. It is still very light as I walk back to camp, but someone turned the moon on in a Botticelli blue-and-pink sky. The horned larks have stopped singing and the crickets converse between the rocks, talking of long days and warm summer evenings.

Down the slope, in a patch of tall grass, a long-billed curlew stalks, a breathtakingly lovely bird with an elegantly curved bill, probing for insects. I watch it move with measured tread, until it finally disappears behind a screen of sagebrush.

In the morning I discover that I have hosted numerous six-leggers who have filtered under my ground cloth: a long-legged spider of incredible speed; numerous tiny, dark-brown, shiny beetles, whom I examine and draw but despair of ever identifying; a darkling beetle of pterodactyl proportions. I feel no breeze, yet the cheatgrass shivers. With warmth and sunlight come the first flight of black flies, leaving shot-down ones in my hand to be examined, tiny transparent-winged rockets of misery.

I make my usual inventory of what toppled into my water cup

last night: an orange-and-black, narrow, wiggly rove beetle, its short elytra leaving most of the abdominal segments showing; a minute black-and-gray beetle; a fly with white-knobbed halteres (the stalklike governors attached to the thorax just behind the front wings that make possible stable two-winged flight), a dark dot on the front edge of its wing, and a humped thorax, is one of the blessed nonbiters. Once out of the water it revives and stumbles over my knuckle. Motes of dust float on the water's surface, but when they are spread out on my hand and dry, they separate into minutiae that crawl away, the unidentifiable meek of the earth.

Behind camp a ridge steps up in a series of small rocky-capped peaks, ballasted by sloping fingers rooting it into the valley below. Flowering plants increase, tucked into rock cracks, growing in shadows, always in places where a little water gathers—death lilies, vivid blue larkspur, blue flax, white phlox, lavender thistles, yellow daisies, a veritable rock garden. The country rock is nearly black, lined with white quartz, which makes individual chunks appear to be tied up with white string like little surprise packages. I trudge across the slope, sometimes on solid rock, sometimes on scree, heading south. The Utah junipers display berries as big as marbles. A stiff breeze gusts. Clouds tack across the sky.

A rock wren chirrups an intermittent commentary. A friendly wind skips by and twines through the rocks. Some of the rock is abrasive, dolomitic, with sharp edges, eaten with circles and dots and disks and shallow solution holes, beset by juniper roots. There are little shallow caves all along, and in them there is often scat, but not a sign of what I expected, a wood rat's nest. I've stowed manuscript in my day pack to work on as I sit in this beneficent solitude, but I am quite content not to do anything except look and be cooled by the wind, dissolved by the rain, and grown over by a juniper of infinite character and wisdom. A jumping spider comes up my sleeve, catapults into my backpack. I don't have to be anywhere until dark. Not since childhood have I felt a day so unstructured, so unprescribed, and when my conscience stops nagging me to go to work, I give my mind permission to go play, and contemplate it contemplating what mischief it might get into—use clouds as stepping-stones? play tiddlywinks with the flat shadows?

While my mind is off playing on the wind, I operate in total lethargy, somewhere half past peace and a third beyond lazy. My biggest task is to watch the cloud shadows define the ridges. When the sun is full out they're all the same color, and difficult to differentiate. Now a cloud shadow falls on one, then another, separating them in depth, showing off the contours.

Here on this ridge Tule Valley stretches in full view, north to south. The valley sags like a hammock, brownish-green, streaked and marbled with chalky patches, with the broad white streak of a salt flat down the middle. Mountains bound the whole east side, one after the other. The mountains have so much sky above them that they are not barricades but adornments: they exist only to create valleys.

Dust devils rise off the lake bed, smoke upward and disappear. Any obstacle that interrupts the wind's flow can start it swirling and spinning. As it rises a dust devil forms a vacuum into which more air rushes, fueling itself with velocities of up to fifty miles per hour within its cone. Several wander off across the playa, blithe spirits of the desert. The Gosiute Indians believed that they themselves came from these windblown dusts and that their ancestors' spirits were embodied in these whirlwinds. The wind orchestrates the dust devils that sweep up the seeds that salt the playa that grow in the desert that bloom in the spring. The soil rolls up heat I can smell, and through it, wisps of sagebrush perfume the air.

22

OF DUST LAKES
AND GLOWWORMS

At the Nevada–Utah border, Terry Tempest Williams and I, on our way east to Simpson Springs, pick up the route that Jedediah Smith followed 160 years ago to the month—June—on his return from California in 1827. The desert looks as if a dust storm has just passed, laying a pall over soil and plant and rock, reducing the landscape to a single monotonous tonality, faded to an ashen sameness, a colorless common denominator. Even the cloudless sky looks dusty.

With few birds, no visible animals, the landscape stretches sterile, as if the dust that lies everywhere has damped all movement, all life. Except for huge Mephistophelean grasshoppers with their startling red-orange wings making high-arced leaps across the desert, nothing moves. Against the leached-out soil, a swath of foxtail grass looks preternaturally green.

Immense ripples, up to five hundred feet wide and three feet high, gouged out by waves in the shallow lake bed of Lake Bonneville, make a roller-coaster ride. The familiar "biscuit" puffiness of the alkali surface may look soft but is hard as a rock. We see the same chalky, dust-in-the-throat landscape as Horace Greeley who judged that if "Uncle Sam should ever sell that tract for one cent per acre, he will swindle the purchaser outrageously."

Where Smith's route swings north, we keep east on the road established by Lieutenant James Simpson, who found Simpson Springs (he named it Pleasant Spring) while exploring for a more southerly route west, one that would avoid the Great Salt Lake Desert and shorten the journey. The route he laid out became the Pony Express route as well as the Lincoln Highway. Although shorter, the route is such a long stretch without water that transcontinental travel still crosses the Great Salt Desert to the north. It is indicative of the desolation of the countryside that it was abandoned as a major highway.

After endless miles of desert on Simpson's road, such a fine dust coats me that it feels uncomfortably part of my skin, clogging my pores and, when I move, emanating from me like a cloud. The powdery dust has its own personality and creates us in its image. I illustrate Mark Twain's description of his fellow stagecoach passengers as being "so deeply coated with ashes that they are all one colorless color."

We reach Simpson Springs after dark. A brisk wind stirs up the hillside and kicks dust in my face when I spread out my sleeping bag. About three in the morning moonrise washes out the stars, illuminating a bird's-nest web of clouds wreathed all around the horizon. A mockingbird sings all night. James Clyman, crossing the Utah desert in 1846, remembered that "long before day was visibele a small Bird of the mocking bird kind was heard to cheer us with his many noted Song an this is the only singing Bird that I have heard for the last 10 days." Terry counts twenty-one different songs.

We slept on the high gravelly slope that marks the "Provo stage" of Lake Bonneville, which inundated this area from Idaho to southern

Utah, coinciding with the last stage of Pleistocene glaciation. This morning, where we stand on the epitome of arid, would then have been awash.

Shortly after 14,260 years ago, when Lake Bonneville was at its highest elevation, it breached a natural alluvial dam at Red Rock Pass in southern Idaho and spewed north into the Snake River drainage. After the break, it has been calculated that the lake fell 10 feet in four days, and for six weeks spewed northward at an estimated massive maximum discharge of some 15 million cubic feet per second, dropping a total of 350 feet. The lake's descent was so rapid that it left no record between the higher Bonneville and the lower Provo shoreline.

The Provo level, kept stable by drainage to the north, persisted at 4,800 feet until some eight thousand years ago. Its prominent shoreline scribes the mountainsides because the lake remained at this level long enough to cut definite features, especially on the east side of the basin. The shoreline is not level, having been upwarped in places because of isostatic unloading—the relieving of the massive weight of water that allowed parts of the lake bed to bend upward.

With the warming and drying climate at the end of the Pleistocene, the lake dropped below its outlet. A change in weather patterns occurred that endures today: the uniform cooling of the sea surface, and the southward movement of atmospheric circulation in the Northern Hemisphere, brought more frontal storms during winter months. Evaporation began to exceed precipitation and inflow. The terminal lake of Lake Bonneville is the Great Salt Lake, its surface some thousand feet lower than its predecessor's at its greatest extent, its waters vastly saltier.

Small white snail shells litter the ground and crunch underfoot, their turreted shapes identifying them as *Lymnaea,* a common genus in lake sediments. Shelves of tufa mark the shoreline and tell of wave action. Grayish-white marl outcrops, calcium carbonate mixed with soil, crumble in my fingers.

I hike up another three hundred feet plus to the highest shoreline of Lake Bonneville, cutting across rough slopes gutted with chutes gouged out by swift erosion. The last fifty feet are hard going, complicated by large boulders interlarded with rolling cobbles. When I finally gain the old demarcation between earth and water, I am breathless and sweating. I scan a cavernous lake bed, an emptiness that stretches the mind's capacity to understand that this was, not too long ago, all water, sparkling, dancing blue, scintillating water, full of fins and fluted shells, creatures scaled and valved, fluttering and snapping and filtering.

I gaze out over the basin below, blanched and simmering in the heat and, in the pulsing of the wind, hear the sound of waves whooshing on shore, the antithesis of desert. Thousands of years ago water would have lapped at my toes and the boulder on which I sit would have gleamed with moisture and crawled with small snails rasping up algae.

Those insolent, isolated mountains in the distance were once underwater anchors for scrabblers and silvery swimmers. Those huge roller-coaster corrugations on the desert floor were scooped out by waves that sloshed like water in a dishpan. The oversize emptiness is that extra emptiness of place where there was once a productive, animate something else. Lake Bonneville evaporated and left a legacy of salt and silence: the ultimate desert.

The flat below Table Mountain, about seven miles south of Simpson Springs, unfolds desolate, burned over two years ago. "Flat" is a euphemism for a hummocky, burrow-ridden, warted, lumpy, bossed terrain, riddled with animal holes and pimpled with plants.

The animals that go here leave their signatures on the flora: edges torn ragged by deer, which have no incisors; edges clean from the sharp incisors of jackrabbits. Seven jackrabbits, despite their smaller size, make as much impact as one sheep because they leave so much cut foliage on the ground uneaten.

Three large openings to a kit fox's den gape a few feet apart, open to the sun, undoubtedly interconnected underground. A five-foot pile of fresh dirt surrounds one opening. At the door of an abandoned den, cracks furrow the dirt and spiderwebs festoon the opening. Dens are probably deserted when the flea population in one becomes too troublesome. Present in every desert, kit foxes, along with coyotes and vultures, are efficient scavengers. With their large ears and inquisitive faces, they epitomize the open country of all our deserts, where there is an abundance of nocturnal rodents. Their range closely coincides with that of the kangaroo rats that furnish their main prey.

Scattered droppings, largely wads of rabbit's hair, surround the opening of the active nest. Horned larks, as well as kangaroo rats and Townsend ground squirrels, serve as prime food for Great Basin kit foxes. Nearly all the adult Townsend ground squirrel females, and the majority of yearling females, produce a litter annually, a reproductive imperative keyed to the insecurity of the desert. Townsend ground squirrels are basic rodents, a head, body, four legs, a modest tail, all an undistinguished gray, the simplest common denominator of little scurrying mammals that, by the thousand, are the herbivores that fuel the next level of consumers.

Reproduction depends on fresh grass in the spring, which ultimately depends on rainfall during the preceding six months. If greens are not available, females do not come into breeding condition and reproduction is suspended. What food there is, is converted into fat stores for hibernation rather than into ovum production. This quick-response reproductive strategy produces abrupt swings in population density and makes possible survival in the desert, especially here in the Great Basin, where annual rainfall is as varied and scattered as it is in any region of the United States.

Foxes, generally one kit fox per two square miles here, often take ground squirrels by plugging up holes in the colony and closing the escape hatches, then digging out the prey. They also often rework ground-squirrel areas. Given the number of predators focusing on ground squirrels, their breeding capacity has to be high.

Kit foxes also dote on the two species of kangaroo rats that are prevalent here. One species, Ord's kangaroo rat, lives in sand. The other, the Great Basin kangaroo rat, inhabits loamy clay soil. Both eat greasewood, but they apportion the plant by eating different parts.

A small hole, rimmed with three feet of dirt in which long claw marks are evident, was likely bored by a badger digging after a ground squirrel, of which it needs to eat an average of one or two per day to survive. The major part of badger diet is the ubiquitous Townsend ground squirrel, which it literally mines with its massive claws.

A short distance away are two large holes, unmistakably badger holes. To my amazement, for badgers are largely nocturnal, I watch the occupant's black-and-white muzzle appear, then the whole big, healthy-looking animal. Its dusty coat ripples like a bear's shag as it slouches across the ground, from one hole to the other and back again, an unusual midday treat.

The thermometer in the shade of my pack indicates 98 degrees F. but this mid-June afternoon feels more like 198. The landscape is like a huge kiln, well fired up. The heat envelops me, permeates me with lassitude. Angel-wing clouds give no respite. I can scarcely talk my mouth is so dry. There is no shade, no refuge. I feel bereft of decision-making capacity. I stumble a lot when I walk, cursing the ill-placed rocks that humble my pace.

Back at Simpson Springs I stop at the shoulder-high water faucet to fill my empty canteen. A wavering silvery column of water splashes coolly on the cement pad beneath the pump. Without thinking I lean forward, put my head under the faucet, and let the life-saving cold water drench and soothe my overheated head and experience the restorative effects of cool water applied directly to the brain.

Never in my whole life have I been so thankful for cool water. No wonder Mr. Chorpenning, who had the overland mail contract a century ago, rushed out here to see Simpson's newly discovered spring, the spring that made possible a desert crossing by providing a place for Pony Express and wagon trains to stop. Here travelers could refresh before continuing to the next spring, fifty long, dust-coating, seat-numbing, eye-stinging, woolly-mouthed miles away.

In the evening Terry suggests walking up a canyon where, earlier in the day, she had heard a great horned owl. She carries a small tape recorder with owl calls, which echo softly off the rocks.

Sitting quietly in the darkness, waiting for an owl rejoinder that never comes, I perceive a tiny glow. In the dark I work my way toward it and find a pinkish glowworm, cashew nut–shaped, clustered with three other insects. In the dim light, I cannot tell if they are winged male glowworms mating with her (the female glowworm mates while in the larval stage) or predators feeding upon her—luminescence is not used to attract the opposite sex, and may provide some protection against predators. Another glowworm gleams faintly, twenty feet farther up the canyon, a comma of light.

The female never goes through metamorphosis to set out on six spindly beetle legs, never feels the pull of wing on thorax, never hunts her meal under a desert moon, never senses the world through probing antennae. She just remains a pudgy pink glowworm, a cold, curled-up light in a deep desert canyon, eternally luminescent and eternally adolescent.

23

OF SPADEFOOT TOADS
AND TWILIGHT

I kick a bootful of snow into the air. On this January day in the Great Salt Desert, the snow falls like a fine, soundless, glittering shower of fireworks. There are no horizons, only thick fog, wrapped like an ermine cape across the shoulders of the land.

All the way down the hill, the snow glistens, paved with ice crystals that rise an inch long and half an inch wide, stacked above the surface like feathers. They are hexagonal structures, striped with clear white lines. I run my hand across the surface and hear a subdued wind-chimes tinkle. Terry Williams says they sound like African thumb pianos. She calls them *Qulu,* an Eskimo term that defines the precise conditions necessary to produce such a magic display of ice crystals.

The temperature is 19 degrees F. The only world that exists is the world at my fingertips, fine and brittle, a vast silence of freezing,

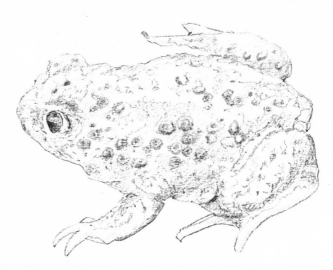

GREAT BASIN SPADEFOOT TOAD
(*Scaphiopus intermontanus*)

swirling mist. The tallest objects in view are the dried sunflower and
ragwort stalks leaning awry like untended fence posts. I cannot see
the springs just down the hill where the Donner party stopped on its
fateful way to California, although Peter Hovingh, who knows the
Great Basin from mountain to floor, assures me they are there.

Ice is everywhere. A glaze of white, breathed over the landscape, coats the ground thatch and branches. The sun blazes behind
the clouds. Then the mists lighten, outlines clear, shapes begin to
gain edges. As the day brightens, colors emerge—an umber stubble
in the field, silvery weathered wooden fence posts strung with
platinum barbed wire, greasewood frosted silver.

Vapors steam off a series of warm springs set in a cold meadow.
Frost bedazzles the plants rimming the pools and puddles with a
quarter-inch covering of crystals. Even as I watch, the crisp points
lose their sharpness. A prairie falcon hunts, the only movement in
the landscape. In the still, steely coldness of this day, it is an act of
faith to imagine this spring resonating with a chorus of spadefoot
toads.

In just a couple of months Great Basin spadefoot toads will
breed in these ponds and springs, setting miles of the desert alive
with their hoarse chortlings after a rain, a breeding invitation that
varies with each species. Their name comes from the flange on their

hind feet with which they burrow into the soil, rotating their sturdy bodies while pushing first with one foot, then the other, digging out of sight in moments. Spadefoot toads belong to the genus *Scaphiopus,* different from the true *Bufo* toads, two of the separating differences being the digging spade and vertical pupils. Most spadefoot toads are keyed to temporary pools and puddles. Great Basin spadefoots, breeding in these more or less permanent springs, are the exception, responding to temperature more than rain.

I walk the edge of the steaming pond, imagining them enduring this crystalline winter. Burrowing enables them to endure a season of both cold and desiccation safely underground. While hibernating, they can store almost a third of their body weight as diluted urine to forestall water loss through their skin to the surrounding soil as the soil dries. Some species may even form impervious cocoons of mud around themselves to reduce desiccation. For nine to ten months they survive without any food, locked away in a Stygian subterranean darkness, metabolic activities reduced to a barely detectable level, mere nuggets of life.

A heavy rain with air temperatures above 52 degrees F. stimulates the magic of the toads' rapid emergence, a breaking through into fresh air, even though they may continue to return to a damp burrow during the day. The incessant calling of a group of male spadefoots attains an amazing volume of sound that buckles up the night air. Male calling attracts the females—males hold onto the slippery-skinned females by their embossed front fingers—and there is an orgy of mating the likes of which hasn't been seen since ancient Rome.

Along with red-spotted toads, the spadefoot's egg and larval development is among the fastest of the amphibians. Eggs hatch in two days (a frog's take a week). In nature's nicety of timing, the nourishment of the egg is gone by the time the mouth parts of the tadpole develop, and the tadpole is able to feed on its own.

In my mind's ear I remember countless pools on countless spring backpack trips into the canyons, little wigglers sometimes scattered, sometimes clustered in dense groups. Toward the end of their water period the tadpoles often aggregate in bundles, an activity apparently thermally controlled. Such aggregation not only increases their body temperatures and their metabolism, but warms the surrounding water, increasing the growth of that upon which they feed. The presence of dead tadpoles in the pools stimulates the growth rate of those remaining. In some species, the tadpoles are both carnivorous and herbivorous, with mouthparts formed accordingly. The carnivorous ones attack and eat their siblings should food become scarce, assuring that at least some will survive, and those cannibalized contribute to the survival of the species.

Scaphiopus tadpoles usually leave the water while their tadpole tails are still attached. They slither out of the pool and complete their metamorphosis, a rapid process that prepares the little swimmer for life on land as a toad in just a few hours. This sudden change in environment demands a whole new behavior. The danger of desiccation with a large surface-to-volume ratio is great and commits them to a nocturnal existence, although they can withstand the highest temperature of all desert amphibians known. On this frigid morning I think of them safely below ground, withstanding the winter buried deep in the mud. I hope their feet are warmer than mine.

Not until early summer do I see the Great Salt Desert west of Salt Lake City again, and the contrast could not be more marked. The clear, crimped edges of mountains define the horizons. Lenticular clouds hang, sheared by high-altitude, high-velocity winds. The sun consumes the sky and there are no shadows. Salt deposits scroll graceful white cartouches on the greige soil. The soil tones are infinitely subtle, a grisaille surface marbled and delicately filigreed with lines of light blue gray, dazzling, and lifeless, but no less dazzling for being so lifeless.

The small hummocks formed around plants look like drops of turpentine dripped on paint, spreading out from the center in furry circles. Thin sandy triangles stream out behind plant hummocks where they've tripped up the wind. Sometimes the placement of hummocks and plants is as regular as pawns on a chessboard. No perennial herbs grow between them although there is an invisible

292

but rich component of blue-green algae hidden underneath the surface.

Alkali powders my boots as the ground whitens into the center of the desert. The soil becomes progressively saltier, until no plants grow at all and light reflects off the surface in a blinding, coruscating, eye-wearing glare that renders sunglasses useless. Ridges reticulate the surface in hexagonal patterns and then disappear, leaving a covering only lightly puckered, interspersed with patches as smooth as white glass. The intermittent flooding and evaporation of the salt flats during uncounted millennia in the past spread forth these innumerable layers of salt. With the retreat of the lake's waters, peripheral land, freed of the weight of the water, rose as much as two hundred feet, leaving a threshold blocking further incursions of water from the Great Salt Lake, preserving a level dry surface, today batiked with blue cloud shadows.

When the normal spring runoff that coats the lake evaporates, it pulls up fresh salts from below and repaves the flats, making them (reputedly) the world's best racecourse for cars and bicycles attempting to set speed records. Captain Howard Stansbury, surveying the Great Salt Lake in 1849, saw this vast expanse as extraneous to man or beast, useful only to "furnish a desirable space on which to measure a degree of the meridian."

Were it not for the dirt roads taking off across the countryside, Terry and I would be seeing the Great Salt Desert as John Charles Frémont saw it on his way to climb and name Pilot Peak in 1843. By the time we reach the Silver Island Range, the aesthetic and homogeneous simplicity of the salt desert disappears. Pointillist shrubs, russets and dark grays, outline ridges or follow drainage lines. The bare ground darkens, a nondescript acier, achromatic. Muckledun. A loggerhead shrike streaks above the flat and drops a lizard.

Terry and I scan the hillsides for Danger Cave. This desolate country, with a scant four and a half inches of annual rainfall, was home to a prehistoric people who occupied caves in the rocky outcrops bordering a long-departed arm of Lake Bonneville. Because of the excavations done in it, and the proposition of a Desert

Culture life-style that came out of it, Danger Cave is one of the best known of the many that dotted the lake edge. Such caves served not as permanent residences but temporary sites, utilized by archaic peoples on their never-ending rounds of hunting and gathering and fishing. Like nearly all archaeological sites of the Great Basin, they lay on the borders of the great Pleistocene lakes.

The people who came and went under these overhangs came up from the valleys carrying their nets and baskets, digging sticks, and chipping tools, fashioning more when needed, finding and taking sustenance when it was seasonally available, with an extensive tribal knowledge of what ripened where and when, utilizing different sites for different activities. They developed no permanent base camps or stable food sources that had to be protected, and therefore developed no talent for war.

We spot a dark gaping hole at the top of a limestone fault scarp and scramble up a steep slope covered with extremely unstable and coarse limestone rocks. The ascent is slippery and treacherous, our effort justified only because of the shadowy cave we want to see.

Hoisting ourselves up the last few feet we enter a broad portal. Angular chunks of black rock veined with white quartz litter its threshold. Inside, the cave extends back to a fire-blackened roof. When I turn and face outward to the west, the view opens to the flats below, and beyond to a fringe of mountains. A single black obsidian chip and an exquisite jaw and leg bone of a tiny mouse lodge in the powdery silt at my feet. Red-tailed hawks and prairie falcons wheel by at eye level. Out of sight a rock wren twitters, then materializes at the lip of the cave, walks about and pokes and putters, tail cocked all the while, for two long bird-watching minutes.

I sit cross-legged at the entrance, looking past the present with ancient eyes, collating the knowledge I have of this century with that of five centuries past. Anthropologist Robert Elston grouped the time sequence of the long-gone people into "good times/hard times" to explain the appearance of various artifacts and the changes in diet and harvesting. In wet times, with more fish and game, more grass, food was easier to come by, and the closer to the top of the food chain it was possible to live. When populations were small during good times, pre-archaic life was very good. But, during bad times of warmer and drier intervals, there was less fresh water, fewer grasses and more scrub, resources were sparser and more widely distributed, making them more difficult to gather and process.

When times were bad and populations were high, life was poor to desperate. But *these* were the times of innovation, invention, and change. Prehistoric people then increased the variety of plants and animals utilized, as well as made more intense use of what was already available; they developed newer and better means of processing and preparing food. Out of these periods of stress came innovation and advances in technology, such as new techniques in basketmaking and harvesting methods. I, twentieth-century woman, sit here, nestled in the silt of centuries, holding the minute thigh bone of a mouse, and find this thought incredibly reassuring.

(Terry finds out some months later that the cave we found was not Danger Cave, close by, lower, but so nearly closed by backfill that we missed seeing it. Instead we had found an unnamed cave just around the corner, commanding a glorious view of the landscape below. Its openness and the sense of being relatively unscathed gave us both a feel of time and place and people that Danger Cave, heavily excavated, churned up, and soiled with graffiti, can no longer convey. We decide that we were blessed with one of those serendipitous occasions: when you get lost, you always discover something better than what you set out to find.)

In the north end of the cave a shaft of light strikes the wall, poured through a high chimney. A four-foot-wide passageway with limestone walls, narrowing to nothing, leads to the base of the chimney. Light from the opening slides across white stains on the upper walls. Trying to peer up the opening to see the sky forces me to push my hand flat against the wall to keep my balance. When I look away from the confined slot of blue and focus on the wall where my hand is, I see afterimages of glowing color and import. I have a visceral sense of knowing something I didn't know before, a recognition of a human presence that is so ephemeral that it may evaporate in the desert wind but nevertheless stains the stone and walks in our footsteps.

I return to the clamshell opening and look out over the desert. In my mind's eye I travel back to other times and other deserts, and the images come through with unbelievable fidelity and clarity: a heavy-bodied grasshopper struggling up a thick agave leaf, a silken playa lapped with velvet water, the grace of bighorn sheep and the playfulness of desert cottontails in a dry wash, ice chests full of desert aromas that translated into drawings on a page, so many sibilant sand dunes with their odalisque curves, a young kangaroo rat struck dead by a rattlesnake, gleaming desert pavements laid with lacquered stones, tiny fish fenced and measured and locked up, little Buddha-like red-spotted toads bleating piteously in the night, me discommoding a scorpion, a rattlesnake discommoding me, the eternal search for three atoms—two hydrogen and one oxygen.

Insights into this beautifully attuned world to which I am not adapted makes the adjustments of those that hop and stalk, scurry and slither in the deserts objects of admiration and respect: a kangaroo rat and a black-throated sparrow that can live well without free water; specialized toads that dream away the bad times underground; minute kangaroo mice that prolong their lives by periods of torpor; canyon wrens that adjust their clutch size to the available food. I think of all the fossorial animals that escape the desert heat underground, of physiological adjustments of blood and urine, hearing and seeing, of adaptations in behavior that make life in the desert not only possible but possible with zest, qualities seen and unseen that spell not only survival, but survival with vigor. I think of plants that can withstand salt and those that cannot, and their different modes of photosynthesis. I number the ingenious seeds that germinate under precise regimes, and their measured sequences, time to remain dormant, time to sprout, time to flower and set seed, and time to dazzle the desert. These deserts are full of good health and good spirits, and a heat that locks in the marrow against the cold and lightless winters.

Looking out over this desert, which has exacted its own tributes of this slow-boned human, remembrances come crowding to my mind of the gifts these desert years have laid on my doorstep, a mosaic of experiences made up of sprigs of creosote bush and sagebrush, an owl feather and a grasshopper wing, a chip of obsidian, all tied up with the song of a spadefoot toad, my own medicine bundle for my own ceremonies of passage.

If there were but one memory I could take away with me—I squint against the sky, thinking, knowing I don't really have to think because it was the answer that instigated the question—it is the talisman I shall have always: an afternoon with a small black-tailed gnatcatcher who so trusted this outlandish earthbound creature that we napped on a torrid desert afternoon, within a wing's reach of each other's dreams.

To the west a single thin cloud poises over the evening mountains, a molten spear illuminated from beneath, a Vasa Murrhina cloud. The only cloud, alone in the sky, it incandesces as I watch, the curve of a bow arcing between two distant points. Then it fades. The ends still glow while the middle darkens to match the mountains beneath. The relationship shifts: the cloud, like a spear thrown from an atlatl, flies to the next mass of mountain, burying its head in the mountain flank.

The sky behind the mountains segues to a pale steely blue, without warmth, bending upward to dusk. Where the sun has departed, the sky bleaches. Dust spirits sleep. The wind abides. Silence streams from the mountains. Black feathers of darkness drift downward.

The desert comes alive.

NOTES

ABBREVIATIONS

PERIODICALS

American Journal of Botany	*Amer. J. Botan.*
American Journal of Physiology	*Amer. J. Physiol.*
American Midland Naturalist	*Amer. Midl. Nat.*
American Naturalist	*Amer. Nat.*
Arizona Highways	*Ariz. Highw.*
BioScience	*BioSci.*
Botanical Gazette	*Botan. Gaz.*
Botanical Review	*Botan. Rev.*
California Historical Society Quarterly	*Calif. Hist. Soc. Quart.*
Chihuahuan Desert Discovery	*Chih. Dsrt. Disc.*
Desert Plants	*Dsrt. Plnts.*
Ecology	*Ecol.*

Ecological Monograph	*Ecol. Monogr.*
Evolution	*Evol.*
Geological Society of America Bulletin	*Geol. Soc. Amer. Bull.*
Great Basin Naturalist	*Great Basin Nat.*
Great Basin Naturalist Memoirs	*Great Basin Nat. Mem.*
Herpetologica	*Herpt.*
Journal of Arachnology	*J. Arach.*
Journal of Arid Environments	*J. Arid Envir.*
Journal of the Arizona Academy of Sciences	*J. Ariz. Acad. Sci.*
Journal of Ecology	*J. Ecol.*
Journal of Geology	*J. Geol.*
Journal of Mammology	*J. Mamm.*
Journal of Wildlife Management	*J. Wildlf. Manag.*
Nature Conservancy Magazine	*Nat. Conserv. Mag.*
Northern Nevada Native Plant Society Newsletter	*NNNPS Newsl.*
Oecologica	*Oecol.*
Proceedings of the California Academy of Sciences	*Proc. Calif. Acad. Sci.*
Science	*Sci.*
Scientific American	*Sci. Amer.*
Scientific Monthly	*Sci. Mon.*
Senate Miscellaneous Documents	*Sen. Misc. Docs.*
Southwestern Naturalist	*Southw. Nat.*
University of California Publications in Zoology	*Univ. Calif. Publ. Zool.*

BOOKS

Arid-Land Ecosystems	*Arid-Land Ecosys.*
Arid Lands Today and Tomorrow	*Arid Lands*
The Big Bend of the Rio Grande	*Big Bend*
Birds of the Great Basin	*Birds*
Transactions of the Symposium of the Biological Resources of the Chihuahuan Desert Region, United States and Mexico	*Chih. Dsrt. Reg.*
Comparative Biochemical Physiology	*Comp. Biochem. Phys.*
Comparative Physiology of Desert Animals	*Comp. Physiol. Dsrt. Anml.*
Convergent Evolution in Warm Deserts	*Conver. Evol.*

Creosote Bush. Biology and Chemistry of Larrea in New World Deserts	Creosote Bush
Deep Canyon, A Desert Wilderness for Science	Deep Cyn.
Desert Animals: Physiological Problems of Heat and Water	Dsrt. Anml.
Desert Biology	Dsrt. Biol.
Biology of Desert Invertebrates	Dsrt. Invert.
Desert Landforms	Dsrt. Landf.
A Study of Desert Surface Conditions	Dsrt. Surf. Cond.
Discovering the Desert	Discov. Dsrt.
Environmental Physiology of Desert Organisms	Envir. Phys. Dsrt. Org.
Exploring Southwestern Trails, 1846–1854, by Philip St. George Cooke, William Henry Chase Whiting, Francoix Xavier Aubry	Expl. Southw. Trails
Geomorphology in Deserts	Geomorph. Dsrts.
Great Basin Cultural Ecology	Great Basin Cult. Ecol.
A Doctor Comes to California. The Diary of John S. Griffin, Assistant Surgeon with Kearny's Dragoons	Griffin
Handbook of Physiology	Handbk. Phys.
Insects, Food and Ecology	Insects and Ecol.
Intermountain Flora. Vascular Plants of the Intermountain West, U. S. A.	Intermt. Flora
Mammals of the Southwest Deserts	Mamm. Southw. Dsrts.
The Mammals of Trans-Pecos Texas including Big Bend National Park and Guadalupe Mountains National Park	Mamm. Texas
Man and the Environment in the Great Basin	Man and Envir.
Mesquite	Mesq.
"Notes of a Military Reconnaissance, from Fort Leavenworth, in Missouri,	

to San Diego, in California," etc.	Notes
Oregon's Great Basin Country	*Oregon*
Origin and Evolution of Deserts	*Orig. Dsrts.*
Reports of Explorations and Surveys, to Ascertain the Most Practicable Route for a Railroad from the Mississippi River to the Pacific Ocean 1853–1856.	*Pac. RR Repts.*
Personal Narrative of Explorations and Incidents in Texas, New Mexico, California, Sonora, and Chihuahua	*Pers. Narr.*
The Physics of Blown Sand and Desert Dunes	*Phys. Blown Sand*
Physical Systems in Semiarid Environments	*Phys. Sys. Semiar. Envir.*
Physiological Adaptations: Desert and Mountains	*Physiol. Adapt.*
The Quaternary Geology of the United States	*Quat. Geol.*
Reference Handbook on the Deserts of North America	*Ref. Handbk. Dsrts.*
Riparian Ecosystems and Their Management	*Ripar. Ecosys.*
The Sagebrush Ecosystem: A Symposium	*Sagebr. Ecosys.*
Salt Marshes and Salt Deserts	*Salt Dsrts.*
Southern Trails to California in 1849	*Southrn. Trails*
Surficial Geology of the Eastern Mojave Desert, California	*Surf. Geol. E. Moj. Dsrt.*
Temperate Deserts and Semi-Deserts	*Temp. Dsrts.*
Terrestrial Vegetation of California	*Terr. Veg.*
Threatened and Endangered Plants	*Threat. Plnts.*
U.S.G.S. Professional Paper	*USGS Prof. Pap.*

1: OF BEGINNINGS AND LECHUGUILLA

PAGE

3 Chihuahuan Desert literature in English is sparse compared to that for the other three major deserts. The broadest and most accessible collection of papers is from two symposia: Roland H. Wauer and David H. Riskind, eds., *Transactions of the Symposium on the Biological Resources of the Chihuahuan Desert Region, United States and Mexico* (Alpine, Tex.: Sul Ross State University, 1974), and Jon C. Barlow, A. Michael Powell, and Barbara N. Timmermann, eds., *Second Symposium on Resources of the Chihuahuan Desert Region* (Alpine, Tex.: Sul Ross State University and the Chihuahuan Desert Research Institute, 1986). Not defined as a biotic province until 1934, the Chihuahuan Desert was first described by Forrest Shreve, "The Desert Vegetation of North America," *Botanical Review* 8 (1942): 195–246; more recent is W. Frank Blair, "The Biotic Provinces of Texas," *Texas Journal of Science* 2(1950): 94, 102–108. Although primarily herpetological, the introduction of David J. Morafka, "A Biogeographical Analysis of the Chihuahuan Desert Through Its Herpetofauna," *Biogeographica* 9(1977): 181–85, and "Is There a Chihuahuan Desert? A Quantitative Evaluation Through a Herpetofaunal Perspective," in *Chih. Dsrt. Reg.* (1974): 437–54, is an excellent overview.

   Thorough essays on each desert appear in the definitive Gordon L. Bender, ed., *Reference Handbook on the Deserts of North America* (Westport, Conn.: Greenwood Press, 1982), including Fernando Medellin-Leal, "The Chihuahuan Desert": 321–81, who derives the euphonious word *Chihuahua* from the Tarahumara Indian word meaning "place of a workshop," a name first used in the 1840s to denote a vague southwestern region.

4 Big Bend: Roland H. Wauer, *Naturalist's Big Bend* (College Station and London: Texas A&M University Press, 1980); an interesting historical account of the area that was to become Big Bend National Park is Ernest J. Palmer, "A Botanical Trip Through the Chisos Mountains of Texas," *Journal of the Arnold Arboretum* 9(1928): 153–72.

5–6 Century plant (*Agave havardiana*) fertilization: Donna Howell, "The Bat-Agave Connection," *Chihuahuan Desert Discovery* 13(1983): 6–8, and 14(1983): 4–6; "Flock Foraging in Nectar-Feeding Bats: Advantages to the Bat and to the Host Plants," *American Naturalist* 114(1979): 23–49; "Bats and Pollen: Physiological Aspects of the Syndrome of Chiropterophily," *Comparative Biochemical Physiology* 48A(1973): 263–76; C. Edward Freeman and William H. Reid,

"Nectar Amino Acids in Four Species of *Agave* (Agavaceae)," *Southwestern Naturalist* 28(1983): 113–15; Joseph F. Kuban, John Lawley, and Robert L. Neill, "The Partitioning of Flowering Century Plants by Black-chinned and Lucifer Hummingbirds," *Southw. Nat.* 28(1983): 143. The definitive book on agaves is Howard S. Gentry, *The Agave Family in Sonora* (Washington, D.C.: U.S.D.A. Agricultural Handbook, 1972).

7   Origin of deserts: J. Rzedowski, "Geographical Relations of the Flora of Mexican Dry Regions," in *Vegetation and Vegetational History of Northern Latin America,* ed. A. Graham (Amsterdam, Neth.: Elsevier, 1973): 61–62; Ronald U. Cooke and Andrew Warren, *Geomorphology in Deserts* (Berkeley and Los Angeles: University of California Press, 1973): 32; William G. McGinnies, *Discovering the Desert* (Tucson: University of Arizona Press, 1981): 29; D. J. Morafka, "Biogeographical Analysis."

7   Origin of Chihuahuan Desert flora: Philip V. Wells, "Post-glacial Origin of the Present Chihuahuan Desert Less than 11,500 Years Ago," in *Chih. Dsrt. Reg.* (1974): 82, and "Late Pleistocene Vegetation and Degree of Pluvial Climatic Change in the Chihuahuan Desert," *Science* 153(1966): 971–73; Ronald P. Neilson, "High Resolution Climatic Analysis and Southwest Biogeography," *Science* 232(1986): 27–34, for recent atmospheric research.

No definitive flora of the Chihuahuan Desert is in print; Marshall C. Johnston "Brief Résumé of Botanical including Vegetational Features of the Chihuahuan Desert Region with Special Emphasis on Their Uniqueness," in *Chih. Dsrt. Reg.* (1974): 335–59, and A. Michael Powell, "Vegetation of Trans-Pecos Texas," *New Mexico Geological Society Guidebook* (31st Field Conference, Trans-Pecos Region, 1980): 299–302, provide the most current information. The best identification book for the layman is unfortunately out of print: W. B. McDougall and O. E. Sperry, *Plants of Big Bend National Park* (Washington, D.C.: U.S. Government Printing Office, 1951).

7–8   Lechuguilla (*Agave lechuguilla*): C. Edward Freeman and William H. Reid, "Aspects of the Reproductive Biology of *Agave lechuguilla* Torr.," *Desert Plants* 7(1985): 75–80.

8   Sotol (*Dasylirion leiophyllum*): Ross Maxwell, *The Big Bend of the Rio Grande* (Austin: University of Texas Bureau of Economic Geology, Guidebook 7, 1979): 99–100, and Rzedowski, "Geographical Relations": 61–72.

10   Shag or Torrey yucca (*Yucca torreyi*): The most common narrow-leaf yucca; the definitive book on yuccas is S. D. McKelvey, *Yuccas of the Southwestern United States.* 2 vols. (Jamaica Plain, Mass.: Arnold Arboretum of Harvard University, 1938–47).

10– Medicinal use of plants: William Booth, "Combing the Earth for
11 Cures to Cancer, AIDS," *Science* 237(4818) (1987): 969–70; Robert
    Mohlenbrock, "Why Should We Save Our Plants?" *The Nature Con-
    servancy Magazine* 37(5): 4–9; J. B. Callicot, "On the Intrinsic Value
    of Nonhuman Species," *The Preservation of Species: The Value of Bio-
    logical Diversity* (Princeton, N.J.: Princeton University Press, 1986):
    138–65.
11– Collared peccary (*Tayassu tajacu*): George Olin, *Mammals of the South-
12 west Deserts* (San Diego: Southwest Parks and Monuments Associa-
    tion, 1982): 4; David Schmidly, *The Mammals of Trans-Pecos Texas
    Including Big Bend National Park and Guadalupe Mountains National
    Park* (College Station: Texas A&M Press, 1977): 160–61; J. E. Ellison
    and W. F. Harwell, "Mobility and Home Range of Collared Peccary
    in Southern Texas," *Journal of Wildlife Management* 33 (1969): 425–27;
    S. M. Zervanos and N. F. Hadley, "Adaptational Biology and Energy
    Relationships of the Collared Peccary (*Tayassu tajacu*)," *Ecology* 54
    (1973): 759–60; William J. Bigler, "Seasonal Movements and Activ-
    ity Patterns of the Collared Peccary," *Journal of Mammology* 55(1974):
    851–55; Carol D. Crosswhite, "The Significance of Cacti in the Diet
    of the Javelina (*Tayassu tajacu*)," *Dsrt. Plnts.* 6(1984): 3–4.
12 "killed a great many . . .": Goode P. Davis, Jr., *Man and Wildlife in
    Arizona: The American Exploration Period 1824–1856* (Scottsdale,
    Ariz.: The Arizona Game and Fish Department, 1982): 16.
14 Calcium oxalate in cactus: Oxalic acid binds with calcium to form
    calcium oxalate as insoluble crystals that cause kidney stones or other
    renal problems in animals; the exception is the wood rat (see p. 126
    and note); see also Bodil Schmidt-Nielson, "Urea Excretion by the
    Vertebrate Kidney," in *Nitrogen Metabolism and the Environment* (New
    York: Academic Press, 1972): 143–47, and O. J. Reichman, I. Prak-
    ash, and V. Roig, "Food Selection and Consumption," in *Arid-Land
    Ecosystems: Structure, Functioning and Management,* ed. D. W. Goodall
    and R. A. Perry (Cambridge: Cambridge University Press, 1979)1:
    700.
16 "the desert, any desert . . .": Edward Abbey, "The Ancient Dust,"
    Beyond the Wall (New York: Holt, Rinehart & Winston, 1984): 154.

2: OF DESERT RIVERS AND PIPISTRELLES

PAGE
18– Chihuahuan Desert lizards: James F. Scudday, "Some Recent
19 Changes in the Herpetofauna of the Northern Chihuahuan Desert,"
    in *Chih. Dsrt. Reg.* (1974): 513–22; Eric R. Pianka, "On Lizard
    Species Diversity: North American Flatland Deserts," *Ecol.*

48(1967): 333–51; K. P. Schmidt and T. F. Smith, "Amphibians and Reptiles of the Big Bend Region of Texas," *Zoological Series of the Field Museum of Natural History* 29(1944): 75–96.

The Chihuahuan Desert Research Institute is an independent research foundation that provides information to both the scholarly community (sponsoring symposia, etc.) and the public at large, as well as developing a study area of Chihuahuan Desert plants north of Alpine, Texas. See "Scudday Leads Research Survey of Lower Canyon," *Chih. Dsrt. Disc.*, no. 20 (Fall 1986): 4.

18   Lizard body temperature: Charles M. Bogert, "How Reptiles Regulate Their Body Temperature," *Scientific American* 200(1959): 105–20; John L. Cloudsley-Thompson, "Temperature Regulation in Desert Reptiles," in *Comparative Physiology of Desert Animals,* ed. G. M. O. Maloiy (New York: Academic Press, 1972): 39–59; William G. Degenhardt, "A Changing Environment: Documentation of Lizards and Plants over a Decade," in *Chih. Dsrt. Reg.* (1974): 533–55.

20   Location of Chihuahuan Desert: Robert H. Schmidt, "Where Is the Chihuahuan Desert?" *Chih. Dsrt. Disc.* 17(1985): 10; Morafka, "Biogeographical Analysis": 59–60; Stephen G. Wells and Donald R. Haragan, eds., *Origin and Evolution of Deserts* (Albuquerque: University of New Mexico Press, 1983).

Robert H. Schmidt, "A Climatic Delineation of the 'Real' Chihuahuan Desert," *Journal of Arid Environments* 2(1985): 243–50, uses an aridity index in which the mean annual precipitation (in millimeters) is divided by the average annual temperature (in degrees Celsius); an index below 10 is considered desert. The Koeppen system draws the boundary between semiarid and arid where evaporation is twice that of precipitation; see R. F. Logan, "Causes, Climates and Distribution of Deserts," in *Desert Biology,* ed. G. W. Brown (New York: Academic Press, 1968): 1:22.

20–   Desert riparian ecosystems and birds: R. Roy Johnson and Lois T.
21   Haight, "Avian Use of Xeroriparian Ecosystems in the North American Warm Deserts," *Riparian Ecosystems and Their Management: Reconciling Conflicting Uses,* coor. R. Roy Johnson et al. (Washington, D.C.: U.S.D.A. Forest Service General Technical Report RM-120, 1985): 156–60.

23–   Desert pocket mice (probably *Perognathus penicillatus*): Daily torpor
24   has been calculated to save about 135 grams of food for each hour spent in torpor (for a 23-gram mouse), according to J. W. Hudson and G. A. Bartholomew, "Terrestrial Animals in Dry Heat: Estivators," in *Handbook of Physiology: Adaptation to the Environment,* ed. D. B. Dill

(Washington, D.C.: American Physiological Society, 1964): 541–50; and Richard E. Macmillen, "Water Economy of Nocturnal Desert Rodents," in *Comp. Physiol. Dsrt. Anml.:* 149–53.

23– Cactus mouse (*Peromyscus eremicus*): A. L. Gennaro, "Northern Geo-
24 graphic Limits of Four Desert Rodents of the Genera Peromyscus, Dipodomys, and Onychomys in the Rio Grande Valley," *American Midland Naturalist:* 492; in the Rio Grande valley its range extends northward nearly to Española, New Mexico, coinciding closely with that of mesquite; also, George A. Bartholomew and William R. Dawson, "Temperature Regulation in Desert Mammals," in *Dsrt. Biol.*:1: 415–16.

24– Snails (*Rhabdotus schiedeanus*): Knut Schmidt-Nielsen, C. Richard
25 Taylor, and Amiram Shkolnik, "Desert Snails: Problems of Survival," in *Comp. Physiol. Dsrt. Anml.:* 1–13, and two works by Clifford S. Crawford, *Biology of Desert Invertebrates* (Berlin: Springer-Verlag, 1981): 50–56, 68–69, 73–76, and "Assimilation, Respiration, and Production: (a) Invertebrates," in *Arid-Land Ecosystems,* eds. D. W. Goodall and R. A. Perry (Cambridge: Cambridge University Press, 1979): 717–41.

25 Candelilla (*Euphorbia antisyphilitica*): Ross Maxwell, *Big Bend:* 95–99. Gary Nabhan, *pers. comm.;* now only half the available shoots are cut and Mexico is currently planting thousands of acres.

28 Thistledown velvet ant (*Dasymutilla gloriosa*): While there are no books on desert insects per se, the more recent field guides do pay more attention to insect fauna, especially James A. MacMahon, ed., *Deserts* (New York: Alfred A. Knopf, Audubon Society Nature Guides, 1985); for western reference, according to Dr. F. Martin Brown, the most useful general book is still the long-out-of-print E. O. Essig, *Insects of Western North America* (New York: The Macmillan Company, 1926). See also E. B. Edney, "Desert Arthropods," in *Dsrt. Biol.*: 2:311–94.

28– Side-blotched lizard (*Uta stansburiana*): C. E. Alexander and W. G.
30 Whitford, "Energy Requirements of *Uta stansburiana," Copeia* 1968 (1968): 678–83; O. Cuellar, "Delayed Fertilization in the Lizard *Uta stansburiana," Copeia* 1966 (1966): 549–52; D. W. Tinkle, "Home Range Density Dynamics and Structure of a Texas Population of the Lizard *Uta stansburiana,"* in *Lizard Ecology: A Symposium,* ed. W. W. Milstead (Columbia, Mo.: University of Missouri Press, 1967): 5–29; D. W. Tinkle, D. McGregor, and S. Dana, "Home Range Ecology of *Uta stansburiana stejnegeri," Ecol.* 43(1962): 223–29; Walter G. Whitford and F. Michael Creusere, "Seasonal and Yearly Fluctuations in Chihuahuan Desert Lizard Communities," *Herpetologica*

33(1977): 54–65; P. D. Spoecher, "Movements and Seasonal Activity Cycles of the Lizard *Uta stansburiana stejnegeri*," *Amer. Midl. Nat.* 77(1967): 484–94; and Richard M. Eakin, *The Third Eye* (Berkeley and Los Angeles: University of California Press, 1973).

29– Lizard water balance: J. R. Templeton, "Salt and Water Balance in
30 Desert Lizards," in *Comp. Physiol. Dsrt. Anml.*: 64, and Knut Schmidt-Nielson and W. R. Dawson, "Terrestrial Animals in Dry Heat: Desert Reptiles," in *Handbk. Phys.*, ed. D. B. Dill (Washington, D.C.: American Physiological Society, 1964): 467–80; Cloudsley-Thompson, "Temperature Regulation": 49: "The physiological adaptations of animals to desert life are concerned with striking a balance between the two incompatible requirements of conserving water for vital purposes and of transpiring it for cooling. How this balance is struck, depends very largely upon the size of the animal concerned."

30 Bird/lizard comparisons: William R. Dawson and George A. Bartholomew, "Temperature Regulation and Water Economy of Desert Birds," in *Dsrt. Biol.* 1: 365–66; Knut Schmidt-Nielsen, *Desert Animals: Physiological Problems of Heat and Water* (Oxford: Oxford University Press, 1964): 31, 213–14; and Bodil Schmidt-Nielsen, "Urea Excretion by the Vertebrate Kidney," in *Nitrogen Metabolism and the Environment,* ed. J. W. Campbell and L. Goldstein (New York: Academic Press, 1972): 81–103.

31 Coprolite studies: V. M. Bryant, Jr., "Prehistoric Diet in Southwest Texas: The Coprolitic Evidence," *American Antiquity* 39(1974): 407–20.

31– Cave dwellers' diet: S. Boyd Eason, Melvin Konner, and Marjorie
32 Shostak, *Design for Living* (New York: Harper & Row, 1988).

32– Whiptail lizards (*Cnemidophorus* sp.): Eric R. Pianka, "Comparative
33 Autecology of the Lizard *Cnemidophorus tigris* in Different Parts of Its Geographic Range," *Ecol.* 51(1970): 703–20; W. W. Milstead, "The Black Gap Whiptail Lizards After Twenty Years," in *Chih. Dsrt. Reg.* (1974): 523–32, and "Changes in Competing Populations of Whiptail Lizards (*Cnemidophorus*) in Southwestern Texas," *Amer. Midl. Nat.* 73(1965): 75–80; John W. Bickham and James A: MacMahon, "Feeding Habits of the Western Whiptail Lizard, *Cnemidophorus tigris,*" *Southw. Nat.* 17(2) (1972): 207.

33 Bipedality in lizards: M. A. Mares and A. C. Hulse, "Patterns of Some Vertebrate Communities in Creosote Bush Deserts," *Creosote Bush: Biology and Chemistry of Larrea in New World Deserts,* ed. T. J. Mabry, J. H. Hunzinker, and D. R. DiFeo, Jr. (Stroudsburg, Pa.: Dowden, Hutchinson & Ross, 1977): 209–26.

33 Western pipistrelle (*Pipistrellus hesperus*): W. Glen Bradley and Michael J. O'Farrell, "Temperature Relationships of the Western Pipistrelle (*Pipistrellus hesperus*)," *Physical Systems in Semiarid Environments,* ed. Clarence C. Hoff and Marvin L. Riesdel (Albuquerque: University of New Mexico Press, 1969): 85–96.

34 Insectivorous bats: W. Glen Bradley and M. K. Yousef, "Small Mammals in the Desert," *Physiological Adaptations: Desert and Mountains,* ed. Mohamed K. Yousef, Steven M. Horvath, and Robert W. Bullard (New York: Academic Press, 1972): 129–33.

3: OF HORSE LUBBERS AND CREOSOTE BUSHES

PAGE

36 Angel trumpet (*Acleisanthes longiflora*): Richard Spellenberg and Rebecca K. Delson, "Aspects of Reproduction in Chihuahuan Desert Nyctaginaceae," *Chih. Dsrt. Reg.* (1974): 273–87.

36– "purple sage": Hugh Mozingo, *Shrubs of the Great Basin* (Reno: Uni-
37 versity of Nevada Press, 1987) : 238, says that Grey was using artistic license and called big sagebrush (*Artemisia tridentata*) by this poetic name; other botanists have suggested *Salvia dorii.* See also Mac-Mahon, *Deserts:* 360.

38 Horse lubber (*Taeniopoda eques*): Ernest R. Tinkham, "Faunistic and Ecological Studies on the Orthoptera of the Big Bend Region of Trans-Pecos Texas, with Especial Reference to the Orthopteran Zones and Faunae of Midwestern North America," *Amer. Midl. Nat.* 40(1948): 549, 603.

38 Glaucous leaves: Thomas W. Mulroy, "Spectral Properties of Heavily Glaucous and Non-Glaucous Leaves of a Succulent Rosette-Plant," *Oecologica* 38(1979): 349–57.

39 CAM: Ting, "Succulents," contains a description with clear diagrams; Tony L. Burgess and Avi Shmida, "Succulent Growth Forms in Arid Environments," *Arid Lands: Today and Tomorrow,* ed. Emily E. Whitehead, et al. (Boulder, Colo.: Westview Press, 1988): 383–95; Irwin P. Ting and Stan R. Szarek, "Drought Adaptation in Crassulacean Acid Metabolism Plants," *Environmental Physiology of Desert Organisms,* ed. N. F. Hadley (Stroudsburg, Pa.: Dowden, Hutchinson & Ross, 1975): 152–65; Park S. Nobel, "Surface Temperatures of Cacti—Influences of Environmental and Morphological Factors," *Ecol.* 59(1978): 986–96, and "Water Relations of Flowering of *Agave deserti*," *Botanical Gazette* 138(1977): 5–6; Tony L. Burgess, "Agave Adaptation to Aridity," *Dsrt. Plnts.* 7(1985): 39–40.

39 Succulents: Irwin P. Ting, "Succulents," *Deep Canyon, A Desert*

Wilderness for Science, ed. Irwin P. Ting and B. Jennings (Palm Desert: Boyd Deep Canyon Desert Research Center, 1976): 125–30; and W. L. Ehrler, "Daytime Stomatal Closure in *Agave americana* as Related to Enhanced Water-Use Efficiency," *Phys. Sys. Semiar. Envir.*: 239–47.

39   Photosynthesis in desert plants: H. Walter and E. Stadelmann, "A New Approach to the Water Relations of Desert Plants," *Dsrt. Biol.* 2: 273; E. J. DePuit and M. M. Caldwell, "Gas Exchange of Three Cool Semi-Desert Species in Relation to Temperature and Water Stress," *Journal of Ecology* 63(1975): 835–58; R. D. Graetz and I. Cowan, "Microclimate and Evaporation," *Arid-Land Ecosys.*: 427; R. K. Gupta, "Integration," ibid.: 666.

40   Rain: John R. Pearson, Big Bend Natural History Association, *pers. comm.,* over the two-day period of misty rain, only .34 to .29 inches fell in the area of Big Bend National Park.

40   Climate: M. Anthony, "Ecology of the Opuntiae in the Big Bend Region of Texas," *Ecol.* 35(1954): 338; W. G. Degenhardt, "A Method of Counting Some Diurnal Ground Lizards of the Genera *Holbrookia* and *Cnemidophorus* with Results from the Big Bend National Park," *Amer. Midl. Nat.* 75(1966): 66–67.

40   Rain shadow: P. F. Logan, "Causes, Climates and Distribution," *Dsrt. Biol.* 1: 21–23; H. P. Bailey, B. B. Simpson, and F. Vervoorst, "The Physical Environment: The Independent Variable," *Convergent Evolution in Warm Deserts,* ed. Gordon H. Orians and Otto T. Solbrig (Stroudsburg, Pa.: Dowden, Hutchinson & Ross, 1977): 28; J. A. Mabbutt, *Desert Landforms* (Cambridge, Mass.: MIT Press, 1977): 3.

41–   Creosote bush (*Larrea tridentata*): At one time, the North American
45   species was considered to be the same as the South American species, *L. divaricata,* and this name appeared in the literature; now the North American species is recognized as separate, *L. tridentata.* See Mabry et al., *Creosote Bush;* Enrique Campos López, Tom J. Mabry, and Salvador Fernandez Tavison, eds., *Larrea* (Saltillo, Coahuilla, Mexico: Consejo Nacional de Ciencia y Tecnologia Insurgentes Sur 1677, 1981); M. G. Barbour, "Germination Requirements of the Desert Shrub *Larrea divaricata,*" *Ecol.* 49(1968): 915; M. G. Barbour et al., "The Structure and Distribution of *Larrea* Communities," *Creosote Bush:* 241–42, 250.

41   The South American origin was recognized in 1898. William L. Bray, "On the Relation of the Flora of the Lower Sonoran Zone in North America to the Flora of the Arid Zones of Chili and Argentina," *Botan. Gaz.* 26(1898): 121–47; recent papers are O. T. Solbrig, "The Floristic Disjunctions between the Monte in Argentina and the

Sonoran Desert in Mexico and the United States," *Missouri Botanic Gardens Annals* 59(1972): 218–23; O. T. Solbrig et al., "The Strategies and Community Patterns of Desert Plants," *Conver. Evol.:* 67–106; and Paul S. Martin and Peter J. Mehringer, Jr., "Pleistocene Pollen Analysis and Biogeography of the Southwest," *The Quaternary Geology of the United States,* ed. H. E. Wright and David G. Frey (Princeton, N.J.: Princeton University Press, 1965): 445; M. G. Barbour, "Patterns of Genetic Similarity Between *Larrea divaricata* of North and South America," *Amer. Midl. Nat.* 81(1969): 54–67; J. H. Hunziker et al., "Geographic Distribution, Morphology, Hybridization, Cytogenetics, and Evolution," *Creosote Bush:* 42–44.

43 Arrival of creosote bush: P. V. Wells, "Post-Glacial Origin," *Chih. Dsrt. Reg.* (1974): 77–79, 82; the oldest documented wood-rat midden with creosote-bush evidence is 10,580 ± 550 in the Sonoran Desert in southwestern Arizona; Wells finds conclusive evidence that the present wide dominance of *Larrea* in the southwestern United States was not accomplished before the Holocene. See also F. C. Vasek, H. B. Johnson, and G. B. Brum, "Creosote-bush: Long-lived Clone in the Mojave Desert," *American Journal of Botany* 64(1975): 246–55, and Thomas R. Van Devender and W. Geoffrey Spaulding, "Development of Vegetation and Climate in the Southwest United States," *Science* 204(1979): 701–10.

43 Polyploidy in creosote bush: David E. Brown, "Chihuahuan Desertscrub," "Biotic Communities of the American Southwest—United States and Mexico," ed. David E. Brown, *Dsrt. Plnts.* 4(1982): 172–73. Anatomical differences parallel morphological: for example, lengthening of plant fibers indicates advancement in evolution and, in the creosote bush, increases in the number of chromosomes, substantiating that the western races evolved from the eastern: H. M. Hull, S. J. Shellhorn, and R. E. Saunier, "Variations in Creosotebush (*Larrea divaricata*) Epidermis," *Journal of the Arizona Academy of Sciences* 6(1971): 196–98. See also three papers by T. W. Yang, "Chromosome Numbers in Populations of Creosote Bush (*Larrea divaricata*) in the Chihuahuan and Sonoran Subdivisions of the North American Desert," *J. Ariz. Acad. Sci.* 4(1967): 183–84, "Ecotypic Variation in *Larrea divaricata,*" *Amer. J. Botan.* 54(1967): 1041–44, and "Major Chromosome Races of *Larrea divaricata* in North America," *J. Ariz. Acad. Sci.* 6(1970): 41–45; also Albert W. Johnson, John G. Packer, and Gerd Reese, "Polyploidy, Distribution, and Environment," in *Quat. Geol.:* 497–99; G. Ledyard Stebbins, Jr., "Aridity as a Stimulus to Plant Evolution," *Amer. Nat.* 86(1952): 33–35.

44 "even mules will not . . .": William Helmsley Emory, "Notes of a Military Reconnaissance, from Fort Leavenworth, in Missouri, to

San Diego, in California, Including part of the Arkansas, Del Norte, and Gila Rivers," *Senate Executive Document No. 7*, 30th Cong., 1st sess. (Washington, D.C.: Wendell & Van Benthuysen, Printers, 1848) [517]: 88.

44 Overgrazing and creosote bush: C. M. McKell and B. E. Norton, "Management of Arid-Land Resources for Domestic Livestock Forage," in *Arid-Land Ecosys.* 2: 455–78.

44 Leaf resins and waxes: B. N. Timmermann, "Practical Uses of *Larrea*," *Creosote Bush:* 252–56, and Tom J. Mabry et al., "The Natural Products Chemistry of *Larrea tridentata* Cav. in the Chihuahuan Desert," in *Chih. Dsrt. Reg.* (1974): 247; the authors point out that the creosote bush is a "rather remarkable chemical factory synthesizing several hundred natural products, which together account for between 30–50% of the dry weight of the leaves and stems. Such synthetic ability is characteristic of many desert plants (although we know of none more prolific and diverse than *Larrea*) and together these plant chemicals constitute one of the least recognized resources of the Chihuahuan Desert." Donald A. Levin, "Plant Phenolics: An Ecological Perspective," *Amer. Nat.* 105(1971): 157–75, for plant chemicals and how they protect against grazing; D. F. Rhoades, "The Antiherbivore Chemistry of *Larrea*," *Creosote Bush:* 135–61.

44 "Indians and Mexicans . . .": Edward Lee Greene, "Botanizing on the Colorado Desert," *Amer. Nat.* 15 (1881): 24.

44– Prehistoric plant use: Ross Maxwell, *Big Bend:* 112; Robert A. Bye,
45 Jr., "Ethnobotany of the Southern Paiute Indians in the 1870s: with a Note of the Early Ethnobotanical Contributions of Dr. Edward Palmer," *Great Basin Cultural Ecology*, ed. Don D. Fowler (Reno, Nev.: Desert Research Institute Publications in the Social Sciences 8, 1972): 96.

45 NDGA and aging: The Nature Conservancy, "Utility of Diversity," *Save the Land* (October 1987): 6.

4: OF BARCHANS AND COTTONWOOD

PAGE
46 White Sands: David Quammen, "Yin and Yang in the Tularosa Basin," *Audubon* 87(1985): 60–68; Richard Atkinson, *White Sands: Wind, Sand and Time* (Globe, Ariz.: Southwest Parks and Monuments Association, 1977), is the best general reference, although an older paper, Fred W. Emerson, "An Ecological Reconnaissance on the White Sands, New Mexico," *Ecol.* 15(1935): 226–33, is still informative. For sand dunes in general, Janice E. Bowers, *Seasons of the*

Wind (Flagstaff, Ariz.: Northland Press, 1986), which includes White Sands: 52–58, 133–34; Roger S. U. Smith, "Sand Dunes in the North American Deserts," *Ref. Handbk. Dsrts.*: 481–524, and the classic R. A. Bagnold, *The Physics of Blown Sand and Desert Dunes* (London: Methuen, 1941); see also Bagnold, "The Physical Aspects of Dry Deserts," *Biology of Deserts*, ed. J. L. Cloudsley-Thompson (London: Institute of Biology, 1954): 7–12.

46   Condensation: Dew is a ready source of moisture for desert animals; tarantulas and spadefoot toads both gain weight from moisture that condenses on them, and others, such as desert night lizards, lick themselves: Robert C. Lasiewski and George A. Bartholomew, "Condensation as a Mechanism for Water Gain in Nocturnal Desert Poikilotherms," *Copeia* (1969): 405–407.

46   "frequently the milk . . .": Pedro Bautista Pino, in *Three New Mexico Chronicles. The Exposición of Don Pedro Bautista Pino, 1812; the Ojeada of Lic. Antonio Barreiro, 1832; and additions by Don José Augustín de Escudero, 1849*, trans., intro., and notes by Carroll H. Bailey and J. Villasana Haggard (Albuquerque, N.M.: The Quivira Society, 1942): 24.

47   Area history: Stewart Udall, "In Coronado's Footsteps," *Arizona Highways* 60(1984): 7–8; Atkinson, *White Sands:* 35–36; and Cyclone Covey, trans. and annot., *Cabeza de Vaca's Adventures in the Unknown Interior of America* (Albuquerque: University of New Mexico Press, 1986).

47   Historical geology: F. E. Kottlowski, "Lake Otero—Second Phase in Formation of New Mexico's Gypsum Dunes," *Geological Society of America Bulletin* 69(1958): 1733–34; F. E. Kottlowski, Maurice E. Cooley, and Robert V. Ruhe, "Quaternary Geology of the Southwest," *Quat. Geol.:* 287–98; and Peter Hendrickson, *Lake Lucero: White Sands National Monument, New Mexico* (Globe, Ariz.: Southwest Parks and Monuments Association, 1983).

48–   Cottonwood (*Populus wislizenii*): L. M. Shields, "Gross Modifica-
49   tions in Certain Plant Species Tolerant of Calcium Sulfate Dunes," *Amer. Midl. Nat.* 50(1953): 226, and for historical interest, Frederick Adolphus Wislizenus, "Memoir of a Tour to Northern Mexico, Connected with Col. Doniphan's Expedition, in 1846 and 1847," *Senate Miscellaneous Documents No. 16*, 30th Cong., 1st sess. [511] (Washington, D.C.: Tippin & Streeper, Printers, 1848).

49–   Dunes: E. D. McKee, "Structures of Dunes at White Sands National
50   Monument, New Mexico (and a Comparison with Structures of Dunes from Other Selected Areas)," *Sedimentology* 7(1966): 1–69, and McKee and John R. Douglass, "Growth and Movement of

Dunes at White Sands National Monument, New Mexico,"
U.S.G.S. Professional Paper 750D (Washington, D.C.: U.S. Government Printing Office, 1971): 108–14.

51– Interdune flats: Both the above papers have information on interdune
52 flats, especially McKee, "Structures": 51–56; see also two papers by L. M. Shields, "Leaf Xeromorphy in Dicotyledonous Species from a Gypsum Sand Deposit," *Amer. J. Botan.* 38(1951): 175, 187–89, and "Zonation of Vegetation Within the Tularosa Basin, New Mexico," *Southw. Nat.* 1(1956): 49–68.

52 Gypsophilous plants: A. Michael Powell and B. L. Turner, "Aspects of the Plant Biology of the Gypsum Outcrops of the Chihuahuan Desert," *Chih. Dsrt. Reg.* (1974): 315–25; B. L. Turner and A. M. Powell, "Deserts, Gypsum and Endemism," *Arid Land Plant Resources,* ed. J. R. Goodin and D. K. Northington (Lubbock: Texas Tech University, 1979): 96–116; U. T. Waterfall, "Observations on the Desert Gypsum Flora of Southwestern Texas and Adjacent New Mexico," *Amer. Midl. Nat.* 36(1946): 456–66, who listed some ninety species at White Sands.

52– Algae: L. M. Shields and L. W. Durrel, "Algae in Relation to Soil
53 Fertility," *Botan. Rev.* 30(1964): 92–128, and L. M. Shields, C. Mitchell, and F. Drouet, "Alga- and Lichen-Stabilized Surface Crusts of Soil Nitrogen Sources," *Amer. J. Botan.* 44(1957): 489–98; E. Imre Friedmann and Margalith Galun, "Desert Algae, Lichens, and Fungi," in *Dsrt. Biol.* 2: 166–86, and Roy E. Cameron, "Communities of Soil Algae Occurring in the Sonoran Desert in Arizona," *J. Ariz. Acad. Sci.* 1(1960): 85–88.

53 Soil microfauna: Perseu F. Santos and Walter G. Whitford, "Seasonal and Spatial Variation in the Soil Microarthropod Fauna of the White Sands National Monument," *Southw. Nat.* 28(1983): 417–21, "The Role of Mites and Nematodes in Early Stages of Buried Litter Decomposition in a Desert," *Ecol.* 62(1981): 664–69, and "The Effects of Microarthropods on Litter Decomposition in a Chihuahuan Desert Ecosystem," *Ecol.* 62(1981): 654–63; Santos et al., "A Comparison of Surface and Buried *Larrea tridentata* Leaf Litter Decomposition in North American Hot Deserts," *Ecol.* 65(1984): 278–84. These extensive studies on microarthropods are currently in progress at the Jornada Experimental Range at Las Cruces, New Mexico, a validation site for the IBP Desert Biome Program.

53– White Sands lizard (*Sceloporus undulatus cowlesi*): Charles H. Lowe
54 and Kenneth S. Norris, "A Subspecies of the Lizard *Sceloporus undulatus* from the White Sands of New Mexico," *Herpt.* 12(1956): 125–27, considered this to be a new subspecies because of its unusually

distinct form; in the laboratory, none changed basic color for a year or underwent color change under different diets or temperatures; hatchlings were the same color as the adults. See also Wilbur Mayhew, "Biology of Desert Amphibians and Reptiles," *Dsrt. Biol.* 1: 244–46; J. R. Dixon, "Aspects of the Biology of the Lizards of the White Sands, New Mexico," *Contributions to Science* (Los Angeles: Los Angeles County Museum) 129(1967): 1–22. Thomas H. Lewis, "The Herpetofauna of the Tularosa Basin and Organ Mountains of New Mexico with Notes on Some Ecological Features of the Chihuahuan Desert," *Herpt.* 6(1950): 1–10, describes reptiles and amphibians here by habitat.

54 Background matching: Kenneth S. Norris and Charles H. Lowe, "An Analysis of Background Color-Matching in Amphibians and Reptiles," *Ecol.* 45(1964): 588; Roy E. Bundy and John Neers, "Color Variation in the Round-tailed Horned Lizard, *Phrynosoma modestum*," *Ecol.* 39(1958): 463–77, in which the lizards matched different soil and rock types in New Mexico and Texas; see also Seth B. Benson, "Concealing Coloration Among Some Desert Rodents of the Southwestern United States," *University of California Publications in Zoology* 40(1933): 1–70 passim.

54 Black coloration: W. J. Hamilton, "Coloration and Its Consequences for Diurnal Desert Insects," *Envir. Phys. Dsrt. Org.:* 75, 87. Warren P. Porter, "Solar Radiation Through the Living Body Walls of Vertebrates with Emphasis on Desert Reptiles," *Ecological Monograph* 37(1967): 294, "the heavily pigmented, though very thin, body wall of a black desert beetle excludes more light from the body cavity than most vertebrates measured." Neil F. Hadley, "Micrometeorology and Energy Exchange in Two Desert Arthropods," *Ecol.* 51(1970): 438–44, describes how darkling beetles and scorpions handle the heat load of the desert; also John Cloudsley-Thompson, "On the Functions of the Subelytral Cavity in Desert Tenebrionidae," *Entomological Monthly Magazine* 100(1964): 148–51.

55 Moisture within dunes: Bagnold, *Phys. Blown Sand:* 245–46.

55– Root systems: H. J. Dittmer, "A Study of the Root Systems of
56 Certain Sand Dune Plants in New Mexico," *Ecol.* 40(1959): 265–73.

55– Sand burial: J. A. McCleary, "The Biology of Desert Plants," in
56 *Dsrt. Biol.* 1: 169, and Shields, "Gross Modifications": 224–30.

56 Thigmomorphogenesis: M. J. Jaffe, "Morphogenetic Responses of Plants to Mechanical Stimuli or Stress," *BioScience* 30(1980): 239–43.

58 Wolf spiders (Lycosidae): S. J. Knost and J. S. Rovner, "Scavenging by Wolf Spiders (Araneae: Lycosidae)," *Amer. Midl. Nat.* 93(1975): 239–44.

5: OF DEAD MEN AND MESQUITE

PAGE

60– Jornada del Muerto: William H. Emory, *Notes:* 89: "The river com-
61 mences to gather its feeble force into the smallest compass to work
its way around the western base of Fra Cristobal mountain. The
Chihuahua road runs on the eastern side, and that part of it is the
dreaded jornado of the traders, where they must go most seasons of
the year ninety miles without water."

Wislizenus, "Memoir," 38: "This awful Jornada, a distance of
about 90 miles, with very little or without any water at all, has to be
resorted to because the Rio del Norte [Rio Grande] below Fray
Cristobal takes not only a very circuitous bend, but rough mountains, too, alongside of it, make it most difficult to follow the water-
course. In the rainy season there is generally plenty of water in the
Jornada, as everywhere else, but in the dry season often not a drop is
found." See also Don Franciso de Valverde, "Investigations of Conditions in New Mexico, 1601," *Don Juan Oñate, Colonizer of New
Mexico 1595–1628*, ed. George P. Hammond and Agapito Rey
(Albuquerque: University of New Mexico Press, 1953): 660.

61 San Marcial: T. M. Pearce, ed., *New Mexico Place Names. A Geographical Dictionary* (Albuquerque: University of New Mexico Press,
1965): 146; John T. Hughes, *Doniphan's Expedition; Containing an
Account of the Conquest of New Mexico; General Kearny's Overland
Expedition to California; Doniphan's Campaign Against the Navajos; His
Unparalleled March upon Chihuahua and Durango; and the Operations of
General Price at Santa Fé* (Cincinnati: U. P. James, 1847): 61, gives a
sad account of the loss of men and stock at Valverde while waiting to
embark on the Jornada, as do Kearny's soldiers.

61– Kearny's expedition: Dwight L. Clarke, ed., *Stephen Watt Kearny,
62 Soldier of the West* (Norman: University of Oklahoma Press, 1961);
A. B. Bender, "Government Explorations in the Territory of New
Mexico 1846–1859," *New Mexico Historical Review* 9(1934): 3–4;
Philip St. George Cooke, *The Conquest of New Mexico and California
in 1846–1848* (1878; reprint ed., Chicago: Rio Grande Press, 1964):
85–86; George D. Lyman, ed., "A Doctor Comes to California. The
Diary of John S. Griffin: Assistant Surgeon with Kearny's Drag-
oons, 1846–1847," introduction and notes, George W. Ames, Jr.,
California Historical Society Quarterly (1943): 2–4.

62 Emory: William H. Goetzmann, *Exploration and Empire* (New York:
Alfred A. Knopf, 1966): 254–57, and Ross Calvin, ed., *Lieutenant
Emory Reports* (Norman: University of Oklahoma Press, 1951): 9–13.

62 "It surprised me . . .": Clarke, *Kearny:* 185. See also Jay W. Sharp, "Jornada del Muerto," *New Mexico Magazine* 63 (1) (1985): 18–20.

62 Gypsum soil: R. S. Campbell and I. F. Campbell, "Vegetation of Gypsum Soils of the Jornada Plain, New Mexico," *Ecol.* 19(1938): 572–77; Waterfall, "Desert Gypsum Flora": 456–66.

62– Jornada bird populations: Two papers by R. J. Raitt and Stuart L.

63 Pimm, "Temporal Changes in Northern Chihuahuan Desert Bird Communities," *Chih. Dsrt. Reg.* (1974): 579–89, and "Dynamics of Bird Communities in the Chihuahua Desert, New Mexico," *Condor* 78: 427–44; also two papers in *Chih. Dsrt. Reg.* (1974), Allan R. Phillips, "Summary of Avian Resources of the Chihuahuan Desert Region": 617–20, and J. Dan Webster, "The Avifauna of the Southern Part of the Chihuahuan Desert": 559–66; R. J. Raitt and R. L. Maze, "Densities and Species Composition of Breeding Birds of a Creosotebush Community in Southern New Mexico," *Condor* 70(1968): 193–205; Keith L. Dixon, "Ecological and Distributional Relations of Desert Scrub Birds of Western Texas," ibid. 61(1959): 407; Anders H. Anderson and Anne Anderson, "Notes on Use of Creosote Bush by Birds," ibid. 48(1946): 179; J. Stokley Ligon, *New Mexico Birds and Where to Find Them* (Albuquerque, N.M.: University of New Mexico Press, 1961).

David E. Brown, "Chihuahuan Desertscrub": 169–79, notes that most Chihuahuan Desert birds are generally desert-adapted western species that have spread farther southeast; the only "characteristic" species are scaled quail (*Callipepla squamata*) and the white-necked or Chihuahuan raven (*Corvus cryptoleucus*), neither of which is confined to Chihuahuan Desert scrub.

63 Creosote-bush expansion: J. L. Gardner, "Vegetation of the Creosotebush Area of the Rio Grande Valley in New Mexico, *Ecol. Monogr.* 2(1951): 378, 401–402, quotes residents who remembered baling hay thirty-five years ago in areas now largely creosote bush; Duane Knipe and Carlton H. Herbel, "Germination and Growth of Some Semidesert Grassland Species Treated with Aqueous Extract from Creosotebush," *Ecol.* 47(1966): 781. Although some of the conclusions in Robert R. Humphrey, "The Desert Grassland, A History of Vegetational Change and an Analysis of Causes," *Botan. Rev.* 24(1958): 193–248, are no longer valid, it is useful for the thoroughness of its comparative historical material.

63 Habitat attrition: Jon C. Barlow, "Effects of Habitat Attrition on Vireo Distribution and Population Density in the Northern Chihuahuan Desert," *Chih. Dsrt. Reg.* (1974): 591–96; S. K. McIlvanie, "Grass Seedling Establishment, and Productivity—Overgrazed vs. Protected Range Soils," *Ecol.* 23(1942): 228–31. For historical per-

spective, J. L. Rich, "Recent Stream Trenching in the Semi-arid Portion of Southwestern New Mexico, a Result of Removal of Vegetation Cover," *American (Silliman's) Journal of Science* 32(1911): 237–45.

63   Running of cattle and sheep: George A. McCall, *New Mexico in 1850: A Military View,* ed. Robert W. Frazer (Norman: University of Oklahoma Press, 1968). The first big sheep drives began in 1850, and Frazer suggests that by 1853 the grazing lands of New Mexico were already depleted. During the same period, the land surface covered by mesquite in this area increased dramatically while grassland cover declined from 90 to 25 percent.

63– Black-throated sparrow (*Amphispiza bilineata*): Michael Smyth and
64   George A. Bartholomew, "The Water Economy of the Black-throated Sparrow and the Rock Wren," *Condor* 68(1966): 447–58; Fred A. Ryser, Jr., *Birds of the Great Basin* (Reno: University of Nevada Press, 1986): 44–45, 483–85; Dawson and Bartholomew, "Temperature Regulation": 367–69, 382–84; Wilbur Mayhew, "Birds," *Deep Cyn.*: 155; O. J. Reichman, I. Prakash, and V. Roig, "Food Selection and Consumption," in *Arid-Land Ecosys.* 1: 693; Schmidt-Nielson, *Dsrt. Anml.*: 213–14; Dawson and Bartholomew, "Temperature Regulation": 1: 365–68.

64– Mesquite (*Prosopis juliflora* var. *glandulosa*): B. B. Simpson, ed.,
65   *Mesquite* (Stroudsburg, Pa.: Dowden, Hutchinson & Ross, 1977), a collection of studies on mesquite; Frank W. Reichenbacher, "Ecology and Evolution of Southwestern Riparian Plant Communities," *Dsrt. Plnts.* 6(1985): 15–22; K. L. Polk and D. N. Ueckert, "Biology and Ecology of a Mesquite Twig Girdler, *Oncideres rhodosticta,* in West Texas," *Annals of the Entomological Society of America* 66(1973): 411–17, suggest that one way of controlling mesquite is via the mesquite twig girdler; see also Bil Gilbert, "A Tree Too Tough to Kill," *Audubon* 87(1985): 84–97; Janet I. Sprent, "Problems and Potentials for Nitrogen Fixation in Deserts," in *Arid Lands:* 1049.

64   Mesquite growth pattern: H. A. Mooney, B. B. Simpson, and O. T. Solbrig, "Phenology, Morphology, Physiology," in *Mesquite:* 30.

65   "most annoying ...": Griffin, "A Doctor Comes to California," *Calif. Hist. Soc. Quart.* (1942): 200.

6: OF CACTUS WRENS AND PLAYAS

PAGE

66– Philip St. George Cooke: "Report of Lieut. Col. P. St. George Cooke
67   of his march from Santa Fe, New Mexico, to San Diego, Upper

California," in "Notes of a Military Reconnaissance, from Fort Leavenworth, in Missouri, to San Diego, in California, Including part of the Arkansas, Del Norte, and Gila Rivers," *Senate Executive Document No. 7*, 30th Cong., 1st sess. (Washington, D.C.: Wendell & Van Benthuysen, Printers, 1848) [517]: 549–62; Cooke also wrote a popular account, *Conquest of New Mexico*: 71, 159; see also Ralph P. Beiber with Averam B. Bender, *Exploring Southwestern Trails, 1846–1854, by Philip St. George Cooke, William Henry Chase Whiting, François Xavier Aubry* (Glendale, Calif.: Arthur H. Clark Company, 1938): 20–23.

67 "a much branc[h]ed shrub . . .": William H. Emory, "Notes," *House Executive Document 41*, October 8, 1846: 89.

67– Cactus wren (*Campylorhynchus brunneicapillus*): Thomas G. Marr
68 and Ralph J. Raitt, "Annual Variations in Patterns of Reproduction of the Cactus Wren (*Campylorhynchus brunneicapillus*), *Southw. Nat.* 28(1983): 149–56, and Robert F. Ricklefs and F. Reed Hainsworth, "Temperature Regulation in Nestling Cactus Wrens: The Development of Homeothermy," *Condor* 70(1968): 121–27; Anders H. Anderson and Anne Anderson, *The Cactus Wren* (Tucson: University of Arizona Press, 1973).

69 Carrion: M. McKinnerey, "Carrion Communities in the Northern Chihuahuan Desert," *Southw. Nat.* 23(1978): 563–76.

71 Buffalo gourd (*Cucurbita foetidissima*): Jennie S. DeVeaux, William P. Darby, Eugene B. Shultz, Jr., and Larry Icerman, "Buffalo Gourd as a Dryland Fuel Alcohol Crop: Development Strategy and Economics for New Mexico," *Arid Lands*: 1299–1304; H. J. Dittmer and B. P. Talley, "Gross Morphology of Tap Roots of Desert Cucurbits," *Botan. Gaz.* 125(1964): 121–26; C. Wiley Hinman, "Potential New Crops," *Scientific American* 255(1986): 32–37.

75 Chihuahuan/Sonoran transitions: Ralph W. Axtell, "Ancient Playas and Their Influence on the Recent Herpetofauna of the Northern Chihuahuan Desert," *Chih. Dsrt. Reg.* (1974): 502–507; C. H. Lowe, "The Eastern Limit of the Sonoran Desert in the United States with Additions to the Known Herpetofauna of New Mexico," *Ecol.* 36(1955): 343–55, considers the crest of the Peloncillo Mountains to be the eastern limit of the Sonoran Desert; also Steven P. McLaughlin, "A Floristic Analysis of the Southwestern United States," *Great Basin Naturalist* 46(1986): 46–65; James A. MacMahon, "North American Deserts: Their Floral and Faunal Components," *Arid. Ecosys.* 1: 59, lists the sibling pairs on either side of the barrier. Morafka, "Biogeographical Analysis": 127–31, 195, 209–16, the quick changes in environment brought about a population of par-

thenogenetic whiptail lizards, one of whose parents was eastern and the other a western species.

75 Lesser earless lizards (*Holbrookia maculata*): Bogert, "How Reptiles Regulate": 105–20; Degenhardt, "Method of Counting": 67; and "A Changing Environment": 549–53.

76 Millipedes (*Orthoporus ornatus*): C. S. Crawford, "Seasonal Water Balance in *Orthoporus ornatus,* a Desert Millipede," *Ecol.* 59(1978): 996–1004, and *Dsrt. Invert.*: 93, 130.

76– Blister beetle (*Meloe* spp.): Howard Ensign Evans, *The Plea-*
77 *sures of Entomology* (Washington, D.C.: Smithsonian Institution Press, 1985): 93–102.

77 "one that even an entomologist . . .": Ibid.: 93.

77 Damage to creosote bush: B. B. Simpson, J. L. Neff, and A. R. Moldenke, "Reproductive Systems of *Larrea,*" in *Creosote Bush:* 99–102.

78 Ants (Formicinae): A. Schumacher and W. G. Whitford, "Spatial and Temporal Variation in Chihuahuan Desert Ant Faunas," *Southw. Nat.* 21(1976): 1–8; two papers by W. G. Whitford and G. Ettershank: "Demography and Role of Herbivorous Ants in a Desert Ecosystem as Functions of Vegetation, Soil and Climatic Variables," *US/IBP Desert Biome Research Memo RM 72–32* (Logan, Utah, 1972), and "Factors Affecting Foraging in Chihuahuan Desert Harvester Ants," *Environmental Entomology* 4(1975): 689–96; W. G. Whitford, C. A. Kay, and A. M. Schumacher, "Water Loss in Chihuahuan Desert Ants," *Physiological Zoology* 48(1975): 390–97; Mark E. Hay and Patricia J. Fuller, "Seed Escape from Heteromyid Rodents: The Importance of Microhabitat and Seed Preference," *Ecol.* 62(1981): 1395–99; O. J. Reichman, "Behavior of Desert Heteromyids," *Great Basin Nat. Mem. No. 7*: 77–90, and F. H. Wagner and R. D. Graetz, "Animal-Animal Interactions," *Arid-Land Ecosys.* 2: 51–83. Two papers by Diane W. Davidson: "Species Diversity and Community Organization in Desert Seed-Eating Ants," *Ecol.* 58(1977): 711–24, and "Foraging Ecology and Community Organization in Desert Seed-Eating Ants," *Ecol.* 58(1977): 725–37; Dennis J. O'Dowd and Mark E. Hay, "Mutualism Between Harvester Ants and a Desert Ephemeral: Seed Escape from Rodents," *Ecol.* 61(1980): 538–39; D. W. Davidson, R. S. Inouye, and J. H. Brown, "Granivory in a Desert Ecosystem: Experimental Evidence for Indirect Facilitation of Ants by Rodents," *Ecol.* 65(1984): 1780–86.

78– Termites (*Gnathitermes tubiformans*): Walter G. Whitford and Diana
79 W. Freckman, "The Role of Soil Biota in Soil Processes in the Chihuahuan Desert," *Arid Lands:* 1063; Crawford, *Dsrt. Invert.*:

156–57, 165–69; J. A. Ludwig and W. G. Whitford, "Short-Term Water and Energy Flow in Arid Ecosystems," *Arid-Land Ecosys.* 2: 293–95; MacMahon, *Deserts:* 521.

79   Playas: Richard O. Stone, "Playas," ed. Thomas Clements, *A Study of Desert Surface Conditions* (Natick, Mass.: Quartermaster Research & Development Center, Technical Report EP-53, 1957): 14–16; various papers by J. T. Neal, among them, "Playa Variation," in *Arid Lands in Perspective,* ed. W. G. McGinnies and B. J. Goldman (Tucson: University of Arizona Press, 1969): 15–25; Mabbutt, *Dsrt. Landf.:* 184; Ronald U. Cooke and Andrew Warren, *Geomorphology in Deserts:* 217–28; J. R. Hendrickson, "Saline Habitats and Halophytic Vegetation of the Chihuahuan Desert Region," *Chih. Dsrt. Reg.* (1974): 289–314.

80   "indurated clay . . .": John Russell Bartlett, *Personal Narrative of Explorations and Incidents in Texas, New Mexico, California, Sonora, and Chihuahua* (New York: D. Appleton & Co., 1856): 1: 246.

81   "As we toiled . . .": Ibid.: 1: 247.

7: OF SAGUARO AND ROADRUNNERS

PAGE

86–   Sonoran Desert flora: "The Sonoran Desert is generally conceded to
87   be the richest, most diverse of all the North American desert types, due to the large number of species—over 3,000 . . . and the great diversity of life forms. . . ." Michael G. Barbour et al., "The Structure and Distribution of *Larrea* Communities," *Creos. Bush:* 232. See also David E. Brown, "Biotic Communities of the American Southwest," *Dsrt. Plnts.:* 180, and Lee R. Dice, "The Sonoran Biotic Province," *Ecol.* 20(1939): 118–29; Raymond M. Turner and David E. Brown, "Sonoran Desertscrub," *Dsrt. Plnts.:* 181–221. The definitive botanical reference is the monumental two-volume work by Forrest Shreve and Ira L. Wiggins, *Vegetation and Flora of the Sonoran Desert* (Stanford, Calif.: Stanford University Press, 1977).

87–   Saguaro (*Carnegiea gigantea*): Along the San Pedro saguaro are at the
88   northeastern limit of their range with the thickest growth around Tucson; their western limit lies against the Colorado River in northwestern Arizona; general references are Paul Griswold Howes, *The Giant Cactus and Its World* (New York: Duell, Sloan & Pearce, 1954), and Gary Paul Nabhan, *A View of Saguaro National Monument and the Tucson Basin* (Tucson: Southwest Parks and Monuments Association,

1986); also, Frank S. Crosswhite, "The Annual Saguaro Harvest and Crop Cycle of the Papago, with Reference to Ecology and Symbolism," *Dsrt. Plnts.* 2(1980): 3–6.

87   Freezing: Warren F. Steenbergh and Charles H. Lowe, "Ecology of the Saguaro: I. The Role of Freezing Weather in a Warm-Desert Plant Population," *Transactions of the National Park Centennial Symposium* (Washington, D.C.: U.S. Department of the Interior, National Park Service Symposium Series, No. 1, 1976): 49–50; P. V. Wells, "Postglacial Origin": 81.

87–   Diminishing saguaro numbers: Warren F. Steenbergh and Charles H.
88   Lowe, *Ecology of the Saguaro: II. Reproduction, Germination, Establishment, Growth, and Survival of the Young Plant* (Washington, D.C.: U.S. Government Printing Office, National Park Service Scientific Monograph Series, No. 8, 1977); Richard I. Yeaton, Richard Karban, and Holliday B. Wagner, "Morphological Growth Patterns of Saguaro (*Carnegiea gigantea*) on Flats and Slopes in Organ Pipe Cactus National Monument, Arizona," *Southw. Nat.* 25(1980): 339–49.

88   Nurse trees: John Vandermeer, "Saguaros and Nurse Trees: A New Hypothesis to Account for Population Fluctuations," *Southw. Nat.* 25(1980): 358–60; Duncan T. Patten and Edward M. Smith, "Heat Flux and the Thermal Regime of Desert Plants," in *Envir. Phys. Dsrt. Org.:* 10–12; R. M. Turner, Stanley M. Alcorn, and George Olin, "Mortality of Transplanted Saguaro Seedlings," *Ecol.* 50(1969): 835–44; M. G. Barbour, "Plant-Plant Interactions," in *Arid-Land Ecosys.* 2: 33–49; Forrest Shreve, "Establishment Behavior of the Palo Verde," *The Plant World* 14(1911): 289–96; Walter T. McDonough, "Interspecific Associations Among Desert Plants," *Amer. Midl. Nat.* 70(1963): 291–99; Charles H. Lowe and D. S. Hinds, "Effect of Paloverde (*Cercidium*) Trees on the Radiation Flux at Ground Level in the Sonoran Desert in Winter," *Ecol.* 52(1971): 916–22; Walter and Stadelmann, "Water Relations" 2: 267; Otto T. Solbrig and Gordon H. Orians, "The Adaptive Characteristics of Desert Plants," *American Scientist* 65(1977): 418; and Gordon H. Orians et al., "Resource Systems," ed. G. H. Orians and Otto T. Solbrig, *Convergent Evolution in Warm Deserts* (Stroudsburg, Pa.: Dowden, Hutchinson & Ross, 1977): 194–95. Richard L. Hutto, Joseph R. McAuliffe, and Lynee Hogan, "Distributional Associates of the Saguaro (*Carnegiea gigantea*)," *Southw. Nat.* 31(4)(1986): 474, consider a saguaro 10 cm. in diameter to be around twenty years old.

89–   Roadrunner (*Geococcyx californianus*): Robert D. Ohmart, "Observa-
90   tions on the Breeding Adaptations of the Roadrunner," *Condor* 75(1973): 140–49; W. A. Calder, "The Diurnal Activity of the Roadrunner, *Geococcyx californianus,*" *Condor* 70(1968): 84–85; C. H. Lowe

and D. S. Hinds, "Thermoregulation in Desert Populations of Road-runners and Doves," *Physiol. Sys. Semiarid Envir.:* 113; O. J. Reich-man et al., "Food Selection and Consumption," *Arid-Land Ecosys.:* 694.

89 Roadrunner diet: John Bartlett, *Personal Narrative* 2: 563: "It might be supposed that the venom of the tarantula, the centipede, the scor-pion, and the rattlesnake would effectually preserve them all from enemies. But such is not the case. A most voracious bird is found here, called by the Mexicans the '*paysano,*' and by the Americans the '*chapporal cock,*' which feeds on these hideous creatures. He even ventures to attack the rattlesnake, and, as if aware of the latter's venom, protects himself from its fangs by using his wing as a shield. Many instances have been related to me by eye-witnesses of contests between the rattlesnake and this bird, in which the latter always came off conqueror. His aim is to seize the reptile by the back of his neck, when he may be considered as vanquished. With the exception of this bird and the hog, every animal has an instinctive dread of rattlesnakes, and will fly at their approach."

89 Fossil roadrunners: Arthur H. Harris and Celinda R. Crews, "Conk-ling's Roadrunner—A Subspecies of the California Roadrunner?" *Southw. Nat.* 28(1983): 407–12.

90 Cainism: Christopher H. Stinson, "On the Selective Advantage of Fratricide in Raptors," *Evolution* 33(1979): 1219–25.

90 Peccaries: James Pattie, *The Personal Narrative of James Ohio Pattie of Kentucky,* ed. T. Flint (Cincinnati: John H. Wood, 1833), noted the banks of the San Pedro well-timbered with cottonwood and willow, and in the bottoms (pp. 67–68), "great numbers of wild hogs . . . foxcolored, with their navel [scent gland] on their back, towards the back part of their bodies. The hoof of their hind feet has but one dew-claw, and they yield an odor not less offensive than our polecat. . . . We killed a great many, but could never bring ourselves to eat them."

Davis, *Man and Wildlife:* 28. Davis (181–88) marks an increase in abundance in javelina in modern times and suggests it may be due to vegetation changes, although their range may have expanded before Americans entered the Southwest.

90– White-throated wood rat (*Neotoma albigula*): James H. Brown, G. A.
91 Lieberman, and William F. Dengler, "Woodrats and Cholla: Depen-dence of a Small Mammal Population on the Density of Cacti," *Ecol.* 53(1972): 310–13.

91– Wood-rat nests: Albert W. Johnson, "The Evolution of Desert Vege-
92 tation in Western North America," in *Dsrt. Biol.:* 107.

91 Wood-rat middens: Van Devender and Spaulding, "Development of Vegetation and Climate": 131–56, also *Science* 204(1979): 701–10.

92   Streamside vegetation: Erik Tallak Nilsen, M. Raoul Sharifi, and Philip W. Rundel, "Comparative Water Relations of Phreatophytes in the Sonoran Desert of California," *Ecol.* 65 (1984): 767–78.

       Cooke, Bartlett, and other historic accounts describe the San Pedro as a running stream with squawfish and suckers.

92–   Arroyo cutting: In 1959, James R. Hastings, "Vegetation Change and
93   Arroyo Cutting in Southeastern Arizona," *J. Ariz. Acad. Sci.* 1(1959): 60–67, and some twenty years later, James R. Hastings and Raymond M. Turner, *The Changing Mile* (Tucson: University of Arizona Press, 1980), find the evidence that overgrazing is the primary cause of arroyo cutting to be equivocal: "For if the changes stem from climatic variation alone, as climatic conditions revert to what they used to be—and they inevitably will—the mesquite will disappear, the grasses will return, and the landscape will again assume an uncluttered aspect. With a return to cooler, moister conditions the paloverdes and the oaks may migrate downslope into their old habitats; conditions for saguaro establishment may improve, and the future again see the development of stands like the one now dying in Saguaro National Monument; the river channels may heal and a cycle of filling commence. The last of these events, the geological record shows, has happened in the past. . . ." Other articles describing the massive change in southwestern streams are S. C. Martin and R. M. Turner, "Vegetation Change in the Sonoran Desert Region, Arizona and Sonora," *J. Ariz. Acad. Sci.* 12(1977): 59–69; Dean A. Hendrickson and Dennis M. Kubly, "Desert Waters: Past, Present, and Future," *Nat. Conserv. Mag.* 34(1984): 6–12; R. R. Humphrey, "Vegetational Change," and R. Roy Johnson and Charles H. Lowe, "On the Development of Riparian Ecology," *Riparian Ecosystems and Their Management*; this report of the First North American Riparian Conference contains other pertinent papers, among them John N. Rinne, "Livestock Grazing Effects on Southwestern Streams: A Complex Research Problem": 295–99. Also R. Roy Johnson and James M. Simpson, "Desertification of Wet Riparian Ecosystems in Arid Regions of the North American Southwest," in *Arid Lands:* 1383–93, and W. L. Minckley and David E. Brown, eds., "Physical Environments of Southwestern Wetlands," *Dsrt. Plnts.* 4(1–4)(1982): 226.

       Charles Bowden, *Killing the Hidden Waters* (Austin, Tex.: University of Texas Press, 1985), and Marc Reisner, *The Cadillac Desert: The American West and Its Disappearing Water* (New York: The Viking Press, 1986) put these changes in the larger context of water use in the desert West.

8: OF DESERT PAVEMENTS AND KANGAROO RATS

PAGE

94– Creosote bush "island": N. E. West, "Nutrient Cycling in Desert
95   Ecosystems," in *Arid-Land Ecosys.* 2: 316; Frits W. Went, "The
     Dependence of Certain Annual Plants on Shrubs in Southern Cali-
     fornia Deserts," *Bulletin of the Torrey Botanical Club* 69(1942): 100–14;
     Jeffrey Lee, "Origins of Mounds Under Creosote Bush (*Larrea triden-
     tata*) on Terraces of the Salt River, Arizona," *Journal of the Arizona-
     Nevada Academy of Science* 21(1986): 23, 27.

95– Phainopepla (*Phainopepla nitens*): Glenn E. Walsberg, "Brood Size
96   and the Use of Time and Energy by the Phainopepla," *Ecol.*
     59(1978): 147.

95   "a beautiful jet black . . .": Elliott Coues, "Birds of the Colorado
     Valley," *U.S. Geological and Geographical Survey of the Territory, Misc.
     Pub. 11* (Washington, D.C.: U.S. Government Printing Office,
     1878): 476.

96   "with precisely the fragrance . . .": Edward Lee Greene, "Botanizing
     on the Colorado Desert," *Amer. Nat.* 14(1880): 29: "This mistletoe,
     upon a close inspection, was found bearing a profusion of small,
     greenish and altogether inconspicuous flowers, with precisely the
     fragrance of pond lilies. . . ."

96   El Camino del Diablo: Kirk Bryan, "The Papago Country,"
     U.S.G.S. Water Supply Paper 499 (Washington, D.C.: U.S. Govern-
     ment Printing Office, 1925): 413–16, describes Kino's trips, begin-
     ning in 1699, as well as those of de Anza in 1775; Herbert H. Bolton,
     Rim of Christendom (New York: Russell & Russell, 1960): 410–15,
     441–42; Elliott Coues, *On the Trail of a Spanish Pioneer, the Diary and
     Itinerary of Francisco Garcés*, vol. 1 (New York: Francis P. Harper,
     1900): 127; Garcés traveled with de Anza. Coues discusses El Ca-
     mino and notes that Sierra de la Cabeza Prieta was also known as
     Cerro de San Pasqual and, more recently, the Mohawk Range (and
     still appears so on some maps today); also, an unpublished manu-
     script, Bernard L. Fontana, "An Archaeological Survey of the Ca-
     beza Prieta Game Range, Arizona," in the Library of the Arizona
     State Museum: 50–52.

     For Kino's account, Herbert E. Bolton, ed., *Kino's Historical Mem-
     oir of Pimeria Alta. A Contemporary Account of the Beginnings of Califor-
     nia, Sonora, and Arizona, by Father Eusebio Francisco Kino, S.J., Pioneer
     Missionary, Explorer, Cartographer, and Ranchman, 1683–1711* (Cleve-
     land: Arthur H. Clark Company, 1919). More recent narrators are

Raphael Pumpelly, *My Reminiscences* (New York: Henry Holt & Company, 1918): 2: 761–76; Charles Bowden, "Adventures in the Shell Trade," *Tucson Citizen,* May 26, 1984; and an essay in *Beyond the Wall* by the quintessential *Rattus desertus,* Edward Abbey (New York: Holt, Rinehart & Winston, 1984): 1–49. William T. Hornaday, *Camp-fires on Desert and Lava* (New York: Charles Scribner's Sons, 1914): 113, says that three hundred to four hundred "wayfarers" died on El Camino.

96–
97
Tanks: Pumpelly, traveling across southern Arizona in 1861, vol. 1: 192: "The only supplies of water to be found, over an area of many thousands of miles, are in the mountains at a few points where the rains had left in natural tanks enough to last for a few weeks." See also Minckley and Brown, "Physical Environments of Southwestern Wetlands": 226.

97
Sonoran Desert birds: S. E. Reichert, "Development and Reproduction in Desert Animals," *Arid-Land Ecosys.:* 802.

97
Sonoran Desert annuals: I. N. Forseth et al., "Field Water Relations of Sonoran Desert Annuals," *Ecol.* 65(1984): 1436–44, gives baseline information on annual phenology for this area.

97
Plantain (*Plantago insularis*): J. J. Mott, "Flowering, Seed Formation and Dispersal," *Arid-Land Ecosys.:* 636–38; for a photograph of the minute 3-mm flower, see Robert I. Gilbreath, *Miniature Flowers. A Desert Search* (Flagstaff, Ariz.: Northland Press, 1985): 3.

Stephen J. Dina and Lionel G. Klikoff, "Carbohydrate Cycle of *Plantago insularis* var. *fastigata,* a Winter Annual from the Sonoran Desert," *Botan. Gaz.* 135(1974): 17–18. Plantain seedlings sprout with less than one inch of rain in the Mojave Desert; see Lloyd Tevis, Jr., "A Population of Desert Ephemerals Germinated by Less than One Inch of Rain," *Ecol.* 39(1958): 688–95.

98
Plant cover on desert pavement: H. Brad Musick, "Barrenness of Desert Pavement in Yuma County, Arizona," *J. Ariz. Acad. Sci.* 10(1975): 227–28.

98–
99
Desert pavement: Mabbutt, *Dsrt. Landf.:* 124–27; Cooke and Warren, *Geomorph. Dsrts.:* 120–29; V. A. Kovda et al., "Soil Processes in Arid Lands," *Arid-Land Ecosys.:* 1: 445–47; Thomas Clements, ed., *Dsrt. Surf. Cond.:* 11–12; Ronald U. Cooke, "Stone Pavements in Deserts," *Annals of the Association of American Geographers* 60(1970): 560–77.

99
Desert varnish: Carleton B. Moore and Christopher Eldridge, "Desert Varnish," in *Ref. Handbk. Dsrt.:* 527–36; R. I. Dorn and T. M. Oberlander, "Microbial Origin of Desert Varnish," *Science* 213(1981): 1245–47; Ronald I. Dorn et al., "Cation-Ratio and Accel-

erator Radiocarbon Dating of Rock Varnish on Mojave Artifacts and Landforms," *Science* 231(1986): 830–33; Roger LeB. Hooke, Houng-yi Yang, and Paul W. Weiblen, "Desert Varnish: An Electron Probe Study," *Journal of Geology* 77(1969): 275–88.

William P. Blake, "Superficial Blackening and Discoloration of Rocks Especially in Desert Areas," *American Institute of Mining Engineers—Transactions* 35(1909): 371–75, is of historical interest; also "Geological Report," in R. S. Williamson, "Report of Explorations in California for Railroad Routes, to Connect with the Routes near the 35th and 32d Parallels of North Latitude," *Reports of Explorations and Surveys, to Ascertain the Most Practicable Route for a Railroad from the Mississippi River to the Pacific Ocean 1853–1856. Senate Executive Document No. 73, 33rd Cong., 2d sess.* (Washington, D.C.: U.S. Government Printing Office) [762]: 117: "Pebbles of various colors . . . lay in profusion on the surface. We had not proceeded far before we found that the ground was literally paved with them, and that, in fact, but little earth or sand was to be seen. These pebbles were not loose, as upon an ordinary gravel-walk, but seemed laid down compactly, as if by art, and all at the same height, as if they had been pressed down by a roller, or otherwise. . . . The size of the pebbles varies from that of a hickory nut to a hen's egg, and larger; but the greater part are not larger than an egg. They consist, as before observed, of various colored porphyries, and of basalt and greenstone, mingled with quartz, agates, and jaspers. The whole surface of the plain was swept clean by the winds, and the upper layer of pebbles was perfectly clean and free from soil, sand, or dust. All the cementing material seemed removed, and they were retained to the surface by a narrow but firm bedding on the under side. Every pebble had the beautifully polished and glistening exterior, and the diversity of colors was increased, and their brilliance heightened, by this singular polish. The glitter of the sun's rays on this plain was like that on the water of a lake in a summer's day, when the surface is thrown by a passing breeze. Each pebble seemed firmly placed, and yet could be readily detached. The galloping of our mules made a strange clinking or rattling sound, but scarcely left a trace of our passage behind us."

100   "an iron-hard, iron-hued . . .": Abbey, *Beyond the Wall:* 151, 152.
101– Kangaroo rat (*Dipodomys merriami*): W. Glen Bradley and Roger A.
104   Mauer, "Reproduction and Food Habits of Merriam's Kangaroo Rat, *Dipodomys merriami*," *J. Mamm.* 52(1971): 503–507; Steven D. Thompson, "Microhabitat Utilization and Foraging Behavior of Bipedal and Quadrupedal Heteromyid Rodents," *Ecol.* 63(1982): 1303–12; James C. Munger, Michael A. Bowers, and W. Thomas

Jones, "Desert Rodent Populations: Factors Affecting Abundance, Distribution, and Genetic Structures," *Biology of Desert Rodents, Great Basin Nat. Mem.* 7(1983): 100–102; Bartholomew and Dawson, "Temperature Regulation in Desert Mammals": 336, 366, 407, 416; Knut Schmidt-Nielson, *Dsrt. Anml.*: 150–52, 160–70, 177–78; and "Recent Advances in the Comparative Physiology of Desert Animals," in *Comp. Physiol. Dsrt. Anml.*: 376.

101– Morphological adaptations: Joyce C. Nikolai and Dennis M.
103 Bramble, "Morphological Structure and Function in Desert Heteromyid Rodents," *Great Basin Nat. Mem.* 7(1983): 44–64; R. E. MacMillen, "Water Economy": 73–74.

103– Seed foraging: J. H. Brown and G. A. Lieberman, "Resource Utili-
104 zation and Coexistence of Seed-Eating Rodents in Sand Dune Habitats," *Ecol.* 54(1973): 788–97; M. A. Mares, "Convergent Evolution of Desert Rodents: Multivariate Analysis and Zoogeographic Implications," *Paleobiology* 2: 32–36; O. J. Reichman, "Relation of Desert Rodent Diets to Available Resources," *J. Mamm.* 56(1976): 731–51; Reichman, Prakash, and Roig, "Food Selection": 1: 696–99; Burt P. Kottler, "Risk of Predation and the Structure of Desert Rodent Communities," *Ecol.* 65(1984): 689–701.

9: OF WHITE-WINGED DOVES AND DESERT BIGHORNS

PAGE

105– *Cabeza Prieta:* School of Renewable Natural Resources, *Cabeza Pri-
107 eta National Wildlife Refuge Management Plan* (Tucson: University of Arizona, 1980): 58–59, "was established in 1939 to protect the dwindling population of desert bighorn sheep in the area. See also *The Cabeza Prieta Game Range* (U.S. Department of the Interior, Fish and Wildlife Service, RL–99-R, June 1965). Also present in the Cabeza are desert antelope; see Charles Bowden, *Blue Desert* (Tucson: University of Arizona Press, 1986): 21–25; and Alberto González-Romero and Patricia Galina-Tessaro, "Wild Bighorn Sheep and Pronghorn Antelope in the Pinacate, Sonora: A Dwindling Resource," in *Arid Lands:* 233–242. For other accounts of this sheepwatch, Bowden, "The Heat Treatment," *City Magazine* 2(1987): 29–31, and William Broyles, "Counting Sheep the Hard Way," *Tucson Citizen,* September 15, 1984.

Bartlett, *Personal Narrative* 2: 209: "If one unused to these remarkable plants should suddenly be brought to this place, where he would see before him a vast plain studded with thousands of these cacti, many of which rise to the height of twenty or thirty feet, in a single stem without a branch, he would be very likely, particularly if he saw them as we did by moonlight, to imagine himself in the midst of the ruins of a magnificent palace, the columns of which were alone left standing."

107– Mesquite fruit, leaves: See a collection of pertinent essays in *Mesquite:*
108   M. A. Mares et al., "*Prosopis* as a Niche Component": 123–49; O. T. Solbrig et al., "Patterns of Variation": 48–50; H. A. Mooney et al., "Phenology": 38–39; Richard S. Felger, "Mesquite in Indian Cultures of Southwestern North America": 152–59, 164, 176. See also J. T. Peacock and C. McMillan, "Ecotypic Differentiation in *Prosopis* (Mesquite)," *Ecol.* 46(1965): 35–51.

108   Flora: Norman M. Simmons, "Flora of the Cabeza Prieta Game Range," *J. Ariz. Acad. Sci.* 4(1966): 93–104.

108   Saguaro seeds: S. E. McGregor, S. M. Alcorn, and G. Olin, "Pollination and Pollinating Agents of the Saguaro," *Ecol.* 43(1962): 266, estimate that a stand of fifteen to twenty mature saguaros per acre could produce two million viable seeds so that seed production is not a limiting factor in saguaro establishment; see also McGinnies, *Discov. Dsrt.:* 27.

110   Ants (Formicinae): Frits Went, Jeanette Wheeler, and George C. Wheeler, "Feeding and Digestion in Some Ants (*Vermessor* and *Manica*)," *BioSci.* 22(1970): 82–88.

110– White-winged doves (*Zenaida asiatica*): S. M. Russell, "Regulation of
12   Egg Temperatures by Incubant White-winged Doves," *Phys. Sys. Semiar. Envir.:* 107–11; S. M. Russell and P. J. Gould, "Population Structure, Foraging Behavior and Daily Movements of Certain Sonoran Desert Birds," *US/IBP Desert Biome Research Memo RM 74-427* (Logan: Utah State University, 1974); Dawson and Bartholomew, "Temperature Regulation": 1: 361, 379, 386.

113– Bee stings: S. A. Minton, "Venoms of Desert Animals," *Dsrt.*
14   *Biol.:*1: 496–97; Albert L. Sheffer, "Anaphylaxis," *Journal of Allergy and Clinical Immunology* 72(2)(1985): 227, 232; David B. K. Golden and Martin D. Valentine, "Insect Sting Allergy," *Annals of Allergy* 58 (1984): 444–48; the Arizona-Sonoran Desert Museum and the Arizona Poison Control System (n.d.), *Venomous Creatures,* advises to *scrape* out the stinger with a fingernail or knife blade, *not* to pull it out with your fingers. See also B. Heinrich, "Thermoregulation and Flight Energetics of Desert Insects," *Environ. Phys. Dsrt. Org.:* 100.

114– Gila monster (*Heloderma suspectum*): Minton, "Venoms": 1:500–501;
15   Mayhew, "Desert Amphibians and Reptiles," ibid.: 1: 234–53.

115   Zebra-tailed lizard (*Callisaurus draconoides*): Mayhew, "Desert

Amphibians and Reptiles": 1: 260–61. John Woodhouse Audubon, *Audubon's Western Journal 1849–1850* (Tucson: University of Arizona Press, 1984): 147–48: "one little beauty with a banded tail runs before us and across our path by dozens. It makes frequent stops, and each time curls its tail on its back, and waves it gently four or five times most gracefully."

115– Thirst: A firsthand account is that of Bill Corcoran, a miner in Death
18   Valley, quoted in Bourke Lee, *Death Valley* (New York: The Macmillan Company, 1931): 154–55: "Three days wanderen around outa my head with angels flyen alongside a me pouren water out of a silver pitcher into a silver bowl. I could hear the rustle of their wings and the splashen water. I could see more water than I ever knew was on earth before. Water was runnen in all directions, and I could hear it rainen plainer than it ever rained when I was myself. I'll never come closer to dyen and not go. I musta fell down all over the country; I busted my ribs and cut my head on the rocks and threw away my shirt and one shoe and didn't know it. When they found me . . . I couldn't talk, my tongue and throat was swollen so. . . . In those three days I was wanderen around in the desert I went down from one hundred and eighty-five pounds to one hundred and twenty-six pounds. Sixty pounds in three days is what I lost. That's some dryen out."

115   "tumid tongue . . .": W. J. McGee wrote the most lurid account of death in the Cabeza, "Thirst in the Desert," *Atlantic Monthly* 81(1898): 483–488, unkindly provided by Bill Broyles (p. 488): "Perhaps the tumid tongue and livid lips dry again as the final spurts from the capillaries are evaporated. Thirsty insects gather to feast on the increasing waste; the unclean blow-fly hastens to plant its foul seed in eyes and ears and nostrils, and the hungry vulture soars low. The wanderer, striving to loosen the tormenting browbands, tears his scalp with his nails and scatters stray locks of hair over the sand; the forbidding cholla, which is the spiniest of the cruelly spined cacti, is vaguely seen as a great carafe surrounded by crystal goblets, and the flesh-piercing joints are greedily grasped and pressed against the face, where they cling like beggar-ticks to woolen garments, with the spines penetrating cheeks and perhaps tapping arteries; the shadow of shrub or rock is a Tantalus' pool, in which the senseless automaton digs desperately amid the gravel until his nails are torn off. Then the face is forced into the cavity, driving the thorns further into the flesh, breaking the teeth and bruising the bones, until the half-stark and already festering carcass arises to wander toward fresh torment."

115– Reaction and adaptation to heat: E. F. Adolph and Associates, *Physiol-*
16 *ogy of Man in the Desert* (New York: Wiley Interscience Publishers,
1947), is a collection of studies on heat exhaustion, thirst, water
requirements, etc., wise reading for anyone spending any length of
time in the desert; see also E. B. Adolph and D. B. Dill, "Observations on Water Metabolism in the Desert," *American Journal of Physiology* 123(1938): 369–78; F. N. Craig, "Sweat Mechanisms in Heat," in
Physiol. Adapt.: 53–64; D. H. K. Lee, "Terrestrial Animals in Dry
Heat," *Handbk. Phys.*: 551–82; Knut Schmidt-Nielsen, "Recent
Advances in the Comparative Physiology of Desert Animals,"
Comp. Physiol. Dsrt. Anml.: 5–6, 10–22; John Bligh, "Evaporative
Heat Loss in Hot Arid Environments," *Comp. Physiol. Dsrt. Anml.*:
357–69; G. E. Folk, Jr., *Textbook of Environmental Physiology* (Phila-
delphia: Lea & Febiger, 1976): 225. Sobering reading is James P.
Knochel et al., "The Renal, Cardiovascular, Hematologic and Serum
Electrolyte Abnormalities of Heat Stroke," *American Journal of Medi-
cine* 30(1961): 299–309.
116– Acclimatization: D. B. Dill, F. G. Hall, and H. T. Edwards,
18 "Changes in Composition of Sweat During Acclimatization to
Heat," *Amer. J. Physiol.* 123(1938): 412–19; H. S. Belding, "Bio-
physical Principles of Acclimatization to Heat," in *Physiol.
Adapt.*: 9–21.

   Dawson and Bartholomew, "Temperature Regulation": 386, note
that white-winged doves that had lost 20 percent of their initial
weight were able to restore 12–15 percent of that within five minutes
after access to water; Jack C. Turner, Jr., "Water, Energy and Electrolyte Balance in the Desert Bighorn Sheep, *Ovis canadensis,*" Ph.D.
dissertation, University of California, Riverside, 1973: 111–13.
118 "radiant with health": Carl Lumholtz, *New Trails in Mexico* (New
York: Charles Scribner's Sons, 1912): 224.
118– Desert bighorn (*Ovis canadensis*): David M. Leslie, Jr., and Charles L.
20 Douglas, "Desert Bighorn Sheep of the River Mountains," *The
Journal of Wildlife Management Mongraphs* 43(1979): 1–56, and
"Human Disturbance at Water Sources of Desert Bighorn Sheep,"
The Wildlife Society Bulletin 8(1980): 284–90; Gale Monson and
Lowell Sumner, eds., *The Desert Bighorn* (Tucson: University of
Arizona Press, 1981); Norman M. Simmons, "Refuge in a Wilderness," *Explorers Journal* 46(1968): 127–33, and "The Social Organiza-
tion, Behavior, and Environment of the Desert Bighorn Sheep on the
Cabeza Prieta Game Range, Arizona," Ph.D. Dissertation, Univer-
sity of Arizona, 1969; Turner, "Water, Energy and Electrolyte Balance": 110–14.

10: OF RED-TAILED HAWKS AND BLACK-TAILED GNATCATCHERS

121   "Not to have known . . .": Joseph Wood Krutch, *The Desert Year* (New York: The Viking Press, 1952): 126.

122   Water-hole birds: B. B. Beck, C. W. Engen, and P. W. Gelfand, "Behavior and Activity Cycles of Gambel's Quail and Raptorial Birds at a Sonoran Desert Waterhole," *Condor* 75(1973): 466–70; Dawson and Bartholomew, "Temperature Regulation": 363–64, 388; Wilbur Mayhew, "Birds," *Deep Cyn.:* 153–59.

122– Black vulture (*Coragyps atratus*): David Costello, *The Desert World*
23   (New York: Thomas Y. Crowell, 1972): 181; Dawson and Bartholomew, "Temperature Regulation": 364; Knut Schmidt-Nielsen, "Recent Advances": 204–205.

123   Harris' (Yuma) antelope squirrel (*Ammospermophilus harrisii*): Dawson and Bartholomew, "Temperature Regulation": 410; W. Glen Bradley and M. K. Yousef, "Small Mammals in the Desert," *Physiol. Adapt.:* 132–42; J. W. Hudson, D. R. Deavers, and S. S. Bradley, "A Comparative Study of Temperature Regulation in Ground Squirrels with Special Reference to the Desert Species," in *Comp. Physiol. Dsrt. Anml.:* 202–207; Knut Schmidt-Nielson, *Dsrt. Anml.:* 139–40; George A. Bartholomew and Jack W. Hudson, "Desert Ground Squirrels," *Sci. Amer.* 205(1961): 107–16, a well-illustrated article; Daniel E. Hatch, "Energy Conserving and Heat Dissipating Mechanisms of the Turkey Vulture," *Auk* 87(1970): 111–24.

124   Gambel's quail (*Lophortyx gambelii*): Most historic accounts note the tremendous numbers of quail; for instance, A. L. Heerman, "Report upon Birds Collected on the Survey," in *Pacif. RR. Reports, Sen. Exec. Doc. No. 73*, 33rd Cong., 2d sess. (Washington, D.C.: Beverley Tucker, Printer, 1859) [767]: 10: 19–20, and J. Ross Browne, *Adventures in the Apache Country* (New York: Harper Brothers, 1869): 76. See also Gordon W. Gullion, "The Ecology of Gambel's Quail in Nevada and the Arid Southwest," *Ecol.* 41(1960): 534–35; also George A. Bartholomew and William R. Dawson, "Body Temperatures in California and Gambel's Quail," *Auk* 75(195–98): 150–56.

125   Kawaiisu legend: Maurice Zigmond, "Some Mythological and Supernatural Aspects of Kawaiisu Ethnography and Ethnobiology," *Great Basin Cult. Ecol.:* 129–34.

125   "the point where days . . .": Sigurd Olsen, *Reflections from the North Country* (New York: Alfred A. Knopf, 1976): 28. "I know now as

men accept the time clock of the wilderness, their lives become entirely different. It is one of the great compensations of primitive experience, and when one finally reaches the point where days are governed by daylight and dark, rather than by schedules, where one eats if hungry and sleeps when tired, and becomes completely immersed in the ancient rhythms, then one begins to live."

125 Bees: V. J. Tepedino, "The Importance of Bees and Other Insect Pollinators in Maintaining Flora Species Composition," *Great Basin Nat. Mem.* 3(1979): 139–50; B. B. Simpson et al., "Reproductive Systems": 105–13; P. D. Hurd and E. G. Linsley, "The Principal *Larrea* Bees of the Smithsonian," *Smithsonian Institution Contributions to Zoology* 193(1975): 1–74; J. C. Schultz, D. Otte, and F. Enders, "Larrea as a Habitat Component for Desert Arthropods," *Creosote Bush:* 176–77, 193–94, 204–205.

126 White-throated wood rat: See Reichman, Prakash, and Roig, "Food Selection": 700; Schmidt-Nielsen, *Dsrt. Anml.:* 143–47; James C. Munger, Michael A. Bowers, and W. Thomas Jones, "Desert Rodent Populations": 91–116; Wagner and Graetz, "Animal-Animal Interactions": 92.

126 Wood-rat utilization of cactus: Bodil Schmidt-Nielson, "Urea Excretion by the Vertebrate Kidney": 143–47: Experiments show that the wood rat absorbs greater quantities of calcium from its intestine than other mammals can and excretes it as calcium carbonate in a higher percentage than other mammals are able to do (high amounts cause kidney stones or other renal damage). Since no mammal is known to be able to metabolize oxalic acid, Schmidt-Nielson suggests that it may be destroyed by intestinal bacteria.

126– Saguaro: R. M. Turner et al., "Transplanted Saguaro Seedlings":
27 835–44; Walter and Stadelmann, "Water Relations": 2: 259–60; R. I. Yeaton and M. L. Cody, "Distribution of Cacti along Environmental Gradients," Sonoran and Mojave Deserts, *J. Ecol.* 67 (1979): 529–41; Yeaton et al., "Morphological Growth-Patterns": 341–48.

127 Desert birds: Dawson and Bartholomew, "Temperature Regulation": 388, suggest that "any bird that can satisfy its other habitat requirements in the desert is a candidate for establishment there, because it is likely to be as effective physiologically as many birds already occupying this environment."

127 Verdin (*Auriparus flaviceps*): M. Max Hensley, "Biological Relations of the Breeding Bird Population of the Desert Biomes in Arizona," *Ecol. Monogr.* 24(1954): 200; Orians et al., "Resource Utilization Systems": 194–95.

127– Costa's hummingbird (*Calypte costae*): Dawson and Bartholomew,
 28 "Temperature Regulation": 370–72.
128 Bighorn mating behavior: This mating behavior is known as *Flehmen;* Alex Vargo, *pers. comm.,* and James W. Greier, *Biology of Animal Behavior* (New York: Times Mirror Mosby College Publishing, 1984): 310.
129 Sonic booms: *Management Plan:* 11, 29.
129 "the water was detestable . . .": John Durivage, "Letters and Journal of John E. Durivage," in Ralph P. Beiber, ed., *Southern Trails to California in 1849* (Philadelphia: Porcupine Press, 1974): 234.
131 Gular flutter: Knut Schmidt-Nielsen, "Recent Advances": 210–12; Ryser, *Birds:* 28–30; Dawson and Bartholomew, "Temperature Regulation": 361. Gular flutter has a high mechanical efficiency because the frequency is related to the resonance of the thoraco–abdominal cavity and remains nearly constant: George A. Bartholomew, R. C. Lasiewski, and E. C. Crawford, Jr., "Patterns of Panting and Gular Flutter in Cormorants, Pelicans, Owls, and Doves," *Condor* 70(1968): 31–34.

11: OF SAND FOOD AND PALM TREES

PAGE
136 "encountered an immense sand drift . . .": William H. Emory, "Notes": 100.
136– Gigantism in dunes: Bowers, *Seasons:* 26–27; Howard C. Stutz,
 38 James M. Malby, and Gordon K. Livingston, "Evolutionary Studies of Atriplex: A Relic Gigas Diploid Population of *Atriplex Canescens,*" *Amer. J. Botan.* 62(1975): 236–75. These saltbushes in the Little Sahara Dunes outside of Delta, Utah, are immense; all saltbushes growing outside the dunes are polyploids; those on the dunes are diploid relicts whose confreres were probably grazed out of surrounding areas, and these remain preserved in the highly specialized dune habitat, where cattle could not go.
138 "which grows into a pear-shaped . . .": Beiber, ed., *Expl. Southw. Trails:* 209.
138 Sand color: R. M. Norris and K. S. Norris, "Algodones Dunes of Southeastern California," *Geol. Soc. Amer. Bull.* 72(1961): 611–12, and WESTEC Services, Inc., *Survey of Sensitive Plants of the Algodones Dunes* (Tustin, Calif.: Bureau of Land Management and WESTEC Services, Inc., 1977); see also Smith, "Sand Dunes": 481–524, and "Geological and Geomorphic Aspects of Deserts," *Dsrt. Biol.* 1:61; Bagnold, *Phys. Blown Sand;* James Eymann, "Dunes," *Dsrt. Surf. Cond.:* 81.

139 "a low bush . . .": Emory, "Notes": 101.

139– Sand food (*Ammobroma sonorae*): Gary Nabhan, *Gathering the Desert*
41 (Tucson: University of Arizona Press, 1985): 51–59; *pers. comm.,* a
similar plant called wild melon grows in the Nagib Desert in Africa;
when eaten by an animal, the seeds pass unaltered through its digestive system. When the animal defecates the seed and urinates upon or
covers the scat with sand, it both effectively fertilizes and protects it.
Although no like observations have been made in the Sonoran
Desert, the possibility exists.

George Yatskievych, "Notes on the Biology of the Lennoaceae,"
Cactus & Succulent Journal 57(1985): 73, suggests revising sand food's
"parasite" designation.

140 Kangaroo rat: James H. Brown, "Species Diversity of Seed-Eating
Desert Rodents in Sand Dune Habitats," *Ecol.* 54(1973): 779–82; the
only kangaroo rats caught in the WESTEC study were *Dipodomys
deserti.*

140 Germination: Clayton Newberry, *pers. comm.,* at the Desert Botanical Gardens in Phoenix, on his germination studies. Hosts for sand
food, with confirmed haustorial connections, are bur sage (*Ambrosia
dumosa*), dune buckwheat (*Eriogonum deserticola*), Palmer's and pleated
tiquilia (*Tiquilia palmeri* and *plicata*), and arrowweed (*Pluchea sericea*).
Gary Nabhan, "*Ammobroma sonorae,* an Endangered Parasitic Plant in
Extremely Arid North America," *Dsrt. Plnts.* 2(1980): 191, adds
Emory's dalea (dune peabush) (*Psorothamnus emoryi*).

140 Endangered plants: Besides sand food, other sensitive plants pro-
posed for endangered-species status are Wiggins' croton (*Croton wig-
ginsii*), dune buckwheat (*Eriogonum deserticola*), Pierson's locoweed
(*Astragalus lentiginosus* var. *piersonii*), Borrego locoweed (*A. l. bor-
reganus*), palafoxia (*Palafoxia arida* var. *gigantea*), and dune sunflower
(*Helianthus niveus* ssp. *tephrodes*). See also Bowers, *Seasons:* 51, 58,
65–66.

141 ORV use: William J. Kockelman, "Management Concepts," *Environmental Effects of Off-Road Vehicles,* ed. Robert H. Webb and Howard G.
Wilshire (New York: Springer-Verlag, 1983): 419–24. Where vehicles congregate, no seedlings appear although they may be abundant
elsewhere. Healthy reproducing populations of all seven endangered
species only occur away from high-usage areas. See also Roger A.
Luckenback and R. Bruce Bury, "Effects of Off-Road Vehicles on the
Biota of the Algodones Dunes, Imperial County, California," *Journal
of Applied Ecology* 20(1983): 265–86, and Richard M. Iverson, Bern
S. Hinckley, and Robert M. Webb, "Physical Effects of Vehicular
Disturbances on Arid Landscapes," *Science* 212(1981): 915–16;
M. D. Sutton, "Recreation and Tourism in Arid Lands," *Arid-Land*

Ecosys. 2: 514: quoting Roger Luckenback "no other current form of recreation is capable of producing such a detrimental 'residue.' Although it may take only a split second for a dirt bike to cover a yard of terrain, the effects of its passing initiate far-reaching and diverse environmental degradation."

142 Coachella Dunes: R. P. Sharp, "Wind Ripples," *J. Geol.* 71(1963): 142 617–36, and *Field Guide to Southern California* (Dubuque, Iowa: Kendall/Hunt Publishing Company, 1976). The Nature Conservancy has acquired 11,749 acres in the 13,000-acre preserve, which includes both palm oases and dunes, under federal and state management: *The Nature Conservancy Annual Report* 37(1987): 9.

142– Desert iguanas (*Dipsosaurus dorsalis*): K. S. Norris, "The Ecology of
43 the Desert Iguana *Dipsosaurus dorsalis,*" *Ecol.* 34(1953): 265–87; Wilbur Mayhew, "Reproduction in the Desert Lizard 'Dipsosaurus dorsalis,'" *Herpt.* 27(1971): 57–77, and "Biology of Desert Amphibians and Reptiles," *Dsrt. Biol.* 1: 252–54, extrarenal nasal secretions, pp. 257–58; J. R. Templeton, "Reptiles," in *Comparative Physiology of Thermoregulation,* ed. G. C. Whittow (New York: Academic Press, 1970): 1: 204–49, and "Salt and Water Balance": 61–77; Cloudsley-Thompson, "Temperature Regulation": 39–59. Knut Schmidt-Nielsen, *Dsrt. Anml.:* 228–39. Most desert iguanas hibernate in the Coachella Dunes about six inches below the surface, going into hibernation fairly early in the fall, according to Raymond H. Cowles, "Observations on the Winter Activities of Desert Reptiles," *Ecol.* 22: 128–29.

144– Sidewinders (*Crotalus cerastes*): Laurence M. Klauber, *Rattlesnakes:*
45 *Their Habits, Life Histories, and Influence on Mankind* (Berkeley and Los Angeles: University of California Press, 1982): 54–56; Mahon Dickerson Fairchild, "A Trip to the Colorado Mines in 1862," *California Historical Society Quarterly* 12(1933): 13–16; traveling at night across the desert in 1862: "These halts and night marches were not without their perils, for, escaping from rough cover, the sidewinder, a small sized 'horned' rattlesnake, very venomous, seemed to fancy the dusty road best, and were numerous in the trail and feared by the animals we were riding, and they, jumping aside to avoid the reptiles, would often encounter the terrible thorns of the cactus."

145– Fringe-toed lizard (*Uma notata*): Walter Mosauer, "The Reptiles of a
46 Sand Dune Area and Its Surroundings in the Colorado Desert, California. A Study in Habitat Preference," *Ecol.* 16 (1935): 17–19, and "Toleration of Solar Heat," *Ecol.* 17 (1936): 56–66; two articles by Jim Cornett, "Uma, the Fringe-Toed Lizard," *Pacific Discovery* 36

(1983): 2–10, and "Interbreeding Between *Uma inornata* and *Uma notata*," *Southw. Nat.* 27 (1982): 223 (these are probably a single species); the Coachella Valley fringe-toed lizard is probably a subspecies of the Colorado Desert lizard since they interbreed; another species inhabits the Mojave Desert, and two more are found in the Chihuahuan Desert. Also Wilbur W. Mayhew, "Reproduction in the Sand-Dwelling Lizard *Uma inornata*," *Herpt.* 21(1966): 39–55, and "Reproduction in the Arenicolous Lizard *Uma notata*," *Ecol.* 47 (1966): 9–18; R. C. Stebbins, "Some Aspects of the Ecology of the Iguanid Genus *Uma*," *Ecol. Monogr.* 14(1944): 311–32, is a detailed study of the genus and its habitat, with an outline of the specific adaptations for living in a loose substrate, well-illustrated; K. S. Norris, "The Evolution and Systematics of the Iguanid Genus *Uma* and Its Relation to the Evolution of Other North American Desert Reptiles," *Bulletin of the American Museum of Natural History* 114 (1985): 253–326. This population of fringe-toed lizards, totally isolated from other populations, is now surrounded by a rapidly growing area that threatens the dunes themselves. Although the lizards are classified as "endangered" by the State of California and "threatened" by the federal government, these designations apply only to federally owned land.

147 Movie-making: Ron Geatz, "California Closes on Coastal Dunes Rich in Movie History," *Save the Land* (October 1987): 2.

147–
49 Palm oases: California's desert palms (*Washingtonia filifera*) were first studied by Robert Henderson, "Where Indians Found a Desert Paradise," *Desert Magazine* 1(1938): 14–15, 31, and "Where Wild Palms Grow," ibid., 28(1965): 26–28.

In a recent study, James W. Cornett counted 1,300. Between 1920 and 1940 there was a decrease in numbers because of lack of fire and other problems, but since then the number has more than doubled and, *pers. comm.*, both tree and grove numbers are increasing: Cornett, *The Desert Palm Oasis* (Education Foundation of the Desert Protective Council, Inc., Educational Bulletin #84-1, 1984). Researchers at Palm Springs Desert Museum calculate a 40 percent increase in wild fan population over the last forty years: "Palm Oases: A Special Desert Riparian Habitat," *Sonorensis* 9(2) (1988): 19. Of historical interest is S. B. Parish, "A Contribution Toward a Knowledge of the Genus Washingtonia," *Botan. Gaz.* 44(1907): 408–31. Richard J. Vogl and Lawrence T. McHargue, "Vegetation of California Fan Palm Oases on the San Andreas Fault," *Ecol.* 47(1966): 532–40, is a good summary of all aspects of palm oases in the California desert although some of the thinking has changed. For palm oases outside of California, see Charles Bowden, "Sun, Silence, Bighorns," *Arizona Highways* 61(1985): 38, 42–45, which describes an Arizona oasis.

It is interesting to compare Frances Carter, "Bird Life at Twenty-nine Palms," *Condor* 39(1937): 210–19, with the resort/military complex of today.

12: OF OLD SEAS AND NEW SEAS

PAGE

150   Paleobotany: D. I. Axelrod, *A Miocene Flora from the Western Border of the Mojave Desert* (Washington, D.C.: Carnegie Institution of Washington, Publication 516, 1939): 123–26.

153– Travertine and tufa: Gerald A. Cole, "Desert Limnology," in *Dsrt.*
54   *Biol.* 1: 432; J. Claude Jones, "The Tufa Deposits of the Salton Sink," ibid.: 79–83. Tufa is forming today on rocks in the Salton Sea, limited to areas where there are resistant materials on which to form.

155– "through the dreariest . . ."; "until one has crossed . . .": Durivage in
56   Beiber, ed., "Letters": 213, 228–29. Mahon D. Fairchild, "Colorado Mines," saw it thus (13–14): "The country through which we had traveled seemed to have been the bed of a sea as the surface of the ground was covered with marine shells and a plainly defined watermark existed upon the western side of an immense valley which stretched to the southward as far as the eye could reach. Though we did not comprehend our situation, we were in fact then below sea level near the head of a former arm of the Gulf of California whose water had been shut off by a natural embankment of silt deposited by the Colorado River."

156   Lake Cahuilla: Norris and Norris, "Algodones Dunes": 606, point out that the name of precedence is Lake LeConte, given in 1902.

Shreve, "Desert Vegetation": 215: "California botanists frequently allude to the part of the Sonoran Desert which lies in their State as the 'Colorado Desert.' This is a rather ambiguous name and overlooks the fact that the area in question has no features which distinguish it from adjacent parts of Arizona, Baja California and Sonora."

156   Colorado Desert: William P. Blake, "Sketch of the Region at the Head of the Gulf of California, A Review and History," H. T. Cory, *The Imperial Valley and the Salton Sink* (San Francisco: John J. Newbegin, 1905): 22, meant the term "Colorado Desert" "to apply strictly to the typical desert area of the lacustrine clays and alluvial deposits of the Colorado where extreme characteristic desert conditions prevail. . . . The appellation may properly be confined to the

regions reached by the deposition of the silt of the Colorado whether in the form of deltas or at the bottom of ancient lakes. I should also include the bordering detrital slopes from the contiguous mountains. So restricted, the area is practically coterminous with the ancient beach-lines and terraces of the lakes which occupied the valley."

156 "old-traveled trail . . .": "The Cahuilla Basin and the Desert of the Colorado," *The Salton Sea,* ed. D. T. MacDougal (Washington, D.C.: Carnegie Institute Publication 193, 1914): 4.

156– Colorado River/Salton Sea: Mildred de Stanley, *The Salton Sea Yester-*
57 *day and Today* (Los Angeles: Triumph Press, 1966); Kottlowski et al., "Quaternary Geology," *Quat. Geol.*: 287–98; W. P. Blake, "The Cahuilla Basin and Desert of the Colorado," *Salton Sea* (Washington, D.C.: Carnegie Institution of Washington Publication 193, 1914): 1–12; F. C. Farr, ed., *The History of Imperial County, California* (Berkeley: Elms & Franks, 1918). Two papers by Godfrey Sykes are of historical interest: "Geographical Features of the Cahuilla Basin," *Salton Sea:* 13–20, and *The Colorado Delta* (Washington, D.C.: Carnegie Institution of Washington Publication 460, 1937): 174.

157– Agribusiness: Steve Gliessman, Agroecology Program, University
58 of California, Santa Cruz, *pers. comm.;* Martha Rosemeyer and Martha Brown, "The Conversion Process: Many Questions Still Unanswered," *The Cultivar* (Summer 1987): 1, point out that abandonment of synthetic pesticides and fertilizers, and conversion to organic farming, is attended with lack of information, and lack of encouragement through tax breaks, subsidies, etc.; the Agroecology Program is beginning extensive studies on productivity changes, costs, and the like. See also V. J. Chapman, *Salt Marshes and Salt Deserts of the World* (London and New York: Interscience Publishers, 1960). A good overview is John Brady Marks, "Vegetation and Soil Relations in the Lower Colorado Desert," *Ecol.* 31 (1950): 176–93; James W. O'Leary, "Saline Environments and Halophytic Crops," *Arid Lands Today and Tomorrow,* ed. Emily E. Whitehead et al. (Boulder, Colo.: Westview Press, 1988): 773–85. V. A. Kovda et al., "Soil Processes in Arid Lands," *Arid-Land Ecosys.* 1: 466.

157– Insecticides: L. B. Brattsten et al., "Insecticide Resistance: Challenge
58 to Pest Management and Basic Research," *Science* 4743 (1986): 1255–60; for alternatives, Frank Graham, *The Dragon Hunters* (New York: E. P. Dutton, 1984).

158 "The deserts should never . . .": John Van Dyke, *The Desert* (New York: Charles Scribner's Sons, 1901): 59: "Grasses, trees, shrubs, growing grain, they, too, may need good air as well as human lungs. The deserts are not worthless wastes. You cannot crop all creation

with wheat and alfalfa. Some sections must lie fallow that other sections may produce. Who shall say that the prenatural productiveness of California is not due to the warm air of its surrounding deserts? Does anyone doubt that the healthfulness of the countries lying west of the Mississippi may be traced directly to the dry air and heat of the deserts. They furnish health to the human; why not strength to the plant? The deserts should never be reclaimed. They are the breathing-spaces of the west and should be preserved forever."

13: OF NIGHT LIZARDS AND SINGING DUNES

PAGE

163 Mojave Desert: Peter Rowlands et al., "The Mojave Desert," in *Ref. Handbk. Dsrt.*: 112–14; John McPhee, *Basin and Range* (New York: Farrar, Straus & Giroux, 1981).

164 Granite Mountains: Bruce A. Stein and Sheridan F. Warrick, eds., *Granite Mountains Resource Survey* (Santa Cruz: University of California, Environmental Field Program, Publication No. 1, 1979), as well as a delightful book, Flora Pomeroy, *Granite Mountain Spring* (Santa Cruz: University of California Field Program, Publication No. 17, 1986). The Granite Mountain Reserve is one of twenty-seven sites, representing the major habitats of California, established by the University of California Natural Land and Water Reserves System, *Terrestrial Vegetation of California,* ed. M. G. Barbour and J. Major (New York: Wiley Interscience, 1977): 92–94; Sara Steinberg Gustafson, *Natural Reserve System* (Los Angeles and Berkeley: University of California, 1985): 24, quotes founder Kenneth Norris, "You can't study nature without a nature to study. The reserves serve as vital bulwarks against further loss for teaching and research."

A good overview of the California deserts is that of Forrest Shreve, "Ecological Aspects of the Deserts of California," *Ecol.* 6(1925): 93–103, as good reading today as it was sixty years ago; see also Marc Reisner, "A Decision for the Desert," *Wilderness* 50(1986): 33–53.

164– Desert night lizard (*Xantusia vigilis*): M. R. Miller, "Some Aspects of
65 the Life History of the Yucca Night Lizard, *Xantusia vigilis,*" *Copeia* (1951): 114–20, and "Further Observations on Reproduction in the Lizard *Xantusia vigilis,*" *Copeia* 1954(1954): 38–40; J. Van Denbergh, "The Species of the Genus *Xantusia,*" *Proceedings of the California Academy of Sciences,* Ser. 2(5): 523–34; R. G. Zweifel and C. H. Lowe, "The Ecology of a Population of *Xantusia vigilis,* the Desert Night

Lizard," *American Museum Novitates* 2247(1966): passim. For its discovery, see Ann Zwinger, *John Xantus, The Fort Tejon Letters 1857–1859* (Tucson: University of Arizona Press, 1986): 147, 149–50.

167– Evergreen shrubs: T. L. Ackerman et al., "Phenology of Desert
70 Shrubs in Southern Nye County, Nevada," *Great Basin Nat. Mem.* 4(1980): 14–16, 19. E. M. Romney et al., "The Role of Shrubs on Redistribution of Mineral Nutrients in Soil and the Mojave Desert," *Great Basin Nat. Mem.* 4(1980): 124–133; Lyman Benson and R. A. Darrow, *Trees and Shrubs of the Southwestern Deserts* (Tucson: University of Arizona Press, 1981), for specific shrubs and their ranges.

167 Throwaway branches: Solbrig and Orians, "Adaptive Characteristics": 418; N. E. West, "Formation, Distribution and Function of Plant Litter in Desert Ecosystems," *Arid-Land Ecosys.:* 651–52; B. R. Strain, "Seasonal Adaptations in Photosynthesis and Respiration in Four Desert Shrubs Growing in Situ," *Ecol.* 50(1969): 511–13.

Productivity of *Lycium* and *Krameria:* S. A. Bamberg et al., "Comparative Photosynthetic Productions of Mojave Desert Shrubs," *Ecol.* 56(1975): 732–35, and "A Comparison of Seasonal Primary Production of Mojave Desert Shrubs During Wet and Dry Years," *Amer. Midl. Nat.* 95(1976): 398–405. The neo-Latin *rhatany* appears in dictionaries, but common spelling in the West is *ratany,* more closely allied to the American Spanish *rataña* or *ratania.*

170– Eastern Mojave flora: Robert F. Thorne, Barry A. Prigge, and James
73 Hendrickson, "A Flora of the Higher Ranges and the Kelso Dunes of the Eastern Mojave Desert in California," *Aliso* 10(1981): 71–89.

173 C_3 and C_4 photosynthesis: G. E. Kleinkopf et al., "Photosynthetic Strategies of Two Mojave Desert Shrubs," *Great Basin Nat. Mem.* 4(1980): 100–109; R. E. Graetz and I. Cowan, "Microclimate and Evaporation": 428; Solbrig and Orians, "Adaptive Characteristics": 418; Janice E. Bowers, "Plant Ecology of Inland Dunes," *J. Arid Envir.* 5(1982): 199–220.

174 "Have you wandered . . .": Robert W. Service, "The Call of the Wild": *Collected Poems of Robert Service* (New York: Dodd, Mead, 1968): 17.

174 Age of dunes: R. S. U. Smith, "Eolian Geomorphology of the Devils Playground, Kelso Dunes and Silurian Valley, California," in *Surficial Geology of the Eastern Mojave Desert, California* (Reno, Nev.: 97th Annual Meeting of the Geological Society of America, 1984): 172–73.

174– Singing dunes: Dennis T. Trexler and Wilton N. Melhorn, "Singing
75 and Booming Sand Dunes of California and Nevada," *California Geology* (1986): 147–52, list Eureka Dunes north of Death Valley, Big

Dune on the Amargosa River south of Beatty, Nevada, and Sand Mountain, east of Fallon, Nevada, as singing dunes; see also P. K. Haff, "Booming Dunes," *American Scientist* 74(1986): 376–81; R. P. Sharp, "Kelso Dunes, Mojave Desert, California," *Geol. Soc. Amer. Bull.* 77(1966): 1045 ff.; D. R. Crisswell, J. R. Lindsay, and D. L. Reasoner, "Seismic and Acoustic Emissions of a Booming Dune," *Journal of Geophysical Research* 80(1975): 4963–75.

175 "a vibrant booming . . .": R. A. Bagnold, *Phys. Blown Sand:* 250.

14: OF JOSHUA TREES AND RED-SPOTTED TOADS

PAGE

177 History of Soda Lake, including the Zzyzx Mineral Springs and Health Resort period: Anne Q. Duffield, *A Short History of Soda Springs* (Archaeographics, 1983); also David M. Elder, "Early Man on Soda Mountain," *Pacific Coast Archaeological Society Quarterly* 18(1982): 46–48.

178 Old Mojave trail: Bureau of Land Management, *East Mojave National Scenic Area* (Riverside: California Desert District Office): 13. Jedediah Smith, in C. Hart Merriam, "The Route of Jedediah S. Smith in 1826: Earliest Crossing of the Deserts of Utah and Nevada to Southern California," *Calif. Hist. Soc. Quart.* 2(1923): 235: "I travelled a West course, fifteen days over a Country of complete Barrens.—generally travelling from morning untill night without water. I crossed a Salt Plane, about 20 miles long & 8 wide [Soda Lake], on the surface was a crust of beautiful fine white Salt, quite thin."

178 Cima lava fields: B. D. Turrin et al., "Geochronology and Eruptive History of the Cima Volcanic Field, Eastern Mojave Desert, California," *Surf. Geol. E. Moj. Dsrt.:* 99; L. D. McFadden et al., "Cumulic Soils Formed in Eolian Parent Materials on Flows of the Cima Volcanic Field, Mojave Desert, California," ibid.:134–49; two papers by S. G. Wells et al., "Types and Rates of Late Cenozoic Geomorphic Process on Lava Flows on the Cima Volcanic Field, Mojave Desert," ibid.: 116–33, and "Late Cenozoic Landscape Evolution on Lava Flow Surfaces of the Cima Volcanic Field, Mojave Desert, California," *Geol. Soc. Amer. Bull.* 96(1985): 1518–29.

178 East Mojave: BLM, *East Mojave:* 1–2; Peter Rowlands et al., "Mojave Desert": 103–104, 108, 112; Alan Cranston, "In Defense of the Desert," *Sierra* (1986): 40–46; Marc Reisner, "Decision for the Desert"; and "California Desert 1988," *Sunset* (March 1988): 97–111, is an excellent (and well illustrated) overview, describing the need for legislation to protect fragile desert areas.

NOTES

180   Kawaiisu legend: Zigmond, "Kawaiisu Ethnography": 131.
180– Joshua trees (*Yucca brevifolia*): Thorne, Prigge, and Hendrickson,
82   "Flora": 95–96. William Manly, *Death Valley in '49*, ed. Milo M.
      Quaife (Chicago: Lakeside Press, 1927): 192–93: "As we went on we
      seemed to be coming to lower ground, and near our road stood a tree
      of a kind we had not seen before. The trunk was about six or eight
      inches through and six or eight feet high, with arms at the top quite
      as large as the body, and at the end of the arms a bunch of long, stiff,
      bayonet-shaped leaves. It was a brave little tree to live in such a barren
      country." See Arthur Cronquist et al.: *Intermountain Flora. Vascular
      Plants of the Intermountain West, U.S.A.*, vol. 1 (New York: New York
      Botanical Garden, 1972), and Arthur Cronquist, "The Biota of the
      Intermountain Region in Geohistorical Context," *Intermountain Bio-
      geography: A Symposium,* ed. K. T. Harper and James L. Reveal, *Great
      Basin Nat. Mem.* 2(1978): 3–15; R. M. Turner, "Mohave Desert-
      scrub," *Dsrt. Plnts.* 4: 157, 165–66; Stephen A. Trimble, *Joshua Tree.
      Desert Reflections* (Twentynine Palms, Calif.: Joshua Tree Natural
      History Association, 1979): 3–4. The yucca moth singular to *Yucca
      brevifolia* is *Tegeticula synthetica,* according to Don C. Force and Mich-
      ael L. Thompson, "Parasitoids of the Immature Stages of Several
      Southwestern Yucca Moths," *Southw. Nat.* 26(1) (1984): 47.
185   Creosote bush–bur sage community: Barbour and Major, eds., *Terr.
      Veg.:* 873–75.
         On clumping, see Turner, "Mohave Desertscrub": 4: 157–68;
      Kleinkopf et al., "Photosynthetic Strategies": 100–109, when cre-
      osote bush receives more rainfall, it tends to grow in clusters; Mich-
      ael G. Barbour, "Desert Dogma Reexamined: Root/Shoot
      Productivity and Plant Spacing," *Amer. Midl. Nat.* 89(1973): 41–57,
      concludes that regularity of spacing is the exception rather than the
      rule. See also Robert W. Wright, "The Distribution of *Larrea triden-
      tata* (D.C.) Colville in the Avra Valley, Arizona," *J. Ariz. Acad. Sci.*
      6(1970): 58–63; Derek J. Anderson, "Pattern in Desert Perennials," *J.
      Ecol.* 59(1971): 555–60.
185   Germination and survival: Thomas L. Ackerman, "Germination and
      Survival of Perennial Plant Species in the Mojave Desert," *Southw.
      Nat.* 24(1979): 399–408; Barbour, "Germination Requirements":
      915–23.
185– Winter annuals: Turner, "Mohave Desertscrub": 4: 160–62; Solbrig
93   et al., "Strategies and Community Patterns": 79; in the southwestern
      United States, the annual flora increases with aridity and variability
      of rainfall, from 1 percent total cover in areas with 20 percent
      coefficient of variation in annual rainfall, to 94 percent in Death
      Valley where the coefficient is larger than 50 percent.

Frits W. Went began the first systematic research on desert annuals: "Ecology of Desert Plants. I. Observations on Germination in the Joshua Tree National Monument, California," *Ecol.* 29(1948): 242–53, and "Ecology of Desert Plants. II. The Effect of Rain and Temperature on Germination and Growth," *Ecol.* 30(1949): 1–15; Went and M. Westergaard, "Ecology of Desert Plants. III. Development of Plants in the Death Valley National Monument, California," *Ecol.* 30(1949): 26–28; Marcella Juhren, F. W. Went, and Edwin Phillips, "Ecology of Desert Plants. IV. Combined Field and Laboratory Work on Germination of Annuals in the Joshua Tree National Monument, California," *Ecol.* 37(1956): 318–30; and Went, "The Ecology of Desert Plants," *Sci. Amer.* 193(1955): 68–72, and "Germination and Seedling Behavior of Desert Plants," *Arid-Land Ecosys.*: 477–489. See also J. J. Mott, "Flowering, Seed Formation and Dispersal," ibid.: 627, 634–35.

Thomas W. Mulroy and Philip W. Rundel, "Annual Plants: Adaptations to Desert Environments," *BioSci.* 27(1977): 109–14, describe summer annuals, none of which is endemic to the Mojave Desert. They are most prevalent where there is summer precipitation, hence there are many more in the Sonoran than the Mojave desert. Response to rainfall must be rapid, seeds must endure irregular and extended periods in dry soil at high temperatures, and photosynthetic mechanisms must allow for rapid growth (all those studied in the Mojave are C_4 species). Because so few plants can grow under such a regimen, there are many fewer summer annual species than winter.

A notable group of papers by Janice C. Beatley include "Survival of Winter Annuals in the Northern Mojave Desert," *Ecol.* 48(1967): 745–50; "Biomass of Desert Winter Annual Populations in Southern Nevada," *Oikos* 20(1969): 261–73; and "Phenological Events and Their Environmental Triggers in Mojave Desert Ecosystems," *Ecol.* 55(1974): 856–61.

185 Dodder (*Cuscuta nevadensis*): A. Wallace, E. M. Romney, R. B. Hunter, "Regulative Effect of Dodder (*Cuscuta nevadensis* Jtn.) on the Vegetation of the Northern Mojave Desert," *Great Basin Nat. Mem.* 4(1980): 98–99.

190 Germination: Two papers by Lloyd Tevis, Jr., "Germination and Growth of Ephemerals Induced by Sprinkling a Sandy Desert," *Ecol.* 39(1958): 681–88, and "A Population of Desert Ephemerals," ibid.: 688–95, refine Went's work.

190 Mojave rainfall and weather patterns: David G. Thompson, "The Mojave Desert Region, California: A Geographic, Geologic, and

344

Hydrologic Reconnaissance," *U.S.G.S. Water-Supply Paper 578* (Washington, D.C.: U.S. Government Printing Office, 1929): 69, 92–93, 108–109; R. F. Logan, "Causes, Climates and Distribution of Deserts," *Dsrt. Biol.* 1: 42–45; Ackerman et al., "Phenology of Desert Shrubs": 6, 16–17; Cooke and Warren, *Geomorph. Dsrts.:* 419–20; Thorne et al., "Flora": 73–75.

190 Bighorn sheep: Charles L. Douglas and David M. Leslie, Jr., "Influence of Weather and Density on Lamb Survival of Desert Mountain Sheep," *J. Wildlf. Manag.* 50(1)(1986): 155.

191– Storksbill seeds: Lars F. Soholt, "Consumption of Primary Produc-
92 tion by a Population of Kangaroo Rats (*Dipodomys merriami*) in the Mojave Desert," *Ecol. Monogr.* 43(1973): 357–76. See also Mulroy and Rundel, "Annual Plants": 111–12.

193 Soil fungi: M. C. Drew, "Root Development and Activities," in *Arid-Land Ecosys.:* 576; Gabor J. Bethlenfalvay et al., "Mycorrhizae in Stressed Environments: Effects on Plant Growth, Endophyte Development, Soil Stability and Soil Water," *Arid Lands:* 1015, 1023; R. K. Gupta, "Integration," ibid.: 663; F. W. Went and N. Stark, "Mycorrhiza," *BioSci.* 18(1968): 1035–39, and "The Biological and Mechanical Role of Soil Fungi," *Proceedings of the National Academy of Science* 60(1968): 497–509; Sara P. Stubblefield, T. N. Taylor, and James M. Trappe, "Fossil Mycorrhizae: A Case for Symbiosis," *Science* 237(4810)(1987): 59–60; and Jennifer Watters, "Mycorrhizae and Agriculture: A Lucrative Partnership," *The Cultivar* 6(1) (1988): 3.

193– Red-spotted toads (*Bufo punctatus*): Lon McClanahan and Roger
95 Baldwin, "Rate of Water Uptake Through the Integument of the Desert Toad, *Bufo punctatus*," *Comp. Biochem. Phys.* 28(1969): 381–88. Thomas B. Thorson, "The Relationship of Water Economy to Terrestrialism in Amphibians," *Ecol.* 36(1955): 114–15, found that species like *Bufo punctatus* that took up water quickly also lost it quickly, and smaller amphibians tolerated water loss better than larger ones as they tend to have a larger proportionate body water content. See also Mayhew, "Desert Amphibians": 209–15, 221.

195 Breeding: B. S. Low, "The Evolution of Amphibian Life Histories in the Desert," *Evolution of Desert Biota* (Austin: University of Texas Press, 1976): 149–95; Frederick B. Turner, "Some Features of the Ecology of *Bufo punctatus* in Death Valley, California," *Ecol.* 40(1959): 175–81; Lloyd Tevis, Jr., "Unsuccessful Breeding of Desert Toads (*Bufo punctatus*) at the Limit of Their Ecological Tolerance," *Ecol.* 47(1966): 766–74, found that toads did not emerge from under-

ground until evening air temperature reached over 64 degrees F. and did not breed until about 75 degrees F.

195– Mojave rattlesnake (*Crotalus scutulatus scutulatus*): Klauber, *Rattle-*
96   *snakes:* 143–44.

196   Brittlebush (*Encelia farinosa*): Like several other desert shrubs, brittlebush produces two kinds of leaves, one set xerophytic and covered with a thick mat of hairs, the other mesophytic and almost glabrous, early noted by Edith B. Shreve, "Factors Governing Seasonal Changes in Transpiration of Encelia farinosa," *Botan. Gaz.* 77(1924): 432–39. The long-time assumption that brittlebush exuded a substance that prevented other plants from becoming established has been disproved; the sparsity of annuals beneath it is more likely due to its single-stem growth, which does not hold debris. Bur sage, which exudes toxic substances but has multiple branching from the ground, holds considerable amounts of ground litter, in which other plants freely root: Cornelius H. Muller, "The Association of Desert Annuals with Shrubs," *Amer. J. Botan.* 40(1953): 53–60; also, Walter H. Muller and Cornelius H. Muller, "Association Patterns Involving Desert Plants That Contain Toxic Products," ibid. 43(1956): 354–61.

198– Giant hairy scorpion (*Hadrurus arizonensis*): Minton, "Venoms": 1:
99   488–91; Mark Twain, *Roughing It* (Hartford, Conn.: American Publishing Co., 1891): 457, gives the impression that scorpion bites are of no more than casual discomfort: "It was such ecstasy to dream, and dream—till you got a bite. A scorpion bite. Then the first duty was to get up out of the grass and kill the scorpion; and the next to bathe the bitten place with alcohol or brandy; and the next to resolve to keep out of the grass in future." Theodore H. Savory, *Spiders, Men, and Scorpions, Being the History of Arachnology* (London: University of London Press, 1961): 20, relates scorpion myths.

See also N. F. Hadley, "Water Relations of the Desert Scorpion, *Hadrurus arizonensis,*" *Journal of Experimental Biology* 53(1970): 547–88, and "Adaptational Biology of Desert Scorpions," *Journal of Arachnology* 2(1974): 11–23; N. F. Hadley and S. C. Williams, "Surface Activities of Some North American Scorpions in Relation to Feeding," *Ecol.* 49(1968): 726–34; J. L. Cloudsley-Thompson, "The Scorpion," *Science Journal* (1965): 35–41, and *Desert Life* (London: Pergamon Press, 1965): 40–46; K. Bud and R. F. Bowerman, "Prey Capture by the Scorpion *Hadrurus arizonensis* Ewing (Scorpiones, Vaejovidae)," *J. Arach.* 7(1979): 243–53; two papers by Philip H. Brownell address the method by which scorpions locate prey, "Compressional and Surface Waves in Sand: Use by Desert Scorpions to Locate Prey," *Sci. Amer.* 197(1977): 479–82, and "Prey Detection by the Sand Scorpion," *Sci. Amer.* 251(1984): 86–97; G. A. Polis and R. D. Farley, "Population

Biology of a Desert Scorpion: Survivorship, Microhabitat, and the Evolution of Life History Strategy," *Ecol.* 61(1980): 620–29, is a fascinating look at how to survive if you are a scorpion.

15: OF ALLUVIAL FANS AND DESERT TORTOISES

PAGE

200 Death Valley: Manly, *Death Valley in '49* (241): "Just as we were ready to leave and return to camp we took off our hats, and then overlooking the scene of so much trial, suffering, and death spoke the thought uppermost in our minds, saying: 'Good-bye, Death Valley!' Ever after this, in speaking of this long and narrow valley over which we had crossed into its nearly central part, and on the edge of which the lone camp was made for so many days, it was called Death Valley. Many accounts have been given to the world as to the origin of the name, but ours were the first visible footsteps, and we the party which gave it the saddest and most dreadful name that came to us first from its memories."

201 Lake Manly: Charles B. Hunt, *Death Valley: Geology, Ecology, Archaeology* (Berkeley and Los Angeles: University of California Press, 1975). Eliot Blackwelder, "Lake Manly: An Extinct Lake of Death Valley," *Geographical Revue* 23(1933): 471, "searched in vain along the mountain sides the entire length of this route for definite traces of old shore lines or lake deposits and for the notches that may have been cut by the outlets of such lakes" and found none. Morrison, "Quaternary of the United States," *Quat. Geol.*: 265–85; Hendrickson and Kubly, "Desert Waters": 7–9; R. leB. Hooke, "Geomorphic Evidence for Late-Wisconsin and Holocene Tectonic Deformation, Death Valley, California," *Geol. Soc. Amer. Bull.* 83(1972): 2086–87, 2093–96.

201 Water needs: Peggy Larson, *The Deserts of the Southwest* (San Francisco: Sierra Book Club, 1970): 183.

202 Salt flats: Clements, *Dsrt. Surf. Cond.*: 8–9; Richard O. Stone, "Playas," ibid.: 21–23; Wallace H. Fuller, "Desert Soils," *Dsrt. Biol.* 2: 60–61; and Hunt, *Death Valley:* passim.

202 Brine flies, etc. (Ephydridae): Essig, *Insects:* 608–609; Jerry A. Powell and Charles L. Hogue, *California Insects* (Berkeley: University of California Press, 1979): 162–64; Edmund C. Jaeger, *California Deserts* (Stanford, Calif.: Stanford University Press, 1948): 52; Charles T. Brues, *Insects, Food and Ecology* (New York: Dover Publications, 1946): 16, 419.

One of the species common to briny pools is *Ephydra hians,* the pupae of which provided the Paiute Indians with a nutritious fatty food called "koochabe." The pupal cases normally attach to rocks but are easily dislodged in numbers by storms, when the Indians collected and dried them.

203– Alluvial fans: Ronald U. Cooke, "Morphometric Analysis of Pedi-
205 ments and Associated Landforms in the Western Mojave Desert, California," *Amer. J. Sci.* 269(1970): 22, defines piedmont plains (alluvial fans) as having a slope of less than 11 degrees; see also C. S. Denny, "Alluvial Fans in the Death Valley Region, California and Nevada," *USGS Prof. Pap. 466* (Washington, D.C.: U.S. Government Printing Office, 1965); R. LeB. Hooke, "Processes on Arid-Region Alluvial Fans," *J. Geol.* 75(1967): 438–60; Mabbutt, *Dsrt. Landf.:* 110–14.

An older paper, Eliot Blackwelder, "Desert Plains," *J. Geol.* 39(1931): 133–40, contains short, clear definitions of desert landforms.

203– Creosote bagworm (*Thyridopteryx meadii*): Edmund C. Jaeger, *Desert*
204 *Wild Flowers* (Stanford, Calif.: Stanford University Press, 1982): 136.

204– Scale insects (Coccidae): Brues, *Insects:* 118, and Schultz, Otte, and
205 Enders, "*Larrea* as a Habitat Component for Desert Arthropods," *Creosote Bush:* 187–88, note that coccinids on creosote bush have not been well studied. An interesting historical note is J. M. Stillman, "On the Origin of the Lac," *Amer. Nat.* 14(1880): 782–87, who found coccinids on only two plants in Arizona, creosote bush and catclaw.

205 Desert algae: E. I. Friedmann, "Ecology of Lithophytic Algal Habitats in Middle Eastern and North American Deserts," *Eco-Physiological Foundation of Ecosystems Productivity in Arid Zone,* ed. L. E. Rodin (Leningrad: U.S.S.R. Academy of Sciences, Publishing House Nauka, 1972): 182–85; Friedmann and Galun, "Desert Algae": 175–76.

205– Caliche: John C. Dohrenwend et al., "Surficial Geology of the East-
206 ern Mojave Desert, California—First Day Road Guide," *Surf. Geol. E. Moj. Dsrt.:* 1–24; McFadden et al., "Cumulic Soils," ibid.: 134–49; R. I. Dorn, "Geomorphological Interpretation of Rock Varnish in the Mojave Desert," ibid.: 150–61; Fuller, "Desert Soils": 41, 54.

207– Creosote bush age and clones: Rowlands et al., "Mojave Desert": 124;
208 Simpson, Neff, and Moldenke, "Reproductive Systems of *Larrea,*" *Creosote Bush:* 92; Vasek, Johnson, and Brum, "Long-lived Clone": 255, think that the early post-pluvial period would have been a suitable time for establishment of the ancient clones that may have "persisted continuously since the first seedlings established in the Mojave Desert at the close of the Wisconsin glaciation." For how these clones form, see Wright, "Distribution of *Larrea tridentata*": 60–61.

208   Growth rings: Michael G. Barbour, "Age and Space Distribution of the Desert Shrub *Larrea divaricata*," *Ecol.* 50(1969): 684.

208   Radiocarbon dating: *Sonorensis* 7(1986): 9.

208   Broomrape (*Orobanche* sp.): Philip J. Wilke, "Ethnography," *Deep Cyn.:* 101, for native use.

208–   Desert tortoise (*Gopherus agassizii*): Cloudsley-Thompson, "Tem-
10   perature Regulation": 39–59; A. M. Woodbury and Ross Hardy, "Studies of the Desert Tortoise *Gopherus agassizii*," *Ecol. Monogr.* 18(1948): 145–200. The desert tortoise was already endangered when the above monograph was written, from being used for food, run over by vehicles, and exploited commercially; the added present-day danger is loss of habitat. See also Howard Lawler, "The Desert Tortoise and Its North American Relatives," *Sonorensis* 7(1986): 7–15. A 27,000-acre fenced, patchwork of public and private lands, the Desert Tortoise Natural Area, has been established in eastern Kern County by the Desert Tortoise Preserve Committee, Inc.; it protects an unusually high population of 200 tortoises per square mile: *Nat. Conserv. Mag.* 38(4)(1988): 27.

210   Death Valley dunes: Bowers, *Seasons:* 126–27; H. A. Mooney, O. Bjorkman, and J. Berry, "Photosynthetic Adaptations to High Temperature," *Envir. Phys. Dsrt. Org.:* 138–51.

210–   Mesquite: Mooney, Simpson, and Solbrig, "Phenology, Morphol-
11   ogy, Physiology," *Mesq.:* 31–43; E. T. Nilsen et al., "Diurnal and Seasonal Water Relations of the Desert Phreatophyte *Prosopis glandulosa* (Honey Mesquite) in the Sonoran Desert of California," *Ecol.* 64(1983): 1381–93, found mesquite tapping ground water four to six meters deep, and even during extreme water stress, physiological adaptations such as osmotic adjustment and seasonally changing stomatal sensitivity gave it great tolerance to drought.

211   Mesquite girdler (*Oncideres pustulatus* and *Megacyllene antennatus*): Jaeger, *California Deserts:* 183–84.

212   Desert cockroaches (*Arenivaga* sp.): Crawford, *Desert Invertebrates:* 58–61, 176; E. B. Edney, "Absorption of Water Vapor from Unsaturated Air by *Arenivaga* sp. (Polyphagidea, Dictyoptera)," *Comp. Biochem. Phys.* 19(1966): 387–408, and "Desert Arthropods," *Dsrt. Biol.* 2: 340–67; E. B. Edney, S. Haynes, and D. Gibo, "Distribution and Activity of the Desert Cockroach *Arenivaga investigata* (Polyphagidea) in Relation to Micro-climate," *Ecol.* 55(1974): 420–27; D. D. Hawke and R. D. Farkley, "Ecology and Behavior of the Desert Burrowing Cockroach, *Arenivaga* sp. (Dictyoptera, Polyphagidea)," *Oecologia* 11(1973): 263–79.

212– Desert holly (*Atriplex hymenelytra*): H. A. Mooney et al., "Photo-
14 synthetic Adaptations": 143–49, and H. A. Mooney, Olle Bjorkman, and John Troughton, "Seasonal Changes in the Leaf Characteristics of the Desert Shrub *Atriplex hymenelytra*" (Washington, D.C.: Carnegie Institute Yearbook No. 73, 1974): 73: 846–52; A. Wallace et al., "Mineral Composition of *Atriplex hymenelytra* Growing in the Northern Mojave Desert," *Great Basin Nat. Mem.* 4: 146–50. A general view of the production of different leaves is G. Orshan, "Surface Reduction and Its Significance as a Hydroecological Factor," *J. Ecol.* 42(1954): 442–44. Olle Bjorkman and Joseph Berry, "High-Efficiency Photosynthesis," *Sci. Amer.* 225(1973): 80–93, discuss the efficiency of the C_4 pathway of photosynthesis, a quality which they suggest may have great utility in hot-climate agriculture.

16: OF PUPFISH AND DESERT RESORTS

PAGE
215 Desiccation cracks: Cooke and Warren, *Geomorph. Dsrts.:* 138.
216– Devil's Hole pupfish (*Cyprinodon diabolis*): Cole, "Desert Limnol-
20 ogy," *Dsrt. Biol.* 1: 476–77; R. R. Miller, "Speciation in Fishes of the Genera *Cyprinodon* and *Empetrichys*, Inhabiting the Death Valley Region," *Evol.* 4(1950): 155–63, and "Correlation between Fish Distribution and Pleistocene Hydrography in Eastern California and Southwestern Nevada, with a map of the Pleistocene Waters," *J. Geol.* 54(1946): 43–53; W. L. Minckley and J. E. Deacon, "Southwestern Fishes and the Enigma of 'Endangered Species,'" *Science* 159(1968): 1424–32; Deacon and Minckley, "Desert Fishes," *Dsrt. Biol.* 2: 409, 415–18, 428–29, 452–53, 459, 469–70; J. E. Deacon and M. S. Deacon, "Research on Endangered Fishes in the National Parks with Special Emphasis on the Devil's Hole Pupfish," *Proceedings, First Conference on Scientific Research in the National Parks* 1(1979): 9–20; David L. Soltz and Robert J. Naiman, *The Natural History of Native Fishes in the Death Valley System* (Los Angeles: Natural History Museum of Los Angeles County, Science Series 30, 1978): 17, 24, describes the habitat of the Devil's Hole pupfish in detail, and thinks that it has been isolated longer than any of the other pupfish, between ten and twenty thousand years; this includes a chapter (pp. 65–73) on the recent pumping in Ash Meadows. Hillary Hauser and Jack McKenney, "Devil's Hole," *Ocean Realm* (Spring 1988): 67–71, is an account of scuba diving to see these pupfish.
217– Endangered species: Edwin P. Pister, "Endangered Species: Costs
18 and Benefits," *Great Basin Nat. Mem.* 3(1979): 151–58. Hendrickson

and Kubly, "Desert Waters": 6, of the thirty-one fishes listed as endangered by the U.S. Fish & Wildlife Service in 1981, twenty-three were desert species. See also Jack E. Williams and James E. Deacon, "Subspecific Identity of the Amargosa Pupfish, *Cyprinodon nevadensis,* from Ash Meadows, Nevada," *Great Basin Nat.* 46(1986): 220–23, and Jack E. Williams and Donald W. Sada, "Status of Two Endangered Fishes, *Cyprinodon nevadensis mionectes* and *Rhinichthys oculis nevadensis,* from Two Springs in Ash Meadows, Nevada," *Southw. Nat.* 30(4)(1985): 475–84.

218 Renal research: Current studies on pupfish are trying to ascertain what protects their kidney system from the concentration of calcium salts that in humans cause renal failure: The Nature Conservancy, "Utility of Diversity," *On the Land* (May 1988): 4.

220–22 Ash Meadows: J. C. Beatley, *Endangered Plant Species of the Nevada Test Site, Ash Meadows, and Central-Southern Nevada* COO-2307-11, COO-2307-12, addendum COO-2307-13 (Washington, D.C.: U.S. Energy Research and Development Administration, 1977), and *Vascular Plants of Ash Meadows, Nevada* (Los Angeles: Laboratory of Nuclear Medicine, Radiation Biology, UCLA 12-845, 1971); P. J. Mehringer, Jr., and C. N. Warren, "Marsh, Dune and Archaeological Chronology, Ash Meadows, Amargosa Desert, Nevada," *Nevada Archaeological Survey Research Paper* 6: 120–51.

222 "this was the Creator's . . .": Manly, *Death Valley in '49:* 165–66.

222 Endemics: Hugh N. Mozingo and Margaret Williams, *Threatened and Endangered Plants of Nevada* (Washington, D.C.: U.S. Government Printing Office, 1980); "Ash Meadows National Wildlife Refuge," *Wilderness* 50(1987): 21–23, cites twelve endemic plant and animal species here.

17: OF BLACKBRUSH AND SAGEBRUSH

PAGE

229–30 Creosote bush does not grow farther north than about 37 degrees latitude.

230 Blackbrush (*Coleogyne ramosissima*) transition community: Janice C. Beatley, "Climates and Vegetation Pattern Across the Mojave/Great Basin Desert Transition of Southern Nevada," *Amer. Midl. Nat.* 93(1975): 53–55, 66–69; Susan E. Meyer, "Some Factors Governing Plant Distributions in the Mojave-Intermountain Transition Zone," *Intermountain Biogeography: A Symposium, Great Basin Nat. Mem.* 2(1978): 197–207; A. A. El-Ghonemy, A. Wallace, and E. M. Romney, "Socioecological and Soil-Plant Studies of the Natural

Vegetation in the Northern Mojave Desert–Great Basin Desert Inter-
face," "Soil-Plant-Animal Relationships Bearing on Revegetation
and Land Reclamation in Nevada Deserts," *Great Basin Nat. Mem.*
4(1980): 73–74; Thorne, Prigge, and Hendrickson, "Flora": 93–94.
MacMahon, "North American Deserts": 42, characterizes this area
as of "extraordinary biological interest."

230– Great Basin Desert: Bowers, *Seasons:* 11; Neil E. West, "Overview
31   of North American Temperate Deserts and Semi-Deserts," Neil E.
     West, ed., *Temperate Deserts and Semi-Deserts* (Amsterdam, Neth.:
     Elsevier, 1983): 321–26; MacMahon, "North American Deserts":
     24–26; Paul A. Kay, "A Perspective on Great Basin Paleoclimates,"
     Man and Environment in the Great Basin: 76–81; Logan, "Causes,
     Climates and Distribution": 1:45; McGinnies, *Discov. Dsrt.:* 29–34;
     McCleary, "Biology of Desert Plants": 143; Raymond M. Turner,
     "Great Basin Desertscrub," in "Biotic Communities of the Ameri-
     can Southwest—United States and Mexico," *Dsrt. Plnts.* 4(1982):
     145–46.

     The Great Basin was not always of interior drainage; several possi-
     ble sites of exterior drainage occurred in the early/middle Pleisto-
     cene, likely from Lake Lahontan westward into the Sacramento or
     Klamath River system; see Morrison, "Quaternary of the United
     States": 271.

232 "the shadows of small clouds . . .": Frederick W. Bachmann and
     William S. Wallace, ed. and annot., *The Land Between* (Los Angeles:
     Westernlore Press, 1957): 100.

232 Great Basin National Park: The 76,800-acre Great Basin National
     Park, the first regional park and the first national park in Nevada,
     was established in 1986 at the site of Humboldt National Forest.
     Some sagebrush desert is included in the park but it is primarily
     higher in altitude.

232– "the Great Basin . . .": John Charles Frémont, *Report of the Exploring
33   Expedition to the Rocky Mountains in the Year 1842, and to Oregon and
     North California in the Years 1843–44* (Washington, D.C.: Gales &
     Seaton, Printers, 1845): 174.

233– Like creosote bush and mesquite, sagebrush has an extensive litera-
34   ture: *The Sagebrush Ecosystem: A Symposium* (Logan: Utah State
     University, 1976) contains a series of papers on various aspects of
     sagebrush, among them James A. Young, Richard E. Eckert, and
     Raymond A. Evans, "Historical Perspectives Regarding the Sage-
     brush Ecosystem": 1–10; they term this symposium (p. 10) a "sol-
     emn wake for sagebrush ecosystem of 1850." See also David L.
     Sturges, "Hydrologic Relations of Sagebrush Lands": 86–88; Neil E.

West, "Basic Synecological Relationships of Sagebrush-Dominated Lands in the Great Basin and the Colorado Plateau": 35–37; Martyn M. Caldwell, "Physiology of Sagebrush": 75–83; H. F. Mayland and R. B. Murray, "Mineral-Cycling Aspects Within the Sagebrush Ecosystem": 63; J. G. Nagy, "Wildlife Nutrition and the Sagebrush Ecosystem": 165–67; Neil C. Frischknecht, "Biological Methods: A Tool for Sagebrush Management": 121. See also West, "Great Basin—Colorado Plateau Sagebrush Semi-Desert," in *Temp. Dsrts.*: 331–40; Cronquist et al., *Intermt. Flora:* 1: 124–25; M. A. Ayyad, "Soil-Vegetation-Atmosphere Interactions," *Arid-Land Ecosys.:* 2: 16.

233– "If we once get safely . . .": Clark, "Diaries": 34.
34

235– Lichen: Lora M. Shields and Francis Drouet, "Distribution of Terres-
36 trial Algae Within the Nevada Test Site," *Amer. J. Botan.* 49(1962): 547–54; L. M. Shields et al., "Algae- and Lichen-Stabilized Surface Crusts of Soil Nitrogen Sources," *Amer. J. Botan.*: 490–97; J. M. Snyder and L. H. Wullstein, "The Role of Desert Cryptogams in Nitrogen Fixation," *Amer. Midl. Nat.* 90(1973): 257–65; W. E. Booth, "Algae as Pioneers in Plant Succession and Their Importance in Erosion Control," *Ecol.* 22(1941): 38–46. The two widely distributed lichen particularly prominent on sagebrush bark are *Santhorina polycarpa* and *Candelariella vitellina*.

236 Hawks: William H. Behle, "Avifaunistic Analysis of the Great Basin Region of North America," *XIII International Ornithological Congress, Proceedings* (1963): 1168–81, and Mayhew, "Birds," *Deep Cyn.:* 156.

236– Pill beetles (Byrrhidae): Richard E. White, *A Field Guide to the Beetles*
37 (Boston: Houghton Mifflin, 1983): 1555–56.

18: OF LAKES AND RATTLESNAKES

PAGE

239 Alvord Desert: Denzel Ferguson and Nancy Ferguson, *Oregon's Great Basin Country* (Bend, Ore.: Maverick Publications, 1982): 5–9, 115, 146, 159–60; Arthur Cronquist et al., *Intermount. Flora*": 86; Henry P. Hansen, "Postglacial Vegetation of the Northern Great Basin," *Amer. J. Botan.* 34(1947): 164–71 documents the changes and development of the flora. For interesting historical reading, see Gerald A. Waring, "Geology and Water Resources of the Harney Basin Region, Oregon," *U.S.G.S Water-Supply Paper 231* (Washington, D.C.: U.S. Government Printing Office, 1909).

239 Overgrazing: Ferguson and Ferguson: 95–97; Jon R. Luoma, "Discouraging Words," *Audubon* 88(1986): 86, 104; Neil E. West, "Great

Basin–Colorado Plateau Sagebrush Semi-Desert," ed. Neil E. West, *Temperate Deserts and Semi-Deserts* (Amsterdam, Neth.: Elsevier, 1983): 341–43, and "Intermountain Salt-Desert Shrubland," ibid.: 384–92.

239– Halogeton (*Halogeton glomeratus*): Costello, *Desert World:* 42; Richard
40   E. Eckert, Jr., and Floyd E. Kinsinger, "Effects of *Halogeton glomeratus* Leachates on Chemical and Physical Characteristics of Soils," *Ecol.* 41(1960): 764–72.

240 Wind: M. Fuchs, "Atmospheric Transport Processes above Arid-land Vegetation," *Arid-Land Ecosys.:* 394–97; John L. Cloudsley-Thompson, *Deserts and Grasslands* (Garden City, N.Y.: Doubleday & Company, 1976): 8–9, 12–13.

240 "a peculiarly Scriptural wind . . .": Twain, *Roughing It:* 160.

241– Alvord Lake: Ira S. Allison, "Dating of Pluvial Lakes in the Great
43   Basin," *Amer. J. Sci.* 250(1952): 907–909, and "Early Man in Oregon, Pluvial Lakes and Pumice," *Scientific Monthly* 62(1946): 63–65; L. S. Cressman et al., *Archaeological Researches in the Northern Great Basin* (Washington, D.C.: Carnegie Institute of Washington Publication 538, 1942). Interesting historically is E. D. Cope, "The Silver Lake of Oregon and Its Region," *Amer. Nat.* 23(1889): 970–82.

Henry P. Hansen, "Early Man in Oregon: Pollen Analysis and Postglacial Climate and Chronology," *Sci. Mon.* 62(1946): 52–62, and "Postglacial Vegetation": 164–71; C. Melvin Aikens, "Archaeology of the Northern Great Basin: An Overview," *Man and Envir.:* 139–55; Donald K. Grayson, "Toward a History of Great Basin Mammals During the Past 15,000 Years," ibid.: 82–101; Robert B. Butler, "The Holocene in the Desert West and Its Cultural Significance," *Great Basin Cult. Ecol.:* 5–12.

The Alvord Creek Formation, exposed on the eastern side of Steens Mountain, contains fossil maples, conifers, etc., that suggest that there was at least twice as much rainfall during late Miocene/ Pliocene times; see Ferguson and Ferguson, *Oregon's Great Basin Country:* 4–5, 40.

241– Jackrabbits (*Lepus californicus*): Ibid.: 43. J. Kent McAdoo and Donald
42   A. Klebenow, "Native Faunal Relationships in Sagebrush Ecosystems," *Sagebr. Ecosys.:* 52–53; Frischknecht, "Biological Methods": 123; West, "Great Basin—Colorado Plateau": 339; Wagner and Graetz, "Animal-Animal Interactions": 65–71; Bartholomew and Dawson, "Body Temperatures": 410–12; Costello, *Desert World:* 47–48, 126–27; Knut Schmidt-Nielsen, *Dsrt. Anml.:* 129–38; O. J. Reichman et al., "Food Selection and Consumption": 1: 696–97; Reichert, "Development and Reproduction in Desert Animals," *Arid-Land. Ecosys.:* 800–804.

244 Horned larks (*Eremophila alpestris*): William H. Behle, "Distribution and Variation of the Horned Larks (*Otocoris alpestris*) of Western North America," *Univ. Calif. Publ. Zool.* 46(1942): 205–316, and "Avian Biogeography of the Great Basin and Intermountain Region," *Great Basin Nat. Mem.*: 67–68, 73; Ryser, *Birds:* 347–50.

245 Western rattlesnake (*Crotalus viridis*): Klauber, *Rattlesnakes:* 36–42.

246 Navajo legend: Terry Tempest Williams, *Pieces of White Shell* (New York: Charles Scribner's Sons, 1984): 145.

19: OF GRASS FIRES AND GROUSE LOCUSTS

PAGE

247– Fire: Mayland and Murray, "Mineral-Cycling Aspects": 65; Carlton
48   M. Britton and Michael H. Ralphs, "Use of Fire as a Management Tool in Sagebrush Ecosystems," *Sagebr. Ecosys.:* 101–109; Cronquist et al., *Intermt. Flora:* 125, lists plant sequence following a fire.

248 Desert soil, fire: S. Adams, B. R. Strain, and M. S. Adams, "Water-Repellent Soils, Fire, and Annual Plant Cover in a Desert Scrub Community of Southeastern California," *Ecol.* 51(1970): 696–700; J. A. Young et al., "Historical Perspectives Regarding the Sagebrush Ecosystem," *Sagebr. Ecosys.:* 7.

248 Sagebrush lizard (*Sceloporus graciosus*): McAdoo and Klebenow, "Native Faunal Relationships": 56; Eric R. Pianka, "On Lizard Species Diversity": 337; Wilmer W. Tanner, "Zoogeography of Reptiles and Amphibians in the Intermountain Region," *Great Basin Nat. Mem.* 2(1978): 43–50.

250 Cheatgrass (*Bromus tectorum*): Janice C. Beatley, "Ecological Status of Introduced Brome Grasses (*Bromus* sp.) in Desert Vegetation of Southern Nevada," *Ecol.* 47(1966): 548–54; James A. Young and Raymond A. Evans, "Downy Brome—Intruder in the Plant Succession of Big Sagebrush Communities in the Great Basin," *Journal of Range Management* 26(1973): 410–15; Young, Evans, and Sherman Swanson, "Snuff the Candles in the Desert," *Northern Nevada Native Plant Society Newsletter* 13(1987): 3–4, document the thoroughness and quickness of cheatgrass takeover. Young et al., "Historical Perspectives": 1, 7, lay the phenomenal success of invaders like cheatgrass to the ability to adjust their genotypes to a changed environmental condition; cheatgrass can even successfully invade bunchgrass stands that have not been burned.

251 Burrowing owls (*Speotyto cunicularia*): Ryser, *Birds:* 267–70; Mayhew, "Birds": 157–58; Uwe George, *The Deserts of This Earth* (New York: Harcourt Brace Jovanovich, 1977): 137–38; R. L. Gleason and

T. H. Craig, "Food Habits of Burrowing Owls in Southeastern Idaho," *Great Basin Nat. Mem.* 39(1979): 274–76; Dennis J. Martin, "Selected Aspects of Burrowing Owl Ecology and Behavior," *Condor* 75(1973): 446–56.

251 "commence chatting and bowing . . .": Dr. Samuel W. Woodhouse, "Mammals and Birds," in "Report of an Expedition down the Zuni and Colorado Rivers by Captain L. Sitgreaves," *Sen. Exec. Doc. No. 59*, 32nd Cong., 2d Sess. [668] (Washington, D.C.: Robert Armstrong, Public Printer, 1853): 62.

Bartlett, *Personal Narrative* 2: 560: "A small brown owl also resides with the prairie dogs, and is almost always found standing on their hillocks, acting perhaps as a sentinel, for which the community has to pay dear. He is undoubtedly an interloper as, from the known habits of this bird, one of which is its fondness for ground mice, moles, and other small quadrupeds, it doubtless seeks the habitations of the prairie dogs to feed on their young. The parent dogs can have little courage to permit a diminutive bird like this to prey upon their offspring."

251 Winnemucca dunes: Jonathan O. Davis, "The Last 35,000 Years in the Lahontan Area," in *Man and Envir.:* 59; Pat Lott, "Winnemucca Field Trip, June 10–11," *NNNPS Newsletter* 4(1978): 4, 9.

252, Grouse locusts (Tetrigidae): Tinkham, "Orthoptera": 562, are char-
56 acterized by "the elongation of the pronotum over the abdomen and by their short fine antennae and small size." In the Big Bend section of the Chihuahuan Desert they occur in damp sand or soil.

256– King's dalea (*Psorothamnus kingii*): Mozingo and Williams, *Threatened*
57 *Plants:* 249.

20: OF GREASEWOOD AND KANGAROO MICE

PAGE

260 Lake Lahontan: I. C. Russell, "Sketch of the Geological History of Lake Lahontan," *U.S.G.S. Annual Report 3* (Washington, D.C.: U.S. Government Printing Office, 1883), is a classic early report; see also Cronquist et al., *Intermt. Flora:* 87–90; H. T. U. Smith, "Geological and Geomorphic Aspects of Deserts," *Dsrt. Biol.* 1: 91–92; Davis, "Last 35,000 Years": 53–71; Morrison, "Quaternary Geology": 276–81; P. J. Mehringer, Jr., "Late Pleistocene Vegetation in the Mojave Desert of Southern Nevada," *J. Ariz. Acad. Sci.* 3(1965): 172.

260– Black Rock Desert: Lindsay Applegate, "Notes and Reminiscences
61 of Laying Out and Establishing the Old Emigrant Trail into Southern Oregon in the Year 1846," *The Quarterly of the Oregon Historical*

Society 22(1921): 31; Samuel G. Houghton, *A Trace of Desert Water: The Great Basin Story* (Glendale, Calif.: Arthur A. Clark, 1976): 44–45; Ferguson and Ferguson, *Oregon's Great Basin Country:* 116. This is not to be confused with the Black Rock Desert in south-central Utah.

Jonathan O. Davis and Robert Elston, "New Stratigraphic Evidence of Late Quaternary Climatic Change in Northwestern Nevada," *Great Basin Cult. Ecol.:* 43–46; C. W. Clewlow, Jr., "Surface Archaeology of the Black Rock Desert, Nevada," *University of California Archaeological Survey Report* 73(1968): 1–94.

260–   Winter fat (*Eurotia lanata*): John P. Workman and Neil E. West,
61   "Germination of *Eurotia lanata* in Relation to Temperature and Salinity," *Ecol.* 48(1967): 659–61; Neil E. West, "Intermountain Salt-Desert Shrubland": 390–91; Dwight D. Billings, "The Plant Associations of the Carson Desert Region, Western Nevada," *Butler University Botanical Studies* 7(1945): 96–97 (reprinted by *Northern Nevada Native Plant Society,* 1980); Cronquist et al., *Intermt. Flora:* 117.

260–   Halophytes: James J. Riley, "Physiological Responses of Plants to
61   Salinity: Plant-Water Relations," in *Phys. Sys. Semiar. Envir.:* 249–54; MacMahon, "North American Deserts": 41; E. M. Romney and A. Wallace, "Ecotonal Distribution of Salt-Tolerant Shrubs in the Northern Mojave Desert," *Great Basin Nat. Mem.* 4(1980): 134–38; Hendrickson, "Saline Habitats": 291–92; W. D. Billings, "The Shadscale Vegetation Zone of Nevada and Eastern California in Relation to Climate and Soils," *Amer. Midl. Nat.* 42(1949): 87–107; M. M. Caldwell, "Physiology of Desert Halophytes," *Ecology of Halophytes,* ed. R. J. Reimold and W. H. Queen (New York: Academic Press, 1974): 355–78.

261   Salt grass (*Distichlis spicata*): Billings, "Carson Desert": 104–105.

261   Black Rock Desert surface: Davis and Elston, "New Stratigraphic Evidence": 47–53.

262   "the young man whom he . . .": J. Goldsborough Bruff, *Gold Rush: Journals, Drawings, and Other Papers,* ed. Georgia W. Read and Ruth Gaines (New York: Columbia University Press, 1949): 2: 571. Bruff's account is entertaining and illustrated.

262   Humboldt River/Sink: Gregory C. Crampton, "Humboldt's Utah, 1811," *Utah Historical Quarterly* 26(1958): 269–81; Dale L. Morgan, *The Humboldt, Highroad of the West* (Lincoln: University of Nebraska Press, 1985): passim; John Bidwell, "The First Emigrant Train to California," *The Century Magazine* 4(1890): 122.

262–   "the meanest river . . .": Horace Greeley, *An Overland Journey from*
63   *New York to San Francisco in the Summer of 1859,* ed. Charles T. Duncan

(New York: Alfred A. Knopf, 1964): 229; and "one of the pleasant-est . . .": Twain, *Roughing It:* 203.

263 could overturn a lightly laden wagon: Bidwell, "First Emigrant Train": 122.

263 Salinity and plants: Howard C. Stutz, "Explosive Evolution of Perennial *Atriplex* in Western America," *Great Basin Nat. Mem.* 2(1978): 161–68; O'Leary, "Saline Environments," *Arid Lands:* 773, 779; Hendrickson, "Saline Habitats": 290–92, 301–302; Walter and Stadelmann, "Water Relations": 279–85, 292–93; West, "Nutrient Recycling": 310, 315; Chapman, *Salt Dsrts.:* 8, 294–98, 300–306; V. A. Kovda et al., "Soil Processes in Arid Lands," *Arid-Land Ecosys.* I: 450–51, 459–61.

266 Honeysweet (*Tidestromia oblongifolia*): Bjorkman and Berry, "High-Efficiency Photosynthesis": 80–93; H. A. Mooney, Bjorkman, and Berry, "Photosynthetic Adaptations to High Temperature," *Envir. Phys. Dsrt. Org.:* 140–42, 149–50.

266 Greasewood sprouting: Michael G. Barbour, "Is Any Angiosperm an Obligate Halophyte?" *Amer. Midl. Nat.* 84(1970): 105–20, thinks that "obligate" may need more definition; his inference is that halo-phytes can grow as well elsewhere but avoid competition by being able to grow in saline situations.

266– Emigrants: W. J. Ghent, *The Road to Oregon. A Chronicle of the Great*
68 *Emigrant Trail* (London: Longmans, Green & Co., 1929): 7, 22–24, 163; W. E. Hollon, *Great American Desert* (New York: Oxford University Press, 1966): 81–84; Catherine S. Fowler, "Settlement Patterns and Subsistence Systems in the Great Basin: The Ethnographic Record," *Man and Envir.:* 123.

267 "We found the water . . .": Bennett Clark, "Diary of a Journey from Missouri to California in 1849," ed. Ralph P. Beiber, *Missouri Historical Review* 23(1928): 39.

267 "the road white with the bones . . .": Twain, *Roughing It:* 150, 201–202: "We camped two days in the neighborhood of the 'Sink of the Humboldt.' We tried to use the strong alkaline water of the Sink, but it would not answer. It was like drinking lye, and not weak lye, either. It left a taste in the mouth, bitter and every way execrable, and a burning in the stomach that was very uncomfortable. We put molasses in it, but that helped it very little; we added a pickle, yet the alkali was the prominent taste, and so it was unfit for drinking. The coffee we made of this water was the meanest compound man has yet invented. It was really viler to the taste than the unameliorated water itself. Mr. Ballou, being the architect and builder of the beverage felt constrained to endorse and uphold it, and so drank half a cup, by

little sips, making shift to praise it faintly the while, but finally threw out the remainder, and said frankly it was 'too technical for *him.*' "

267– "Taking the general aspect . . .": Clark, "Diary": 34, 41.
68

268 Carson Desert: Hollon, *American Desert:* 81–82; West, "Great Basin—Colorado Plateau": 344; Billings, "Carson Desert": 89–91; Davis, "The Last 35,000 Years": 53–75. Young, Eckert, and Evans, "Historical Perspectives": 4, the first ranches in the valley were stocked with animals abandoned on the Forty Mile Desert.

268 Ricegrass (*Oryzopsis hymenoides*): Young, Evans, and Swanson, "Snuff the Candles," *NNNPS Newsl.*

268– Pallid kangaroo mouse (*Microdipodops pallidus*): James H. Brown and
69 George A. Bartholomew, "Periodicity and Energetics of Torpor in the Kangaroo Mouse, *Microdipodops pallidus,*" *Ecol.* 50(1969): 705; Michael L. Rosenzweig and Philip W. Sterner, "Population Ecology of Desert Rodent Communities: Body Size and Seed-Husking as Bases for Heteromyid Coexistence," *Ecol.* 51(1970): 217–24; Bartholomew and Dawson, "Temperature Regulation": 1: 408; Kottler, "Risk of Predation": 689–99.

269– Smoke bush: (*Dalea polydenius*) was first collected by Torrey near the
70 Carson Desert, described by Sereno Watson, "Botany," *United States Exploring Expedition of the Fortieth Parallel* (Washington, D.C.: U.S. Government Printing Office, 1871): 64 and Pl. IX, "sprinkled with conspicuous elevated reddish glands." Billings, "Carson Desert": 97–100, describes this plant community.

21: OF SALT DESERT AND PRONGHORNS

PAGE

271 Gunnison and Humboldt: Nolie Mumey, *John Williams Gunnison (1812–1853), The Last of the Western Explorers: A History of the Survey Through Colorado and Utah with a Biography and Details of His Massacre* (Denver: Artcraft Press, 1955): 113–22; see also Gregory C. Crampton, "Humboldt's Utah, 1811": 26(1958): 275.

272 Lake Bonneville: Donald R. Currey and Steven R. James, "Paleoenvironments of the Northeastern Great Basin and Northeastern Basin Rim Region: A Review of Geological and Biological Evidence," *Man and Envir.:* 27–52; and Morrison, "Quaternary Geology": 273.

272– Horned lizard (*Phrynosoma platyrhinos*): Lorus J. Milne and Margery J.
73 Milne, "Notes on the Behavior of Horned Toads," *Amer. Midl. Nat.* 44(1950): 721, 723; Mayhew, "Biology of Desert Amphibians": 229–41; Cloudsley-Thompson, "Temperature Regulation": 45–47, 55;

Wagner and Graetz, "Animal-Animal Interactions," *Arid-Land. Ecosys.* 2: 73; E. R. Pianka, "Diversity and Niche Structure in Desert Communities," ibid. 2: 340–49.

272 "as if conscious . . .": Bartlett, *Personal Narrative* 1: 248.

274 Greasewood (*Sarcobatus vermiculatus*): F. S. Crosswhite, "John C. Frémont: Explorer, Plant Collector and Politician," *Dsrt. Plnts.* 6(1984): 62; Irving McNulty, "The Effect of Salt Concentration on the Growth and Metabolism of a Succulent Halophyte," in *Phys. Sys. Semiar. Envir.:* 255–56, 262; Chapman, *Salt Dsrts.:* 305; Ferguson and Ferguson, *Oregon:* 79–80.

276 Snowy plover (*Charadrius alexandrinus*): Ryser, *Birds:* 171–73.

276 Black flies (Simuliidae): Frank R. Cole, *The Flies of Western North America* (Berkeley and Los Angeles: University of California Press, 1969): 108.

276 Tule Valley: Peter Hovingh, "Tule Valley," in *The Hiker's Guide to Utah,* ed. Dave Hall (Billings, Mont.: Falcon Press, 1982): 103–105.

278– Pronghorn (*Antilocapra americana*): Olin, *Mamm. Southw. Dsrts.:* 20;
79 R. R. Lechleitner, *Wild Mammals of Colorado* (Boulder: Pruett Publishing Co., 1969): 222–24; Schmidly, *Mamm. Texas:* 166–68; Ferguson and Ferguson, *Oregon:* 49–50; McAdoo and Klebenow, "Native Faunal Relationships": 51.

279 Long-billed curlew (*Numenius americanus*): Ryser, *Birds:* 187–89.

281 Dust devils: Rudolf Geiger, *The Climate Near the Ground* (Cambridge, Mass.: Harvard University Press, 1966): 91–92.

281 Gosiute spirits: Flo Krall, *Basin and Range Landscape. A Bioregional Guide to the Stansbury Mountains* (Salt Lake City: Utah Museum of Natural History, 1983): 5.

22: OF DUST LAKES AND GLOWWORMS

PAGE

282 Jedediah Smith: Dale Morgan, ed., *The Great Salt Lake* (Indianapolis: Bobbs-Merrill, 1947): 86–87, and *Jedediah Smith and the Opening of the West* (Indianapolis: Bobbs-Merrill, 1953): 86–87, 100–104; John Caughey, "Southwest from Salt Lake in 1849," *Pacific Historical Review* 6(1937): 143–44.

283 Ripples: Ronald L. Ives, "Desert Ripples," *Amer. J. Sci.* 244(1946): 492–94.

283 "Uncle Sam . . .": Greeley, *An Overland Journey:* 225.

283 Simpson: Frank McNitt, ed. and annot., *Navajo Expedition. Journal of a Military Reconnaissance from Santa Fe, New Mexico to the Navajo Country Made in 1849 by Lieutenant James H. Simpson* (Norman: Uni-

versity of Oklahoma Press, 1964): lxvi–lxvii, 234–39; James H. Simpson, "Report of Reconnaissances, etc., in the Territory of Utah, in the Months of August, September and October, 1858, under Instructions from Brevet Brigadier General A. S. Johnson, USA, Commanding the Dept. of Utah; with a map of Wagon Roads in Utah Territory," *Sen. Exec. Doc. No. 40*, 35th Cong., 2nd Sess. [984], describing the landscape around "Pleasant Spring" (later Simpson Springs), October 24, 1858 (p. 31): "The desert as level as a floor, and in spots perfectly smooth and divested of every vestige of vegetation, and even of that universal plant in this country, the wild sage. The soil is clay, slightly intermixed with fine sand, and packs hard. . . . The general appearance of the soil of the desert is that of a baked surface checkered by cracks, sprinkled thinly with small artemisia, with now and then a patch smooth and denuded, and looking like polished clay floor."

283 Pony Express: Bureau of Land Management, Salt Lake District, "Pony Express Trail," 1982.

283 Lincoln Highway: Drake Hokanson, "To Cross America, Early Motorists Took a Long Detour," *Smithsonian* 16(1985): 64, who was "vastly pleased to get across that nightmare."

283 "so deeply coated . . .": Twain, *Roughing It:* 142–43.

283 "long before day . . .": James Clyman, "The Journal of James Clyman," ed. J. Roderic Korns, *West from Fort Bridger: The Pioneering of the Immigrant Trails Across Utah, 1846–1850* (Salt Lake City: Utah State Historical Society, 1951): 35.

283– Lake Bonneville: Morrison, "Quaternary Geology": 273–82; Currey
84 and James, "Paleoenvironments": 31–34; K. T. Harper and G. M. Alder, "Paleoclimatic Inferences Concerning the Last 10,000 Years from a Resampling of Danger Cave, Utah," in *Great Basin Cult. Ecol.:* 19; David B. Madsen, Donald R. Currey, and James H. Madsen, "Man, Mammoth, and Lake Fluctuations in Utah," *Selected Papers* (Utah Division of State History, Antiquities Section) 2(1976): 43–58; Richard H. Jackson and Dale J. Stevens, "Physical and Cultural Environment of Utah Lake and Adjacent Areas," *Great Basin Nat. Mem.* 5(1981): 5–6; Harold E. Malde, "Snake River Plain," *Quat. Geol.:* 261.

285– Kit fox (*Vulpes macrotis*): Harold J. Egoscue, "Ecology and Life His-
86 tory of the Kit Fox in Tooele County, Utah," *Ecol.* 43(1962): 491–97, and "Notes on Kit Fox Biology in Utah," *Southw. Nat.* 29(3)(1984): 361–62.

286 Townsend ground squirrels (*Citellus townsendi*): Graham W. Smith and Donald R. Johnson, "Demography of a Townsend Ground

Squirrel Population in Southwestern Idaho," *Ecol.* 66(1985): 171–78; Hudson, Deavers, and Bradley, "Temperature Regulation in Ground Squirrels," in *Comp. Physiol. Dsrt. Anml.:* 191, 208–11.

288 Glowworm (Phengodidae): Darwin L. Tiemann, "Observations on the Natural History of the West Banded Glowworm *Zarhipis integripennis* (Le Conte) (Coleoptera: Phengodidae)," *Proc. Calif. Acad. Sci.* (4th series) 35(1967): 262.

23: OF SPADEFOOT TOADS AND TWILIGHT

PAGE

289– Snow: Terry Tempest Williams and Ted Major, *The Secret Language of*
90 *Snow* (San Francisco, New York: Sierra Club/Pantheon Books, 1984).

290– Spadefoot toads (*Scaphiopus* sp.): A. N. Bragg, *Gnomes of the Night.*
92 *The Spadefoot Toads* (Philadelphia: University of Pennsylvania Press, 1965), and "Further Study of Predation and Cannibalism in Spadefoot Tadpoles," *Herpt.* 20(1964): 17–24; W. W. Mayhew, "Adaptations of the Amphibian, *Scaphiopus couchi,* to Desert Conditions," *Amer. Midl. Nat.* 74(1965): 95–109, and "Biology of Desert Amphibians," 1: 209–14, 222–23; Roger S. Seymour, "Energy Metabolism of Dormant Spadefoot Toads (*Scaphiopus*)," *Copeia* 1973 (1973): 435–45; R. Ruibal, Lloyd Tevis, Jr., and Virginia Roig, "The Terrestrial Ecology of the Spadefoot Toad," *Copeia* 1969(1969): 571–84; V. H. Shoemaker, L. McClanahan, Jr., and R. Ruibal, "Seasonal Changes in Body Fluids in a Field Population of Spadefoot Toads," ibid.: 585–92, located burrowed spadefoot toads and measured the concentrations in their body fluids; they found no evidence that spadefoots reabsorbed bladder urine or that they were under water stress; and three papers by Lon McClanahan, "Adaptation of the Spadefoot Toad, *Scaphiopus couchi,* to Desert Environments," *Comp. Biochem. Physiol.* 20(1967): 73–99; "Changes in Body Fluids of Burrowed Spadefoot Toads as a Function of Soil Water Potential," *Copeia* 1972 (1972): 209–16; and "Nitrogen Excretion in Arid-Adapted Amphibians," *Envir. Physiol. Dsrt. Org.:* 107–108.

292– Great Salt Desert: Howard Stansbury, *An Expedition to the Valley of the*
93 *Great Salt Lake* (Ann Arbor, Mich.: University Microfilms, 1966): 110: "The first part of the plain consisted simply of dried mud, with small crystals of salt scattered thickly over the surface. Crossing this, we came upon another portion of it, three miles in width, where the ground was entirely covered with a thin layer of salt in a state of deliquescencce [*sic*], and of so soft a consistence that the feet of our

mules sank at every step into the mud beneath. But we soon came upon a portion of the plain where the salt lay in a solid state, in one unbroken sheet, extending apparently to its western border. So firm and strong was this unique and snowy floor, that it sustained the weight of our entire train, without in the least giving way or cracking beneath the pressure. Our mules walked upon it as upon a sheet of solid ice. The whole field was crossed by a network of little ridges, projecting about half an inch, as if the salt had expanded in the process of crystallization. I estimated this field to be at least seven miles wide and ten miles in length. How much farther it extended northward I could not tell; but if it covered the plain in that direction as it did where we crossed, its extent must have been very much greater. The salt, which was very pure and white, averaged from one-half to three-fourths of an inch in thickness, and was equal in all respects to our finest specimens for table use." By spring, 1987, the "West Desert" had been heavily diked in preparation for pumping excess water out of the Great Salt Lake.

292–
93   Vegetation: Neil W. West, "Intermountain Salt-Desert Shrubland": *Temp. Dsrts.:* 389.

293   "furnish a desirable space . . .": Stansbury, *Expedition:* 119.

293–
95   Danger Cave: Jesse D. Jennings, "Danger Cave," *American Antiquity* 23(2)(1957): 1–328; although some of the precepts have changed, this is a masterly statement of prehistoric life in the Great Basin. Jennings suggests (p. 285) that basketry and probably other weaving techniques were in wide use in western North America, and harvesting and milling techniques in place, before they appeared in the Near East, and may have migrated from here to Eurasia. See also Harper and Alder, "Paleoclimatic Inferences": 19.

293–
94   Desert Culture: James M. Adovasio and G. F. Fry, "An Equilibrium Model for Culture Change in the Great Basin," *Great Basin Cult. Ecol.:* 67–68; Jackson and Stevens, "Utah Lake": 3–23; Don D. Fowler and Jesse D. Jennings, "Great Basin Archaeology: A Historical Overview," *Man and Envir.:* 105–20; C. Melvin Aikens, "Archaeology": 139–55; Jesse D. Jennings and Edward Norbeck, "Great Basin Prehistory: A Review," *American Antiquity* 21(1955): 1–11.

ANNOTATED
BIBLIOGRAPHY

The books cited here are those I have found particularly useful, enjoyable, and fascinating, and might be of interest to an inquisitive reader wishing to know more about the deserts of the United States. Many excellent books are available at specific monuments and parks, cited in the notes but not here because they are specific in content and not widely available. A perusal of the yearly indices of *Ecology, Great Basin Naturalist, Southwestern Naturalist,* and *American Naturalist,* to name a few, will show many articles on deserts that encapsulate current research in highly readable form. The excellent *Desert Plants* is devoted entirely to desert botany, and various Southwestern museum publications, such as *Sonorensis* (Arizona–Sonora Desert Museum), are available through membership.

ABBEY, EDWARD. *Beyond the Wall*. New York: Holt, Rinehart & Winston, 1984. The quintessential desert rat, in a series of superb essays, defining one man's desert.

ADOLPH, E. F., and Associates. *Physiology of Man in the Desert*. New York: Wiley Interscience Publishers, 1947. A collection of research articles that explore man's reaction to heat.

BAGNOLD, R. A. *The Physics of Blown Sand and Desert Dunes*. London: Methuen, 1941. A pioneer work of mathematical precision, with lyrical descriptive passages that the English do so well.

BARLOW, JON C.; POWELL, A. MICHAEL; and TIMMERMANN, BARBARA N., eds. *Second Symposium on Resources of the Chihuahuan Desert Region*. Alpine, Tex.: Sul Ross State Chihuahuan Desert Research Institute, 1986. This and the first (see Wauer and Riskind) symposium are invaluable.

BARTLETT, JOHN RUSSELL. *Personal Narrative of Explorations and Incidents in Texas, New Mexico, California, Sonora, and Chihuahua*. 2 vols. New York: D. Appleton & Co., 1856. Bartlett traveled the southwestern deserts while surveying the boundary between Mexico and the United States in 1852–53; his intelligent firsthand narrative encompasses a lot of country, much of which is just the same as when he first saw it.

BENDER, GORDON L., ed. *Reference Handbook on the Deserts of North America*. Westport, Conn.: Greenwood Press, 1982. More than you ever wanted to know about deserts and so an essential reference book: thorough, readable essays on each of the deserts, on desert geology, biology, botany, etc., plus definitive bibliographies.

BENSON, LYMAN, and DARROW, R. A. *Trees and Shrubs of the Southwestern Deserts*. Tucson: University of Arizona Press, 1981. Large format with thorough illustrations, which make it very useful for identification; good text with common names.

BOWDEN, CHARLES. *Blue Desert*. Tucson: University of Arizona Press, 1986. A collection of fine essays by a superb writer and keen observer of the modern desert.

BOWERS, JANICE E. *Seasons of the Wind*. Flagstaff, Ariz.: Northland Press, 1986. A lovely book on dunes, how they are formed, plant and animal life, written with scholarship and charm.

BROWN, DAVID E., ed. "Biotic Communities of the American Southwest, United States and Mexico." *Desert Plants* 4(1–4)(1982). Although this is a magazine article, it gives such a concise overview of all the deserts that is indispensable for the interested layman.

BROWN, G. W., JR. *Desert Biology*. vols. 1 and 2. New York: Academic Press, 1965 and 1974. Authoritative essays by various authorities on different facets of the desert. Excellent.

CLEMENTS, THOMAS, ed., with MERRIAM, RICHARD H.; STONE, RICHARD O.; EYMANN, JAMES L.; and READE, HAROLD L. *A Study of Desert*

Surface Conditions. Natick, Mass.: Quartermaster Research & Development Center, Environmental Protection Research Division, Technical Report EP-53, 1957. A study that leaves no stone unturned.

CLOUDSLEY-THOMPSON, JOHN L., ed. *Biology of Deserts.* London: Institute of Biology, 1954. Cloudsley-Thompson's books are both erudite and pleasant reading.

————. *Desert Life.* London: Pergamon Press, 1965.

————. *Deserts and Grasslands.* Garden City, N.Y.: Doubleday & Company, 1976.

COOKE, RONALD U., and WARREN, ANDREW. *Geomorphology in Deserts.* Berkeley and Los Angeles: University of California Press, 1973. Basic to an understanding of why and where deserts are where they are.

COSTELLO, DAVID. *The Desert World.* New York: Thomas Y. Crowell, 1972. Popular and accurate treatment of the western American deserts.

CRAWFORD, CLIFFORD S. *Biology of Desert Invertebrates.* Berlin, New York: Springer-Verlag, 1981. A thorough and readable treatment of the most neglected desert inhabitants.

DILL, D. B.; ADOLPH, E. F.; and WILBER, C. G., eds. *Handbook of Physiology. Sect. 4. Adaptation to the Environment.* Washington, D.C.: American Physiological Society, 1964. A series of essays on what desert heat requires of those who live or work there.

FERGUSON, DENZEL, and FERGUSON, NANCY. *Oregon's Great Basin Country.* Bend, Ore.: Maverick Publications, 1982. Although local in character, this is the only book about the area, and that makes it, in its thoroughness and affection for the country, a valuable resource.

FOWLER, DON D., ed. *Great Basin Cultural Ecology: A Symposium.* Reno, Nev.: Desert Research Institute Publications in the Social Sciences 8, 1972. A collection of provocative, imaginative essays on the anthropology of a vast section of desert.

FRÉMONT, JOHN CHARLES. *Report of the Exploring Expedition to the Rocky Mountains in the Year 1842, and to Oregon and North California in the Years 1843–44.* Washington: Gales & Seaton, Printers, 1845. Although the report is concerned with his whole exploration of the West, Frémont's view of the Great Basin is a fascinating firsthand account of discovery and the rigors of desert travel.

GEORGE, UWE. *The Deserts of This Earth.* New York: Harcourt Brace Jovanovich, 1977. Popular treatment, easy reading.

GOETZMANN, WILLIAM H. *Exploration and Empire.* New York: Alfred A. Knopf, 1966. A superb book in which are some insights on the role North American deserts have played in the westward movement and how they have affected history.

GOODALL, D. W., ed. *Evolution of Desert Biota*. Austin: University of Texas Press, 1976. A search into sources and reasons.

———; PERRY, R. A.; and HOWES, K. M. W., eds. *Arid-Land Ecosystems: Structure, Functioning and Management*. Cambridge: Cambridge University Press, 1979. A well-done series of papers with a cosmic viewpoint of desert life and living.

HADLEY, NEIL F., ed. *Environmental Physiology of Desert Organisms*. Stroudsburg, Pa.: Dowden, Hutchinson & Ross, 1975. Indispensable.

HOLLON, W. E. *The Great American Desert*. New York: Oxford University Press, 1966. Mostly the far western deserts; good information and reading.

HORNADAY, WILLIAM T. *Camp-Fires on Desert and Lava*. New York: Charles Scribner's Sons, 1914. An entertaining, macho, historic view of the Pinacate region of the Sonoran Desert, on the border between Arizona and Mexico; included here because it gives an insight into how deserts were viewed seventy years ago.

HOWES, PAUL G. *The Giant Cactus and Its World*. New York: Duell, Sloan & Pearce, 1954. A detailed study of the most famous plant in the Sonoran Desert; although replaced by more current research, it is pleasant and informative.

HUNT, CHARLES B. *Death Valley: Geology, Ecology, Archaeology*. Berkeley and Los Angeles: University of California Press, 1975. Although this is a local-focus publication, it is of such excellence and so comprehensive that it should be included.

INGRAM, D. L., and MOUNT, L. E. *Man and Animals in Hot Environments*. New York: Springer-Verlag, 1975. Research on how to work and survive in the desert, and how different vertebrates handle heat.

JAEGER, EDMUND C. *The California Deserts*. Stanford, Calif.: Stanford University Press, 1948. A concise, beautiful little book, which has not been bettered in forty years.

———. *Desert Wild Flowers*. Stanford, Calif.: Stanford University Press, 1982. Although focused on California, most of these plants occur elsewhere, descriptions are brief and concise with interesting information, every plant is illustrated, and its value far exceeds its limited locality.

———. *Desert Wildlife*. Stanford, Calif.: Stanford University Press, 1961. Although confined to the California deserts, most of the animal species are found elsewhere; handy.

LARSON, PEGGY. *The Deserts of the Southwest*. San Francisco: Sierra Club Books, 1977. Required reading for anyone walking our deserts—or even thinking about it. Good to take into the field.

MABBUTT, J. A. *Desert Landforms*. Cambridge, Mass.: MIT Press, 1977.

Describes and explains all the characteristic landforms; indispensable.

MABRY, T. J.; HUNZIKER, J. H.; and DIFEO, D. R., JR., eds. *Creosote Bush. Biology and Chemistry of Larrea in New World Deserts.* Stroudsburg, Pa.: Dowden, Hutchinson & Ross, 1977. More than you ever wanted to know about creosote bush and weren't going to ask, a well-written collection of scholarly essays on all facets of the most prevalent plant in the southern deserts.

MACMAHON, JAMES A., ed. *Deserts.* New York: Alfred A. Knopf, Audubon Society Nature Guides, 1985. If you can take only one book into the desert, this is it. More illustrations and more concise information in one softcover book than is available elsewhere in one volume, plus a superbly written introduction by one of the most versatile desert scholars.

MADSEN, DAVID, and O'CONNELL, JAMES F., eds. *Man and Environment in the Great Basin.* Washington, D.C.: Society for American Archaeology, Papers No. 2, 1982. How ancient man and deserts interrelated provides some provocative thought for present-day man.

MALOIY, G. M. O., ed. *Comparative Physiology of Desert Animals.* New York: Academic Press, 1972. Never mind the stuffy title—good reading.

McGINNIES, WILLIAM G. *Discovering the Desert.* Tucson: University of Arizona Press, 1981. A solid book by one of today's most respected desert scholars.

NABHAN, GARY PAUL. *Gathering the Desert.* Tucson: University of Arizona Press, 1985. An ethnobotanist with the pen of a poet documents ancient and modern-day plant use; a beautiful lyrical book, exquisitely illustrated.

ORIANS, G. H., and SOLBRIG, OTTO T., eds. *Convergent Evolution in Warm Deserts.* US/IBP Synthesis Series, vol. 3. Stroudsburg, Pa.: Dowden, Hutchinson & Ross, 1977. A wider view of deserts with wide implications; thoughtful reading.

SCHMIDT-NIELSON, KNUT. *Desert Animals: Physiological Problems of Heat and Water.* Oxford: Oxford University Press, 1964. Superb work by a dean of desert researchers.

SHREVE, FORREST, and WIGGINS, IRA L. *Vegetation and Flora of the Sonoran Desert.* Stanford, Calif.: Stanford University Press, 1977. This monumental two-volume work is definitive and includes an unparalleled introductory essay.

SIMPSON, B. B., ed. *Mesquite: Its Biology in Two Desert Scrub Ecosystems.* Stroudsburg, Pa.: Dowden, Hutchinson & Ross, 1977. The ultimate on mesquite.

TRIMBLE, STEVEN. *The Sagebrush Sea. A Natural History of the Great Basin.*

Reno, Nev.: University of Nevada Press, 1989. One of a series of handsomely done books on different aspects of the Great Basin; there are also fine volumes on shrubs, birds, etc.

TWAIN, MARK. *Roughing It.* Hartford, Conn.: American Publishing Company, 1891. Twain in the Great Basin Desert is pure delight.

UTAH STATE UNIVERSITY. *The Sagebrush Ecosystem: A Symposium.* Logan: Utah State University, 1978. The ultimate on sagebrush, which covers the northern part of the United States deserts as creosote bush covers the southern.

WAUER, ROLAND H., and RISKIND, DAVID H., eds. *Transactions of the Symposium on the Biological Resources of the Chihuahuan Desert Region, United States and Mexico.* Alpine, Tex.: Sul Ross State University, 1974. Indispensable for lovers of the least-known desert in the United States.

WELLS, STEPHEN G., and HARAGAN, DONALD R. *Origin and Evolution of Deserts.* Albuquerque: University of New Mexico Press, 1983. A collection of detailed essays on the recentness of desert ecosystems.

YOUSEF, MOHAMED K.; HORVATH, STEVEN M.; and BULLARD, ROBERT W., eds. *Physiological Adaptations: Desert and Mountains.* New York: Academic Press, 1972. An interesting juxtaposition of two extreme environments and the adjustments required of their inhabitants.

ACKNOWLEDGMENTS

My grateful thanks to all those who made possible so many of many trips into the desert: Judy von Ahlefeldt, Charles Bowden, William Broyles, Peter and William Hovingh, Steve McDowell, Gary Nabhan and Karen Reichhardt, Alan Romspert, Mary Savina, Judy Sellers, Sara Whitman, Anita Williams, Terry Tempest Williams. The professionalism of The Pilot, Herman Zwinger, enabled me to enjoy the view from ten thousand feet, and loving thanks also to other members of my family who accompanied the author on various forays into the deserts: Earl Milner, Susan Zwinger, and Sara Roberts.

I am grateful to those knowledgeable people who read, reviewed, and criticized the manuscript, especially those in the scientific community. I am especially indebted to Dr. James MacMahon, Utah State University, Logan, Utah, who read the entire manuscript and commented carefully. For specific areas: Alan Brenner, Jon Frost, Dr. James Scudday (Chihuahuan Desert); Janice Bowers, William Broyles, Dr. David M. Leslie, Dr. Gary Nabhan and Karen Reichhardt, David Nordstrom (Sonoran Desert); Dr. Lon McClanahan, Dr. Kenneth Norris, and Alan Romspert

(Mojave Desert); Terry Tempest Williams (Great Basin). I also thank Anne Cross, Judy Sellers, and Terry Tempest Williams, who read the manuscript in its entirety and made perceptive suggestions. Timilou Rixon's help was extended, unstinting, and invaluable. And especially Nellie Donovan Teale, who read the manuscript in the peace and quiet of Trail Wood.

I appreciate those who generously provided necessary background information: Charles Bowden and William Broyles, Tucson, Arizona; Jeffrey Cooper, Natural Historian, Wickenburg Inn, Arizona; Dr. Donald Currey, University of Utah, Salt Lake City, Utah; Dr. W. R. Gardner, head of Soil and Water Science, University of Arizona; Linda Hagen and Stephen Van Riper, Cabeza Prieta National Wildlife Refuge, Ajo, Arizona; Julian Hayden, Tucson, Arizona; Roy Johnson, Office of Arid Land Studies, University of Arizona, Tucson, Arizona; Dr. Lon McClanahan, California State University, Fullerton, California; Dr. Gary Nabhan and Clayton Newberry, Desert Botanical Garden, Phoenix, Arizona; Dr. Kenneth S. Norris and Dr. Steve Gleissman, Environmental Field Studies Program, University of California at Santa Cruz; Amadeo Rea, San Diego Museum of Natural History, San Diego, California; Karen Reichhardt, Phoenix, Arizona; Alan Romspert, Coordinator, and Dr. Jerry Sherpa, Desert Studies Center, Zzyzx, California; Dr. Walter Whitford, Jornada Experimental Range, Las Cruces, New Mexico. Wendy Hodgeson, Curator of the Desert Botanical Garden in Phoenix, Arizona, and a fine botanical illustrator, checked my drawings and updated nomenclature. If any errors have slipped through their intellectual fine-tooth combs, they regrettably are mine.

Many gave generous and kindly help and local information: Dr. Richard Beidleman, Department of Biology, Colorado College, and F. Marvin Brown, Colorado Springs, Colorado; Mr. and Mrs. Frank Broyles, Tucson; Joella Buffa, Bureau of Land Management; Louis and LaNai Fouchet, and Father Thomas Megen, Winnemucca, Nevada; Manny Gamboa at White Sands National Monument, New Mexico; Mr. and Mrs. Cecil Garland, Callao, Utah; Jane Grunt, 29 Palms Inn, Twentynine Palms, California; Julie Jones-Eddy, Reference Librarian, and her staff, Colorado College; Dr. David Nordstrom, Fitzsimmons Hospital, Denver, Colorado; John Pearson, Big Bend Nature Association, Big Bend National Park, Texas; John Paul Prude, Prude's Dude Ranch, Davis, Texas; Bill Ratcliffe, Orem, Utah; Dr. W. Ann Reynolds, Chancellor, California State University System, Long Beach, California; Dr. Mary Savina and members of the Carleton College Death Valley Seminar—John Bernstein, Nancy Braker, Perdita Butler, Laura Day, Reid Fischer, Sharon Frank, Kate Heimes, Roger Huddleston, Glenn Lee, Jan Schlamp; Eric Parkman Smith, Concord, Massachusetts; Dr. Alexandra Vargo, Department of Biology (Entomology), Colorado College; Michael Ward, Furnace Creek, Death Valley; Mr. and Mrs. Charles Williams, Mexicali, Mexico. For their many courtesies—a place to stay, the loan and recommendations of books I wouldn't otherwise have known about, the loan of equipment, local information, encouragement and suggestions—I thank them all.

Herman wishes to thank the FBOs who provided courteous, safe, and efficient service: Alpine Aviation, Alpine, Texas; Daggett Aviation, Inc., and West Winds Aviation at Twentynine Palms, California. My thanks to all those hearty, no-nonsense women in all the oases-in-the-desert small-town and smaller cafés, who dispensed iced tea, burritos, homemade pies and donuts, nests of jelly bean eggs on Easter, and efficient remedies for insect bites: Benson, Elfrida, Tombstone, Ajo, and Truth or Consequences, Arizona; Trona and Lone Pine, California; Denio, Baker, Ely, Garrison, Lovelock, Tonopah, and Winnemucca, Nevada; Frenchglen and Harney, Oregon; Vernon, Delta, and Pioche, Utah. They are a book in themselves.

My thanks to Fran Collin, a thoughtful and supportive agent. For helping me keep my programs and head on the same disk, Jeff Eichengreen, Jim Mallory, Dave Nordstrom, Bob Schork; and for helping me keep my head, Kathryn Redman, and Kate Belden, gofer extraordinaire. And to Truman Talley, for suggesting this book in the first place; and to Nancy Etheredge, Earl Tidwell, Julia McGown, and Mary Wagstaff for their care in putting it together.

John T. Hughes, *Doniphan's Expedition; Containing an Account of the Conquest of New Mexico; General Kearny's Overland Expedition to California; Doniphan's Campaign Against the Navajos; His Unparalleled March upon Chihuahua and Durango; and the Operations of General Price at Santa Fe*, concludes his 1848 account of survival on the Jornada del Muerto with the hope of every nonfiction author:

> The author has now finished his labors, and if he has afforded entertainment for the curious, truth for the inquisitive, novelty for the lover of romance, instruction for the student of history, or information for the general reader, he feels himself amply rewarded for his pains. Should any one, however, think that the narrative herein given of the expedition, is unfaithful, or incomplete, let him consider how difficult it is to write history; how impossible it is to feast every appetite; and how diverse are the sentiments of mankind.

ANN H. ZWINGER
February 1988

INDEX

Page references for illustrations are in **boldface** type.